VISITOR'S G
USA

World Travellei

CW00435203

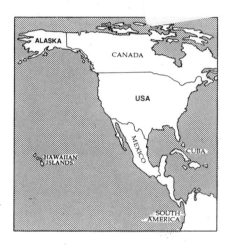

he Author

he author is an American who has travelled widely in his native country.
fter 4 years 'touring' America with the Air Force, he spent 10 years
·arketing computer systems in Britain. In 1989 Brian formed a travel
riting team with his photographer-wife, Jackie, who recieved her first
·notography award aged 10. They have negotiated 34,000 miles of
·merican highway this trip, in their motorhome and have re-visited every
·ate in the USA. Brian is also the author of the *Visitor's Guide: Florida.*

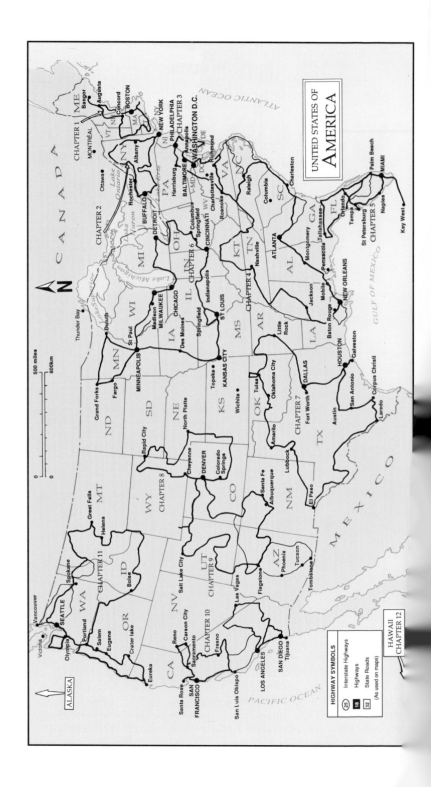

VISITOR'S GUIDE
USA

Brian Merritt

MPC

HUNTER
PUBLISHING INC

Published by:
Moorland Publishing Co Ltd,
Moor Farm Road West,
Ashbourne, Derbyshire
DE6 1HD
England

Published in the USA by:
Hunter Publishing Inc,
300 Raritan Center Parkway,
CN 94, Edison, NJ 08818

Front cover: Detroit Tigers *(Detroit CVB)*
Rear Cover: Havasu Falls, Supai, Grand Canyon *(MPC Picture Collection)*

MPC Production Team:
Editor : John Robey
Designer: Dan Clarke
Cartographer: Alastair Morrison

ISBN 0 86190 465 6

British Library Cataloguing in
Publication Data.
A catalogue record for this book is
available from the British Library.

Colour origination by:
P & W Graphics Pte Ltd, Singapore

Printed in the UK by:
Richard Clay Ltd, Bungay, Suffolk

Note on the Maps
The maps drawn for each chapter, while comprehensive, are not
designed to be used as route maps, but rather to locate the main cities,
towns and places of interest.

While every care has been taken to ensure that the information in this book is as
accurate as possible at the time of publication, the publisher and author accepts
no responsibility for any loss, injury or inconvenience sustained by anyone
using this book.

CONTENTS

Key to Symbols Used in Text and on Maps

⌂	Church/Ecclesiastical site	🚶	Recommended walk
⊓	Archaeological site	⊞	Building of interest
🏞	Beautiful view/Scenery, Natural phenomenon	🏰	Fort
🏛	Museum/Art gallery	🦌	Zoo/Animal interest
❋	Other place of interest	♣	Park*
🌼	Garden	♿	Handicapped accessible

* Parks in the USA can range from National Parks to Recreational Parks

Abbreviations

COC	Chamber of Commerce	NMP	National Military Park
CVB	Convention & Visitors' Bureau	NM	National Monument
		NP	National Park
NHP	National Historic Park	SHP	State Historic Park
NHS	National Historic Site	SP	State Park

Key to Maps

●▢	Town/City	— · — · —	National boundary
———	Route	———————	Regional boundary
———	Optional Route	～⌒～	Rivers/Lakes

How To Use This Guide

This MPC Visitor's Guide has been designed to be as easy to use as possible. Each chapter covers a region or itinerary in a natural progression which gives all the background information to help you enjoy your visit. MPC's distinctive margin symbols, the important places printed in bold, and a comprehensive index enable the reader to find the most interesting places to visit with ease.

At the end of each chapter an Additional Information section gives specific details such as addresses and opening times, making this guide a complete sightseeing companion.

At the back of the guide the Fact File, arranged in alphabetical order, gives practical information and useful tips to help you plan your holiday — before you go and while you are there.

The maps of each region show the main towns, villages, roads and places of interest, but are not designed as route maps and motorists should always use a good recommended road atlas.

INTRODUCTION

Founded by adventurers and freedom seekers, America is a land of dreams and visions. The challenge is to experience it to the full — the fantastic images of Walt Disney, the man-made marvels of Manhattan, and all the natural wonders of a new world.

For convenience, the United States has been divided into bite-sized tours. Each traveller's taste will suggest which region is for starters, which the main course, and how many helpings of dessert are desirable. For drivers, routes are chosen for scenery and interest, with options to combine tours into longer trips. Non-drivers may follow many of the itineraries using package tours. The format has made it possible to include thousands of those 'hidden treasures' which allow the traveller to truly experience America.

Land of Opportunity

An inspired Dr Samuel Frances Smith wrote of majestic purple mountains and fruited plains in his song *America the Beautiful*. Add some great lakes, mighty rivers, the island archipelago of Hawaii, and President Seward's 'great folly', Alaska, and the total reaches $3^1/_2$ million square miles ($9^1/_3$ million square km).

The geologically ancient Appalachian Mountain Range separates the eastern seaboard from the Central Plains. The land is flat and fertile from the southern Atlantic coast, rising to the gentle rolling Piedmont, while the northeast was scoured by glaciers. Farmland abandoned during the big push west is gradually returning to the great eastern forests.

The massive Mississippi Basin, fed by the Tennessee, Ohio, Missouri, Arkansas, and innumerable other rivers, empties into the Gulf of Mexico. The Central Plains east of the mighty Mississippi are punctuated by the Ozark Mountains. New methods of irrigation and plant varieties continue to make the Central Plains the 'breadbasket of America'.

To the west, the Great Plains sweep up to the Rocky Mountains, backbone of the American continent. The massive uplift which created the Rockies made vast mineral resources accessible, including the gold and silver which drew prospectors west in the 1800s. Massive quantities of coal, oil, and valuable ores invite new investment in remote areas of Wyoming and Utah, even today.

Peaks and troughs between the Rockies and the Pacific Ocean are a geological roller coaster. Folds like Death Valley and the High Sierras were formed under immense pressure, while erosion has worked to great effect in the

Grand Canyon and Zion Canyon. At the singularly scenic California coastline, the mountains meet the sea.

The youthful United States treated its massive resources as though they were unlimited, but fortunately conservationists, such as John Muir and President Theodore (Teddy) Roosevelt, slowed the headlong rush of progress in time. Visitors can still experience the delicately balanced ecosystem of the Everglades, thrill to every bend of Glacier National Park's 'Going to the Sun Road', or peer back to the earth's beginnings at the Grand Canyon.

Flora and fauna vary with region and climate, from sub-tropical southeast to arctic northwestern mountains. Wildlife is not restricted to national parks and forests, and casual travellers often see as many varieties alongside highways as do hikers in remote regions.

The Making of America

When and how humans first reached the American continent is a matter of controversy. However, the 'New World' was first colonized between 12,000 and 45,000 years ago, probably via a land bridge between Siberia and Alaska during the last Ice Age. Climatic changes and loss of easy prey (giant bison, mammoth and mastodon), required paleo-Indians to specialize, adapting tools and techniques for local environments. Smaller game was supplemented by foraging, which for many evolved into agriculture.

By 1500, few Native Americans followed herds of buffalo or lived true nomadic lifestyles. In the Southwest descendants of the Anasazi cultivated maize, squash, beans, and cotton. They built adobe cities, dubbed Pueblos by Spaniards, and produced fine black pottery. In the Northeast, five Indian nations formed the Iroquois Confederacy in opposition to their rivals, the Hurons and Algonquins. Iroquois lived in long houses, grouped together and protected by a log palisade, with crops planted in surrounding fields. Although fierce towards their enemies, the Iroquois League of Nations was dedicated to peace.

Apart from short-lived Norse settlements and, perhaps, the briefest visit by a legendary Irish Saint, some five to twenty million Indians lived in North America without external aid or interference before the coming of white men.

Christopher Columbus set sail for the Indies and although he returned from the Bahamas virtually empty-handed his glowing reports sparked the first American gold rush. Spanish Conquistadors plundered Aztec, Mayan, and Inca civilizations, sending ship after gold-laden treasure ship home. Spanish soldiers easily overcame civilizations wracked by diseases they had brought, and the Church and Monasteries adopted the survivors. Meanwhile the French, Dutch, and British were searching for the legendary northwest passage. Attempts to colonize the New World were interrupted by European disputes, with redoubled efforts after the Spanish Armada was defeated.

Jamestown became Britain's first permanent colony in 1607. Cursed with the wrong crops, a hot climate and high mortality rate, it was nearly abandoned until a growing market for tobacco provided economic security. In 1620 the Plymouth Colony was settled by Pilgrims, victims of religious persecution in Europe. Survivors of that first inhospitable winter thanked God and Indian helpers for a bountiful harvest.

Other charters were given, one to the prolific Massachusetts Bay Company, and the east coast became peppered with English colonies. Meanwhile Champlain led the French in establishing the fur trade and Quebec. The Dutch founded New Amsterdam, purchasing the site from Manhatoe Indians for 60 guilders in 'the greatest real estate bargain in history'. For a time, everyone except the Indians had room to grow.

The plantation system, imported from the West Indies, took root in the south. New Englanders believed that riches were Heaven's reward for hard work, and established commerce based on trading and shipping. In between was a melange of Dutch, Swedes, Irish, Scots and, at the behest of William Penn, a number of German Quakers.

Fuelled by attempts to dominate lucrative trade with the Orient and the New World, Europe's internecine rivalry spilled across the Atlantic to the colonies. New Amsterdam was annexed, becoming New York, but the main struggle was between English and French, with Indian allies on both sides adding to the carnage. English colonists discovered that help was far away, and became increasingly self-reliant. Land won from the French was often returned to the 'enemy' by European diplomats. Finally, with British and Iroquois aid, the French were overcome. Vast tracts of land between the Appalachian Mountains and the Mississippi, claimed for France by La Salle, became suddenly available.

Britain was reluctant for eager colonists to plunge into the interior; Indian allies who owned the land might start an expensive war, and trade could be diverted down the Mississippi to Spain. Extra taxes imposed to defray America's escalating defence costs proved unpopular with the increasingly independent colonists. British products were boycotted, led by Boston reactionaries. The Bostonian mob attacked British soldiers, sparking the 'Boston Massacre' when several stone-throwers were shot. After numerous incidents were ignored, ' The Boston Tea Party' finally forced King George III to act. He wrote to Lord North, ' The die is now cast. The colonies must either submit or triumph.'

Although most colonists desired only restoration of earlier freedoms, on 4 July 1776 the Declaration of Independence was signed. However, the poorly provisioned Continental Army of George Washington was incapable of defeating an army backed by German mercenaries and an Imperial Navy. City after coastal city was lost, yet the British Army was loth to venture inland. Farmers, unwilling to join a long war, would rise up against invaders within striking distance. While Washington honed leadership skills by maintaining an Army short of men, supplies, and funds, Benjamin Franklin and others practised diplomacy in Europe. With French aid the war ended in 1783. Washington had insufficient money to pay his staunch men, so he thanked them heartily, gave them their muskets, and went home.

The Revolutionary War had been fought by thirteen Independent States, each jealously guarding *its* rights. The colonies felt that any federal government was likely to be worse than British Rule. Nevertheless, they met in Philadelphia to draft the American Constitution. A system of 'checks and balances', amended by a bill outlining fundamental human rights, was eventually adopted and is still in use. George Washington, president of the Constitutional Convention, was unanimously elected first President of the United States, 13 years after the Declaration of Independence.

The new nation had its work cut out. Thomas Jefferson, first Vice-President, favoured the farmers and plantations. Cheap land, low interest rates, and America would become a nation of contented farmers. Alexander Hamilton, first Secretary for the Treasury, was for commerce, manufacturing, and progress. High interest rates would guarantee foreign investment, while expensive land would make labourers in cities happy to work for low wages.

Both visions were at least partially realized. The Louisiana Purchase added a vast tract of land beyond the Mississippi, while explorers Lewis and Clark claimed fertile Oregon, giving the United States access to the Pacific. The Monroe Doctrine was formed, outlining America's 'Manifest Destiny', the phoenix of a new, free world arising from the ashes of war-torn Europe. A great exodus west began, requiring pioneers who, in turn, needed clothing and manufactured goods from the east.

In northern states, commerce was king and an industrial base became established. In the south, tobacco had depleted the soil but there was always more land. Mexico had encouraged Americans to settle in Texas, and that was annexed with the war cry, 'Remember the Alamo!' In 1846 the 49th parallel became the Canadian Border, while two years later Mexico ceded California and what was to become the American Southwest.

A new crop, cotton, gave life to old plantations. Slavery, in decline since 1776, was reborn with the advent of the cotton gin. The seeds of conflict, planted in the founding of Jamestown and Plymouth, had found new, fertile soil. Southerners did all the hard work — growing cotton and reinvesting hard-earned money in land and slaves to work it — to find the 'Damn Yankees' made fortunes just by spinning and distributing it. *And* they had the nerve to tell Southerners how to live.

Signs heralded the Civil War long before the first state seceded. Railways had opened up western territories and both sides wanted *their* new states ratified. In Kansas, John Brown brought guns in cases labelled 'Beecher Bibles' for the abolitionist cause. In Washington DC the Supreme Court decided that negro slave Dred Scott was not a citizen and could not sue in a federal court. Also, Congress could not deprive citizens of their property ie slaves. John Brown's attempt at Harper's Ferry to hijack weapons with which to free and arm slaves hardened both sides.

Abraham Lincoln, Republican Party candidate, was the final catalyst. Before he could be inaugurated the South formed the Confederate States of America. Lincoln promised to uphold individual states' rights regarding slavery, but refused to allow them to secede. More Americans died in the Civil War that followed than all others combined. The Union had capital, industry, a large population, and the navy. Against them were a Confederacy possessing skilled officers and soldiers fresh from the Mexican wars, fighting for their lives and homes. Despite Union naval blockades, Confederates inflicted heavy casualties on the Yankees in numerous engagements.

Lincoln, fearing European support for the South and growing political opposition in the North, passed the Emancipation Proclamation. By Independence Day 1863 the tide was turning. Grant took Vicksburg, last Confederate stronghold on the Mississippi, while Lee had been halted at Gettysburg

Americans have all sorts of pastimes including quilt making

Ice hockey has a popular following

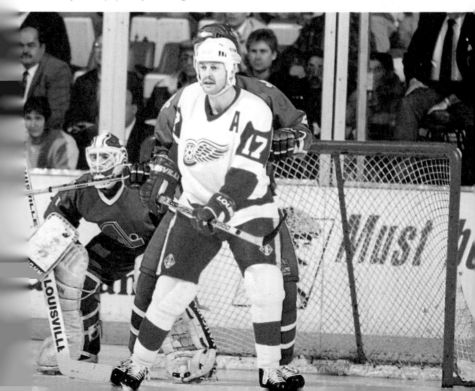

the previous day. Lee surrendered at Appomattox Court House nearly two years later, but not before the South had been devastated. The reconstruction of the South which Lincoln planned went awry after his assassination.

Many Confederate soldiers and former slaves joined the western exodus, and for a brief time the cowboy had his day. Men like Wyatt Earp and Judge Roy Bean made their own laws. But trails were pushed ever west as the free range became settled. Indians forced onto unwanted land were relocated again when valuable minerals were discovered. Many were resigned to the great white tide, but hot-heads on both sides spawned massacres. The end was hastened by the destruction of the buffalo and Custer's unfortunate collision with Crazy Horse, which spurred public opinion and the military against the Indians. By 1890 the West was considered won.

The growth of the West fuelled eastern expansion. A great industrial belt formed from the Atlantic to the Great Lakes states. Coal became king with competition from a relative newcomer — oil. Fortunes were made, and names like Carnegie and Rockefeller became synonymous with success. Imported European labour became fodder for 'The Captains of Industry', soon renamed 'The Great Robber Barons'. Trade unions were formed, and farmers formed the Populist Party, hoping for a return to Thomas Jefferson's ideals. Rough-riding President Teddy Roosevelt earned the nickname 'the trust-buster', and President Woodrow Wilson continued to carry out Roosevelt's monopoly reforms and conservation efforts.

Business was back, bigger than ever after World War I, but wealth was more evenly distributed. Excesses of business and society in the 1920s lead to prohibition, the crash, and the depression. The American economy bounced back after Franklin Roosevelt's New Deal, spurred on by World War II. The prosperous 1950s became the swinging 1960s. A new conscience was born from the birth pains of the Black Civil Rights movement, the fiasco of Vietnam, and realization that America's resources, great as they are, must be carefully husbanded. Yet technology continued to rush apace, culminating in the message from the moon on 21 July 1969: 'The Eagle has Landed.'

With the thawing of the Cold War, the United States is cautiously optimistic, and the 'Great Experiment' continues.

The Facts

Government

The constitution of 1787 defined three bodies: the Legislature, Executive, and Judiciary, which comprise the United States Federal Government. The Legislature (Congress) combines the House of Representatives, where each state has members in proportion to its population, and the Senate, with two members from each state. Elections for President, the Chief Executive, occur every four years, and no person may be elected more than twice. The Supreme Court heads the judiciary, with final responsibility for determining constitutional meaning. The system of checks and balances built into the constitution and its amendments protect rights of state and the individual, and ensure that no single body usurps the power of the Federal Government.

Population

According to the 1990 Census, just under 250 million people live in the United States with a racial mix as follows:

White	80.3%
Black	12.1%
Asian & Pacific Islanders	2.9%
Native Americans	0.8%
Other	3.9%

Hispanics comprise 9% of the above.

The People

Ethnic variety amongst Americans is most apparent in larger cities, but rural areas such as the Pennsylvania Dutch Country make for interesting exceptions. English is the official language, occasionally supplemented by Spanish. The cultural diversity of New York City is renowned, while perhaps the greatest ethnic mix is in Hawaii, meeting place of the Pacific. Martin Luther King Jr refined the 'melting pot' concept, describing America as a great vegetable soup, with each ingredient distinct, yet adding to the whole.

Food and Drink

Advertising has elevated American hot dogs, hamburgers, and fizzy drinks to pop art, with fast food franchises spread throughout the world. For a real treat, sample regional cuisine — the most popular types are widespread. Spicy Cajun and Creole dishes from New Orleans are available in Seattle and Boston, while Las Vegas restaurants advertise cut-price Maine lobsters. Tex-Mex, Mexican cooking Texas style, has reached cult status at Taco Bell, while real Mexican food is available north of the border at select restaurants.

Chinese restaurants are ubiquitous, although locations like San Francisco's and New York's Chinatown do add atmosphere. Vietnamese, Taiwanese, and Malaysian styles are other Oriental offerings, with regional Japanese cuisine big in larger cities. Fine Italian and French restaurants are hard to beat, and for a change, try a Californian or local wine — 21 years is the legal drinking age in most states. Some communities, especially in the Mid-West and South, have retained prohibition, but locals always know the nearest 'wet' town.

Entertainment and Leisure

The United States is activity orientated, even when spectating. While the three big sports — baseball, football, and basketball — are uniquely American, virtually every other sport has a following. Culture and nightlife are best in major cities, whether a philharmonic orchestra or late night jazz session. The same is true of shopping, and a growing number of stores never close. Washington, New York, and Chicago are justly famous for their fine museums, while the big cities of California have come of age with world-class museums surrounded by landscaped parks.

The outdoor enthusiast has options ranging from strolling in Central Park to hiking into remote wilderness areas, with perhaps a mule or lama to take the strain. White water rafting, parascending and ballooning add spice to a holiday, or opt for the more sedate adventures of calm river rafting, a helicopter flight, or a scenic harbour cruise. Diving is fantastic off the Florida Keys,

Hispanic culture adds zest to the Southwest

Americans love a parade

Hawaii, Californian coast, and also the Great Lakes. Downhill skiing challenges beginners to experts, while cross-country trails or snowmobiles open up the scenic beauty of Yellowstone and other national parks along the American snow belt. Horse lovers can visit Bluegrass Kentucky for the famous Derby, or go out West to experience a dude ranch or rodeo.

Deciding where to go

Each chapter of this book contains a brief outline, with main highlights, time required, and best seasons for travel. Long tours, like California and the South, can be halved if time is short. If one particular attraction comes to mind, like Walt Disney World or the Grand Canyon, go there — but take in other pleasures in the vicinity. Shorter tours like New England or the Mid-Atlantic states are designed to build confidence and expertise. Both will be useful for the great romp across the Pacific Northwest in Chapter 11, perhaps the most demanding, yet most rewarding, tour of all.

The Arches National Park—one of the USA's scenic wonders

1

NEW ENGLAND

Picturesque New England stirs up images of tranquil village life in settings of almost impossible beauty. Green is a predominant colour, splashed with the riotous rainbow of autumn leaves and pierced by the tall white spire of a New England church.

Boston

The heart of New England, **Boston** is colonial and cosmopolitan, high-tech and historic. Founded by Puritans in 1630, the seaport outpaced rivals to become the largest British settlement. Although Boston suffered for its patriotic outbursts during the War of Independence, the city soon bounced back. Modern Boston remembers its past but looks to the future, its fine universities leading the way.

The Freedom Trail

Begin a tour of the city at **Boston Common**, 'ye oldest publik park' in America. The information kiosk heads the **Freedom Trail**, a blood red line which slices a 2 mile historic swath through Boston — allow a day and wear comfortable shoes. The trail crosses Boston Common to the **State House**, where the Massachusetts State Legislature meets, then along the common's edge to Park Street Church. Three signatories of the Declaration of Independence and Paul Revere are among patriots interred at **Granary Burying Ground**. King's Chapel, the first Anglican church in New England, is a side step north before

---

New England in Brief

Historic Boston is the gateway to New England. Follow the coastline of Cape Cod before visiting Newport, Rhode Island, to see the homes of America's elite. Beyond Mystic Seaport and the Connecticut River Valley are the lakes, rivers and mountains of Vermont and New Hampshire. The grand finale is the incomparable coastline of Maine.

Two weeks are best for the 1,500 mile (2,400km) tour. Autumn is considered *the* time to tour New England, but spring and summer are equally pleasant. The ski resorts of New Hampshire, Maine and Vermont have much to offer the winter sports enthusiast.

Into and Around Boston

Logan Airport is conveniently located just a few miles from downtown Boston via a tunnel under the Charles River. Shuttle buses connect the five main terminals to the 'T', Boston's rapid transit rail network. With streets laid out by colonial cattle, downtown Boston is a driver's nightmare. Fortunately, Boston is best seen on foot, with most historic sites found along the 'Freedom Trail'. The 'T' is available for longer jaunts, while others opt for sightseeing bus tours from Boston Common.

Downtown Boston is central within the peninsula formed by the Charles River and Fort Point Channel, with the Italian North End at the tip and the condominium-lined waterfront to the east. Boston Common is west of downtown, surrounded by the upper-crust homes of Beacon Hill to the north and Back Bay to the west. The Charles River Reservation, a popular park for jogging, cycling or relaxing, lines the Charles River, with cerebral Cambridge opposite. Pleasant drives follow the Charles River and the Back Bay Fens in Fenway. Returning east towards central Boston, the towering buildings of the Prudential Center are south of Back Bay, followed by the rediscovered town houses of South End. Chinatown, due south of downtown, completes the circuit.

the trail returns to School Street.

The Old Corner Bookstore published works by Longfellow and Emerson while Samuel Adams signalled the Boston Tea Party at the **Old South Meeting House**. The national park service has a visitor centre on State Street, with a documentary film, book shop, and historical exhibits. The **Old State House**, Boston's oldest public building, is now a history museum.

Faneuil Hall, the 'Cradle of Liberty', has a long history as meeting place and market, and the shops and eateries of **Faneuil Hall Marketplace** still attract crowds. The trail next leads to North Hill, Boston's Italian quarter. The **Paul Revere House**, the oldest in Boston, contains colonial furnishings and Revere memorabilia. Beyond the *Ride of Paul Revere* statue is the Old North Church, from which beacons signalled the approaching British troops. Their gift shop and museum houses a rare copy of the 'Vinegar' Bible.

The **USS *Constitution*** at Charlestown Naval Yard was dubbed 'Old Ironsides' after British cannon balls bounced off her heavily planked sides. Guided tours are free at this historic landmark, the oldest commissioned ship in the US Navy. The adjacent museum exhibits the fighting history and preservation of the ship. Final stop along the Freedom Trail is the Bunker Hill Monument.

The waterfront saw frenetic activity during Boston's heyday as a shipping port. The notorious Boston Tea Party took place there, commemorated by a full-scale replica of the original ship. Across Fort Point Channel are the Boston Fire, Children's and Computer Museums, while north along the channel is the excellent **New England Aquarium**. Whale-watching cruises and round trip tickets to Fort Warren on Georges Island are available at Long Pier.

The **African Meeting House** was an early focus of Black community activities in Boston. The 'Underground Railroad' ferried ex-slaves into Canada and

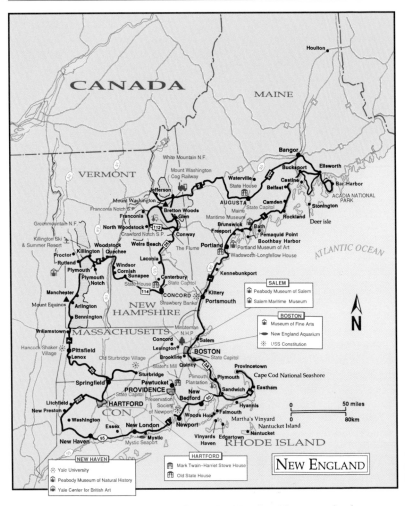

freedom, and Boston's **Lewis and Harriet Hayden House** and others provided shelter and protection. Also along the **Black Heritage Trail** are the Museum of Afro-American History and the Boston African American National Historic Site.

The arts are strong in Boston, commencing with the visual **Museum of Fine Arts**, Isabella Stewart Gardner Museum, and the Institute of Contemporary Art. **Symphony Hall** houses the Boston Symphony and Boston Pop Orchestras. The Hatch Memorial Shell by the Charles River gives free open-air concerts on summer evenings. Most theatres and the Opera House are south and east of Boston Common. The **Science Park** straddles the Charles River Dam off Martha Road.

Shopping in Boston starts at **Copley Place**, boasting Neiman-Marcus, Yves St Laurent, Gucci and other fine stores. Quincy Market, part of the Faneuil Hall complex, offers a diverse selection of delectable edibles with specialty shops to match. Shopping malls are near major Interstate junctions, while the Pru

*The Boston
skyline
by night*

*Boston's
colourful market*

dential Center is scheduled to complete its renovations in 1993, providing more shops and restaurants in central Boston.

Around Boston

Harvard, oldest university in America, is across the Charles River in **Cambridge**. The Harvard Information Center on Massachusetts Avenue gives free tours daily in summer. One admission covers all four **Museums of Natural History**. The **Longfellow National Historic Site**, the poet's home while a professor at Harvard, is where 'The Song of Hiawatha', 'Paul Revere's Ride', and other poems were composed. The **Sackler Museum** concentrates on Oriental and Islamic Art, while the **Fogg Art Museum** tends more towards European. Cambridge is also home to the Massachusetts Institute of Technology (**MIT**). Look for the MIT and Harvard rowing teams on the Charles River.

The evolution of New England architecture is revealed in the environs of **Old Cambridge**, which radiates outward from Harvard Square. Brattle Street was known as 'Tory row' after the well-to-do British sympathizers who once lived there. **Brookline**, west of Boston, is home to the Frederick Law Olmsted and John Fitzgerald Kennedy National Historic Sites. The Kennedy birthplace has been restored to that period, while Olmsted designed New York's Central Park.

From Cambridge follow Memorial Drive west along the scenic Charles River, picking up US2 and following signs for historic **Lexington**. The first conflict of the Revolutionary War occurred in the spring of 1775, *before* the Declaration of Independence, when British General Gage sent 700 troops to retrieve arms cached in Concord. Visit Monroe Tavern, British headquarters and field hospital during the battle, and the free Museum of our National Heritage. Afterwards, stroll Lexington Common. The Minuteman Statue depicts Captain John Parker, who stated, '... if they mean to have a war, let it begin here.' Massachusetts Avenue leads through **Minute Man National Historic Park**, where ranger programs at Battle Road commemorate the struggle.

The engagement commenced at the park's North Bridge section in **Concord**, where 'the shot heard round the world' was fired. In a later period, Concord witnessed a renaissance in American literature. Louisa May Alcott was born at the **Wayside**, later sold to Nathaniel Hawthorne, and she perfected *Little Women* next door at **Orchard House**. Concord has also preserved Ralph Waldo Emerson's House, and the site of Henry David Thoreau's cabin at tranquil *Walden*.

New England Grand Tour

To Plymouth Colony and Cape Cod

The SR3 south is quickest to Plymouth, but SR3A takes in **Adams National Historic Site** in Quincy, commemorating the birthplaces of two American presidents. **Plymouth** was the Pilgrims' first permanent settlement, founded in December 1620. Their first Thanksgiving is celebrated throughout America but relived in Plymouth. The **Plimoth Plantation** re-creates that Pilgrim era, as does the **Mayflower II**, where costumed crew and colonists tell of 'their' amazing voyage. The **Pilgrim Hall Museum** exhibits Pilgrim artifacts and memorabilia.

Whale watching and harbour cruises are other activities in seaside Plymouth, as is browsing through antique shops and sampling free drinks at the **Cranberry World Visitor Center**. Chief Massasoit, who gave the Pilgrims aid and the colony's name (Massachusetts), has a statue on Coles Hill. Some say the Pilgrims disembarked at **Plymouth Rock**.

Follow SR3 south to Sagamore Bridge, then 6A west for picturesque **Cape Cod**. Heritage Plantation exhibits classic cars, Currier and Ives prints, and antique firearms in a garden setting at **Sandwich**. The Glass Museum recalls the village's heyday as an early glass manufacturing site. Brewster is peppered with antique shops and art galleries, and has an aquarium amongst its museums. At Orleans join US6 north for the delightful if widespread **Cape Cod National Seashore**. The visitor centre at Eastham provides maps and orientation.

Provincetown is an artists' colony and a principle Cape Cod resort. Shops, restaurants and boutiques line the streets, while the 252ft **Pilgrim Monument** towers above the town. Cruise boats leave MacMillan Pier regularly, with a chance of seeing whales and dolphins. On Commercial Street, the Heritage Museum boasts the world's largest model of a schooner, while the Art Association Museum exhibits works by local artists. From Provincetown head north for Race Point Beach, part of Cape Cod National Seashore. Beyond the visitor centre are miles of shoreline backed by windswept dunes, perfect for strolling or dolphin-spotting.

Follow SR28 along southern Cape Cod to Chatham, a haven for sport and commercial fishermen. Next comes **Hyannis**, another popular cape resort which offers **Cape Cod Railway** trips to Sandwich and Sagamore. Hyannis is also the gateway to charming **Nantucket Island**, famed for cobblestone streets, Quaker architecture, and its treacherous shoals. Reservations for automobiles are required in summer, or leave the car in Hyannis. Museums and points of interest include the Maria Mitchell Science Center, with an aquarium and museum of natural science. The Whaling Museum and other structures owned by the Nantucket Heritage Association depict early island life.

Martha's Vineyard, the other major island off Cape Cod, has a year-round ferry service from Woods Hole near Falmouth. Beaches and wildlife sanctuaries draw visitors — those without cars get around by bicycle or shuttle bus. Edgartown and Vineyard Haven are main centres of activity.

From Cape Cod, US6 continues west to New Bedford, a fishing and former whaling port whose Seamen's Bethel (chapel) was described in Herman Melville's *Moby Dick*.

Rhode Island

The 'Ocean State' is less developed than many expect, boasting a picturesque countryside delimited by a meandering coast. Stop first at **Pawtucket**, where

Slater Mill Historic Site demonstrates early spinning and weaving technology 'borrowed' from English Industrialist Sir Richard Arkwright by Slater.

The capital of Rhode Island is **Providence**, where Roger Williams thanked God for deliverance from intolerant Pilgrims. The city remembers its founder with the Roger Williams National Memorial, and Roger Williams Park, home to the Natural History Museum and Providence Zoo. The white marble **State Capitol** is open for tours on weekdays. The Providence Preservation Society gives historical tours of the city including Benefit Street, where colonial homes are concentrated. The John Brown House is headquarters for the Rhode Island Historical Society while the **Rhode Island School of Design** is located in the 1775 Market House. From Providence, take I-195 east and then SR114 south.

As a bustling city, **Newport** rivalled Boston and New York until occupied by British troops — today the resort is famous for its elite mansions. Details of tours, harbour cruises and accommodation are available from the Convention and Visitors Bureau on America's Cup Avenue. Explore the quaint shops and sea food restaurants along the narrow downtown streets on foot. For a driving tour of Newport head south on America's Cup Avenue, then take consecutive right turns onto Thames Street, Wellington Avenue, and Harrison Avenue; pausing en route to enjoy picturesque Newport Harbor and its fine yachts. Fort Adams State Park has a commanding view of Newport, and its Museum of Yachting recounts the sport's history. Further south along Harrison Avenue is **Hammersmith Farm**, 'Summer White House' during the Kennedy Presidency. The estate was designed by Frederick Olmsted, best known for New York's Central Park, and is open for tours.

Ocean Avenue passes the select shore-front properties of coastal Rhode Island. A right on Coggeshall leads to mansion-lined **Bellevue Avenue**. Dubbed 'cottages' by the aristocratic owners, most homes are now managed by the Preservation Society of Newport County, with concessionary rates when visiting two or more. Belcourt Castle and Beachwood Mansion are managed separately. The Louis XIII fantasy of **Belcourt Castle** was built for Oliver Hazard Perry Belmont. His wife, Alva, won the nearby **Marble House** from William K. Vanderbilt in a divorce settlement. Living history tours at **Beachwood Mansion** re-create the busy social scene of the former owners, descendents of the fur trade magnate John Jacob Astor.

The Grand Trianon of Versailles was the inspiration for **Rosecliff**, while **Chateau-sur-Mer** set the standard for Newport mansions until **The Breakers** was designed by Richard Morris Hunt for Cornelius Vanderbilt II. Resembling a seventeenth-century Genoese palace, the grounds were landscaped by Olmsted, with furnishings by Allard et Fils. Other mansions include **The Elms** and **Kingscote**. For a different view of the mansions, take Memorial Drive east and hike the 3 mile (5km) **Cliff Walk**.

Return towards downtown Newport via Bellevue Avenue and Touro Street. The **Art Museum**, Touro Synagogue, and the Newport Historical Society Museum are near Touro Park. The Quaker Friends Meeting House is in northern Newport, while at Washington Street, **Hunter House** was headquarters for French Admiral de Ternay during the Revolutionary War. SR138 west over Newport Bridge leads to US1 south.

Connecticut

Quinnehtuqut was Indian for the tidal river which divides the state. Connecticut boasts village greens surrounded by crisp, white cottages. While farms were the backbone of colonial Connecticut, the sea was its lifeblood — a heritage preserved in **Mystic**.

The pride of **Mystic Seaport** is the 1841 *Charles W. Morgan*, the last great whaling ship and a national historic landmark. The small maritime museum of 1928 has grown enormously, and now craftsmen demonstrate time-honoured skills in the bustling nineteenth-century seaport. Several buildings house exhibits on maritime New England, and the Children's Museum depicts the life of children at sea. Preservation shipyard coordinates conservation efforts, while the boat shop uses traditional methods to build new boats. Also at Mystic are the **Marinelife Aquarium** and the **Denison Homestead**, recalling eleven generations of the Denison family. Voyager and Windjammer Cruises cater for multi-day and shorter sailings aboard schooners and replica clippers.

At **New London** the Thames River forms Connecticut's deepest harbour. Razed during the Revolutionary War, New London rebounded to become a major whaling town. The Joshuah Hempsted and Nathaniel Hempsted Houses survived the fires, as did the 1756 Shaw Mansion, home of Captain Nathaniel Shaw. Monti Cristo Cottage, boyhood home of dramatist Eugene O'Neill, was the setting for *Long Day's Journey into Night*. The downtown historic district includes the schoolhouse where martyred patriot Nathan Hale taught, and the impressive homes of Whale Oil Row. Continue westbound from New London along the Connecticut coast, where several villages were settled during the 1630s and '40s, not long after Plymouth. Consider a detour inland to Essex for the **Connecticut River Museum** and its reproduction *Turtle*, David Bushnell's 1775 submarine.

New Haven was a planned town, laid out as nine squares in 1638. The centre square, **New Haven Green**, has three fine New England churches built between 1812 and 1815. The **Eli Whitney Museum** in nearby Hamden highlights this Yale graduate's efforts, of which the cotton gin (short for engine) was most famous. Favourite son Roger Sherman, Eli Whitney and Charles Goodyear, another Yale graduate and inventor of vulcanized rubber, rest at the old Grove Street Cemetery.

Guided tours of Ivy League **Yale University** start at the Phelps Gate. Heart of the old campus area is Connecticut Hall, where Nathaniel Hale stayed before graduating in 1773. The 221ft Harkness Tower, a Yale landmark, is across High Street among the relatively newer Georgian and Gothic additions. Points of interest include **Yale University Art Gallery**, founded by John Trumball; **Yale Center for British Art**, boasting the largest collection outside the United Kingdom; and the dinosaur fossils and Indian artifacts of the **Peabody Museum of Natural History**.

Take I-91 north to Hartford if time is pressing, pausing at Wethersfield to see its many Colonial homes. Alternatively, SR34 follows the Housatonic River to I-84 west, after which US202 leads north through the gentle mountains of western Connecticut. At New Preston drive around scenic Lake Waramaug and perhaps detour south on SR47 through the Shepaug River gorge. Both the

American Indian Archaeology Institute, with its reproduction Native American village, and the Historical Museum of the Gunn Library are in Washington. **Litchfield**, birthplace of Harriet Beecher Stowe and Ethan Allen, is known for its charming colonial houses. Continue east on US202 to Avon and follow signs for Hartford.

The insurance corporations of modern **Hartford** imply restraint, but in 1687 the colony openly rebelled against the British Crown. In the Connecticut Charter, King Charles II had granted self rule and land west to the Pacific, but when new Governor Edmund Andros was examining the document for King James II, the candles were blown out. The charter was spirited away and hidden in the 'Charter Oak', where a memorial now stands.

Colonial Hartford is no more, apart from the memorial and the Ancient Burying Ground, but the city has sites of historic and literary interest. Samuel Clemens is typically pictured at his childhood home in Hannibal or during the California Gold Rush, not his seventeen years in **Mark Twain House**. An architectural oddity, visitors are immediately confronted with Clemens' love for ostentatious ornamentation in his Victorian Gothic 'farmhouse'. Nearby is the more staid **Harriet Beecher Stowe House**, purchased after *Uncle Tom's Cabin* brought her fame.

The well proportioned Federal architecture of the **Old State House** contrasts sharply with the white marble **State Capitol**. The Museum of Connecticut History in the State Library Building displays a collection of firearms by Sam Colt, inventor of the revolver. The **Wadsworth Atheneum** has been the cultural centre of Hartford since 1844.

The Berkshires and Central Massachusetts

The seventeenth-century trading post of **Springfield** became a manufacturing centre when the National Armory was established in 1794. The Armory National Historic Site collection of arms includes Longfellow's 'Organ of Muskets'. The Indian Motorcycle Museum exhibits the first gasoline powered motorcycles in America, while the **Springfield Library and Museums** are a complex of historical and fine arts museums surrounding the city library.

 Village life in 1830s Massachusetts is the theme of **Old Sturbridge Village**. Found east of Springfield on the Massachusetts Turnpike, allow a day to explore the forty restored buildings. Artisans and trained volunteers re-create a fascinating period when age-old crafts flourished yet manufactured goods were appearing. Homemaking, farming, milling, printing and the trades are all represented. Collections include an outstanding clock gallery, folk and decorative arts, and firearms. Activities change to reflect the passing seasons, while the annual calender is peppered with events. Meals and accommodation (call ahead) are available within the village, and shops stock period books and crafts.

The Berkshires are west of Springfield on US20. Water powered mills brought early industry, but the Berkshires were not spoilt, and have been a resort for the past century. **Stockbridge** was founded to bring Christianity to local Indians, depicted at the 1739 Mission House, home of Reverend John Sergeant. Naumkeag is typical of stately homes in the Berkshires, and was the summer estate of the ambassador to England, Joseph Choate. The **Norman**

Rockwell Museum has an extensive collection of Rockwell's works. Nearby Monument Mountain inspired many artists, and there authors Herman Melville and Nathaniel Hawthorne became firm friends.

Tanglewood near Lenox is summer home to the Boston Symphony Orchestra, with performances in July and August. Nathaniel Hawthorne wrote *The House of Seven Gables* here, and Hawthorne Cottage has since been reconstructed. The Mount, built for novelist Edith Wharton, embodied her ideals of symmetry and privacy. Tours of other fine homes in Lenox are available during summer weekends.

Pittsfield is largest city in the Berkshires. Visitor Bureau maps outline tours of the surrounding countryside including Arrowhead, where Herman Melville wrote *Moby Dick*. West of Pittsfield is **Hancock Shaker Village**, an active Shaker community until 1960. Now a living museum, the Shaker ideals of simplicity, celibacy, and equality permeate the village. Continue north on US7 through Williamstown.

Vermont

Even the name proclaims its title — 'The Green Mountain State'. Four distinct seasons make Vermont a year-round recreational paradise. Least populated of the New England states, Vermont specializes in healing stress-scarred refugees from beyond its quiet borders.

At **Bennington**, Ethan Allen and his Green Mountain Boys rebelled against New York and its claim to Vermont land. Despite the squabble, the 'boys' prevented General John Burgoyne from reaching vital supplies, contributing to the British defeat at Saratoga. The 306ft-high Battle Monument and Bennington Battle Weekend, held in mid-August, commemorate the event. **Bennington Museum** exhibits Americana and paintings by Grandma Moses, plus an old schoolhouse she attended. The white clapboard **Old First Church**, one of New England's finest, is the official shrine of Vermont. Poet Robert Frost is buried in its cemetery.

The Ethan Allen Highway, SR7A, continues north into Vermont. The thirty-five room Victorian Park-McCullough House in North Bennington was home to two Vermont governors. The Shaftburys, a series of eighteenth-century villages settled from Connecticut and Rhode Island, line SR7A. Among other places, Norman Rockwell lived in Arlington, and the painter's works and life are depicted at the Norman Rockwell Exhibition.

Manchester is gateway to the Green Mountain National Forest and its Bromley, Stratton, and Magic Mountain Ski Areas. A toll road climbs Mount Equinox for views of New England, New York, and Canada. In summer Bromley Mountain runs an alpine slide and scenic chair lift, while the Stratton Mountain Resort holds its art festival during the autumn foliage season. The Southern Vermont Art Center and **Hildene**, summer home of Abraham Lincoln's son Robert Todd Lincoln, are south of the town centre. The nearby **Appalachian Trail** runs from Georgia to Maine — most hikers opt for just a sample.

After Manchester rejoin US7 for the Quaker settlement of Danby, where Pearl S. Buck spent her last years. **Rutland** is dubbed 'Marble City', while nearby Proctor has sidewalks paved with marble and their **Vermont Marble**

Exhibit is a monument to its beauty. Stained glass windows, Tiffany chandeliers and an elaborate grand staircase are a few delights of the thirty-two room **Wilson Castle**, set in 115 acres of prime Vermont.

US4 east leads to recreation-packed Sherburne, best known for the nearby **Killington Ski and Summer Resort**. In summer visitors take a gondola or chair lift to its observation deck. Continue east on US4, with a short detour south to Plymouth for the **President Coolidge Birthplace**. Plymouth Notch has been completely preserved, from the Coolidge birthplace and homestead, to his one-room schoolhouse and outbuildings.

Noted for its village green and quaint covered bridges, **Woodstock** is near the Suicide Six Ski Area and the less violently named Sonnenburg. Dairy farming is an important part of Vermont agriculture, but at the **Billings Farm** **and Museum** the old 1890 methods are still used. East of Woodstock is **Quechee Gorge**, the 'Little Grand Canyon of Vermont'. At the village of Quechee the old woollen mill houses a collection of specialty shops. Take US5 south to Windsor, where Old Constitution House was the 'Birthplace of Vermont'. The long covered bridge across the Connecticut leads to Cornish.

New Hampshire

Boasting the highest mountains in northeastern America, New Hampshire also has its fair share of lakes and streams, businesses and industry. Despite its reputation for being a hard-working state, recreation is number one.

Saint-Gaudens National Historic Site near Cornish was a tavern before

(opposite) New England is a winter wonderland

The 1830's are recreated at old Sturbridge Village

becoming home to the famed sculptor, and a visit includes two studios and exhibits of contemporary art. Travel south to Claremont then follow SR103 east, taking time to enjoy **Sunapee**. Meaning 'wild goose water', regular boat excursions depart from the harbour. Mount Sunapee State Park offers walking trails in summer and both downhill and cross-country skiing in winter.

Concord is capital of New Hampshire, where legislature still meets in its original chambers of the 1819 **State House**. The building houses paintings of famous citizens and artifacts pertaining to state history, as does the New Hampshire Historical Society Museum on Park Street. The Pierce Manse was home to President Franklin Pierce, who practiced law in Concord before being elected. The Conservation Center combines technology with common sense to create the energy efficient home. The educational **Christa McAuliffe Planetarium** is a memorial to the school teacher-cum-astronaut who perished in the Challenger disaster. From Concord take SR106 north, perhaps detouring to Canterbury Village for the **Shaker Village** museum and living history centre. Nearby Franklin was the birthplace of Daniel Webster, where a reconstructed two-room farmhouse shows his early possessions.

Laconia is headquarters for the White Mountains National Forest, although the town is better known as gateway to massive Lake Winnipesaukee. **Weirs Beach** provides a boardwalk plus amusement and water parks to entertain guests, while the lake is one of New England's most picturesque. The M/S *Mount Washington* sails regularly from the dock at Weirs Beach, visiting quaint Wolfeboro on the lake's eastern edge. The **Winnipesaukee Railroad** runs between Weirs Beach and Meredith in summer along the lakeside.

White Mountains Grand Tour

Sites of interest are legion within New Hampshire's **White Mountains**, whether one prefers the scenic pleasures of nature or activity oriented resorts. A number of hikes, including the **Appalachian Trail**, pass through the White Mountain National Forest. Other facilities include scenic waysides, campgrounds, and picnic areas.

From Lake Winnipesaukee take SR25 then 16 northeast to bustling resort communities **Conway** and **North Conway**. The energetic make for the Attitash Alpine Slide or the Mount Cranvale Ski Area, while the Conway Scenic Railway is more sedate. Although fast food is available and inexpensive, the Conway area offers fine dining with myriad cuisines. Cathedral Ledge in Echo Lake State Park has views guaranteed to whet an appetite.

At Glen turn left onto US302 through **Crawford Notch**. Near this scenic slice through the White Mountains are the 200ft high Arethusa Falls, a moderate $1^1/_2$ mile hike, and the popular roadside Silver Cascade. Willey House is headquarters for Crawford Notch State Park, encircled by the White Mountains National Forest. The Mount Washington Hotel at Bretton Woods has been a retreat since 1902, perfectly situated for the **Mount Washington Cog Railway**. Trips are subject to weather conditions, and advance bookings are essential in summer for this 3-hour steam up northeastern America's highest mountain at 6,288ft (1,917m). Bring warm, windproof clothing.

At Twin Mountains take US3 south, with an optional scenic detour west or SR18 to Franconia, home of poet Robert Frost. Continue south on US3 through the celebrated Franconia Notch. Stops en route include Echo Lake and the Ol

Man of the Mountains — photographers should have a zoom lens of 200mm or greater. The Cannon Mountain Aerial Tramway is popular in summer and winter alike, with the New England Ski Museum at the bottom.

A wheelchair accessible walk leads down to **The Basin**, a glacier smoothed granite pothole. Franconia Notch has an extensive network of foot trails and bicycle paths. **The Flume**, south of the Basin, has a boardwalk through an 800ft-long chasm created by a glacier. The admission fee includes a bus to the Flume if desired. Fantasy Farm and Clark's Trading Post, both popular tourist attractions, are near the resort town of North Woodstock.

The 34 mile (55km) **Kancamagus Highway** travels an undisturbed section of the White Mountains. The Loon Mountain Gondola Skyride is near the western entrance, then the highway winds up the Kancamagus Pass and down along the Swift River, passing national forest campgrounds, picnic areas, covered bridges, and marked trails en route. Having completed the loop at Conway, take SR16 north towards Pinkham Notch. Just outside Glen is **Heritage New Hampshire**, an audio-visual extravaganza tracing three centuries of New Hampshire History. Kids love nearby **Story Land**, which combines nursery rhyme characters with amusement rides.

Near Pinkham Notch, scenic SR16 passes the Glen Ellis Falls area, where the Tuckerman Ravine Trail traverses several cascades. Wildcat Mountain Gondola is east of SR16, while the substantial Presidential Range is west. The peaks named after American Presidents are crowned by Mount Washington, accessible via the **Mount Washington Auto Road**. From Gorham take US2 east to the state of Maine.

Southern and Coastal Maine

Maine crams 3,500 miles of shoreline into a coast only 225 miles long, as the seagull flies. But first comes inland Maine, 'The Pine Tree State', a land of rolling forested hills interspersed with rivers and lakes. Follow US2 along the Androscoggin River and then SR17 south to US202 west to **Augusta**, the state capital. The legislature meets at the **Maine State House**, which offers tours. Augusta State Park leads down from the capitol to the Kennebec River. The excellent **Maine State Museum** has dioramas of Maine natural history, while 'Made in Maine' exhibits nineteenth-century manufacturing and crafts. Also visit Fort Western, a 1754 shingle-covered log fort along the Kennebec. From Augusta, take I-95 northeast.

The confluence of the Sebasticook and Kennebec Rivers became Waterville, where the Reddington Museum depicts nineteenth-century life, including a well-stocked apothecary. Further west is **Bangor**, shipping and retail centre of

---

Tips for touring the Maine Coast

When planning a visit, remember that seaside resorts and Mount Desert Island are just as scenic in spring or autumn, and significantly less crowded. US1 is the main coastal route, but allow time for detours, as no one road could follow the thousands of miles of Maine coast. The scenic side trips take in those cameos of New England life, the picture-postcard fishing villages of Maine.

New England is noted for its exceptional autumn colours

Life in early New England is recalled at Strawberry Banke, Portsmouth

northern Maine. The city's raucous lumber days have passed, but giant Paul Bunyan still welcomes visitors to the Bangor Auditorium, where the State Fair is held. The **Cole Land Transportation Museum** collection ranges from a Conestoga wagon to steam logging tractors. The **Bangor Historical Society Museum** on Union Street has free walking tour maps and, in summer, bus tours of the 'Best of Bangor'.

From Bangor follow US1A to Ellsworth, where SR3 leads to the seaside resort of **Bar Harbor**. Nestled among the art and antique galleries are seafood restaurants serving delectable Maine lobsters. Stone mansions line Frenchman Bay, and one is now the Natural History Museum. Alternatively, experience nature first hand on a harbour or whale-watch cruise in summer. The MV *Bluenose* car and passenger ferry cruises to Yarmouth, Nova Scotia. Allow several days and bring passports and automobile insurance documents.

Acadia National Park sprawls across the incredibly beautiful Mount Desert Island. From the main visitor centre at Hulls Cove, north of Bar Harbor, the Loop Road embarks on a super-scenic tour of the park. Waysides overlook Bar Harbor and Frenchman Bay, and other stops include Sand Beach, one of Maine's finest. After Otter Cove comes Seal Harbor, a seaside resort just outside the park. The main loop returns past Jordan Pond for the grand finale atop Cadillac Mountain, highest point on the island. Sieur du Mont Spring is trailhead for several scenic walks, one of many offerings away from the loop road. For a longer drive, SR3 continues past Seal Harbor to Northeast Harbor, where Sargent Drive follows Somes Sound. SR198 and then 102 south leads past Echo Lake and its beach to Southwest and Bass Harbors. The Hio Road near the latter leads to Seawall, overlooking the Cranberry Isles. Southwest Harbor houses the Mount Desert Oceanarium and Wendell Gilley Museum. Trails from nearby Long Pond climb Bernard Mountain or follow the lake shore. SR102 forms a complete loop, returning north via Seal Cove Pond and Pretty Marsh.

Return to Boston along the Maine coast via Ellsworth and US1. Blue Hill, Deer Isle, and Stonington offer a scenic detour, returning via **Castine**. The latter is home to the Maine Maritime Academy, where the *State of Maine* is berthed except during training exercises.

Near Bucksport, a pulp and paper town, **Fort Knox State Park** commands an excellent view of the Penobscot River and still musters a cannon or two for visitors. The **Penobscot Marine Museum** in Searsport is a collection of historic buildings, and **Belfast**, another shipbuilding town, also has a local museum and bay cruises. **Perry's Nut House** combines a gift shop with curiosities collected by the late Mr Perry during his world travels.

Camden is regarded as northern border of 'Down East' Maine. Look for an album, tape, or transcript of *Bert and I*, the definitive collection of Down East humour. Camden is a year-round resort, with boat cruises in summer and skiing in winter. Continuing down the coast, **Rockland** is a busy fishing port where old fashioned Main Street is still an active shopping centre. The Farnsworth Art Museum exhibits works by artists with strong Maine connections. Owl's Head is a popular side trip from Rockland, offering good views of the islands across Penobscot Bay, a ferry's ride from Rockport.

Continuing south, the scenery along US1 remains pleasant but only the longest inlets reach the main road. For a better view of the wandering coastline, explore the peninsulas which extend to **Pemaquid Point** and the **Boothbay Harbor** region. Cod fishermen worked the Maine coast long before the Puritans set sail, and **Bath** has built ships since 1607, an activity continued by the Bath Iron Works. The **Maine Maritime Museum** keeps alive the rich shipbuilding heritage with models, artifacts and a boat-building Apprenticeshop programme. The Grand Banks Schooner *Sherman Zwicker* is often in port.

Bowdoin College at **Brunswick** has a list of famous former students. Hubbard Hall includes a museum to explorers Robert Perry and Donald MacMillan. Longfellow and Hawthorne attended the college, and Harriet Beecher Stowe wrote *Uncle Tom's Cabin* there while her husband taught. A sermon at the nearby 1717 First Parish Church was her inspiration. The Walker Art Building houses the Bowdoin College Museum of Art. Built by two sea captains, the Skolfield-Wittier House is now the Pejepscot Museum, with the personal effects of the captains displayed.

Freeport is home to **L. L. Bean**, a sporting and outdoor recreation goods complex that never closes. The popularity of L.L. Bean has brought hundreds of factory outlets and speciality stores to Freeport. After a hard day's shopping, attack a lobster (restaurants show how to eat them) or sample old-fashioned 'Down East' clam or fish chowder. The depot information sign directs visitors to their favorite shops and outlet stores.

Portland is Maine's largest city and its cultural capital. Visual arts are well represented at the **Portland Museum of Art**, and check for events at the Performing Arts Center. The **Wadsworth-Longfellow House** exhibits poet Henry's possessions. Other impressive homes include the Tate House, built by a 'Mast Agent' for the British Navy, and the Morse-Libby House, known locally as the **Victoria Mansion**. The nineteenth-century buildings at the Old Port Exchange on the waterfront now house restaurants, shops,and boutiques. Several boat tours leave from Commercial Street wharfs for the 365 Calendar Islands. **Portland Head Light** in South Portland was commissioned by George Washington, yet is still operational.

From South Portland, take Routes 77 and 207 south to SR9, which follows the coast. **Kennebunkport**, a summer resort for the past century, received additional publicity when George Bush was elected President, as his summer home is here. Maine ends at **Kittery**, an important shipbuilding centre in a time recalled by the Kittery Historical and Naval Museum, and at Fort McClary State Historic Site. John Paul Jones, the Errol Flynn of the American Revolutionary Navy, had *The Ranger* built in Kittery, then outfitted in nearby Portsmouth.

From Portsmouth to Boston

New Hampshire has a short coastline, but those few miles boast several beaches, seaside towns, and historic **Portsmouth**. Originally settled in 1630 a **Strawbery Banke**, the early seaport is preserved as a living museum and crafts centre. Also a pleasant town for shopping or exploring, Portsmouth has other historic homes along the 'Portsmouth Trail'.

Take US1A south into Massachusetts, stopping at **Salem**. Best known for its infamous witchcraft trials, Salem has witnessed considerable history. Important downtown museum complexes include the nautically orientated

Peabody Museum of Salem and the **Essex Institute Museum Neighborhood**. The **Salem Maritime National Historic Site** preserves much of waterfront Salem. Nearby is the **House of the Seven Gables** complex, which includes Nathaniel Hawthorne's birthplace and the building which inspired his book. Pickering Wharf has been redeveloped for shopping, while downtown Essex Street is a pedestrian mall. Many fine privately owned colonial homes are a short walk west on Essex; return along Chestnut Street. Last but certainly not least, combine history and hysteria at the Salem Witch Museum and the Witch House.

Additional Information

State Tourism Bureaux

*Connecticut Economic
    Development*
865 Brook St
Rocky Hill, CT 06067-3405
☎ 800-CT-BOUND
or 203-258-4293

Maine Publicity Bureau
97 Winthrop St
Hallowell, ME 04347
☎ 207-289-6070

*Commonwealth of
    Massachusetts*
Office of Travel and Tourism
100 Cambridge St,
13th Floor
Boston, MA 02202
☎ 617-727-3201

New Hampshire Tourism
PO Box 856
Concord, NH 03301
☎ 603-271-2666

Rhode Island Tourism Division
7 Jackson Walkway
Providence, RI 02903
☎ 800-556-2484
or 401-277-2601

Vermont Travel Division
34 State St
Montpelier, VT 05602
    802-828-3236

Regional Information

Bar Harbor COC
PO Box 168, Cottage St
Bar Harbor, ME 04609
☎ 207-288-5103

Boston CVB
Prudential Plaza West
PO Box 490
Boston, MA 02199
☎ 617-536-4100

Hartford CVB
One Civic Center Plaza
Hartford, CT 06103
☎ 203-708-6789

New Haven CVB
195 Church St
New Haven, CT 06510
203-777-8550

Newport County CVB
23 America's Cup Ave
Newport, RI 02840
☎ 800-326-6030
or 401-849-8048

Mount Washington Valley CVB
Box 2300
North Conway, NH 03860
☎ 800-367-3364
or 603-356-5701

Plymouth Area COC
91 Samoset St
Plymouth, MA 02360
☎ 508-746-3377

Portland COC
142 Free St
Portland, ME 04101
☎ 207-772-2811

Portsmouth Tourism
1000 Market St, Suite N
Portsmouth, NH 03801
☎ 800-221-5623
or 603-436-7678

Providence CVB
30 Exchange Terrace
Providence, RI 02903
☎ 800-233-1636
or 401-274-1636

Rutland Region COC
PO Box 67, 7 Court Square
Rutland, VT 05701
☎ 802-773-2747

Salem CVB
13 Washington Square
Salem, MA 02199
☎ 508-745-2268

Local Events

Check locally for exact dates

March
St Patrick's Day Parade
South Boston, MA

April
Paul Revere Rides Again
Boston, MA

Battle of Lexington & Concord
Lexington & Concord, MA

May
Street Performers Festival
Boston, MA

Lobster Fest
Mystic Seaport, CT

June
Cambridge River Festival
Cambridge, MA

Festival of Historic Houses
Providence, RI

Yale-Harvard Regatta
Thames River
New London, CT

Sea Music Festival
Mystic Seaport, CT

A Taste of Hartford
Constitution Plaza
Hartford, CT

Newport Music Festival
Newport, RI

Market Square Weekend
Strawbery Banke
Portsmouth, NH

July
Boston Harborfest
Boston, MA

Riverfest
Hartford, CT

Somes Sound Rowing Regatta
Southwest Harbor, ME

Open House Tour
Litchfield, CT

Bangor State Fair
Bangor, ME

July-Aug
Killington Music Festival
Killington, VT

August
Seafest
Nantucket, MA

Maine Lobster Festival
Rockport, ME

Bennington Battle Weekend
Bennington, VT

Early September
Waterfront Festival
Providence, RI

Vermont State Fair
Rutland, VT

Taste of Rhode Island
Newport, RI

October
Dutch Celebration
Plimoth Plantation
Plymouth, MA

Fall Festival
Strawbery Banke
Portsmouth, NH

Harvest Weekend
Old Sturbridge Village, MA

November
Thanksgiving Week
Old Sturbridge Village, MA

December
Boston Tea Party
Boston, MA

Places of Interest

Augusta, ME
Maine State Museum
State House Complex
Augusta, ME 04333
☎ 207-289-2301
Open: 9am-5pm Mon-Fri, 10am-4pm Sat, 1-4pm Sun.
Free. Gifts, &

Bangor, ME
Bangor Historical Society Museum
159 Union St
Bangor, ME 04401
☎ 207-942-5766
Open: noon-4pm Tue-Fri & Sun

Bar Harbor, ME
Acadia NP
Bar Harbor, ME 04609
☎ 207-288-3338
Open: 8.30am-4.30pm.
Admission for loop road only.
Visitor centre, gifts, walks, &

Bath, ME
Maine Maritime Museum
243 Washington St
Bath, ME 04530
☎ 207-443-1316
Open: 9.30am-5pm except major holidays
Gifts, snacks in summer, part &

Boston, MA
Museum of Fine Arts
465 Huntington Ave
Boston, MA 02114
☎ 617-742-1854
Open: 10am-5pm Tue-Sun, 10am-10pm Wed
Gifts, food, part &

New England Aquarium
Central Wharf
Boston, MA 02110-3309
☎ 617-742-8870
Open: 9am-5pm, 9am-6pm weekends, 9am-8pm Fri
Aquariums, dolphin show, gifts, food, &

USS Constitution
Charlestown Navy Yard
Boston, MA
☎ 617-242-5670
Open: 9.30am-3.50pm
Tours

Bretton Woods, NH
Mount Washington Cog Railway
SR302
Bretton Woods, NH 0358
☎ 800-922-8825 or 603-84 5404
Open: mid Apr-Oct, call for times

Cambridge, MA
Longfellow NHS
105 Brattle St
Cambridge, MA
☎ 617-876-4491
Open: 10am-5.30pm
except major holidays

Concord, MA
Minute Man NHP
Box 160
Concord, MA 01742
☎ 508-369-6993
or 617-862-7753
Open: 8.30am-5pm,
extended in summer.
Free
2 visitor centres, gifts, ♿

Eastham, MA
Cape Cod National Seashore
US6
Eastham, MA
☎ 508-255-3421
or 508-487-1256
Open: 8.30am-5pm, closed
winter. Free
Visitor centres, beaches,
part ♿

Franconia, NH
The Flume
US3
Franconia, NH 03580
☎ 603-745-8391
Open: 9am-4.30pm
Memorial Day to mid-Oct
Gifts, food, bus

Freeport, ME
L.L. Bean
95 Main St
Freeport, ME 04032
☎ 800-341-4341
Open: always
Outdoor goods, ♿

Glen, NH
Heritage New Hampshire
R16
Glen, NH
☎ 603-383-9776
Open: 9am-5pm Memorial
Day to Oct
Gifts, ♿

Hartford, CT
*Mark Twain & Harriet
  Beecher Stowe Houses*
Farmington Ave & Forest St
Hartford, CT 06105
☎ 203-525-9317
Open: 9.30am-4pm Tue-
Sat, Noon-4pm Sun. Also
Mon in summer
Visitor centre, gifts, tours

Old State House
800 Main St
Hartford, CT 06103
☎ 203-522-6766
Open: 10am-5pm Mon-
Sat
Free. Exhibits, gifts, ♿

State Capitol
210 Capitol Ave
Hartford, CT 06106
☎ 203-240-0222
Open: call for tour times.
Free
Exhibits, tours, gifts, ♿

Killington, VT
*Killington Ski & Summer
  Resort*
Killington Road
Killington, VT 05751
☎ 802-422-3333
Open: hours vary
Gondola, chairlift, food,
gifts

Laconia, NH
*White Mountains National
  Forest*
PO Box 638
Laconia, NH 03247
☎ 603-528-8721
Free
Hike, picnic, camp, scenic
drives, sections ♿

Mystic, CT
Mystic Marinelife Aquarium
55 Coogan Blvd
Mystic, CT 06355-1997
☎ 203-536-3323
Open: 9am-4.30pm, 9am-
5.30pm summer
Dolphin & whale shows,
gifts, aquariums, ♿

Mystic Seaport
50 Greenmanville Ave
Mystic, CT 06355-0990
☎ 203-572-0711
Open: 9am-4pm, ex-
tended in summer
Food, gifts, boat rides, ♿

New Haven, CT
*Peabody Museum of Natural
  History*
170 Whitney Ave
New Haven, CT 06511
☎ 203-432-5050
Open: 10am-5pm Mon-
Sat, noon-5pm Sun
Gifts, ♿

Yale Center for British Art
1080 Chapel St
New Haven, CT 06520
☎ 203-432-0822
Open: 1-4pm Tue-Thu,
closed Aug & holidays.
Free

Newport, RI
*Preservation Society of New-
  port*
118 Mill St
Newport, RI 02840
☎ 401-847-1000
Open: 10am-5pm May-
Sep, reduced hours in
winter.
Tours of Newport mansions

Pawtucket, RI
Slater Mill Historic Site
Roosevelt Ave., PO Box
727
Pawtucket, RI 02862
☎ 401-725-8638
Open: 10am-5pm Tue-
Sat, 1-5pm Sun June to
Labor Day

Pittsfield, MA
Hancock Shaker Village
US 20, 5 miles west
Pittsfield, MA
☎ 413-443-0188
Open: 9.30am-5pm
tourist season, 10am-3pm
winter

Plymouth, MA
Plimoth Plantation
Box 1620, SR 3A
Plymouth, MA 02360
☎ 508-746-1622
Open: 9am-5pm, closed
winter
Food, gifts, living history

Portland, ME
Portland Museum of Art
7 Congress Sq
Portland, ME 04101
☎ 207-775-6148
Open: 10am-5pm Tue-
Sat, Noon-5pm Sun
Gifts

*Wadsworth-Longfellow
   House*
487 Congress St
Portland, ME 04101
☎ 207-774-1882
Open: 10am-4pm Tue-Sat
Jun to mid-Oct
Gifts

Portsmouth, NH
Strawbery Banke
PO Box 300
Portsmouth, NH 03801
☎ 603-433-1100
Open: 10am-5pm May-
Oct & 1st half of Dec
Gifts, crafts, tours, part ♿

Rutland, VT
*Norman Rockwell Museum
   of Vermont*
SR4 East, Box 7209
Rutland, VT 05701
☎ 802-773-6095
Open: 9am-6pm
Gifts

Salem, MA
Peabody Museum of Salem
East India Square
Salem, MA 01970
☎ 508-745-9500
Open: 10am-5pm Mon-
Sat, 1-5pm Sun & holi-
days
Gifts, ♿

Salem Maritime NHS
Custom House, Derby St
Salem, MA 01970
☎ 508-744-4323
Open: 8.30am-5pm. Free
Gifts, tours

Sandwich, MA
Heritage Plantation
PO Box 566
Sandwich, MA 02563
☎ 508-888-3300
Open: 10am-5pm, closed
winter

Sturbridge, MA
Old Sturbridge Village
1 Old Sturbridge Road
Sturbridge, MA 01566
☎ 508-347-3362
Open: 9am-5pm tourist
season, 10am-4pm Tue-
Sun winter
Gifts, food, lodging, crafts,
♿

Weirs Beach, NH
M/S Mount Washington
PO Box 5367, Lake Ave
Weirs Beach, NH 03247
☎ 603-366-5531
9am & 12.15pm sailings
$3^1/_2$-hour cruise, food

2
NEW YORK

M anhattanites acknowledge only one New York, the city, ignoring the gentle Hudson River Valley, rugged Adirondacks, thundering Niagara Falls, and two Great Lakes. The 'Big Apple' and Upstate New York are fine taken singly, but together form the perfect duet.

New York City

The Big Apple is heart of a conurbation comprising some 18 million people across three states. Foremost in US trade and finance, New York City is also the cultural capital of America. The city's five boroughs are Manhattan Island, Brooklyn and Queens east on Long Island, Richmond (Staten Island), and the Bronx, the only mainland borough. Most places of interest to visitors are concentrated in Manhattan, which for convenience has been divided into **Lower Manhattan** (Battery to 14th Street), **Midtown** (14th to 59th Streets), and **Uptown** to the north.

Lower Manhattan: The Tip to 14th Street

When the Dutch first settled in New Amsterdam, the southern tip at **Battery Park** was a jumble of tide-swept rocks. **Castle Clinton**, a war fortification of 1812, now preserved as a national monument, has exhibits depicting the changing shoreline.

Arrive early or follow the crowds to ticket booths for **The Statue of Liberty** ✳

New York in Brief

Manhattan is more than cosmopolitan, it's vibrant and alive! After experiencing Uptown and Lower Manhattan — and sights between — tour that other New York, the state. Perhaps America's best kept secret is Upstate New York, which combines New England style villages with the finest outdoor recreation, and numerous scenic drives for the motorist.

Two weeks are sufficient for the 1,500 mile tour. Spring and autumn are great touring seasons, while winter is best for skiers. Walking around Manhattan can be hot and tiring during July and August — opt for air conditioned bus tours. Non-residents should request a multiple entry United States visa if visiting the Canadian side of Niagara Falls.

NEW YORK
(CITY PLAN)

The Metropolitan Museum of Art

Birds-eye view of New York, Manhattan Bridge and the Brooklyn Bridge

Into and Around New York City

John F. Kennedy, **La Guardia**, and **Newark International** (the latter in New Jersey) comprise New York City's three major airports, all with shuttle bus and helicopter connections to Manhattan. Taxi transfers are more convenient for hotels than buses, and the extra expense may be defrayed by sharing. JFK airport has a subway connection via a short bus hop to Howard Beach Station. Passenger trains stop at **Grand Central Station** *or* **Pennsylvania Station**, while the **Port Authority** is the main bus terminal, including Greyhound. The Queen Elizabeth II docks at the **Passenger Ship Terminal** on the Hudson.

Manhattan is best seen on foot, but conserve energy by taking public transport (subway, bus, or taxi) between areas of interest. Avenues are north-south trunk routes, streets are closer together and separated into east and west by 5th Avenue. Most subway lines run north-south through Manhattan, but like Broadway are not ruler straight. Lines are numbered (1-7) or lettered (A-S), and most share the few tracks through downtown. Subway cross connections are available at 14th, 42nd, 53rd and 60th streets; 42nd street being the Grand Central Station and Times Square Shuttle. Transport maps are readily available, and remember that express trains skip stops — avoid them if unsure. At night, most Manhattanites on the town take taxis.

Sightseeing bus tours are supplemented by helicopter flights and ferry boats. Circle Line leaves Pier 83, due west from Times Square. Car parking charges often exceed rental fees, making automobiles redundant until leaving for the New York State tour. Those hiring a car might allocate a certain number of days to see Manhattan, *then* pick up a previously booked vehicle. To visit Atlantic City in New Jersey, take a bus from Port Authority, drive south down the Garden State Parkway, or fly.

and Ellis Island Ferry, all under the National Park Service. This double-barrelled treat first visits the statue on Liberty Island, which is actually over the state border in New Jersey. Lady Liberty carries a new torch, a present for her hundredth birthday, while the museum in the base tells her story. Hot, crowded summer afternoons are *not* the time to climb to the top — take the elevator up to the base viewing platform. Despite a $160 million refurbishment for visitors, Ellis Island pulls no punches. A combination of life-size pictures, extracts from letters and diaries, and the immigrants' own voices transport guests back to when Ellis Island was America's main entry point, passed by some 16 million people. Leaving from east of Battery Park, Staten Island Ferry passes Liberty Island for only a nominal charge, but is not nearly so educational or moving as a visit to Ellis.

Traffic encircles the 1907 Custom House north of Battery Park; follow it anticlockwise to Pearl Street. At **Fraunces Tavern**, still serving the public today, George Washington bade farewell to his officers. Further north is **Wall Street**, now financial capital of America but originally a wooden palisade against Indian or British incursions. George Washington was inaugurated at **Federal Hall**, now a national monument, while the famed **New York Stock**

Exchange gives free tours; arrive early for tickets. Across Broadway from Wall Street, **Trinity Church** is the third on its site. Early Dutch colonists, Alexander Hamilton, and steamboat entrepreneur Robert Fulton are interred there.

The unmistakable twin towered **World Trade Center** is northwest of the Broadway-Wall Street junction. South Tower has the 107th floor observation deck, while North Tower offers the Windows on the World complex of lounges and restaurants. **St Paul's Chapel** is New York's oldest, and contains George Washington's personal pew. Continuing east on Fulton Street leads to the famed fish market and **South Street Seaport Museum**, with harbour excursions, a selection of sailing vessels to board, and exhibits on waterfront New York City. Brooklyn Bridge crosses East River just north of the seaport, with Manhattan Bridge beyond.

Returning to the centre, City Hall Park is a pleasant spot, but book weeks ahead to tour City Hall. Follow Center Street north, and from Foley Square take Worth Street east to Chatham Square, starting point of the Bowery. For Mott Street, heart of **Chinatown**, go north a few blocks on Bowery and west on Pell. Like many Chinatowns, New York's is thriving, and Chinese shops and restaurants continue beyond the original northern border at Canal St. **Little Italy**, a block west on Mulberry, has some fine restaurants despite emigration of Italians to the suburbs. Manhattan Neighborhood Trolley Inc runs a thirty-passenger trolley tour of Chinatown and Little Italy which includes the **Lower East Side** — perfect for tired feet. Broadway is found west of Little Italy on Grant or Canal Street.

West of Broadway are **The Villages**, a collection of trendy neighbourhoods with hot nightspots, great food, and good theatre. **Greenwich Village**, best known of the communities, is north of Houston. **Washington Square Park**, its heart, is west of Broadway on 4th Street, or straight down 5th Avenue from Midtown. To sample the Village and its shops, stroll along 4th Street west from the park, take Seventh Avenue north, and return via Perry and Greenwich Avenue. Local artists often exhibit their works in Washington Square by day, while village life picks up at nightfall.

SoHo, short for South of Houston, became chic after Greenwich Village was too established. Bohemian artists and poets flocked to deliciously archaic SoHo and renovated the derelict cast-iron buildings, giving an *avant-garde* touch to an architecturally interesting area. Inevitably others discovered SoHo, leading some to leave, colonizing the triangle below Canal Street, shorting the name to **Tribeca**.

Midtown Manhattan: 14th Street to 59th Street

Broadway, following an old Indian trail, is the one street which mars the perfect grid pattern of Midtown Manhattan. **Times Square** is the triangular junction of Broadway, Seventh Avenue and 42nd Street, and is easy to miss in daylight without the neon signs. Theatregoers should be aware that establishments classified as 'Broadway' refer to size, rather than exact location. Conversely, Times Square also boasts 'off-Broadway' theatres, although more are in Greenwich Village and Uptown. The Theater District is spread from 41st to 53rd Streets between Sixth and Eighth Avenues, with most concentrated on 44th and 45th Streets. Current theatre is listed in 'New York' and *The New Yorker* magazines, and the papers, including *Variety*, an entertainment weekly which also lists off-Broadway shows. Apart from each box office, tickets are available through agencies listed in the information section. TKTS booths on Broadway and 47th and at 2 World Trade Center mezzanine sell half-price tickets on the day of the performance; remember that the best shows are sold out. Between Times Square and the Port Authority Bus Terminal on 8th Avenue are the 24 hour sex cinemas and the discount shops of 42nd Street.

East on 42nd Street leads past Bryant Park and the Beaux Arts styled **New York Public Library** to **Fifth Avenue**. South is the **Empire State Building**, which also houses the Guinness Book of Records. Some visitors enjoy the 86th floor views so much that they forget the 102nd. **Lord and Taylor**, New York's first department store, is on 5th Avenue and 38th Street. Continuing south, eventually Madison Square Park and the Flatiron Building are reached. 42nd Street west leads to **Grand Central Terminal**, constructed by transportation tycoon Cornelius Vanderbilt. The art deco **Chrysler Building** on Lexington Avenue houses the Con Edison Conservation Center. The Ford Foundation is on 43rd Street, while on 45th is the entrance to the **United Nations**. Tours highlight the General Assembly Hall, where unique UN stamps and postmarks are prized by collectors, while the **UN Gifts Center** has handicrafts and goods on sale from around the world. If returning to 5th Avenue via 50th Street, visit Waldorf Astoria and **St Patrick's Cathedral**.

The **Rockefeller Center** is a massive example of private urban renewal, converting twenty-two deteriorating acres into prime Manhattan real estate. Who else but John D. Rockefeller could get a $44 million mortgage during the depression? Upper floors are offices, while beneath are the shops, restaurants, and art works commissioned by the Rockefellers. The golden statue in lower Rockefeller Plaza is fire-bringer Prometheus; in winter, dining tables are removed and the lower plaza becomes a skating rink. Within the complex, Radio City Music Hall and NBC Studios provide tours. The latter is in the RCA building, which takes diners to new heights in the 65th floor Rainbow Room.

Uptown Manhattan is famous for museums, but the acclaimed **Museum of Modern Art** is one of America's finest. Also on West 53rd Street is the **American Craft Museum**, while the **Museum of Broadcasting** is on East 53rd. The aircraft carrier which recovered returned astronauts now houses the **Intrepid Sea-Air-Space Museum**, on West 46th Street at the Hudson River.

Famous stores like **Saks**, **Cartier**, and **Tiffany's** line 5th Avenue between 47th Street and Central Park, along with the brown and bronze Trump Tower foyer. Ladies enjoy the classy collections of **Bergdorf Goodman**, but not all stores are on 5th Avenue. **Macy's** is south on 34th and Broadway in the Garment District. Madison Square Garden sport and convention complex and Penn Central Railroad Station are near Macy's. **Bloomingdale's** is on 3rd Ave and 59th, while **Abraham and Straus** are on 6th and 33rd. Wallach's is in the Empire State Building among other locations.

Returning north, **Carnegie Hall** is west on 8th Avenue and 57th. The **Plaza Hotel** off Fifth Avenue is known for fine shops, lounges, and restaurants — a favourite Manhattan haunt for Frank Lloyd Wright and that young scamp Eloise. The Grand Army Plaza outside leads to the southwest corner of Central Park.

Uptown Manhattan: Central Park and Beyond

Central Park occupies 840 acres of landscaped grounds, trees, and lakes, about 5 percent of Manhattan. The section south of 86th Street has been considerably refurbished, as safe in *daytime* as any major city. Central Park is especially alive on sunny weekends, when motorized traffic is prohibited and New Yorkers take to skates, skateboards, bicycles, and pedicabs. Cycles are rented near the southern border, while paths offer quieter strolls away from road-bound joggers and cyclists.

From the Grand Army Plaza, East Drive goes north through the park while West Drive does the same on its western edge. Near the plaza entrance are the pond, bird sanctuary, and Wollman Memorial Skating Rink. Meandering north leads to the information centre, with a path west to the popular **Children's Zoo**. From the dairy go north over 65th Street Transverse to the statue and tree-lined Mall. **Sheep Meadow**, perfect for picnics or sunbathing, is to the left, while the bandstand up the Mall holds summer concerts. Past Bethesda Fountain is the lake, with Loeb Boathouse on its northeastern edge. Hans Christian Anderson's statue is across East Drive and, north of Conservatory Pond, the delightful bronze of Alice in Wonderland. Return to the fountain and follow the lake west to Bow Bridge.

Beyond the wooded Ramble and 79th Street Traverse is Belvedere Castle and **Delacorte Theater**, the latter presenting free Shakespearean plays in summer. The path between Great Lawn and Belvedere Lake leads east to **Metropolitan Museum of Art**. Take time to appreciate the Met — each visit encourages another. The extensive and eclectic collection exceeds 3 million works, and in addition to major art treasures are whole 'environments', such as an Egyptian Temple, a Romanesque Chapel, and a Ming Dynasty garden court. Among grand donations are Michael C. Rockefeller and Lila Acheson Wallace wings and Lehman Pavilion. Banker Robert Lehman insisted that his fabulous collection must include his home.

Return to Delacorte Theatre and turn west to Shakespeare Garden, where only plants mentioned by the playwright are to be found. South is **Strawberry Fields**, given in memory of John Lennon by Yoko Ono. The subway can be caught at Central Park West (8th Avenue) and 72nd Street, and beyond is the Tavern on the Green at Columbus Circle.

The Metropolitan Museum of Art and Museum of Modern Art are only two of Manhattan's major art establishments. The **Frick Collection** offers exquisite pieces arranged as if the former mansion's owner had just stepped out. The **Solomon R. Guggenheim Museum** building, fresh from a major renovation in 1991, was designed by Frank Lloyd Wright. The cylindrical museum has a downward spiral ramp leading past the works. The **Whitney Museum of Art**, exclusively dedicated to 20th-century American works, was founded by sculptress Gertrude Vanderbilt Whitney. Constantly changing exhibits and *avant-garde* films keep the Whitney and its satellites at Equitable Center and Philip Morris fun and full.

The elegant **Upper East Side** of New York has long attracted the wealthy. Their patronage has brought fine antique shops, exquisite galleries, and the height of *haute couture* to Madison Avenue, between 55th and 79th Street. Museums in Upper East Side along 5th Avenue include the Cooper Hewitt

(Smithsonian Institution's National Museum of Design), Jewish Museum, Museum of the City of New York, and El Museo del Barrio, showcasing works of Puerto Rican and Latin American artists. Between 61st and 71st, Park Avenue boasts the Asia Society and Museum of American Illustration, while the **Abigail Adams Smith Museum**, part of 2nd President John Adams' former estate, is east on 61st between 1st and York Avenues.

Harlem is named after the Dutch city of Haarlem. 'Black Harlem' is from 110th Street to 168th Street, bounded by Morningside Heights and Columbia University. Turn-of-the-century Harlem attracted wealthy Blacks from other cities and the South — here they could rent fine properties. During the 1920s heyday it was fashionable for New Yorkers to visit local bars and jazz clubs, but the depression put Harlem into a spin. The 1980s saw considerable improvement, with financially stable Blacks staying to help the community. Outsiders are warned not to wander through Harlem on their own — take a tour offered by the Black community, such as Harlem Spiritual Inc.

Upper West Side is becoming chic, undoubtedly stimulated by the **Lincoln Center** performing arts complex. Metropolitan Opera House alone seats some 3,800, while New York State Theater is home to New York City Ballet and City Opera. September to May is New York Philharmonic's concert season in Avery Fisher Hall, with 2,700 seats and, since a 1976 remodelling, near perfect acoustics. *West Side Story* was filmed on location in slums since replaced by the Lincoln Center.

The **American Museum of Natural History** and **Hayden Planetarium** give another cultural boost to the Upper West Side. The Museum of Natural History has four floors of exhibits, including a special Discovery Room for children. Hayden Planetarium has a high-tech Sky Theater, multi-screened Guggenheim Space Theater *and* Hall of the Sun. **New York Historical Society** museum and library is just south, while Upper West Side also has the Mormon Visitors Center and the Children's Museum on West 83rd. The **Cathedral of St John the Divine** is north (avoid Morningside Park behind it), as is Columbia University and **The Cloisters** at Fort Tryon Park (take 190th Street subway exit or bus line 4 from Madison Avenue north to its end). The Cloisters, another example of Rockefeller patronage, has an extensive collection of mediaeval art and artifacts. Enjoy a day at the Cloisters and Fort, but avoid Inwood Hill Park on quiet days.

Other Boroughs

The Bronx has the acclaimed **Bronx-Zoo, New York Botanical Gardens**, and **Yankee Stadium**. By subway, exit at East Tremont Avenue (lines 2 and 5) for the zoo, Bedford Park Boulevard (line D) for the gardens, and Yankee Stadium (line 4) for great baseball from spring to autumn. **Prospect Park in Brooklyn** has Brooklyn Botanic Garden and Brooklyn Museum (lines 2 and S). In summer thousands still crowd the **Coney Island** boardwalk and New York Aquarium. **Queens** is the largest borough, mostly taken up with residential areas, La Guardia and JFK Airports. **Shea Stadium** is home to New York Mets and Flushing Meadows Park hosts the US Open Tennis Championships in August. A car is needed to explore Richmond, better known as **Staten Island**. Less developed than other boroughs, Richmond was only connected to New

Jersey until the Verrazano Narrows Bridge linked it to Brooklyn.

Queens and Brooklyn are located on **Long Island**, and beyond is still a residential extension of New York City, officially Nassua County. Elite New Yorkers have sumptuous mansions along the northern 'Gold Coast', off-bounds for mere mortals as even the shoreline is private property. Conversely, the **Hamptons** are a pleasant and accessible collection of southeastern villages, where public beaches are complemented by **Fire Island National Seashore**. ♣

New York State

Upstate New York beckons — and the drive will rest tired feet. From JFK and La Guardia Airports pick up I-678 north to the Bronx, then I-95 southbound. From Manhattan, follow Henry Hudson Parkway north along the river, then I-95 south. Once across the Hudson River, take SR9W north (Lemoine Avenue).

The gently scenic **Hudson River Valley** is remote from bustling New York City, with state and historic parks along both banks of the river. Bear Mountain has a lookout point over the valley, although its namesakes are long gone. Beyond is **West Point** US Military Academy. The visitor centre has information on cadet parades and places of interest, such as West Point Museum in Olmsted Hall. General George Washington made Newburgh headquarters for his Continental Army until hostilities ended with the Treaty of Paris. Take I-84 east over the Hudson River, and continue north on US9.

Poughkeepsie was a Dutch settlement, and at one time served as New York state capital. Beyond is the **Franklin D. Roosevelt National Historic Site** with a library and museum dedicated to America's longest serving president. Hyde Park houses the Culinary Institution of America, while the **Vanderbilt Mansion National Historic Site** is just beyond town. The Beaux-Arts residence was built for Frederick Vanderbilt, the Commodore's grandson. New York State administers nearby Mills Mansion, also pleasantly situated on the Hudson River.

Return across the Hudson via SR199 then SR28 west for the **Catskill Mountains**. This setting for *Rip van Winkle* seems hardly to have changed, but keep awake for the views. From Stony Hollow go clockwise around Ashokan Reservoir, returning on SR28 east. The village of Woodstock is north from West Hurley, and the picturesque Hudson Valley is regained east on 212 then back along scenic SR9W.

Although many assume New York City is the state's capital, that role belongs to **Albany**. Rockefeller Plaza, heart of the city, is a massive complex with the New York **State Capitol**, **State Museum**, and other interesting structures including **The Egg** performing arts centre. View Albany from the 44 storey Corning Tower, then enjoy 'Presidential' Washington and Lincoln Parks, Albany Institute of History and Art, and Schuyler Mansion State Historic Site. From Albany, I-87 is the quickest route north while US4 runs parallel to the Hudson. In late September the skies of Glens Falls are full of colourful balloons, while Lake George Opera Festival takes place early Au-

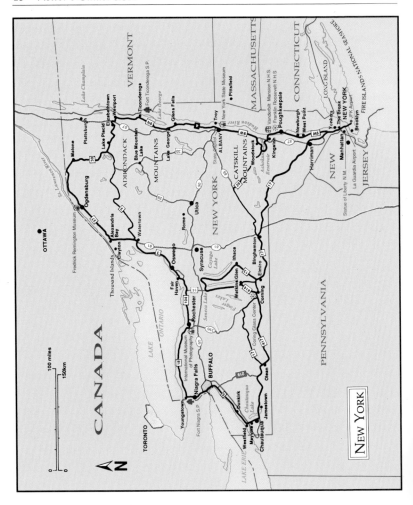

gust. The Hyde Collection of European art and period pieces is open year-round.

Adirondack Park encapsulates some 6 million acres of forests, lakes and mountains of upstate New York. Almost half is wilderness, while scenic roads through the remainder pass friendly villages and a few developed resorts. Starting between Glens Falls and Lake George, the park comes within 20 miles of the Canadian border. Begin the Adirondack experience at **Lake George Village**, including canon fire and musketry practice at **Fort William Henry Museum**, replicating the *Last of the Mohicans* fort. Two operators offer excursions on the 32 mile (51 km) lake, and do not miss the numerous factory outlet stores.

Follow the lake north on SR9N to **Fort Ticonderoga**. Constructed by the French and strengthened by the British, it was taken by Ethan Allen, of Vermont's Green Mountain Boys fame. British General Burgoyne regained Ticonderoga, razing it during his retreat south. This reconstructed fort offer

Adirondack Lake

The Niagara Falls

historically orientated cruises on Lake Champlain aboard the M/V *Carillon*, the fort's name under French occupation. Continue north along Lake Champlain on SR9N, which turns inland (west) at Westport. Beyond Elizabethtown, home of the Adirondack Center Museum, continue northwest between the mountains on SR73.

Lake Placid hosted the 1932 and 1980 Winter Olympics, although the resort is equally popular in summer. Golf courses and tennis courts complement biking and hiking trails, the latter used for cross-country skiing in winter. Lake Placid and nearby Mirror Lake have beaches, boat rides and rentals. **Olympic Center** gives tours, offering an excellent groomed cross-country trail system in winter. Ski jumping is limited to professionals, but the complex is open to the public, and athletes train even in summer, using plastic mats for snow. Shopping, dining, and accommodation are all excellent as befits a world-class resort.

Travellers with sufficient time can follow SR30 north to Malone, then SR37 west along the **St Lawrence Seaway** for the **Frederick Remington Museum** and the famed **Thousand Islands**. Ranging from mere points to village sized, the 1,700 islands are best seen from Alexandria Bay tour boats. The Skydeck on Thousand Islands International Bridge offers excellent views on clear days; foreign visitors should have a multiple entry visa if visiting Canada. Clayton also offers Thousand Islands excursions. Those not taking the St Lawrence detour should follow SR3 west through the Adirondacks to Watertown, where all proceed west along SR3, the Seaway Trail.

At 7,425 square miles (19,230 square km), **Lake Ontario** deserves the title 'Great' — it dwarfs the state of Connecticut. SR104 passes through Oswego at the lake's edge, and 104A dips down to Fair Haven. This is apple country, with blossom in spring and delicious eating in autumn. **Rochester** is the home of Eastman-Kodak, where the **International Museum of Photography** at Eastman House traces photographic developments. After the wild Adirondacks, urbanites will appreciate shopping malls, while Eastman Theater is heart of Rochester culture, regularly presenting the Philharmonic and Broadway shows. The Main Street Visitor Center at the Genesee River gives directions to the **Strong Museum, Rochester Museum and Science Center**, and the interesting **Genesee Country Village** in Mumford. When leaving Rochester, head west and pick up I-390 northbound for the Ontario Lake Parkway and SR18.

Enjoy the picnic facilities and beaches along Lake Ontario, but do not miss **Fort Niagara State Park** near Youngstown. Boasting the only French 'Castle' on American soil, Old Fort Niagara has been restored to its original 1727 appearance, complete with quarters, trading post and chapel. In summer, costumed volunteers drill at this once strategic post where the Niagara River joins Lake Ontario. SR18F follows the river south past the Niagara power stations.

Niagara Falls attracts honeymooners and holidaymakers alike. The American Falls are 185ft high and just over 1,000ft across, while the curved horseshoe of Canadian Falls has a 2,200ft crest and drops 175ft. The right-hand bend in the Niagara at the Falls makes the Canadian side better for an overview, but for sheer exhilaration take a boat trip on the *Maid of the Mist*.

From the American side the *Maid* leaves Prospect Point, which also has films in the Niagara Festival Theater and an Observation Tower with elevators down to the gorge. The information centre is on Niagara Street between 3rd and 4th, with Bus'N Boat Tours leaving the nearby transportation centre. **Goat Island** has excellent views of both falls — it sits between them, with walks along the rapids leading to the overlooks. The American Falls side has a footbridge to Luna Island for a bird's eye view of Bridal Falls, smallest of the Niagara Falls.

Unless visiting the Canadian side for more than a day, walk across Rainbow Bridge. Carry a good waterproof and picture identification (foreigners require passports with multiple-entry visas). Currency exchange is not necessary, but be aware of the current rate. Amusements between Rainbow Bridge and Canadian Falls include a Ripley's, Louis Tussaud's, Guinness Records, and several towers. **Queen Victoria Park** is a pleasant stroll along the cliff top, with excellent views of the falls. Up close, water plummeting over the edge is exhilarating if a trifle disorientating. For an even better look, take Table Rock House's elevator to the observation platform. Niagara Falls Theatre gives an IMAX-eye view on a six-storey screen.

Buffalo, New York's second largest city, was catapulted from a village into the industrial age by the Erie Canal. Buffalo residents enjoy the revitalized theatre district, nightspots along Elmwood Avenue, and the spicy Buffalo Wings, which are actually chicken. Sites include the Albright-Knox Art Gallery, Buffalo and Erie County Historical Society in Delaware Park, and Theodore Roosevelt Inaugural National Historic Site, where rough-riding Teddy Roosevelt was invested after President McKinley's assassination. From Buffalo, SR5 southbound runs parallel to Lake Erie en route to Dunkirk and Westfield. Larger but shallower than Lake Ontario, Lake Erie has begun recovery from the 1900s petrochemical and industrial excesses.

Follow SR394 inland at Westfield for Mayville and Lake Chautauqua. The steam-powered *Chautauqua Belle* plies the waters of this more human-sized lake. **Chautauqua Institution** is an activity-oriented education and entertainment centre which presents symphony, theatre, opera, dance, and bible studies, all open to the public.

Eastbound SR17 is a fast but scenic route from Jamestown to New York City, 10 hours away. If more time is available, take SR417 east from Olean through the northern Allegany Mountains. **Corning's Rockwell Museum** includes a large collection of western art, but is better known for its glass. **Corning Glass Center** exhibits both historical and high-tech aspects of glassmaking, while Stueben Factory demonstrates the time-honoured skills of hand fashioning glass. From Corning, travellers can follow SR414 north to **Watkins Glen** and the Finger Lakes, glacial gouges said to resemble elongated fingers. Watkins Glen, best known for its summer car racing season, has vineyards second only to California's. A short visit could include cruising Lake Seneca, picnicking and wine sampling at Chateau Lafayette Reneau, and viewing the rock formations and falls within Watkins Glen State Park. If time is short, return south on SR14 to Elmira. To explore the region further, follow SR14 north along Lake Seneca, turning east at Geneva and touring Cayuga lakeside on SR89, visiting Taughannock Falls State Park en route. **Ithaca** has high-ranking and beautifully situated **Cornell University**, founded in 1865. Students lead tours from Day Hall.

Further education is also of interest at **Elmira**. Samuel Clemens married local girl Olivia Langdon and Elmira College has preserved his study. The Clemens family are buried in Woodlawn Cemetery, where Samuel's monument is 2 fathoms high — Mark Twain — the depth required by a Mississippi riverboat.

If returning to New York City along SR17, pick up US 6 east near Harriman and take Palisades Parkway south, returning to Manhattan over George Washington Bridge or via Lincoln Tunnel. If another pass through the Catskills and Hudson River Valley is desired, follow I-88 northeast from Binghamton, taking either SR23 or 28, both being scenic, east from Oneonta.

Additional Information

State Tourism Bureaux

New York State Tourism
One Commerce Plaza
Albany, NY 12245
☎ 800-225-5697
or 518-474-4116

Regional Information

Albany County CVB
52 South Pearl Street
Albany, NY 12207
☎ 800-622-8464
or 518-434-1217

Buffalo CVB
107 Delaware Avenue
Buffalo, NY 14202
☎ 716-852-0511

Lake George CVB
Warren County Municipal Center
Lake George, NY 12845
☎ 518-792-7078

Lake Placid CVB
Olympic Center
Lake Placid, NY 12946
☎ 800-833-2521
or 518-523-2445

New York City CVB
2 Columbus Circle
New York, NY 10019-1823
☎ 212-397-8200

Niagara Falls CVB
345 Third St 101

Niagara Falls, NY 14303
☎ 716-285-2400

Watkins Glen COC
100 North Franklin Street
Watkins Glen, NY 14891
☎ 607-535-4300

Local Events

Check locally for exact dates

January or February
Chinese New Year
Chinatown
New York, NY

March
St Patrick's Day Parade
5th Ave
New York, NY

June
International Festival of the Arts
Throughout New York City
New York, NY

Shakespeare in the Park
Delacorte Theater
New York, NY

Empire State Regatta
Albany, NY

International Folk Festival
Rochester, NY

Camel Continental Grand Prix
Watkins Glen, NY

June-July
Lake Placid Horse Show
Lake Placid, NY

July
Independence Day Celebrations
Manhattan waterfront &
Albany, NY

Empire State Games
Albany, NY

August
Collegiate Figure Skating Champs.
Lake Placid, NY

September
New York Film Festival
Lincoln Center
New York, NY

November
Macy's Thanksgiving Day Parade
Central Park West, Broadway & 7th Ave
New York, NY

December
Christmas Tree Lighting
Rockefeller Plaza
New York, NY

New Year's Eve
Times Square
New York, NY

Places of Interest: New York City

American Museum of Natural History
Central Park West & 81st Street
New York, NY 10024
☎ 212-769-5900
Open: 10am-5.45pm;
10am-9pm Wed, Fri & Sat
Films, planetarium, gifts, HA

Bronx Zoo
185th Street & Southern Boulevard
The Bronx
New York, NY 10460
☎ 212-220-5198
Open: 10am-5pm, 10am-5.30pm Sun
Gifts, food , HA

Carnegie Hall
57th Street & 7th Avenue
New York, NY 10019
☎ 212-903-9790
Open: call for times
Performances, tours, HA

Circle Line Cruises
Pier 83
New York, NY 10036
☎ 212-563-3200
Call for sailings
Circles Manhattan, snacks

The Cloisters
Fort Tryon Park
New York, NY 10040
☎ 212-923-3700
Open: 9.30am-4.45pm
Tue-Sun
Medieval exhibits

Empire State Building
350 5th Avenue
New York, NY 10118
☎ 212-736-3100
Open: 9.30am-11.30pm
Views, gifts, food

Frick Collection
5th Avenue & 70th Street
New York, NY
☎ 212-288-0700

Open: 10am-6pm Tue-Sat, 1-6pm Sun
No children under 10 years.
European masters

Guggenheim Museum
5th Avenue & 89th Street
New York, NY
☎ 212-360-3500
Open: 11am-4.45pm Tue-Sat, 11am -7.45pm Tue
Modern art, Lloyd building

Harlem Spirituals Inc
1457 Broadway, Suite 1008
New York, NY 10036
☎ 212-302-2594/5
Open: call for times
Harlem gospel & evening tours

Lincoln Center
Broadway & 64th Street
New York, NY 10023
☎ 212-877-1800 (tours) or 212-877-2011 (tickets & events)
Call for schedule
Opera & Philharmonic, HA

Metropolitan Museum of Art
5th Avenue & 82nd Street
New York, NY 10028
☎ 212-535-7710
Open: 9.30am-5.15pm
Tue-Sun, 9.30am-8.45pm
Fri & Sat
Food, books, gifts, HA

Museum of Modern Art
11 West 53rd Street
New York, NY 10019
☎ 212-708-9480
Open: 11am-6pm Thu-Tue, 11am-9pm Thu
Food, gifts, HA

New York Historical Society
170 Central Park West
New York, NY 10024

☎ 212-873-3400
Open: 10am-5pm Tue-Sun
Gifts

New York Stock Exchange
20 Broad Street
New York, NY 10004
☎ 212-656-5168
Open: 9.15am-4pm
trading days
Free tickets, arrive early

Shea Stadium
Flushing, Queens
New York, NY 11368
☎ 718-507-1234
Call for games
Mets baseball, tours, HA

South Street Seaport
210 Front Street
New York, NY 10038
☎ 212-619-4500/1000
Open: 10am-5pm
Museum, boat trips, gifts, food

Statue of Liberty & Ellis Island
Battery Point
New York, NY 10004
☎ 212-363-3200 (park service)
or 212-269-5755 (ferry)
Open: 9am-4pm
Gifts, food, HA

United Nations
1st Avenue & 64th Street
New York, NY 10017
☎ 212-963-1234/7713
Open: 9.15am-4.45pm
except major holidays
Tours, worldwide gifts, HA

Whitney Museum of Art
945 Madison Avenue @ 75th
New York, NY 10021
☎ 212-570-3676
Closed Mon & hols. HA

Yankee Stadium
161st Street & River Ave
The Bronx

New York, NY 10451
☎ 212-963-6012
Call for game times
Yankees baseball, tours,
HA

Theatre Ticket Agencies

Advance Entertainment
  New York
261 West 35th St,
Suite 800
New York, NY 10001
☎ 212-239-2570

Downtown Theatre Ticket
  Agency
71 Broadway
New York, NY 10006
☎ 212-425-6410
or 800-843-7469

Edwards & Edwards
1 Times Square Plaza,
Suite 2000
New York, NY 10036
☎ 212-944-0290
or 800-843-7469

Theatre Service Americana
335 West 52nd Street,
Suite 2A
New York, NY 10019
☎ 212-581-6600

Places of Interest: New York State

Albany, NY
New York State Museum
Empire State Plaza
Albany, NY 12230
☎ 518-474-5842
Open: 10am-5pm. Free
Gifts, HA

Chautauqua, NY
Chautauqua Institution
SR394
Chautauqua, NY 14722
☎ 800-333-0884
or 716-357-6200
Call for events
Arts, theatre, HA

Corning, NY
Corning Glass Center
Centerway
Corning, NY 14831
☎ 607-974-2000
Open: 9am-5pm except
major holidays
Film, exhibits, gifts, HA

Hyde Park, NY
Franklin Roosevelt NHS
c/o 249 Albany Post Road
Hyde Park, NY 12538
☎ 914-229-9115
Open: 9am-5pm; closed
Tue & Wed in winter
Homes & grounds, &

Vanderbilt Mansion NHS
c/o 249 Albany Post Road
Hyde Park, NY 12538
☎ 914-229-9115
Open:10am-6pm Thu-Sun
winter, 9am-6pm daily
summer
Mansion, &

Lake George, NY
Lake George Steamboat Co
Steel Pier
Lake George, NY 12845
☎ 800-553-2628 or 518-
668-5777
Open: daily May-Oct,
check times
Food, entertainment, &

Lake Placid, NY
Olympic Jumping Complex
Olympic Center
Lake Placid, NY 12946
☎ 518-523-1655
Open: 9am-4.30pm
Jumps, elevator, &

Mayville, NY
Chautauqua Belle
SR 394
Mayville, NY 14757
☎ 716-353-7823
Open: Jun-Sep, call for
times
Steamboat

Niagara Falls, NY
Maid of the Mist
Prospect Point SP
Niagara Falls, NY 14303
☎ 716-284-8897
Open: 9.15am-6pm May-
Oct
Boat trip, &

Odgensburg, NY
Frederick Remington
  Museum
303 Washington Street
Odgensburg, NY 13669
☎ 315-393-2425
Open: 10am-5pm Mon-
Sat, 1-5pm Sun
Galleries, gifts, &

Rochester, NY
International Museum of
  Photography
George Eastman House
900 East Avenue
Rochester, NY 14607
☎ 716-271-3361
Open: 10am-4.30pm Tue-
Sat, 1-5pm Sun
Home, museum, cinema, &

Ticonderoga, NY
Fort Ticonderoga State Park
PO Box 390 (SR74)
Ticonderoga, NY 12883
☎ 518-525-2821
Open: 9am-5pm
Fort, living history

West Point, NY
West Point
Visitors Center, Bldg 2107
West Point, NY 10996
☎ 914-938-2638
Open: 9am-4.45pm
Museum, gifts, tours, &

Youngstown, NY
Fort Niagara State Park
Old Fort Niagara
  Association
Youngstown, NY 14174
☎ 716-745-7611
Open: 9am-dusk except
major holidays
Fort, living history

3

THE MID-ATLANTIC STATES

Washington DC makes a capital introduction to the United States, where monuments to past presidents and the treasures of the Smithsonian Institution are all free. The surrounding Mid-Atlantic states are America in microcosm, whether reliving the Colonial era, retracing the Civil War, or simply enjoying the great cities and contrasting villages.

Washington DC

While the business of Washington is undoubtedly government, tourism comes a strong second with 20 million visitors annually. Ethnic and cultural variety add spice, a counterpoise to the museums, memorials and monuments of 'Postcard Washington'.

President Washington asked Charles L'Enfant for a capital befitting his grand new nation, but the design proved ambitious. After insisting that nothing less would suffice, 'L'Enfant terrible' was replaced and his design scaled to within the young republic's means. As budgets grew his vision became reality, and the soldier-architect was reburied with full honours in Arlington National Cemetery.

Visit **Washington Visitor Information Center** first, found on Pennsylvania Avenue just east of **The White House**. In winter queue directly for White House tours, at other times tickets become available at the Ellipse Park tour booth on tour days from 8 am. Tours include the variously coloured rooms

The Mid-Atlantic States in Brief

Kick off this event-packed tour with Washington DC, then compare bustling Baltimore with quaint Annapolis, Maryland's capital. Cross scenic Chesapeake and Delaware Bays for glittering Atlantic City, casino capital of eastern America. Philadelphia, the 'Cradle of Liberty', remembers its past, while the Pennsylvania Dutch still live theirs. Skyline Drive winds along the Blue Ridge Mountains of Virginia, followed by Colonial Williamsburg and the stately James River Plantations.

This two-week tour packs considerable interest in 1,600 miles. Washington's cherry trees blossom in spring while the Blue Ridge bursts into colour in autumn, both fine touring seasons. Summers are best on the Blue Ridge Mountains or beaches, while air-conditioning cools those hot cities.

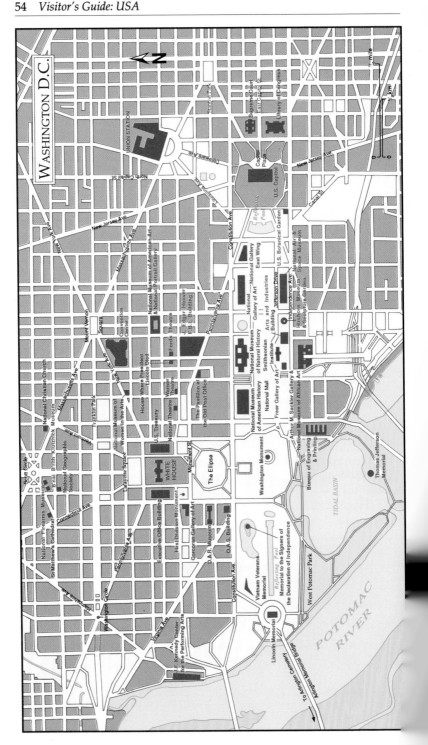

Into and Around Washington DC

Washington National Airport is conveniently located just across the Potomac River, while Washington Dulles International and Baltimore Washington International are respectively 26 miles west and 34 miles northeast. Washington Flyer provides express connections between airports, some services linking into city hotels. Greyhound is at 1st and L Streets, NE, while Amtrak uses Union Station on 1st and Massachusetts, north of Capitol Hill.

The Metro has an excellent bus and subway network, complemented by tourist orientated Tourmobile and Old Town Trolley Tours. Both offer on-off privileges, the Tourmobile focused on 'Postcard Washington' and allowing multiple circles, with optional excursions to Mount Vernon and/or the Frederick Douglass Home. The trolley's scope is broader, taking in more hotels and shops but with fewer stops. Grey Line offer escorted tours from Union Station and major hotels. Numbered streets run north-south, lettered streets east-west, those named after states are diagonal. The city is divided into quarters from the US Capitol, with downtown and the White House in the NW

Washington suffers urban blight and a higher crime rate outside downtown and tourist areas; play safe by sticking to tours or cars in outlying areas. Conversely, automobiles are an unnecessary burden in 'Postcard Washington', where curbside parking is limited and improperly parked cars towed away. If renting, arrange to pick up the car when leaving the city. Washington's big plus side is the strollable expanses of green park among world-class museums and monuments.

used for state functions and the East Room, used for press conferences. In 1814, an uninvited British Admiral George Cockburn torched the White House, but the East Room's Stuart Gilbert portrait of George Washington was saved by First Lady Dolly Madison. Lafayette Square, popular with protestors, is north of the White House, with the Treasury Building to the east and Executive Office in the west.

Several interesting non-governmental buildings are between 17th and 18th Streets west of the White House and the Ellipse. The **Octagon**, an architectural museum, was temporary home to President and Dolly Madison after the British invasion. **Corcoran Gallery of Art** has a fine collection of American and European art, while the **DAR Museum** (Daughters of the American Revolution) displays items from colonial times. The **Organization of American States** exhibits Latin American arts in their nearby museum.

Capitol Hill houses Congress (legislative) and Supreme Court (judicial) branches of government, boasting impressive buildings in a park setting. Commanding views down National Mall to the Potomac River, the **US Capi-** **tol** is entered via the great east-facing staircase. Guided tours begin in the Rotunda, while maps for handicapped guests are near the wheelchair entrance beneath the east stairs. The old Senate, Supreme Court, and House of Representatives Chambers, the latter now utilized as Statuary Hall, are included on the tour.

Flags fly when the legislature is in session, Senate in the north wing and House of Representatives in the south. Non-residents may visit either gallery by showing identification and requesting an International Pass. US residents should obtain a pass from their senators' or representatives' offices; a good excuse to use the underground Capitol Hill shuttle. Weekday tours are also available of the **Supreme Court** and **Library of Congress** buildings. The latter has reading rooms, exhibition halls, and a programme of summer readings and concerts. Nearby Folger Shakespeare Library also gives readings and concerts, and presents independent theatre groups in its Elizabethan Theatre playhouse.

James Smithson, the British scientist who donated his fortune to a country never visited, galvanized a young America into forming the world's largest museum complex. From the US Capitol looking west along National Mall, virtually every building flanking the mall is the **Smithsonian Institution**, affectionately dubbed 'America's attic'. The **National Gallery of Art** is first right, with an outstanding collection of American and European Fine Arts in two wings. North of the mall is their **National Museum of American Art** and **National Portrait Gallery**. Back at the Mall, the **National Museum of Natural History** has excellent exhibits on Asian, Pacific, African, and Native American cultures. The **National Museum of American History** recounts change in US technology and social/political history. Some allow days for each museum — others never get beyond the excellent gift and book shops.

First on the left are two 'non-Smithsonian' institutions, the **US Botanic Garden** with its orchids and azaleas and the US Information Agency, which gives weekday tours of its *Voice of America* program. The acclaimed **National Air and Space Museum** *is* Smithsonian, and like the others has excellent hands-on exhibits. Displays include history-making air and spacecraft, complemented by an IMAX theatre and Albert Einstein Planetarium. The unmistakable **Smithsonian Institution Building**, 'The Castle', houses the main information centre and administrative offices. Surrounding it are the Hirshhorn Museum, Arts and Industries Building, National Museum of African Art, Arthur M. Sackler Gallery, Freer Gallery, and S. Dillon Ripley Center, the latter an underground museum and education complex. Also Smithsonian are the **Anacostia Museum** in southeast Washington, presenting the history and culture of African Americans, the **Renwick Gallery** with its focus on American crafts, and the **National Zoological Park**, with its lovely pandas.

The tall obelisk of **Washington Monument** is right in the heart of 'Postcard Washington'. An elevator takes visitors to the 500ft high observation room, just below the peak. Heat and humidity become oppressive on summer afternoons, making early morning and late evening tours best. The Bureau of Engraving and Printing is southeast. See American currency being printed, but no photographs or samples, please.

In spring, blossoming cherry trees accentuate the soft neoclassical lines of the **Thomas Jefferson Memorial**. Additional trees line the Tidal Basin and also the Potomac riverbank east from the Jefferson Memorial to the National Park Service Visitor Center, the administrators of Washington DC parks and monuments.

West along the Potomac is the **Lincoln Memorial**, where his marble statue gazes towards Capitol Hill. Constitution Gardens north of the reflecting pool has the Signers of the Declaration of Independence Memorial and the more recent Vietnam Veterans Memorial, naming 58,000 lost servicemen and women on polished black granite. The Tourmobile leaves Lincoln Memorial for **Arlington National Cemetery**. Arlington House is the Robert E. Lee Memorial, where he freed his slaves but resigned his US commission. The Tomb of the Unknown Soldier and the Kennedys are among those interred. The Theodore Roosevelt Monument and Lady Bird Johnson Park both occupy islands accessible from the west bank of the Potomac.

Downtown is generally between Pennsylvania and Massachusetts Avenues in the northwest quarter. The F Street shopping precinct is east of the White House, with more shops and eateries at the **Old Post Office Pavilion** on Pennsylvania. Theatre goers find National and Warner Theatres on E Street, and **Ford's Theatre** on 10th. Lincoln was shot at Ford's, across from which is 'The House Where Lincoln Died'. The J. Edgar Hoover Building, home of the **FBI**, gives tours on weekdays. The former Masonic Grand Lodge houses the **National Museum of Women in the Arts**, with intriguing exhibits accentuated by an interesting building.

Amtrak's headquarters are in **Union Station**, a renovated 1900s structure with shops, restaurants and a large cinema, in addition to trains for Baltimore, New York City and beyond. From the station, a drive west down **Massachusetts Avenue** passes much of Washington DC. The Convention Center is south of Mount Vernon Square, while the National City Christian Church at Thomas Circle gives organ recitals on Thursday at noon and tours most days. Southeast of Scott Circle are the B'nai B'rith Klutznick Museum with its Jewish ceremonial art, and the National Firearms Museum. **St Matthew's Cathedral** has a white marble altar inlaid with semi-precious stones — the same *pietra dura* technique as the Taj Mahal. Explorers Hall at the **National Geographic Society** displays memorabilia from their sponsored expeditions and an 11ft globe. Explorers Den sells National Geographic publications, while the adjacent auditorium hosts guest lecturers.

Hundreds of embassies are west along Massachusetts Avenue from Scott Circle, starting with the Australian. The Historical Society of Washington DC is down New Hampshire Avenue from Dupont Circle. Back on Massachusetts, the Anderson House Museum focuses on the American Revolution, with plenty to exhibit since its society was founded by General George Washington and his officers. Sheridan Circle has the greatest concentration of embassies, and just beyond is Woodrow Wilson House, the only presidential museum within Washington. The adjacent Textile Center exhibits virtually every facet of carpets and cloths. Washington has no mountains but Mohammed came anyway, via the **Islamic Center** — women must cover themselves to participate.

Rock Creek Park's scenic drive crosses Massachusetts Avenue beyond Sheridan Circle. The Smithsonian Institution's National Zoological Park, Pierce Mill, Fort De Russy ruins, and the Nature Center are north along the creek. The parkway south follows Rock Creek to the Potomac River and the **Kennedy Center for Performing Arts**, just north of the Lincoln Memorial. The British Embassy and a few others are further west on Massachusetts Avenue near the US Naval Observatory, and beyond is the Gothic **Washington Na-**

The Smithsonian Castle is a Washingon DC landmark

The Stars and Stripes flying at half-mast on Memorial Day at the Washington Memorial

Maryland crab feast

The Pride of Baltimore II *under sail at Annapolis*

tional Cathedral, completed in 1990 after over 80 years. Woodrow Wilson and Helen Keller are interred there.

Other points within Washington include the **National Shrine of Immaculate Conception**, the largest Catholic church in America and the **US National Arboretum**, both in northeastern Washington. The US Postal Service Headquarters and Philatelic Sales Center are in L'Enfant Plaza, an underground shopping and office complex south of the National Air and Space Museum.

Maryland

The original royal grant to Cecil Calvert, second Lord Baltimore, established a haven for Catholics, although the colony saw more Protestant pilgrims than Catholic. Much of today's Delaware and Pennsylvania was included in the liberal charter, later truncated by Mason and Dixon. Chesapeake Bay nearly divides Maryland in two, resulting in a claw-like shape reminiscent of the Bay's main delicacy, Blue Crab. These are best sampled in **Baltimore**, Maryland's largest city.

From Washington follow I-95, exiting on SR2 North for **Inner Harbor**, once a seedy dockside but now Baltimore's pride. An all-day ticket makes the Water Taxi perfect for exploring bayside Baltimore, starting with **Harborplace**, the shopping, dining and entertainment centre. Baltimore Maritime Museum highlights mankind's conquest of the sea, while the nearby **National Aquarium** relates the natural environments of marine mammals and fish in a seven-storey complex. **US Frigate** *Constellation* was built in 1797, one of America's oldest man o'wars. Other stops include the Maryland Science Center, from which a pleasant stroll leads to Federal Hill, a bit of old Baltimore. **Baltimore City Life Museums** and ethnic Little Italy are a few blocks from another stop, while Baltimore Museum of Industry has its own wharf. Water Taxi operators are helpful, often suggesting the best restaurants and nightspots. **Fort McHenry National Monument** can be visited via the Baltimore Patriot, one of several harbour cruise companies. While watching British ships bombard Fort McHenry during the War of 1812, Francis Scott Key wrote *The Star Spangled Banner*. Set to the British drinking song *To Anacreon in Heaven*, Key's poem became the American National Anthem, and in his honour, the fort is restored to the early 1800s.

The Inner Harbour visitor centre has information on Baltimore Orioles games, as will the **Babe Ruth Birthplace**. Nearby is the **B & O Railroad Museum**, with locomotives and ancillary gear from the Baltimore and Ohio Railroad. John Pope designed the Smithsonian's National Gallery after completing the **Baltimore Museum of Art**. Fine Arts on display include the Cone collection, noted for its impressionists' works. Druid Hill Park contains Baltimore Zoo and Schaefer Conservatory, housing rare tropical and desert plants. Francis Scott Key's manuscript of *The Star Spangled Banner* is an exhibit at the **Maryland Historical Society**.

The tremendous growth of Baltimore eclipsed **Annapolis**, Maryland' charming state capital. Long after progress steamrollered other cities Annapolis has retained its historic landmarks and eighteenth-century character. Found south on SR2 from Baltimore, pocket-sized Annapolis is bes explored on foot. Parking spaces are hard to find on the narrow streets, but Navy Football Stadium on SR70 provides free parking and buses. Both City Dock and State House visitor centres provide maps for independent sightseers, while Three Centuries Tours give walks with guides in period costume. Maryland **State House** depicts George Washington resigning as Commander-in-Chief of the Continental Army, which he did there. Also within State Circle is the Old Treasury building, with St Anne's Church visible along School Street.

City Dock and environs are heart of 'tourist' Annapolis, where quaint buildings house craft shops and restaurants; a most pleasant place to browse or relax. Excursions on Chesapeake Bay leave from the dock, including a day-long tour on *Annapolitan II*, visiting Chesapeake Maritime Museum in picturesque St Michaels. Colonial architecture is most evident between the State House and City Dock on Francis and Cornhill Streets, and also Prince George Street. The nearby **US Naval Academy** is the Annapolis equivalent of West Point. **William Paca House** and **Hammond-Harwood House** are the best known historic homes, both predating the War of Independence. Before embarking east for the Atlantic coastline, consider a short detour south to Edgewater and **London Town Publik House and Gardens**, a 1760 ferry tavern restored to period.

Chesapeake Bay, Maryland's most prominent feature, cannot be missed while westbound on the bay bridge via US50. **St Michaels** and its **Chesapeake Maritime Museum** are west of Easton on SR33. Isolated from western Mary- land until the Chesapeake Bay Bridge was completed, this area is pleasantly unspoilt, boasting numerous coves and inlets. Further south on US50, Cambridge tells of its long nautical tradition at Brannock Maritime Museum. In the book *Chesapeake*, James A. Michener described High Street Cambridge as 'one of the most beautiful streets in America'. **Ocean City** is the seaside resort of Maryland, nestled between Delaware and Assateague National Seashore, the latter famous for its Chincoteague Ponies. After enjoying the boardwalk and amusement parks of Ocean City, follow the coastline north.

Delaware and New Jersey Coastline

Rehoboth Beach is the closest oceanside resort to Washington DC and Baltimore, popular in summer along with the surrounding Delaware Seashore and Cape Henlopen State Parks. The **Lewes** Historic Complex on Ship Carpenter and 3rd Streets remembers its seagoing and land-based heritage, while Lewes Zwaanendael Museum recalls the earliest Dutch who colonized the cape. The Cape May to Lewes Ferry provides regular crossings to New Jersey. Those forgoing the Atlantic City experience may head north for Dover, state capital of Delaware, and historic Wilmington en route to Philadelphia.

Cape May, New Jersey, is known for its Victorian gingerbread houses, being one of the seaboard's established resorts. The Cape May Chamber of Commerce has information on tours of its historical districts and tips on chartering fishing or sightseeing boats. The Garden State Parkway is the quickest route to Atlantic City, while scenic SR585 passes the seaside towns of southern New Jersey.

MID-ATLANTIC STATES

80 miles
120km

NEW JERSEY

PHILADELPHIA
Independence N.H.P.
Philadelphia Art Museum

WILLIAMSBURG
Busch Gardens
Colonial Williamsburg

BALTIMORE
Baltimore Museum of Art
Fort McHenry N.M.
National Aquarium

NEW YORK
Newark
NEW YORK
Scranton
Allentown
TRENTON
PHILADELPHIA
Camden
Atlantic City
Atlantic City Expressway
Cape May
Wilmington
Delaware Bay
Rehoboth Beach
Lewes
Ocean City
DELAWARE
Salisbury
DOVER
Easton
St Michaels
Cambridge
Chesapeake Bay
Hampton
Newport News
Norfolk
Virginia Beach
Yorktown
Colonial N.H.P.
Jamestown
Williamsburg
RICHMOND
State Capitol
Valley Forge N.H.P.
Intercourse
Lancaster
Columbia
York
Gettysburg
BALTIMORE
Frederick
Harpers Ferry
N.H.P.
Thurmont
Gettysburg N.M.P.
State Capitol
HARRISBURG
PENNSYLVANIA
PITTSBURGH
OHIO
NEW YORK
LAKE ERIE
CLEVELAND
Wheeling
Parkersburg
WEST VIRGINIA
Martinsburg
Charles Town
Front Royal
Luray
New Market
Waynesborough
Skyline Drive
BLUE RIDGE
Charlottesville
Monticello
Fredericksburg
Stafford Hall Plantation
Tappahannock
Warsaw
Shirley Plantation
Berkeley Plantation
Appomattox Court House N.H.P.
Museum and White House of the Confederacy
Lynchburg
VIRGINIA
Lexington
Natural Bridge
Roanoke
Mabry Mill
Huntington
CHARLESTON
State Capitol
KENTUCKY
COLUMBUS
OHIO
WASHINGTON DC
London Towne
Annapolis
State Capitol
N

Atlantic City combines a five-mile long Boardwalk with the glitter of Las Vegas. Gambling is confined to large casino complexes, which also provide excellent dining, entertainment, and nightlife. Connections are good, and visitors to New York City, Washington DC, Philadelphia, and Baltimore may reach Atlantic City via air, rail, or bus. The Atlantic City Expressway (toll) is the main route from inland cities, passing the Amtrak station and bus depot before reaching the sea. Atlantic Avenue is the main east-west thoroughfare, paralleled by Pacific, one block closer to the boardwalk.

Those following the coast north reach Atlantic Avenue, with most casinos to the right, strung along the Boardwalk. The main exceptions are Harrah's Marina and Trump Castle in the Absecon area. Caeser's occupies prime position at Atlantic Expressway's end, which in Atlantic City separates into Missouri and Arkansas Avenue. Parking is available on the streets which dead-end at the Boardwalk while car parks have security, a sensible precaution.

Gambling brings considerable money into Atlantic City — odds always favour the house — with the excess renovating the fabulous piers which decorated the seaside city. Some offer shopping, others amusements, and for a real Atlantic City touch, take a spin along the Boardwalk in a wicker pushmobile. Unless 'jumping tours' for New York City, follow US30 from northeastern Atlantic City across the Garden State to Philadelphia. Those taking the faster Atlantic City Expressway should still cross the Delaware River into Philadelphia via US 30 and the Benjamin Franklin Bridge.

Pennsylvania

Pennsylvania honours William Penn in name and deed, fitting for this noted Quaker who made religious freedom the law. Quakers were joined by Amish, Mennonites, Moravians, and Dunkards; Germanic peoples collectively known as Pennsylvania Dutch. If left to the peace-loving Quakers and Germans, Pennsylvania would have ignored the call for independence, but the Scottish and Irish catapulted 'the city of brotherly love' into the Revolutionary War.

Philadelphia *is* the 'Cradle of Liberty', where the Declaration of Independence was signed, the Constitution born, and early American government formed — an era still alive at **Independence National Historical Park**. Those crossing Ben Franklin Bridge from New Jersey will find ample parking for the historic sites left on 6th Avenue, left again on Chestnut, and right down 2nd Avenue. The visitor centre between 2nd and 3rd provides exhibits, an orientation film, and a map highlighting places of interest. First of these is Carpenters' Hall, meeting place of the first Continental Congress. The Army-Navy Museum, Marine Corps Memorial Museum, and several houses are open for tour; get tickets for the homes at the visitor centre. Walk north to Franklin Court to learn more of Philadelphia's favourite son. Cards and letters sent from Ben's post office bear the 2-B-Free postmark. The Benjamin Franklin underground museum is in the block's centre.

The Second Bank of the United States, west on Chestnut, is now the park's portrait gallery, exhibiting illustrious citizens of the Revolutionary period. When French friend and ally Lafayette re-visited Philadelphia after the war, he asked to see the 'Hall of Independence'. Since then the Pennsylvania State House has been **Independence Hall**, with ranger guided tours of where the second Continental Congress adopted the Declaration of Independence. **Liberty Bell Pavilion** is north of the hall, housing America's famed, albeit slightly cracked, symbol of freedom. Rangers provide interesting background to the bell's history, originally made in Loughborough, England. Nearby are the free Quaker Meeting House and early money maker, the **United States Mint**.

Pennsylvania Dutch Country

This area was settled by Amish, Mennonites and others of Germanic origin. Many of the 'Plain People' forego modern conveniences, such as electricity, automobiles, and television; visitors find Dutch Country a curiously refreshing blend of old and new. Farmers use combine harvesters pulled by horse, while families go out in horse drawn carriages. Dress is deliberately old-fashioned, reminding the Amish they live in an earlier world. Traditional crafts bring money into the community, as tourists value their finely made quilts, woodwork, and delightful old-fashioned foodstuffs such as sausages, souse, and shoofly pie. Discretion is requested of photographers, as Mennonites and Amish interpret the Bible literally regarding graven images — quick snaps which exclude faces are considered a reasonable compromise.

Arch Street has another Friends Meeting Place and Betsy Ross House, where that most famous seamstress created the first American flag. Elfreth's Alley is lined with quaint colonial homes and a museum, all part of William Penn's 'Greene Countrie Towne'.

Numerous signatories of the Declaration of Independence worshipped at **Christ Church**, which preserves William Penn's baptismal font. The church is on 2nd Street, while Benjamin Franklin and other signatories are interred at its 5th Street burial grounds. **Penn's Landing** along the Delaware River has a nautical museum, historical ships, and often hosts festivals and concerts. Washington Square, south of the historical park, contains the Tomb of the Unknown Revolutionary War Soldier, while nearby Norman Rockwell Museum exhibits the famed artist's works.

Modern Philadelphia boasts numerous shops, many along **Market Street** between the historical area and the delightful extravaganza of City Hall — inspired by the Louvre. Behind the Gallery and One Reading Center on Market Street is the bus station and Philadelphia's Chinatown, with a gate on 10th and Arch Street. The Masonic Temple complex north of City Hall is open to visitors, where architectural connoisseurs will find a variety of styles. Penn Center Station is northwest of City Hall, near downtown Philadelphia Visitor Center.

Fairmount Park is situated along both sides of the other Philadelphia River the Schuylkill. From Arch and 16th Street, drive northwest on Benjamin Franklin Parkway. The Academy of Sciences and **Franklin Institute Museum**, respectively a natural history museum and a hands-on science centre are near Logan Circle. First within Fairmount Park is the Rodin Museum followed by the eclectic **Philadelphia Museum of Art**. Kelly Drive follows the Schuylkill's east bank past Lemon Hill, first of many mansions open to the public. Concerts by the noted Philadelphia Symphonic Orchestra are performed in the Mann Music Center across the river. The Japanese House and Gardens and Horticultural Center are nearby. When leaving Philadelphia follow I-76 north, found from downtown by taking Vine Street west Franklin Square.

George Washington's Continental Army was encamped at **Valley Forge** f six months during the winter of 1777-8. Today a national historical park with ⊓ memorial arch and chapel pay tribute to long-suffering troops, including thousands who never saw spring. George Washington's headquarters and reconstructed encampment are part of the self-guided tour. From Valley Forge pick up US202 then US30 west.

For an excellent introduction to Pennsylvania Dutch Country, leave US30, taking SR10 north to Compass then SR340 west to **Intercourse**. Visitors soon forget the incongruous name when browsing craft shops, watching locals and learning about their fascinating way of life. The **People's Place** is an informative heritage centre with associated handicraft outlets and a quilt museum, all owned and operated by the Pennsylvania Dutch. Traditional crafts and homemakers' supplies, such as cloth, are excellent value. The Country Store and innumerable others sell foodstuffs and handicrafts, from trinkets to wooden gazebos.

Continuing west, Bird-in-Hand was named after a tavern, the present being the fourth on the site. **Lancaster** is self-proclaimed heart of Pennsylvania Dutch Country, and while few of the 'Plain People' are seen downtown, the visitor centre will point travellers towards surrounding places of interest. **Landis Valley Museum** recalls a nineteenth-century Pennsylvania Dutch village, while certain Amish farms and homesteads are available for tours. Visit the Mennonite Information Center to learn more of their faith and culture, including the more conservative Amish.

Harrisburg is Pennsylvania state capital, found northwest of Lancaster along the Susquehanna River. Freeway 283 is quickest, or detour west to Columbia for their fascinating **Watch and Clock Museum** and follow the river north. The massive **State Capitol** and **State Museum** is situated within the 13-acre Capitol Park. Exhibits include Charles II's original charter to William Penn. Events at the Pennsylvania Farm Show Complex vary from a springtime circus to an autumn equestrian show. Market Street bridge leads across the Susquehanna to US15.

Like the battle before it, **Gettysburg National Military Park** encircles the ⊓ town of Gettysburg. The park visitor centre is first stop, where visitors may supplement the park map with a book or copy of Lincoln's Gettysburg Address. Before embarking upon an auto or bicycle tour of the battlefield, visit the electronic map, invaluable for understanding Gettysburg's chronology and geography. The nearby Cyclorama depicts Pickett's charge in a sound-and-light show centred around Paul Philippoteaux's painting. Take the tour slowly, especially around High Water Mark, where the Confederates were halted on aptly named Cemetery Ridge, and at Virginia Memorial on Seminary Ridge, from which Pickett's charge broke cover to cross the mile-long stretch of field. Included on the tour are the National Cemetery, observation tower, and Oak Hill's Eternal Light Peace Memorial.

Eisenhower National Historic Site is administered by Gettysburg, with a ⊓ shuttle bus from the visitor centre to the 34th President's home. Book early as space is limited. Outside the park are the Lincoln Room Museum, where he finalized his famous address, and Lee's Headquarters and Museum. Programs at 'The Conflict' review the soldier's view, the battle itself, and the whole civil war.

Continue south on US15 through Maryland, pausing perhaps at Thurmont to enjoy nearby Catoctin Mountain Park before taking US340 west beyond Frederick.

The Virginias

A colony named after Elizabeth I, the Virgin Queen, famous Virginia sons include George Washington, Thomas Jefferson, and Robert E. Lee. During the Civil War the question of slavery was superceded by the issue of secession, over which the state split into Virginia and West Virginia.

Trouble came earlier to **Harpers Ferry**, West Virginia. Abolitionist John Brown attempted to rob the national armory, intending to free and arm slaves who would use guerilla tactics from surrounding mountains. Today this small town along the Shenandoah River is a peaceful national historic park and living history centre, with river rafting and other excursions offered by local tour companies. John Brown was hung at nearby Charles Town, which preserved the one-room courthouse where he was tried. Most visitors come to Charles Town for the races, both horses and cars running regularly except in winter.

Continue on US340 southwest to Front Royal, Virginia, gateway to **Shenandoah National Park**, whose famed Skyline Drive winds along one of the most scenic sections of the **Blue Ridge Mountains**. The area is also famous for its caverns, and both Luray and New Market have spectacular examples off Skyline Drive. Alternatively visit Front Royal's own Skyline Caverns before taking to the hills. The park itself is a natural wonderland, and drivers must watch for bounding deer and foraging raccoons, especially near dusk and dawn.

Dickey Ridge is the main visitor centre for southbound drivers, while Big Meadows offers food, supplies, camping, and lodging — book ahead in summer. Big Meadow is often overrun with deer; the usual restrictions against feeding apply. Scenic overlooks along Skyline Drive are supplemented with numerous trails, varying from short walks to the Appalachian Trail, linking Georgia to Maine in New England. Rangers advise on moderate trails for the visitor to enjoy.

Near Waynesborough, Skyline Drive becomes the **Blue Ridge Parkway**, with an interesting diversion east on US 250 or I-64 to Charlottesville for **Monticello**, former home of Thomas Jefferson and one of Virginia's most impressive estates. The home and grounds have been restored to Jefferson's era, complimented by an exhibition with details of his life. A 'Presidents Pass' combines Monticello with Ash Lawn-Highland, home of fifth president James Monroe, and **Historic Michie Tavern**.

The Blue Ridge Parkway is lined with scenic turnouts, picnic areas, and pleasant walks, with wild flowers in May and June, autumn foliage in October. Accommodation is available at popular Peaks of Otter Lodge, Rocky Knob, and the nearby towns of Lynchburg, Bedford, and Roanoke. Each visitor centre has its own character, Humpback Rocks having a reconstructed mountain farm, James River the canal, and Peaks of Otter an area of outstanding scenic beauty. Possible detours include **Lexington**, home of Stonewall Jackson, and **Natural Bridge**, named after the area's most outstanding feature

Travellers who follow the Blue Ridge Parkway to **Mabry Mill** will not be disappointed — it is America's most photographed mill. Return north to **Roanoke**, commercial and cultural capital of western Virginia. Their Center on the Square has an arts museum, historical society museum, science museum and a fine theatre.

East from Roanoke on US460 leads to Lynchburg, an important Civil War supply depot. Beyond is **Appomattox Court House National Historical Park**, where Confederate General Lee surrendered to Union General Grant and also where, in summer, uniformed troops and costumed villagers recreate 1865. Those retracing the civil war will find the park service maintains Petersburg, Richmond, Fredericksburg, Spotsylvania, Chancellorsville and Manassas Battlefield Parks, and also several National Cemeteries between Appomattox and Washington.

Richmond is state capital and gateway to colonial Virginia, although the city itself lost many structures during the Civil War. The visitor centre off I-64 exit 14 has details of living history tours. After **The Capitol** visit the White House of the Confederacy at the nearby **Museum of the Confederacy**. Also in Richmond are the **Valentine Museum** and John Marshall House, home to much respected Supreme Court Chief Justice Marshall. One structure predates even the colonial era, Agecroft Hall, built in Lancashire during the late fifteenth century, while the Poe Museum is Richmond's oldest surviving house, with exhibits about the author. Other fine museums include **Virginia Historical Society** and **Virginia Museum of Fine Arts**. Evening entertainment includes dinner cruises on the historic James River.

From Richmond follow SR5 east for the **James River Plantations**. Stately homes include **Shirley Plantation**, where ancestors of the resident Carter-Hill family include Robert E. Lee's mother. **Berkeley Plantation** was once home to the Harrison Family, boasting a Declaration of Independence signatory and two presidents. Berkeley has witnessed enough history to fill a book (several have been written), and visitors also enjoy the gardens. At Green Spring follow SR614 south to Jamestown.

Colonial National Historical Park encompasses Jamestown, where the British Colonies were founded, and Yorktown, where British rule ended with the surrender of General Cornwallis. Despite being the first 'permanent' British settlement, **Jamestown** had a distinctly unhealthy climate — 90 per cent of the colonists died in 1610. Eventually healthier Middle Plantation prospered (later renamed Williamsburg) but Jamestown lives on in memory. The park visitor centre offers an orientation map, necessary since much of the site is archaeological. The national park's living history program is complemented by nearby **Jamestown Settlement**, which has recreated three-cornered James Fort, an Indian settlement, a historical museum and reproduction ships near the original site. From Jamestown, follow the Colonial Parkway north.

Williamsburg occupied 220 acres in 1699 when it became capital of Britain's largest and wealthiest colony. In an unparalleled act of reconstruction, virtually the entire eighteenth-century town has been painstakingly restored or reproduced, creating **Colonial Williamsburg**, living history capital of America. The visitor centre complex is first port of call, signposted from Colonial Parkway. Food, lodging and support services surround the massive car park, with Colonial Williamsburg to the south followed by the popular Williamsburg Inn and Williamsburg Lodge and Conference Center.

Ticket options are Basic Admission, good for one day and most buildings, Royal Governor's Pass, a multiple day ticket which adds the Governors Palace and DeWitt Wallace Gallery, and the annual Patriot's Pass, with admission to Carter's Grove Plantation and the Rockefeller Folk Art Center, both outside the historical area. Access to Colonial Williamsburg itself is free, including entry rights to shops and restaurants, but many walk-in visitors return with a Governor's or Patriot's Pass for the historic buildings and crafts exhibits.

Highlights of Colonial Williamsburg are many, including the restored Capitol, Governor's Palace, Wallace Decorative Arts Gallery, period homes, and numerous crafts demonstrations. Most wandering eighteenth-century characters are found on Duke of Gloucester Street. The experience is educational and enjoyable, including innumerable shops and at least four taverns open for dining. Events are a daily occurrence, with extra celebrations at holidays, and a special series of annual learning forums covering gardening, crafts, antiques, and related interests.

Also within or near Williamsburg is **Abby Aldrich Rockefeller Folk Art Center**, exhibiting a fantastic collection in its expanded galleries, the College of William and Mary, America's second college after Harvard, and **Bassett Hall**, home to John D. Rockefeller Jr and wife Abby while they lovingly restored Colonial Williamsburg. **Carter's Grove** plantation and mansion is included with the Folk Art Center in the Patriot's Pass — allow plenty of time for each. **Busch Gardens — The Old Country** is a fun-filled park. Although the theme is seventeenth-century Europe, the rides and amusements are all high-tech, offering an excellent break for holidaymakers and travellers alike.

Yorktown is the third leg of Virginia's 'Historical Triangle', where British General Corwallis had his regimental band play *The World Turned Upside Down*. Yorktown Battlefield National Historical Site is part of Colonial National Park, awaiting the driver at the northern end of Colonial Drive. Nearby is **Yorktown Victory Center**, recounting the final days of the American Revolution.

Before returning north to Washington, the driver may visit Newport News, Norfolk, and Virginia Beach. The latter with 29 miles of beach, 3 miles lined by boardwalk, with various recreational watersports. The Virginia Maritime Science Museum has interesting hands-on exhibits, including a computerized 'create-a-fish' centre. Norfolk is known for its fine harbour and one of the world's largest Naval facilities, while Newport News has another harbou and interesting Mariner's Museum.

Take US17 north to Tappahannock, crossing the Rappahannock River to Warsaw, then north again along SR3. Stratford boasts **Stratford Hall Plantation**, an outstanding colonial plantation and home to four generations of the Lee family. The hall has been restored to its antebellum finest, when Robert E Lee was born there. Nearby is the George Washington Birthplace National Monument. **Fredericksburg** has preserved **Mary Washington House**, owne by the first President's mother, and **Kenmore**, where his sister lived. Su rounding Fredericksburg are its Civil War battlefields.

Mount Vernon is the final stop en route to Washington, signposted fro northbound US1. This particularly well restored early plantation belonged

George and Martha Washington. The home and outbuildings have been lovingly refurbished, with costumed volunteers and artisans recreating the colonial atmosphere. The museums, which examine Washington's life and exhibit his favourite possessions, are neatly fitted within the plantation outbuildings. An agreeable spot, visitors can sit on the great lawn, explore the gardens, or simply watch ships pass along the Potomac. Return along George Washington Memorial Parkway, a picturesque drive along the Potomac River, passing through historic Alexandria before returning to bustling Washington DC.

Additional Information

State Tourism Bureaux

Delaware Tourism Office
99 Kings Highway, PO Box 1401, Dept RB
Dover, DE 19903
☎ 800-441-8846
or 302-736-4271

Maryland Office of Tourism
217 East Redwood St
Baltimore, MD 21202
☎ 800-543-1036
or 301-333-6611

New Jersey Travel & Tourism
20 West State St, CN-826
Trenton, NJ 08625-0826
☎ 800-537-7397
or 602-292-2470

Pennsylvania Bureau of Travel
453 Forum Bldg
Harrisburg, PA 17120
☎ 800-847-4872
or 717-787-5453

Virginia Division of Tourism
1021 East Cary St, Tower II
Richmond, VA 23219
☎ 804-786-1919

West Virginia Tourism & Parks
101 Washington St, E
Charleston, WV 25305
☎ 800-225-5982
or 304-348-2286

Regional Information

Annapolis CVB
6 Dock St
Annapolis, MD 21401
☎ 301-268-8687
or 301-280-0445

Atlantic City CVB
2314 Pacific Ave
Atlantic City, NJ 08401
☎ 609-348-7100

Baltimore CVB
One East Pratt St, Suite 14
Baltimore, MD 21202
☎ 301-837-4636
or 301-659-7300

Gettysburg Travel Council
35 Carlisle St
Gettysburg, PA 17325
☎ 717-334-6274

Pennsylvania Dutch CVB
501 Greenfield Road
Lancaster, PA 17601
☎ 717-299-8901

Philadelphia CVB
1515 Market St, Suite 2020
Philadelphia, PA 19102
☎ 800-225-5745
or 215-636-3300

Rehoboth Beach COC
73 Rehoboth Avenue
Rehoboth Beach, DE 19963
☎ 800-345-4444
or 302-422-3301

Richmond Visitors Center
1700 Robin Hood Rd or
Capital Square
Richmond, VA 23200
☎ 804-358-5511
or 804-786-4484

Washington DC CVB
1212 New York Ave, NW (mail)
1455 Pennsylvania Ave, NW (visit)
Washington, DC 20005
☎ 202-789-7000

Williamsburg CVB
PO Drawer GB
Williamsburg, VA 23187
☎ 804-253-0192

Local Events

Check locally for exact dates

February
Washington's Birthday
Mount Vernon, VA

April
Virginia State Horse Show
Richmond, VA

Cherry Blossom Festival
Washington, DC

Festival of American Folklife
Washington, DC

White House Spring Garden Tour
Washington, DC

May
Preakness Stakes
Pimlico
Baltimore, MD

May
Bayfest
Sandy Point State Park
Annapolis, MD

Philadelphia Open House
Philadelphia, PA

May-July
Prelude to Independence
Williamsburg, VA

June
Mountain Heritage Arts & Crafts
Harpers Ferry, WV

June-July
Civil War Heritage Days
Gettysburg, PA

June-September
Mann Music Center Concerts
Philadelphia, PA

July
Independence Day
Washington, DC

Freedom Festival
Philadelphia, PA

Best Body on Beach Contest
Rehoboth Beach, DE

July-September
Harborlights Music Festival
Pier 6 Pavilion
Baltimore, MD

August
Pennsylvania Dutch Festival
Philadelphia, PA

Atlantic City Race Week
Farley Marina
Atlantic City, NJ

September
Virginia State Fair
Richmond, VA

Publik Times
Williamsburg, VA

Renaissance Festival
Annapolis, MD

Miss America Pageant
Convention Hall
Atlantic City, NJ

Maryland Seafood Festival
Sandy Point State Park
Annapolis, MD

Defender's Day Program
Fort McHenry NM
Baltimore, MD

October
National Tobacco Festival
Richmond, VA

Baltimore on the Bay
Inner Harbor
Baltimore, MD

December
Christmas in Williamsburg
Williamsburg, VA

Lighting the Nation's Christmas Tree
Washington, DC

Places of Interest

Annapolis, MD
Maryland State House
State Circle
Annapolis, MD 21401
☎ 301-974-3275
Open: 9am-5pm
Visitor centre, tours, ♿

Appomattox, VA
Appomattox Court House NHP
PO Box 218
Appomattox
VA 24522-0218
☎ 804-352-8987
Open: 9am-5pm, reduced in winter
Museum, tours, living history, ♿

Arlington, VA
Arlington National Cemetery
Near Washington DC
Arlington, VA 22211
☎ 703-692-0931
Open: 9.30am-4.30pm Oct-Mar, extended in summer. Free
Arlington House, memorials, parts ♿

Baltimore, MD
Baltimore Museum of Art
Wyman Park
North Charles & 31st
Baltimore, MD 21218
☎ 301-396-7101
Open:11am-6pm weekends, 10am-4pm Tue-Fri, -7pm Thu
Gifts, café

Fort McHenry NM
East Fort Ave
Baltimore, MD 21230-5393
☎ 301-962-4299
Open: 8am-5pm, extended in summer
Gifts, ♿

National Aquarium
Pier 3, 501 East Pratt St
Baltimore, MD 21202
☎ 301-567-3810
Open: 10am-5pm, 10am-8pm Fri
Gifts, aquarium & rain forest

Charlottesville, VA
Monticello
PO Box 316
Charlottesville, VA 2290
☎ 804-295-8181

Open: 9am-4.30pm,
extended in summer
Gifts, tours, &

Gettysburg, PA
Gettysburg NMP
SR134
Gettysburg, PA 17325
☎ 717-334-1124
Open: 8am-5pm, roads
open longer
Cemetery, drive, tours,
gifts, Eisenhower NHS

Harpers Ferry, WV
Harpers Ferry NHP
Box 65
Harpers Ferry, WV 25425
☎ 304-535-6371
Open: 8am-5pm
Gifts, food, walks, museum

Harrisburg, PA
Pennsylvania State Capitol
Main Capitol
Harrisburg, PA 17125
☎ 717-787-6810
Open: 9am-4pm Mon-Sat
Tours

Intercourse, PA
People's Place
Main St
Intercourse, PA 17534
☎ 717-768-7171
Open: 9am-5pm except Sun
Crafts, gifts, film, books

Lewes, DE
Cape May/Lewes Ferry
Ferry Terminal, SR 9
Lewes, DE
☎ 302-645-6313 (Lewes)
or 609-886-2718 (Cape May)
Sailing times vary
Car ferry, snacks, &

Luray, VA
Shenandoah NP
(HQ) SR 4, Box 348
Luray, VA 22835
☎ 703-999-2229
Open: visitor centres
9am-5pm

Lodge, food, camp, hike,
picnic, parts &

Mount Vernon, VA
Mount Vernon
Mount Vernon Ladies Assn
Mount Vernon, VA 22121
☎ 703-780-2000
Open: 9am-4pm, 9am-
5pm Mar-Oct
Tours, gifts, food, parts &

Natural Bridge, VA
Natural Bridge
PO Box 57
Natural Bridge, VA 24578
☎ 800-336-5742
or 703-291-2121
Open: 7am-dusk & light
show at night
Lodge, gifts, food,
waxworks, &

Philadelphia, PA
Independence NHP
313 Walnut St
Philadelphia, PA 19106
☎ 215-597-8974
Open: 9am-5pm, ex-
tended in summer
Independence Hall,
Liberty Bell, gifts, tours,
parts &

*Philadelphia Museum of
Art*
26th & Ben Franklin Pkwy
Philadelphia, PA 19101
☎ 215-787-5498
Open: 10am-5pm Tue-
Sun; free Sun. 10am-1pm
Food, gifts, &

Richmond, VA
*Museum & White House of
the Confederacy*
1201 East Clay St
Richmond, VA 23219
☎ 804-649-1861
Open: 10am-5pm Mon-
Sat, 1-5pm Sun
Museum &, house is not,
gifts

Stratford, VA
Stratford Hall Plantation
SR 214
Stratford, VA 22558
☎ 804-493-8038
Open: 9am-4.30pm
Tour house & outbuild-
ings, gifts

Valley Forge, PA
Valley Forge NHP
SR 23
Valley Forge, PA 19481
☎ 215-783-7700
Open: 8.30am-5pm
Carillon, tours, gifts

Washington, DC
Ford's Theatre
511 10th St, NW
Washington, DC 20004
☎ 202-426-6924
Tours 9am-5pm except
during matinees
Light theatre

*Kennedy Center for
    Performing Arts*
New Hampshire Ave &
    Rock Creek Parkway
Washington, DC 20566
☎ 202-467-4600
Tours 10am-1pm
Drama, dance, opera,
cinema, food, &

*National Geographic
Society*
17th & M Streets
Washington, DC 20036
☎ 202-857-7588
Open: 9am-5pm Mon-Sat,
10am-5pm Sun. Free
Explorers Hall, globe,
gifts

Smithsonian Institution
The Castle, National Mall
Washington, DC 20560
☎ 202-357-2700
or 202-357-2020 (recorded)
Open: 10.30am-5pm
except Christmas. Free
14 museums, gifts, food, &

US Capitol
National Mall East
Washington, DC 20510
☎ 202-224-3121
or 202-225-6827
Tours 9am-3.45pm, open
9am-8pm. Free
Tours, gifts, ᵭ

Washington Monument
National Mall @ 15th St
Washington, DC 20242
☎ 202-426-6841
Open: 9am-5pm, 9am-
midnight summer. Free
Elevator, snacks, gifts

White House
1600 Pennsylvania Ave, NW
Washington, DC 20500
☎ 202-456-7041
or 202-472-3369

Open: 10am-Noon Tue-Sat,
tickets from 8am in sum-
mer. Free, arrive early
Tours, wheelchair access
at NE gate

Williamsburg, VA
*Busch Gardens — The Old
    Country*
One Busch Gardens Blvd
Williamsburg, VA 23187
☎ 804-253-3350
Open: 10am-7pm Apr-Oct,
extended mid-summer
Food, gifts, brewery tour,
rides, parts ᵭ

Colonial Williamsburg
Box C
Williamsburg, VA 23187
☎ 800-447-8679
or 804-220-7286
Open: 9am-5pm Jan-Feb,

8.30am-8pm Mar-Dec
Lodge, food, gifts, tours,
parts ᵭ

Jamestown Settlement
SR 31 & 359
South of Williamsburg
VA 23185
☎ 804-253-4838
Open: 9am-5pm
Villages & fort, living
history, gifts, ᵭ

Yorktown, VA
Colonial NHP
Attn Superintendent
Yorktown, VA 23690
☎ 804-898-3400
Open: 8.30am-5pm
Jamestown & Yorktown,
picnic, hike, gifts, parts ᵭ

4

THE SOUTH

To many the South is a land of legend, where Scarlet O'Hara awaits, sipping mint juleps on some Southern colonel's porch. To others it is Nashville, capital of country music, or the year-round party of New Orleans. Throw in a selection of antebellum plantations, sun-soaked beaches, fields of fluffy cotton, blossoming magnolias and the mighty Mississippi River — the reality is all this and more.

Atlanta, Georgia

Atlanta is capital of the New South, confirmed when the city was awarded the 1996 Summer Olympics. Smartly dressed office workers, tall buildings and high technology are the trademark of this rapidly growing city. Coca Cola and CNN (Cable News Network) are among Fortune 500 companies based in

The South in Brief

Compare modern, bustling Atlanta with Savannah and Charleston, where the old South lingers. From the sun-drenched Atlantic resorts rise to the Blue Ridge and Great Smokey Mountains. Compare Kentucky, the blue grass state, with bluegrass and country music at Nashville, home of the Grand Ole Opry. From Memphis follow the mighty Mississippi past antebellum Natchez to New Orleans and the antics of Bourbon Street. Sample the Gulf of Mexico shores and gracious Mobile before returning to Atlanta.

Three to four weeks are required for the entire 3,100 mile tour — demanding yet rewarding if time and budget allow. Alternatively, split the South into two week tours. Georgia and the Carolinas comprise the Atlantic states, Mississippi, Louisiana and Alabama the Gulf Coast states, while central Tennessee and Kentucky can be included with either tour or visited separately. For a week's vacation, chose Nashville, New Orleans, Atlanta or one of the seaside resorts.

Spring pilgrimages to the antebellum South coincide with blossoming dogwoods and azalea — late March and early April along the gulf coast states, April to early May along the Atlantic. Autumn Pilgrimages are also catching on, while humid summers are best spent relaxing on coastal beaches or in the mountains. Little snow reaches the Deep South, but nightly frosts occasionally spill over into day.

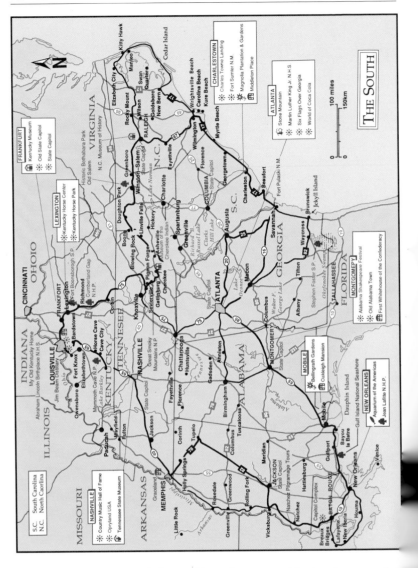

Atlanta. Famous sons include two kings, former president and peacemake:
Jimmy Carter, the 'Peanut King', and that firebrand of non-violence, Marti:
Luther King Jr.

   While other cities wonder how to revitalize downtown, Atlanta barely ha
enough space for its office, shopping, and dining complexes. **Peachtre**
Center and its associated hotels, speciality stores, and eateries seem larger o
every visit. The Merchandise and Apparel Mart complexes tend toward
wholesale, unlike large department stores Macy's and Rich's. The latter is nea
Five Points, crossroads of the South and heart of the MARTA light ra:
network.

Into and Around Atlanta

Formerly known as Terminus, Atlanta is still an important hub in America's transportation network. William B. Hartsfield (Atlanta) International Airport supplements taxi and limousine services with Atlanta Airport Shuttle and Northside Airport Express, together covering main hotels and downtown business centres. Amtrak runs from Peachtree Station and Greyhound from International Boulevard. MARTA is the regional bus and rail network.

Road improvements for the Olympics occasionally delay central thoroughfares, but the city's external connections radiate in every direction, interconnected by the I-285 ring road. Atlanta has numerous car parks but one drawback. Over thirty streets, roads, circles and avenues begin with Peachtree. The main Peachtree Street runs north from Peachtree Center downtown, diverging into Peachtree and West Peachtree Streets before becoming Peachtree Road.

Underground Atlanta is east of Peachtree Street and Five Points. The below ground section of this shopping, dining, and entertainment complex is a remnant of Terminus, the original railway town. Once full of honky-tonks and bars, the revitalized Underground has attracted **World of Coca Cola**, bringing ✳ millions annually to the area. Admission to this nostalgic romp through Coca Cola's past includes unlimited drinks from around their world. Memorabilia collectors should not miss their gift shop. The nearby visitor centre offers an Atlanta guidebook and map, plus information on events and theatre productions.

Atlanta was less than 30 years old when it was steamrollered by Sherman's 'March through Georgia'. Instead of old buildings the city offers excellent shopping, culture and sport. The 1920s **Fox Theatre** on Peachtree Street was built when cinema was supreme; today it adds live theatre, concerts, and Atlanta Ballet. The Atlanta Symphony Orchestra is complemented by the Atlanta Chamber Orchestra, while another twenty dance and theatre groups call Atlanta home. **Atlanta/Fulton County Stadium** is home to Braves baseball in spring-summer and Falcons football in autumn-winter, while the Omni Coliseum indoor sports palace hosts Hawks basketball among its events. Georgia Tech, State University, and University of Georgia matches are also worth seeing.

The **State Capitol** is southeast of World of Coca Cola, while **CNN** is west of ✳ downtown. Cable News Network offers tours on a first come basis — arrive early to see news preparation and live broadcast. Next door to Civic Center is **SciTrek**, Atlanta's hands-on science and technology learning centre. **Wren's Nest** was home to Joel Chandler Harris, whose 'Uncle Remus Animal Stories' told delightful tales of Brer Rabbit adapted for *Song of the South*.

The **Martin Luther King Jr Historic Site** is west of downtown along 'Sweet' ✳ Auburn Avenue, where the Jackson Street kiosk provides maps and tour information. Atlanta preserves his birthplace and grave, and Ebenezer Baptist Church where he and his forefathers preached. Atlanta had a reputation, even during segregation, as a city where Blacks could better themselves, and Sweet

Auburn harkens to that era. East beyond the district is the **Carter Presidential Center**, highlighting the former President's period in office.

Grant Park southeast of downtown presents **Atlanta Cyclorama**, a sound and light re-enactment of the 1864 Battle for Atlanta, and Zoo Atlanta. Piedmont Park to the north enjoys Atlanta Botanic Gardens. Peachtree Street north from downtown passes the excellent **High Museum of Art** and **Woodruff Arts Center**. Further north, Atlanta Historical Society maintains its complex of buildings at Buckhead.

Amusements outside the city include **Six Flags over Georgia**, themed for excitement, and **Georgia's Stone Mountain Park**. The latter boasts an antebellum plantation, scenic railroad, auto and music museum, a carillon, and hikes or a skylift up Stone Mountain. Carved on this massive granite dome are the figures of Stonewall Jackson, Robert E. Lee, and Jefferson Davies, former President of the Confederate States of America. Activities include golf, tennis, ice-skating, beaches along the lakes, and even a riverboat cruise.

Georgia and The Carolinas — Atlantic States Tour

Serene Savannah awaits east on I-16, perhaps visiting **Macon** en route for its springtime cherry blossoms or a symphony at the Grand Opera House. Fine Macon homes include the birthplace of Sidney Lanier, Georgia's foremost poet, and the Italian Renaissance Hay House. Nearby **Ocmulgee National Monument** protects an extensive Native American mound complex, with interpretive help via the visitor centre.

If time permits, head south to **Waycross** and experience the vast **Okefenokee Swamp** through the Swamp Park's exhibits, films and boat trips. Nearby Okefenokee Heritage Center examines the human aspects of swamp life. The southwestern Stephen Foster State Park entrance point, where the Suwanee River emerges, has fewer people and more alligators. From Waycross continue east on US82 to the Atlantic coast, perhaps pausing at **Jekyll Island** resort.

Savannah was Georgia's first settlement, a buffer against Spanish encroachment. General Oglethorpe laid out Savannah as a series of wards centred around public squares, which were soon surrounded by fine homes and public buildings. The farsighted Historic Savannah Foundation has helped the city grow without losing its beauty and heritage. Formerly deserted buildings along the riverfront now house specialty shops and restaurants, while the Savannah River is sailed by Cap'n Sam and his cruises. The **Ships of the Sea Maritime Museum**, itself an old warehouse, exhibits a replica of the *Savannah*, first steam-powered ship to cross an ocean.

Bay Street parallels the river, intersected by Bull and Abercorn Street and Martin Luther King Jr Boulevard. The **Savannah Visitor Center** and **Savannah History Museum** are on the latter. For a sample of Savannah, stroll up Bull from City Hall to Forsyth Park, then back along Abercorn, passing the city's finest squares en route. Tour operators include Gray Line, Helen Salter, Old Savannah and Historic Savannah Foundation; trolley rides are by Colonial Historic Tours. **Fort Pulaski National Monument**, east on US80, recreate Civil War garrison life not far from quaint **Tybee Island** resort.

Coastal South Carolina

The Palmetto State's coastline is renowned for sunny beaches and super getaways, like **Hilton Head Island Resort**. Named after a British captain, not the hotel chain, nevertheless the eight planned communities (locally known as plantations) boast numerous resort hotels, rental and timeshare villas. Not the bargain basement of the oceanside resorts, island guests have a choice of twenty-four golf courses, and a surfeit of scenic walks, tennis courts, cycle paths, and beaches. Take coastal SR170 north for quaint **Beaufort**, a picturesque old port and gateway to nicely natural Hunting Island State Park.

Charleston is indisputably *the* Southern Belle of the Atlantic Coast, where cast iron balustrades decorate fine houses and the city's many churches number among structures of historical significance and character. The city was not spared by the Civil War, for the North could not forget that Charleston fired upon Fort Sumter, commencing the hostilities. Nevertheless many homes remain, with the South's finest plantations nearby.

Historic Charleston, at the confluence of the Ashley and Cooper Rivers, has the parks and gardens of the **Battery** along its southern tip. East Bay Street parallels the Cooper River, leading to Queen, Market, and Calhoun Streets. The main historical area is south of Market Street between East Bay and King Street. Maps and tour information are available at the Visitor Information Center on Calhoun and at Preservation Society offices on King Street. The former shows 'The Charleston Adventure' slide show; the latter, 'Dear Charleston: The Motion Picture'.

Historical area parking can be found on Meeting Street between King and Broad, on Cumberland Street south of the Market, and outside the Visitor Information Center. Walkers might miss some of Charleston's finer details without a guide or guidebook, both are available, and wear comfortable shoes. Alternatively, the horse and carriage tours add atmosphere and an interesting perspective.

Historical Charleston Foundation hosts the annual Festival of Houses and Gardens in March and April; reservations are recommended. Foundation homes include **Nathaniel Russell House**, an 1808 Federal stately home on Market, and **Edmondston-Alston House** on East Battery, while their centre on Broad Street sells finely crafted reproductions of original Charleston antiques — proceeds furthering their preservation goals. Notable Charleston homes and churches include the 1772 Heyward-Washington House on Church, the 1803 Manigault House on Meeting, the Huguenot Church (with Protestant services in French and English), and St Michael's Episcopal on Broad and Meeting, inspired by St Martin's-in-the-Fields. Victorian **Calhoun Mansion** is extravagantly decorated with fine woods and boasts perhaps Charleston's most magnificent ballroom.

Charlestown Museum may be America's oldest, focusing on the city and its environs. **Charles Towne Landing** across the Ashley River is a reconstruction of the first settlement on its original site. Boats to **Fort Sumter National** **Monument** leave from the Municipal Marina along the Ashley and across the Cooper River at Patriots Point. Three years of bombardment reduced the fort's defences to rubble, which proved a better shield than traditional brickwork redoubts, and Fort Sumter stood defiantly until Charleston fell. Fort Sumter, and nearby Fort Moultrie which fired upon it, were rebuilt utilizing knowl-

Atlanta is the capital of the New South

The Okefenokee swamp is full of alligators

edge gained from the contest.

Each plantation surrounding Charleston has its own distinct character. **Middleton Place**, home of Henry Middleton, President of the First Continental Congress, has landscaped grounds worthy of Capability Brown. **Magnolia Plantation and Gardens** supplements camellias and azaleas with a petting zoo, biblical garden, topiary, bike paths, miniature horses, and Audubon Swamp Garden, a waterfowl sanctuary. **Boone Hall Plantation** has a stately tree-lined drive leading to the Georgian mansion, often seen on television and films. Slave Street is of particular interest, a collection of nine houses utilized by household servants and gifted Black artisans. **Drayton Hall**, a Palladian Georgian mansion, appeals to those who appreciate fine lines and unmodernized elegance.

Follow US17 along the coast towards Myrtle Beach, perhaps visiting Georgetown and **Brookgreen Gardens** near Murrells Inlet. Business 17 leads to the heart of **Myrtle Beach**, seaside playground for millions of Americans. Calling itself the 'Grand Strand', some 60 miles of beach are lined with resort hotels, amusement parks, top-quality golf courses and natural state parks surrounding a central boardwalk. Festivals are frequent and big-name hotels offer entertainment, while the Carolina Opry offers a taste of Nashville.

North Carolina

The sunny coastline continues to North Carolina, where **Wilmington** is gateway to Wrightsville, Carolina and Kure Beach Resorts. Wilmington itself is home to the **USS *North Carolina* Battleship Memorial**, the 'Showboat', now a museum offering tours plus a sound-and-light show on summer evenings. Nearby Brunswick Town was principal seaport in Colonial times, now an archaeological State Historic Site. Fort Anderson's earthworks are also there, while larger Fort Fisher near Kure Beach saw a major Civil War battle.

Cape Hatteras National Seashore and the **Wright Brothers National Memorial** at Kitty Hawk make an interesting and scenic diversion. Reservations are essential for Cedar Island and Swan Quarter ferries, especially in summer. Alternatively, US64 links to Manteo and the Outer Banks north of Cape Hatteras National Seashore, making a longer overland route. Return on US158 north, visiting Kitty Hawk, then pressing inland at Elizabeth City for Raleigh. If time is short, head directly from Wilmington to Raleigh.

Raleigh was named after Sir Walter, known for his tobacco. Capital of North Carolina, Raleigh is also a 'Cigarette City', once dominated by tobacco but gradually diversifying. The Capital Area Visitor Center is on Blount Street, just north of the **State Capitol**. Other points within downtown Raleigh include the informative **North Carolina Museum of History**, the Executive Mansion, and Museum of Natural Sciences. **North Carolina Museum of Art** is on Blue Ridge Boulevard.

Continuing west, Durham is another 'Cigarette City', with tobacco auctions in late autumn. At the **Guilford Courthouse National Military Park** northwest of Greensboro, British General Cornwallis and his hardened troops routed the much larger force of Nathanael Greene. Americans celebrate the battle, for Cornwallis' victory was Pyrrhic, and his weakened forces withdrew to Yorktown, where he surrendered.

Less advertised than the Pennsylvania Dutch, the Moravians brought their special brand of Christianity to **Winston-Salem** in 1753, naming their main colony Salem, Hebrew for 'peace'. **Historic Bethabara Park** off University Parkway was their first settlement, an excellent introduction to their ways being provided by volunteer Moravian guides. Then visit **Old Salem**, their restored town with costumed craftsmen and a dozen buildings open to the public. Services at the **Moravian Church** are open to visitors, with members available to answer questions in early afternoons, excepting winter. Easter Sunrise Service, New Year's Eve Watch Night Service, and Christmas Love feast are among ceremonies celebrated, the latter involving mugs of hot coffee and home-baked rolls. Tobacco and fabric built the combined city of Winston-Salem. **R. J. Reynolds Tobacco** offers plant tours, **Tanglewood Park** was a Reynolds family gift, and guests may visit Reynolda House.

The **Blue Ridge Parkway** in North Carolina is one of eastern America's most picturesque drives. From Winston-Salem follow US421 west, picking up US21 northbound then the parkway south. Doughton Park has maps, information, and the old Brinegar Cabin on its outskirts. The Northwest Trading Post and Moses H. Cone Parkway Craft Center offer glimpses of traditional mountain crafts. Daniel Boone's Trace cuts across the parkway at mile 285.1, while nearby Boone town presents 'Horn In the West' about their hero. Blowing Rock has the Tweetsie Railroad and its namesake formation, where snow falls upwards.

The trail network includes moderate walks at Julian Price Memorial Park, Crabtree Meadows and Craggy Gardens. Between them, Linville Falls has strolls and short hikes among falls and scenic cascades. The Museum of North Carolina Minerals and Crabtree Meadows are along the parkway, then take the SR128 side trip to **Mount Mitchell State Park**. Highest point east of the Mississippi, the 6,684ft (2,037m) mountain has excellent views from its lookout tower.

Beyond the Folk Art Center is **Asheville**, where pride of place goes to the **Biltmore Estate**. Designed by Richard Morris Hunt for George Washington Vanderbilt, grandson of the 'Commodore', this French Renaissance chateau is heart of a 7,500 acre working 'gentleman's country estate'. Fine period furnishings and fittings are augmented by interesting curios, such as the chess set Napoleon brought to St Helena. An optional behind-the-scenes tour looks at rooms still being renovated (the chateau has 250). Sections of the grounds are landscaped with plentiful gift shops and restaurants. The Deerpark offers European and American cuisine in a pleasant courtyard setting, with a nearby picnic area. In keeping with the French-styled chateau, the estate has its own winery, offering tours, free samples, and a large gift shop. Special events include its Festival of Flowers in spring, candlelight tours in summer, and Christmas cheer through December.

South of Asheville is the highest point on the parkway, 6,053ft (1,845m) at Richland Balsam. **Cherokee**, at the base of the Great Smoky Mountains, is home to tribe members whose ancestors hid or returned after the 'Trail of Tears'. Downtown has numerous Indian crafts and jewelry shops, while the fascinating **Museum of the Cherokee Indian** presents their culture, history, and leaders. Native American crafts are also displayed at **Oconaluftee Indian Village**, while exploits of Cherokees great and small are related at 'Unto These Hills'.

US441 west leads to the **Great Smoky Mountains National Park**. Beyond ♣ the Oconaluftee Visitor Center and Pioneer Homestead the road winds over the Smokies, crossing into Tennessee at Newfound Gap.

Tennessee and Kentucky — the Inland States Tour

Visitors are drawn by the rugged mountains, whether venturing into remote sections of the Great Smoky Mountains National Park or taking the aerial tramway to Ober Gatlinburg on Mount Harrison. **Gatlinburg** is gateway to less disturbed areas while its tourist zone boasts a Guinness World Records 🏠 Museum, American Historical Wax Gardens, and Christus Gardens, with dioramas based upon Christ's life.

Dollywood at **Pigeon Forge** offers a large theme park with musical production, numerous amusements, and traditional crafts beloved by Dolly Parton. Concerts with big-name stars and special events, such as the American Quilt Showcase, supplement the regular features. Nearby **Dixie Stampede** provides an all-American evening of entertainment. Those following *only* the first half of the Southern tour may return to Atlanta via **Knoxville**, famed for blossoming dogwood trees, and **Chattanooga**, where the renowned **Choo Choo** railroad depot, cars and all, is now a fine hotel.

Others may take US411 northeast from Sevierville, then US25E northwest at Newport for Kentucky and **Cumberland Gap National Historical Park**. ⊓ The gap was used by Native Americans and local wildlife, but achieved fame as Daniel Boone's Wilderness Road. From 1775 to 1800 some 200,000 pioneers trekked over the gap into Kentucky and beyond. Several scenic trails are available; alternatively drive up to Pinnacle Overlook from the visitor centre.

At Corbin, home of Colonel Sanders of Kentucky Fried Chicken fame, take US25 north. Berea College Appalachian Museum, famed for preserving mountain crafts, and Levi Jackson Wilderness Road State Park and its Mountain Life Museum are en route to Richmond, which relives the Daniel Boone tradition, at **Fort Boonesborough**. Also north of town is **White Hall State** ⊓ **Historic Site**, home of emancipationist Cassius Marcellus Clay.

Lexington is heart of Kentucky Bluegrass, famed for fine thoroughbreds and air-cured tobacco — the latter hung in ancient roadside barns. Lexington Center (Rupp Arena) is beyond Broadway and Triangle Park, giving information on tours of the Bluegrass and events at Keenland Race Course and Red Mile. **Mary Todd Lincoln House**, girlhood home of Abraham Lincoln's wife, ⊞ is next door.

The famed horse farms are open only via tours or by appointment, but the countryside should be seen regardless. For a driving tour of the Bluegrass, turn south from Main Street onto Tucker then right onto Manchester Street. Manchester becomes the **Old Frankfort Pike Road**, with traditional horse farms on both sides. The Headley-Whitney Museum has an interesting collection of bibelots, artistically ornamented 'trinkets', then backtrack slightly and turn north onto Yarnallton Pike. Right onto Iron Works Pike leads to **Kentucky Horse Park**, showcase of the Bluegrass, with films, daily Parade of Breeds, and museums which trace horse's history and sports. Trams and jitneys tour the complex, horse and pony rides are available, and the park regularly holds major equestrian events. For the driving tour, turn right onto Paris Pike, pausing at the **Kentucky Horse Center**, where the best thorough-breds are trained. Since workouts are early, keen visitors may book for the following morning, perhaps followed by a sojourn to Pleasant Hill with its charming **Shaker Village**, now a living history centre.

Frankfort, charming capital of Kentucky, can be reached either west on I-64 or more scenically via Old Frankfort Pike Road. Delightfully schizophrenic Frankfort outgrew its Capitol, so the entire government moved to a new site, sparing the historic old buildings. The visitor centre is south of the Kentucky River on Capitol Avenue, followed by the **State Capitol** with its unusual floral clock. North is the **Kentucky Historical Museum**, the **Old State Capitol**, and the **Old Governor's Mansion**, plus several fine eighteenth-century homes. Wilkinson Street leads to the **Ancient Age Distillery**, offering weekday tours in the tourist season.

Louisville is famous for the Kentucky Derby, which takes place at Churchill Downs on the first Saturday in May. The city is also heart of a conurbation extending across the Ohio River into Indiana. The 1st Street visitor centre has information on attractions and events, such as the Bluegrass Music Festival in autumn and cruising the Ohio River on the Belle of Louisville. **Fort Knox** is south on US31W, and while the gold is not on show, the General Patten Museum of Cavalry and Armor is accessible. Just north on 31W, SR44 east leads to Shepardsville, where **Clermont** and **Jim Beam's American Outpost** are south on SR61 then west on 245. The famous bourbon distillery is not included with the tour, and samples are unavailable in 'dry' Clermont, but the outpost has exhibits on distilling and cooperage and their original still may be America's oldest.

Biltmore Estate in the heart of the Blue Ridge Mountains, North Carolina

Historic **Bardstown** is famous for *My Old Kentucky Home,* now a state park. ♣
Stephen Foster's inspiration for the song came from his cousin's plantation,
Federal Hill, where costumed guides evoke old Kentucky. The outdoor musical 'Stephen Foster Story' is presented on summer evenings and Saturday
matinees. Bardstown Tourmobile takes in local sights, including the Heaven
Hill Distilleries, which provide guided tours. Limestone Springs is the terminus of My Old Kentucky Dinner Train. **Old Bardstown Village** has added the
multimedia Kentucky Show to its collection of historic structures. Continue
south on US31E, which passes the **Kentucky State Railway Museum** in New 🚂
Haven.

Travellers often confuse the replica Lincoln's Boyhood Home cabin for
Abraham Lincoln Birthplace National Historic Site, south of Hodgenville. π
'Honest Abe' might find the marble mausoleum surrounding his birthplace
cabin ostentatious, but the historic park has interesting highlights about
Lincoln's early years and the harsh life faced by the Kentucky pioneers.
Continuing south, take SR218 west to US31W southbound. Horse Cave and
Cave City are two tourist resorts which sprang up around the region's exten-

*Lexington is heart of
the Kentucky
Bluegrass*

sive networks of caves. Most famous is **Mammoth Cave National Park**, west of Cave City, with some 300 miles of explored passages and five entrances. Tours range from one to six hours, chosen according to taste and physical capability (dress warmly). Ticketron handles advance reservations, recommended in summer. The park encompasses 52,000 acres above ground, and road-weary travellers may relax or explore trails through forests and over streams. Return south to Tennessee on I-65.

Nashville is capital of country music and also of Tennessee. Nashville has more than enough to occupy visitors not fond of country music while friends hit the 'high spots'. Downtown boasts a fine **State Capitol**, the comprehensive **Tennessee State Museum** in the Polk Cultural Center, and the **Museum of Tobacco Art and History**. Alongside the Cumberland River is **Fort Nashborough**, a replica of the original settlement. South of downtown is the Cumberland Science Center while **The Hermitage** in the northeast was home of President Andrew Jackson. Other impressive homes include the Greek revival Belle Meade Mansion, a style beloved in the South, and Belmont Mansion, an Italianate villa built for Adelicia Acklen, one of Americas wealthiest women during the 1850s. Just west is **The Parthenon**, a life-sized replica of Athens' most famous monument, which houses the city's art treasures. Riverboat cruises on the Cumberland include the **Belle Carol Riverboats** and **General Jackson**, part of the Opryland USA Complex.

Opryland USA is to Nashville what The Disney Company is to Orlando. **Opryland** itself is a theme park with numerous revues highlighting America's musical heritage, from gospel to rock, plus amusements, thrill rides, crafts demonstrations and 'a whole mess of fun'. Plan rides and amusements around the shows and timed demonstrations.

The **Grand Ole Opry** is America's longest running radio show, where country fans watch favourite singers and musicians perform live. Tickets should be purchased in advance, but the Opry reserves some, putting them on sale Tuesdays for the upcoming performances. An Opryland USA Passport includes the Grand Ole Opry, space permitting, plus a multiple day Opryland pass, a musical evening at the Acuff Theatre, and an excursion aboard the showboat *General Jackson*. **TNN**, The Nashville Network, is the country capital's own cable television network, and studio audience tickets are free. The

---

Into and Around Nashville

Rapidly expanding Nashville International Airport offers excellent domestic connections, with a growing list of non-stop international flights. Many hotels provide free courtesy buses, the Opryland Hotel being the main exception. The bus network is good, but cars are more convenient for far-flung attractions. Interstates 40, 65 and 265 encircle downtown Nashville, the visitor centre being near I-65 junction 85, east of downtown. Opryland is east of Nashville; either take I-65 north and exit 89 east, or I-40 east to exit 215, then north on the Briley Parkway. Nashville International Airport is southeast off I-40, exit 216A. Music Row is southwest of downtown on Demonbruen, take I-40 exit 209 if south or eastbound, 209b if north or westbound.

Opryland Hotel is open to visitors, boasting two massive courtyards, one botanical, the other a series of waterfalls. Together they occupying 2 acres *within* the hotel. Explore the maze of speciality shops, restaurants, lounges (with entertainment), and restaurants — or ask guest services for a map.

Music Row is the business side of country music, but with plenty of room for entertainment, the name of the Nashville game. Rows of shops neatly flanked by wax-works museums and car collections are in the Demonbruen/ Music Square area. Of especial interest is the **Country Music Hall of Fame and** **Museum**, with such delights as memorabilia of stars past, treasured posses- sions donated by the latest headliners, and Elvis Presley's 'Solid Gold Cadillac' (press its button). Cherished stars have their own museums, such as Barbara Mandrell Country and Hank Williams Jr Museum. Those not in Music Row or Opryland are found in Hendersonville (Twitty City and House of Cash) or Madison Area (Jim Reeves and Kitty Wells Museums).

See the heart of Music Row on a short walk south along East Music Square, returning via West. Inside those quaint homes and occasional office block lies the power behind Nashville, the producers, promoters, and recording compa- nies. RCA's **Studio B**, where Elvis and others recorded, offers behind-the- ✳ scenes tours. Habitues of Music Row, whether taxi drivers, grocery clerks, or secretaries, are *all* budding country singers and/or instrumentalists. Buskers in the tourist area provide entertainment, some looking for coins, all searching for stardom.

While music plays an important role in **Memphis**, the mighty Mississippi River comes first in commerce, making Memphis Tennessee's largest city and American 'Queen of Cotton'. Drivers westbound on I-40 from Nashville should take exit 1A for downtown Memphis, heading southwest to Front Street, where the visitor centre has useful maps and information. While there, check the schedule for the Peabody Ducks. Living in a penthouse atop the Peabody Hotel on Union Street, these ducks daily descend via elevator to the foyer, following the red carpet to the hotel's ornate fountain. After a leisurely afternoon they return to their rooftop residence, where they often entertain visitors.

Beale Street was the birthplace of the blues, where W.C. Handy blew its first sweet and sour notes. While Handy is no more, **A. Schawbs** on Beale Street is a survivor. This family run shopping institution boasts, 'if you can't find it here, you don't need it!' Also on Beale is the **Center for Southern Folklore**, ✳ offering walking tours of Beale Street and films on the locality. Several Beale Street nightspots offer jazz and blues.

Mud Island is not descriptive of the riverside park, entertainment complex and Mississippi River heritage centre. Reproduction riverboats, a large thea- tre and numerous exhibits make 'Old Man River' fun to learn about. Espe- cially well presented is a five-block long, scale model of the lower Mississippi to paddle in. The Great American Pyramid is a recent addition, offering excellent views across the river, with more delights inside. Those parked downtown can take the monorail across to the island. The *Memphis Queen* and other riverboats depart from the nearby waterfront, offering daytime sight- seeing and evening dinner cruises.

Graceland is former home of and shrine to the King of Rock and Roll, Elvis Presley. From the waterfront near downtown take Riverside Drive then I-55

Opryland, an event-filled day in Nashville

Mardis Gras is a state of mind in New Orleans

south, following signs down Elvis Presley Boulevard. The ticket complex arranges mansion tours, with rooms as the King left them. After the mansion comes the trophy room and gardens, where Elvis is interred. Surrounding the ticket complex are his private jet, customized tour bus, car collection, and museum; these may be toured individually or via a combination ticket. Arrive early unless a tour is reserved.

Mississippi, Louisiana and Alabama — Gulf of Mexico Tour

Welcome to the Deep South, rich in traditions yet presenting the year-round party that is New Orleans. From Memphis there is a choice of two picturesque routes south. First scenic option is Third Street (US61) southbound from Memphis, which drives through the fertile farmland surrounding 'Old Man River'. Take SR322 west then SR1 south to Rosedale, where the **Great River Road State Park** recalls the Mississippi River as the South's busiest 'highway'. The **Greenville** 'riverboat' welcome centre helps visitors to understand the levee system. Between towns are great fields of cotton, soy beans and rice, with waterfowl amid oxbow lakes forgotten by the meandering Mississippi. Return to US61 at Rolling Fork, picking up the narrative at Vicksburg and Jackson.

The alternative inland scenic route takes US78 south from Memphis, pausing for the historic homes of Holly Springs. In **Tupelo**, a memorial park dedicated to Elvis Presley includes his birthplace. From Tupelo retrace US78 west for **Natchez Trace Parkway**, America's great Nashville to Natchez scenic byway. Divert north briefly for the informative visitor centre at mile 266 before plunging south along the parkway. Early trace users include Chickasaw Indians and Hernando de Soto, who wintered nearby during 1540-1 before finding the Mississippi River. The original trace crosses the parkway at mile 221.4, while the Jeff Busby complex has an observation point on the 660ft (201m) Little Mountain. The campsite store sells foodstuffs, useful if a sudden urge to picnic develops. French Camp Academy Museum off the parkway is housed in an 1840 cabin and period-furnished stately home, with quilting and other craft demonstrations. The Ridgeland Crafts Center is before Jackson, where the parkway disappears, emerging at US20 in Clinton.

Jackson, the Mississippi state capital, was named after President Andrew Jackson. General Sherman boasted the Union need fear no further resistance from Jackson; the city was razed and the countryside burned for 10 leagues. The governor's mansion, used as Sherman's headquarters, survived. The new **State Capitol** houses each branch of government, while **Old Capitol** is now the Historical Museum. The **Mississippi Agriculture and Forestry Museum** adjacent to the Smith-Wills Stadium incorporates innumerable implements, a living-history farm, an arboretum, and a selection of vintage crop dusters. Follow I-20 west to Vicksburg, taking exit 4 for the city information centre.

Strategically located **Vicksburg**, commanding views across the Mississippi River, was critical to Union success. Today **Vicksburg National Military Park** offers a scenic drive, supplemented by a park visitor centre, living history programs, and the resurrected ironclad gunboat *Cairo*, first ship sunk by electrically controlled mines. Vicksburg town opens its arms and many fine antebellum mansions to visitors during the Spring Pilgrimage. Fourth of July weekends are especially explosive, remembering the Siege of Vicksburg.

Most stately homes have a tale to tell, and the following are also open outside the pilgrimage. Confederate President Jefferson Davies gave an address from the balcony of Greek Revival **Anchuca**, Native American for 'happy home'. Mary Green of **Duff Green Mansion** bore a son christened Siege during an exchange of cannon fire, while **Cedar Grove** has a shell embedded in its parlor wall. Another cannonball was removed from **Balfour House**, which was conducting a celebratory ball when news came of approaching Union ships, so the Confederate officers reassembled at the city's defenses.

From Vicksburg follow Clay Street west under I-20, turning south onto US27 and again for the Natchez Trace Parkway. At Rocky Springs a short trail leads through the old townsite, now forested with unusual remnants, such as an old safe, poking out from the undergrowth. The old trail is evident at sunken trace, where countless feet made a lasting impression. Mount Locust, a rough farmhouse become an even rougher inn, but early travellers found it more convenient than sleeping with Indians and highwaymen. The parkway ends before Natchez; take US61 for the remaining distance.

An important port before the Civil War, **Natchez** has nevertheless retained perhaps America's finest collection of antebellum homes. Spring and Autumn Pilgrimages are high points on their busy events calendar, with a choice of six half-day tours visiting some thirty fine homes. Evening entertainment in spring includes the 'Confederate Pageant', the old South in song and dance, and 'Southern Exposure', a send-up of the pilgrimage and pilgrims. 'The Mississippi Medicine Show' tops autumn entertainment.

Natchez Pilgrimage Tours on Canal and State Streets are practiced at helping visitors select from the dozen antebellum homes open throughout the year. Interesting examples include octagonal **Longwood**, massively colonnaded **Dunleith** and particularly magnificent **Stanton Hall**. Downtown Natchez boasts numerous homes and historic structures between Commerce Street and Broadway. Historic Jefferson College is open to the public in northeast Natchez, then head southeast on US61. The **Grand Village of the** **Natchez Indians** recreates Native American life, a living heritage centre as much as a museum, with several annual pow-wows.

Continue south on US61 for **Louisiana**, the 'Bayou State'. Rosedown Plan- tation and Gardens and Audubon State Commemorative Area are near quaint **St Francisville**. Rosedown is especially colourful in early spring, and the commemorative area was Oakley Plantation House while Audubon worked there on his *Birds of America*.

The Louisiana capital is **Baton Rouge**, named after the red cedar staves once marking tribal borders. The 34-storey building is the **State Capitol**, with folk exhibits in the basement and great views up top. North Boulevard has the Old State Capitol and Old Governor's Mansion, now the Louisiana Arts & Sciences Center. Riverside Museum is housed in a former railway depot alongside the Mississippi River, across from the Old Capitol. Louisiana State University Complex has a free natural science museum and Museum of Geoscience combining archaeology with geology. The University's **Rural Life Museum** is out on Burden Lane, with a working nineteenth-century plantation and examples of Louisiana rural life from prehistoric times.

Samuel Clemens Riverboat offers excursions around Baton Rouge Harbor with optional catfish cruises. Baton Rouge has a wealth of restaurants serving Creole cookin' straight from New Orleans and Cajun dishes plucked right out of Bayou Teche. One of the best for Cajun atmosphere with music nightly is Mulate's on Bluebonnet Road.

I-10 east leads directly to New Orleans. However, travellers wishing to delve deeper into Cajun Country can take a scenic long-cut via I-10 west. Breaux Bridges is the self-styled 'Crawfish Capital of the World' — their Crawfish Festival in early May is *not* to be missed. Good Cajun restaurants include another Mulate's and Crawfish Kitchen. Nearby **Lafayette** is heart of Cajun country, formed when French Acadians fled Nova Scotia down the Mississippi. The **Lafayette Museum** exhibits period furnishings, Acadian memorabilia and Mardi Gras costumes in a building owned by Jean Mouton, the city's founder. For nineteenth-century Cajun culture and customs, sample living history programs at **Acadiana Village** or **Vermilionville**. Other inter- esting towns include St Martinville, whose Evangeline was immortalized by Longfellow, and antebellum New Iberia. The delta city of **Houma** offers various boating excursions through bayou country, viewing alligators and waterfowl. Then head northeast on US90 for 'Sin City'.

New Orleans deserves its reputation as a party city. While many Southern towns celebrate Mardi Gras, New Orleans is a year-round carnival. The craziest period is the two week build up to Mardi Gras, literally 'Fat Tuesday' — the last day for excesses before Lent. Rex, King of Carnival, leads the morning parade and festivities while Comus, God of Revelry, welcomes night with a torchlight parade.

Vieux Carré, the old square, is the **French Quarter** — heart of New Orleans.

Into and around New Orleans

New Orleans International Airport has good domestic and international connections, with transport to downtown hotels provided by Airport Rhodes. The Union Passenger Terminal on Loyola Avenue serves Amtrak and local rail networks, while Greyhound operate a terminal on Loyola and Tulane, near the Civic Center. I-10 is the major east-west route, while I-55 runs north to Chicago and I-59 links to I-20 and Atlanta. The excellent bus network is supplemented by Riverfront Streetcars along the Mississippi levees between the French Quarter and the Convention Center. The St Charles Avenue Streetcars boast 1920s cars on a line founded in 1835, America's oldest continuously operating street railway. This links the business district south of Canal Street to the Garden District and Audubon Park Zoo.

Explore the French Quarter on foot, as many streets are pedestrian only, especially at night. Hotels located near the French Quarter's border with Canal Street are within walking distance of the frivolities. Most visitors will enjoy New Orleans more away from Mardi Gras — there is always plenty of excitement. Stick to frequented tourist spots, walk in groups, avoid ostentatious dress and old cemeteries — these precautions will help guests join the millions that visit New Orleans annually in safety.

Nineteenth-century townhouses add character to the area, with narrow streets shaded by overhanging balconies festooned with lacy wrought iron work. Like its people, Creole architecture is an intriguing melange of Spanish and French. Facing the levees which hold back the Mississippi, **Jackson Square** on Decatur is the starting point. Street performers and artists enliven the square by day, while nearby eateries like the Café du Monde add local touches like the Beignet, a confectioned doughnut. St Louis Cathedral overlooking the square is amongst America's oldest. An important focal point in New Orleans, the cathedral is flanked by the Cabildo, former state house for the Spanish Governor, and the Presbytère, both part of the Louisiana State Museum.

The Pontalba apartment buildings bordering the square are mostly residences, while the State Museum administers the 1850 House. Rangers from Jean Lafitte National Historic Park Visitor Center often take groups through the French Quarter, where pirate Lafitte resided. Interesting homes include Madam John's Legacy on Dumaine, and Gallier House on Royal. A stroll down Gallier Street passes picturesque homes and shops.

Up from Royal is lewd and licentious **Bourbon Street**. Boasting a year-round carnival of bars and strip joints, jazz clubs and gospel choirs, Bourbon Street awakes with nightfall. Beer and cocktails can be bought from bars or street-side kiosks, most explore the various venues with cup in hand. A queue is the trademark of **Preservation Hall** on St Peter Street, just off Bourbon, with old-time jazz played to a standing-room audience. The hall is not licensed, but drinks can be brought in. The area's accent is not entirely alcohol — Creole and Cajun cuisine is available throughout the French Quarter in some of New Orlean's finest restaurants.

Beyond Jackson Square is the riverfront, where the *Natchez* Riverboat steams up customers on its calliope. To the north, shoppers and browsers enjoy the **French and Farmer's Markets**. Beyond is the **Old US Mint**, also part of the Louisiana State Museum. In the opposite direction is Jackson Brewery complex, Riverfront Park, and acclaimed **Aquarium of the Americas** Riverfront streetcars link the attractions and continue south past the International Cruise Ship Terminal and World Trade Center to the Convention Center and **Riverwalk**, a rejuvenated warehouse district-cum-shopping and dining complex.

Also within New Orleans are **Audubon Park** and its respected **Zoological Gardens**. New Orlean's first wealthy Americans founded the **Garden District**, centred around First Avenue and Coliseum. The famed St Charles Avenue Streetcar runs about seven blocks in from the Mississippi River from Canal Street, passing both First Street and Audubon Park. **City Park** has a golf course, stadium, and the New Orleans Museum of Art. From Lake Shore Drive north of the park, Lake Pontchartrain and its famous causeway disappear in the distance.

Return east via US-90, following the Gulf of Mexico past the beaches and fishing ports of Coastal Mississippi. **Beauvoir**, shrine to Confederate President Jefferson Davies, is a few miles before the resort city of **Biloxi**. Sample delicious Biloxi shrimp and oysters, or catch a shrimping trip from City Dock to experience the Gulf first hand. Also in Biloxi are the Old Lighthouse, Science Marine Education Center, and Seafood Industry Museum. Embark on the P

American to Ship Island for **Gulf Islands National Seashore**. Day trippers can play Robinson Crusoe or visit the island's old fort.

In **Alabama**, take SR188 east through Bayou La Batre, where main street is a bayou, packed with shrimp trawlers. Dauphin Island, south on SR193, is a Gulf Coast barrier island. Dauphin is part beach resort, part Audubon bird sanctuary, part Civil/Spanish War fortification. SR193 returns north, passing fabulous **Bellingrath Gardens** and stately home en route to **Mobile**, Southern Belle of the Gulf Coast. Boasting a number of historic districts, the chamber of commerce visitor centre provides maps and information. Fort Conde, a reconstructed outpost occupied by French, Spanish, British and American contingents, also maintains a welcome centre. **Oakleigh Mansion** was a focal point for Mobile society, and when a family member married a Vanderbilt, the *latter* became eligible for the Blue Book, America's first social register. The free Museum of the City of Mobile has interesting exhibits, including masks and costumes from earlier Mardi Gras — the first American celebrations took place in Mobile. Mardi Gras is a big event on the Mobile calendar, with parades and balls held weekly until Shrove Tuesday, start of the Azalea Trail Festival and Mobile Historic Homes Tour. **Battleship Park** preserves the USS *Alabama*, the submarine USS *Drum*, World War II fighter planes and a B-52 bomber.

Follow I-65 inland to **Montgomery**, Alabama's foremost city. After the **State Capitol** see nearby **First White House of the Confederacy**. Although the Confederate capital was later moved to Richmond Virginia, Jefferson Davis was sworn in as President in Montgomery and the order to fire upon Fort Sumter, beginning hostilities, was given here. Also near the Capitol on Washington and Hull is the **Civil Rights Memorial**, sponsored by the Southern Poverty Law Center. A circular black marble table recalls martyrs of the civil rights movement, Black and White. The backdrop is inscribed with Amos 5:24 from the *Old Testament*, used in Martin Luther King Jr's speech, 'I Have A Dream'.

Also in Montgomery, the State Archives History Museum has exhibits from early Indian to recent times. **Old Alabama Town** is a fascinating collection of historical buildings, including craft centres and an audiovisual presentation in a former tavern. The Museum of Fine Arts houses an excellent collection and Saturday afternoon concerts. The State Theatre hosts the **Alabama Shakespeare Festival**, closing only for September and October. Return to Atlanta by I-85 direct or via I-65 and Birmingham.

Additional Information

State Tourism Bureaux

Alabama Tourism & Travel
532 South Perry St
Montgomery, AL 36104
☎ 800-252-2262
or 205-242-4169

*Georgia Dept of Industry &
   Trade*
PO Box 1776
Atlanta, GA 30301
☎ 404-656-3590

*Kentucky Travel Develop-
   ment*
Capital Plaza Tower
Frankfort, KT 40601
☎ 800-225-8747
or 502-564-4930

Louisiana Office of Tourism
PO Box 94291, 900
Riverside North
Baton Rouge
LA 70804-9291
☎ 800-334-8626
or 504-342-8100

Mississippi Dept. of Econ Dev
Tourism Division, Box 849
Jackson, MS 39205
☎ 800-647-2290
or 601-359-3414

*North Carolina Travel &
Tourism*
430 North Salisbury St
Raleigh, NC 27611
☎ 800-847-4862
or 919-733-4171

*South Carolina Parks &
   Tourism*
Inquiry Div, Box 71
Columbia, SC 29202
☎ 803-253-6318

Tennessee Dept of Tourism
PO Box 23170
Nashville, TN 23170
☎ 615-741-2158

Regional Information

Asheville Tourism
PO Box 1011
Asheville, NC 28802
☎ 800-257-1300
or 704-258-3916

Atlanta CVB
233 Peachtree Street NE,
Suite 2000
Atlanta, GA 30303
☎ 404-521-6688

Baton Rouge CVB
PO Drawer 4149
Baton Rouge, LA 70821
☎ 800-527-6843
or 504-342-7317

Charleston CVB
PO Box 975 (office)
85 Calhoun St (visitor centre)
Charleston, SC 29402
☎ 803-722-8338
or 800-845-7108

Jackson CVB
PO Box 1450
Jackson, MS 39215-1450
☎ 800-354-7695
or 601-960-1891

Lexington CVB
400 W Vine, Suite 363
Lexington, KT 40507
☎ 800-848-1224 or 606-
233-1221

Louisville CVB
400 S First
Louisville, KT 40202
☎ 800-626-5646
or 502-582-3732

Memphis CVB
50 N Front St., Suite 450
Memphis, TN 38103
☎ 901-576-8181

Mobile Tourism
150 S Royal St

Mobile, AL 36602
☎ 800-252-3862
or 205-434-7304

Montgomery CVB
PO Box 79
Montgomery, AL 36101
☎ 205-240-9452

Nashville COC/CVB
161 Fourth Avenue N
Nashville, TN 37203
☎ 615-242-7747
or 615-242-5606

Natchez CVB
311 Liberty Road
Natchez, MS 39120
☎ 800-647-6724
or 601-446-6345

New Orleans CVB
1520 Sugar Bowl (office)
529 St Ann St (visitor centre)
New Orleans, LA 70112
☎ 504-566-5031

Raleigh CVB
PO Box 1879, 225
Hillsborough St, Suite 400
Raleigh, NC 27602
☎ 919-834-5900

Savannah CVB
301 Martin Luther King Jr
Blvd (West Broad)
Savannah, GA 31499
☎ 912-944-0456

Vicksburg CVB
PO Box 110
Vicksburg, MS 39181
☎ 601-636-9421
or 800-221-3536

Local Events

Check locally for exact date

February/March
Mardi Gras
Mobile, AL

Mardis Gras
French Quarter
New Orleans, LA

March-April
Natchez Spring Pilgrimage
Natchez, MS

Vicksburg Spring Pilgrimage
Vicksburg, MS

Festival of Houses and
   Gardens
Charleston, SC

March/April
Spring Fiesta
Garden District & French
   Quarter
New Orleans, LA

April-May
Festival of Flowers
Biltmore Estate
Asheville, NC

April
Dogwood Festival
Atlanta, GA

French Quarter Festival
French Quarter
New Orleans, LA

Night in Old Savannah
Savannah, GA

Opryland American
   Music Festival
Grand Ole Opry & Acuff
   Theatre
Nashville, TN

May
Cajun Country Opry &
   Fais Dodo
Houma, LA

Memphis-in-May
Memphis, TN

Crawfish Festival
Breaux Bridge, LA

Kentucky Derby
Churchill Downs
Louisville, KT

May-June
Spoleto Arts Festival
Charleston, SC

Summer Lights Festival
Downtown
Nashville, TN

June
Sun Fun Festival
Myrtle Beach, SC

Country Music Fan Fair
Fairgrounds & Opryland
Nashville, TN

Blessing the Shrimp Fleet
Bayou La Batre, AL

July
Vicksburg Civil War Re-
   enactment
Vicksburg, MS

August
Kentucky State Fair &
   Music Show
Louisville, KT

Louis Armstrong Jazz
   Festival
New Orleans, LA

September
Arts Festival
Atlanta, GA

Festival Acadiens
Lafayette, LA

Memphis Musical Herit-
   age Festival
Memphis, TN

Tennessee State Fair
Nashville, TN

Georgia Music Festival
Atlanta & Statewide, GA

September-October
Mississippi State Fair
Jackson, MS

October
Cajun Country Opry &
   Fais Dodo
Houma, LA

Fall Homes and Gardens
   Tour
Charleston, SC

Natchez Fall Pilgrimage
Natchez, MS

October-November
Greater Baton Rouge
   State Fair
Baton Rouge, LA

December
Christmas at Biltmore
Asheville, NC

Places of Interest

Asheville, NC
Biltmore Estate
US 25
Asheville, NC
☎ 800-543-2961
or 704-255-1700
Open: 9am-6pm home,
9am-7pm grounds
Tours, food, gifts, winery,
parts ຆ

Blue Ridge Parkway
700 Northwestern Plaza
Asheville, NC 28801
☎ 704-259-0701
Open: Visitor centres
9am-5pm, extended
summers. Free
Scenic highway, walk,
camp, lodge, food, gifts,
parts ຆ

Atlanta, GA
Georgia State Capitol
Capitol Square
Washington Street
Atlanta, GA 30334
☎ 404-656-2350
Open: 9am-5pm Mon-Fri,
11am-3pm Sat, 1-3pm
Sun. Free
Tours weekdays, exhibits,
ຆ

Georgia's Stone Mountain
Highway 78
Atlanta, GA 30086
☎ 404-498-5600
Open: 10am-5.30pm,

extended summers
Skylift, golf, tennis, train,
homes, &

Martin Luther King Jr NHS
449 Auburn Ave (visitor
    centre)
526 Auburn Ave NE (HQ)
Atlanta, GA 30312
☎ 404-524-1956
Open: 9am-5.30pm
Tomb, birthplace, church

Six Flags Over Georgia
7561 Six Flags Road
I-20 West
Atlanta, GA 30059
☎ 404-739-3400
Open: 10am-late
Rides, food, gifts, &

World of Coca Cola
44 Martin Luther King Jr
    Drive SW
Atlanta, GA 30303
☎ 404-676-6745
Open: 10am-9.30pm
Mon-Sat, noon-6pm Sun
Gifts, memorabilia, &

Bardstown, KT
My Old Kentucky Home
PO Box 323
Bardstown, KT 40004
☎ 502-348-3502
Open: 9am-5pm, ex-
tended summers
Tour home, gifts, Stephen
Foster Musical

Baton Rouge, LA
*Capitol Complex Visitors
    Center*
Foundation for Historical
Louisiana, 900 North Blvd
Baton Rouge, LA 70802
☎ 504-342-1866
Open: 10am-4pm Tue-
Sat, 1-4pm Sun. Free
LA Heritage, crafts, State
Capitol, &

Charleston, SC
Charles Towne Landing
1500 Old Towne Rd
(SR 171)
Charleston

SC 29407-6099
☎ 803-556-4550
Open: 9am-5pm, 9am-
6pm summer
Replica town, gardens,
mini-train, gifts, &

Fort Sumter NM
17 Lockwood (mail)
Charleston, SC 29401
☎ 803-722-1691
Cruise times vary
Fort, tours, &

*Magnolia Plantation and
    Gardens*
Rt 4, SR61
Charleston, SC 29407
☎ 803-571-1266
Open: 8am-dusk
Gardens, petting zoo,
gifts, food, wildfowl area,
&

Middleton Place
Rt 4, SR61
Charleston, SC 29407
☎ 803-556-6020
Open: 9am-5pm
Home & Gardens, parts
&

Cherokee, NC
*Museum of the Cherokee
    Indian*
PO Box 770-A
Cherokee, NC 28719
☎ 704-497-3481
Open: 9am-5pm, ex-
tended summers
Tours, gifts, &

Frankfort, KT
Kentucky State Capitol
Capitol Ave
Frankfort, KT 40601
☎ 502-564-6980
Open: 9am-4.30pm Mon-
Fri, 9am-4pm Sat, 1-5pm
Sun
Free, tours, floral clock, &

Gatlinburg, TN
Great Smoky Mountains NP
C/O Superintendent
Gatlinburg, TN 37738

☎ 615-436-1200
Open: 9am-6pm mid-Mar
to Oct. Free
Mill, walk, picnic, camp,
gifts, parts &

Lexington, KT
Kentucky Horse Center
3380 Paris Pike
Lexington, KT 40511
☎ 606-293-1853
Tours 9am, 10.30am & 1pm
Thoroughbred training
(mornings)

Kentucky Horse Park
4089 Iron Works Pike
Lexington, KT 40511
☎ 606-233-4303
Open: 9am-5pm daily
Apr-Oct, Wed-Sun winter
Museums, rides, gifts,
food, shows, parts &

Mammoth Cave, KT
Mammoth Cave NP
C/O Supervisor
Mammoth Cave
KT 42259
☎ 502-758-2251 (info),
502-758-2328 (cave tours),
502-758-2225 (lodging)
Cave tour times vary
Cave tours, boat, lodge,
camp, gifts, food, hike, &

Memphis, TN
Graceland
PO Box 16508, 3734 Elvis
Presley Blvd
Memphis, TN 38186-0508
☎ 800-238-2000 or 901-
332-3322
Open: 9am-6pm, ex-
tended summers
Home & grave, trophies,
gifts

Mobile, AL
Bellingrath Gardens
12401 Bellingrath Rd
Theodore, AL 36582
☎ 205-973-2217
Open: 7am-dusk
Home, garden, gifts

Oakleigh Mansion
350 Oakleigh Place
Mobile, AL 36604
☎ 205-432-1281
Open: 10am-4pm Mon-
Sat, 2-4pm Sun
Tours, gifts

Montgomery, AL

*Alabama Shakespeare
Festival*
No 1 Shakespeare Festi-
val Dr
Montgomery, AL 36117
☎ 205-272-1640
Evenings & weekend
matinees, Wed-Sun
Open: Nov-Aug, Tues-
Sun Sept-Oct
Classical and contempo-
rary productions

Old Alabama Town
310 North Hull St
Montgomery, AL 36104
☎ 205-263-4355
Open: 8.30am-3.30pm
Mon-Sat, 1.30-3.30pm Sun
Tours, crafts & gifts

Nashville, TN

*Country Music Hall of
Fame*
4 Music Square E
Nashville, TN 37203
☎ 615-256-1639
Open: 9am-5pm, 9am-
pm summer
xhibits, Studio B tours,
ifts, &

Opryland USA
302 Opryland Drive,
oom 1503
ashville, TN 37214
615-889-6611
pen: 10am Memorial-
bor Day, closing times
ry
eme park, TNN, Grand
e Opry, Hotel, gifts,
d, &

Tennessee State Museum
505 Deaderick St
Polk Cultural Center
Nashville, TN 37423-1120
☎ 615-741-2692
Open: 10am-5pm Mon-
Sat, 1-5pm Sun
Historical exhibits &
crafts, gifts, &

Natchez, MS

Natchez Pilgrimage Tours
PO Box 347, Canal St
Natchez, MS 39121
☎ 800-647-6742
or 601-446-6631
Open: 9am-5pm, tour
times vary
Tours, call for &

New Orleans, LA

Aquarium of the Americas
PO Box 4327, 111 Iberville St
New Orleans, LA 70178
☎ 504-861-2537
Open: 9.30am-9pm
(9.30am-8pm Thu)
Aquarium, gifts, &

Jean Lafitte NHP
French Quarter Unit
916 N Peters St
New Orleans, LA 70116
☎ 504-589-2636
Open: 9am-5pm. Free
LA folklife, ranger tours,
gifts, &

Raleigh, NC

*North Carolina Museum of
History*
109 E Jones St
Raleigh, NC 27601-2807
☎ 919-733-3894
Open: 9am-5pm Tue-Sat,
1-6pm Sun
Free, tours, &

Tupelo, MS

Natchez Trace Parkway
RR 1, NT-143 (HQ)
Tupelo, MS 38801
☎ 601-842-1572
Open: Visitor centres
8am-5pm. Free
Camp, hike, picnic, gifts,
parts &

Vicksburg, MS

*Vicksburg National Mili-
tary Park*
3201 Clay St (HQ)
Vicksburg, MS 39180
☎ 601-636-0583
Open: 8am-5pm, 8am-
7pm summer
Tours, cemetery, gifts, &

Waycross, GA

Okefenokee Swamp Park
US1 south then SR177
Waycross, GA 31501
☎ 912-283-0583
Open: 9am-5.30pm, 9am-
6.30 summer
Boat, wildlife, exhibits,
picnic

Winston-Salem, NC

Historic Bethabara Park
2147 Bethabara Road
Winston-Salem, NC
27106
☎ 919-924-8191
Open: 9.30am-4.30pm
Mon-Fri, 1.30-4.30pm Sat-
Sun. Free
Visitor centre, congrega-
tion hall, tours

Old Salem
600 South Main St,
Drawer F, Salem Station
Winston-Salem, NC 27108
☎ 800-441-5305
or 919-721-7300
Open: 9.30am-4.30pm
Mon-Sat, 1.30-4.30pm
Sun
Historic homes, gifts,
food, tours

5

FLORIDA

F lorida is the 'Sunshine State', a fantasy land of magic kingdoms and space ports surrounded by a water enthusiast's heaven on earth. Most visitors are drawn by the beaches, tropical climate and fun-filled theme parks. The state's alter ego, 'real' Florida, combines America's finest state parks with the diverse Everglades ecosystem and the historic 'footprints' of Ponce De Leon, Hernando de Soto, and Sir Francis Drake.

Walt Disney World and Orlando

✳ **Walt Disney World**, southwest of Orlando, is first on most visitor's agendas. This massive complex incorporates three blockbuster theme parks, some twenty resort hotels, three par-72 championship golf courses, and lakes bursting with marinas and beaches. This kingdom within Florida also has two water parks, cool and calm **River Country** and thrill packed **Typhoon Lagoon**, where flumes hit 30mph. **Disney Village Marketplace** is a shoppers delight, perfect for last minute gifts and Disney memorabilia. For those over 21, **Pleasure Island** offers New Year's Eve nightly.

✳ The **Magic Kingdom** theme park *is* the old Disney Magic, a mixture of Cinderella Castle and Mickey Mouse. Free monorails and ferryboats transport guests from the car parks into another world. First comes Main Stree*

Florida In Brief

Orlando and Walt Disney World kick off the Florida frolics — a figure-of-eight through the sunshine state. Sample the Gulf Coast resorts before braving the Everglades for Miami and the fabulous Florida Keys. Rocket up the Gold Coast from Fort Lauderdale to Kennedy's Spaceport USA, then visit historic St Augustine, America's oldest City. Tallahassee, a real Southern belle, and the Emerald Coast are the grand finale.

Miami, Orlando, and Tampa are all gateways; start the tour where convenient. Florida is a genuine bargain, where rental cars and motels are inexpensive, saving hard-earned money for the excellent shopping, dining and theme parks. Take two to three weeks for the whole tour or simply visit the places of particular interest. The best (and busiest) time for Florida is early spring for the southern sections, slightly later for the north, although the state is a year-round holiday destination.

Into and Around Walt Disney World/Orlando

The much expanded Orlando International Airport offers virtually every amenity. The area's resorts and theme parks are spread out, but package holidays should include transfers and some motels offer free shuttles to the theme parks — check before booking. Rental cars in Florida are amongst the least expensive in America, especially by the week, but book before leaving home. Orlando Airport is on the Beeline Expressway, with the main north-south route, I-4, to its west. Universal Studies and Sea World are near their junction, with downtown Orlando north and Walt Disney World to the south.

Plan Walt Disney World ahead for extra enjoyment. Gates officially open at 9am, but arrive early. Follow signs from I-4 or US192 for desired theme park, and note the parking lot, row, and position. Write in advance if *The Disabled Guests Guide Book* would be useful. Rental wheelchairs and motorized convenience vehicles are available on a first-come basis, but bring a physically able companion to help get onto rides. Food may not be brought into theme parks, but restaurants and snack bars abound. The One Day Pass is good for *one* theme park, while Four and Five Day Passes allow visiting each park daily (get hands stamped at each exit) and use of Walt Disney World's transportation network. Tickets can be pre-purchased from the Disney Company and selected tour operators.

USA, America as it should have been. The street combines shops, eateries, and customer convenience centres. City Hall has the daily events schedule, such as the Disney Character Hit Parade. Walt Disney World Railroad steams from Main Street, circumnavigating the Kingdom with stops along the way.

The Magic Kingdom is a collection of themed areas, such as Adventureland, where Audio-Animatronics adventures include the Tiki Room and swashbuckling Pirates of the Caribbean. Frontierland has the Big Thunder Mountain Railroad and Diamond Horseshoe Jamboree, with *real* dancing girls — book early. Each themed area offers a lively mixture of rides, amusements, and stalls selling Disney memorabilia. During summer months and selected holidays Magic Kingdom hours are extended and additional events are staged, such as Main Street Electrical Parade and Fantasy in the Sky Fireworks. An evening meal at the Liberty Tree and King Stefan's may be booked during the day, after which rested and replenished guests can revisit favourite attractions before the grand finale.

The two main thrusts of Disney's **EPCOT Center** theme park are world ✳ harmony and the marvels of technology. Future World focuses on discovery and scientific achievement while World Showcase presents the architecture, art, cuisine, music, entertainment, and crafts of selected nations. Most guests start with the 180ft-high geosphere of Spaceship Earth, unmistakable symbol of EPCOT, so save that for last. Earth Station is the home base for the WorldKey Information Service — book here early for popular World Showcase restaurants.

The seven major themed areas at EPCOT's Future World include energy, health, transportation, imagination, the land, the sea, and alternative environ-

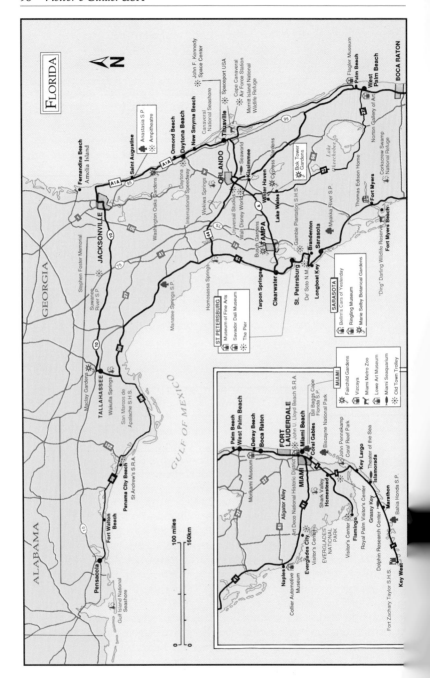

Sea World shows are fun and informative
Sailing lessons at Clearwater Beach

ments. Each section is entertaining and educational, and they are only half of EPCOT. World Showcase propels the visitor through eleven (soon to be thirteen) countries, each with 'pop-up' entertainment, cultural exhibits, and quality souvenirs. Local cuisine is an important part of the experience — where else can one have croissants for breakfast, sushi for lunch, afternoon tea, and a choice of Mexican, Chinese, or Italian for dinner? The countries surround one of Walt Disney World's many lakes, by night reflecting the colourful 'IllumiNations'.

✳   **Disney-MGM Studios Theme Park** combines motion picture and television highlights with the latest in special effects. After seeing how old favourites were made, guests see the future revealed on the backstage tour. Being working studios, more *may* be seen on weekdays. The Production Information Window highlights production activities, shooting schedules, and studio audience ticket availability. Write important times, such as the Indiana Jones Stunt Spectacular, on the Theme Park Map. Look for famous stars, at least one appears daily, and for 'pop-up' Disney characters. The Great Movie Ride is a romp through cinema history, while Disney's animation secrets are revealed in the not-to-be-missed Disney-MGM Studios Animation Tour.

🦌   Halfway between Orlando and Walt Disney World are more theme parks, including **Sea World**. Shows are spectacular and entertaining, but the Sea World programmes are also informative. Hands-on encounters with stingrays and sea urchins are positively encouraged. James Earl Jones narrates 'Shamu: New Visions', where the action takes place in the 5 million gallon habitat that Shamu calls home. Sea lions, otters and a wacky walrus also put on a good show, as do their human counterparts in the water-ski extravaganzas. New shows are presented each night, including a laser and fireworks spectacular during the peak summer season and selected holidays.

✳   **Universal Studios** is the largest film and television studio outside Hollywood, where the audience are launched into dramatic highlights from *Ghost Busters*, *Back to the Future*, *King Kong*, *ET*, and *Earthquake*. Wear comfortable shoes and be prepared to participate. In the evening the Dynamite Nights Stunt Spectacular is pure mayhem, while the world's largest **Hard Rock Café** is open to all.

As the gateway to central Florida, **Orlando** offers excellent shopping and entertainment, especially near International Drive in its southwest. **Mercado Mediterranean Village** has a wide range of shops and restaurants, plus the Orlando & Orange County Visitor Center and the Mardi Gras Dinner and Variety Show. King Henry's Feast, one of many dinner extravaganzas, is nearby, while shopping excels at **Belz Factory Outlet World** and **Florida Mall**.

Church Street Station is heart of downtown Orlando, with specialty shops plus entertainment at Rosie O'Grady's and associated showplaces, offering a complete selection of music. Orlando is a city of tall buildings, clean streets and plenty of parks, such as Lake Eola with its fountain. **Loch Haven Park** is

the cultural centre of Orlando, with numerous museums and various performances at the Civic Theater. The dogwood, azaleas and camellias of **Le** **Botanical Gardens** harken back to the genteel life of a southern farmer. For the real 'natural' Florida visit **Wekiwa Springs State Park**, a short excursion to the north. The refreshing waters of the spring can be swum year-round, while rental canoes are available to explore local waterways.

Between Walt Disney World and **Kissimmee** on US192 are a menagerie of motels, fast food, and amusements of all descriptions, including at least four dinner extravaganzas. Also in the Kissimmee area is the Flying Tigers Warbird Air Museum and Alligatorland Safari Zoo, one of Florida's innumerable alligator-themed attractions.

Southwest Florida

Tampa has been a gateway to Florida since Ponce De Leon; nowadays it is a busy tourist centre, studded with resorts and golf courses. Thought it has no beaches of its own, a fantastic coastline awaits on its doorstep. Tampa International Airport, one of America's finest, has excellent facilities, and the city provides public transportation via the HART Line with its main terminus on Marion Street.

Undisputed king of Gulf Coast attractions is **Busch Gardens, The Dark Continent**. State-of-the-art thrill rides and America's fourth largest accredited zoo are combined in this turn-of-the-century Africa themed entertainment complex. As the world's largest brewer, Busch offer samples to those over 21. Visitors should arrive early at Busch Gardens, and plan for a full day there, wearing comfortable clothes and shoes. Specially priced combination tickets add the water-bourne thrills of nearby **Adventure Island**.

Tampa's **Lowry Zoo** has a 12-acre Florida Wildlife Center, with native animals and habitats from wetlands to prairie to coral reefs. Star of the show is the endangered manatee. Surrounding the zoo is **Lowry Park**, boasting shaded picnicking plus an amusement park and safety village for children. Families also enjoy the **Museum of Science and Industry**, where their hurricane experience offers more than 'hands-on'. Probability indicates that the chance of winning big money at **Bobby's Seminole Indian Village** is higher than scooping the Florida Lottery, with an adjacent Indian trading post, culture centre and village.

Tampa Bay Performing Arts Center offers numerous shows and concerts in its Festival Hall, Playhouse, and the intimate Jaeb Theater. Tampa Theater, a 1926 movie palace resembling a Moorish courtyard, holds additional productions. The Moorish architecture and the minarets of the former Tampa Bay Hotel, now the University of Tampa, house the **Henry Plant Museum** in the south wing. Tampa offers shopping at Harbour Island near the Convention Center and at historic Ybor Square, erstwhile Cuban enclave of Tampa. **Tarpon Springs**, west of Tampa on SR580 then north on US19, offers Greek food and boat tours from its famed sponging docks. Follow US19A south, visiting Honeymoon Island's beaches en route.

The 'Sun Capital of America' is **St Petersburg's** claim to fame — 768 consecutive days of sunshine. St Petersburg and nearby Clearwater are surrounded by suburbs and resort communities, making Pinellas the most densely populated county in Florida. Clearwater Beach is ideally suited to holidaymakers who want a bustling, suburban resort atmosphere, but access to theme parks via connecting highways is slow.

The Pier is *the* St Petersburg landmark, boasting a five-storey inverted pyramid full of specialty shops, snack bars, lounges, and restaurants, plus an aquarium and roof-top observation deck. Just north is the **Museum of Fine Arts**, with exhibits to suit most tastes, while south are the **Salvador Dali Museum** and **Great Explorations**, a high-tech hands-on science museum.

Gulf of Mexico beaches line a chain of barrier islands between St Petersburg and Clearwater, with resorts geared for every conceivable water sport. **Clearwater Beach** has parking (arrive early), accessible from Tampa via US60. South along the coast is Crabby Bills, an inexpensive, homestyle answer to fast food. Before Treasure Island is a collection of designer shops known as **John's Pass Village**, resembling a shanty fishing village. After upmarket Treasure Island and St Petersburg Beach resorts comes **Fort De Soto Park**. The five keys (islands) connected by roads make a popular escape — bring a picnic lunch, towel, and plenty of suntan lotion.

The scenic Sunshine Skyway, I-275, leads south from St Petersburg — watch for playful dolphins from the causeway. Manatee County visitor centre at the I-75 and US301 junction provides useful maps and complimentary orange juice. Follow US301 west to colonnaded **Gamble Plantation State Historic Site**, an antebellum home on a former sugar plantation. South Florida Museum in Bradenton has reproduced the sixteenth-century church and home of Hernando de Soto, contrasting sharply with the living history at **De Soto National Monument**, which depicts the explorer's lifestyle in the American wilderness.

Return to civilization at cultured **Sarasota**. Once home to John and Mable Ringling of the Greatest Show on Earth fame, the **Ringling Museum Complex** incorporates Ca'd'Zan, their palatial Venetian-style residence, and one of America's largest collections of baroque art. The complex hosts the Medieval Fair in early May and regular performances at the New Asolo Theater, with others held at Van Wezel Hall. Across from Ringling Museum is **Bellm's Cars and Music of Yesterday**, with vintage cars and an outstanding collection of old music boxes. Also in Sarasota are the renowned orchids and bromeliads of **Marie Selby Botanical Gardens**.

Longboat, Lido and St Armands Keys boast some of America's finest beaches, and **St Armands** is known for fine shopping and dining around St Armands Circle. To learn more about local sealife, visit **Mote Marine Aquarium**. South of Sarasota are more beaches on Siesta and Casey Keys. Inland on SR72, the 28,875-acre **Myakka River State Park** provides airboat and tram rides for holidaymakers with excellent bird watching, canoeing and hiking for nature lovers.

No railway reached **Fort Myers** when Thomas Edison made it his winter residence in 1886, where an impressed young Henry Ford bought the house next door. Tours of the **Edison Ford Complex** include the homes, an Edison museum, and his laboratory. Beaches near Fort Myers include twin islands **Sanibel** and **Captiva**, where excellent shelling and the Ding Darling Wildlife Refuge attract excessive traffic in Spring. **Fort Myers Beach** has seven miles of sand, plus plenty of T-shirt shops, restaurants, and nightlife. Lovers Key and Carl Johnson Park offer beaches away from the crowds.

Continuing south on US41, **Naples** is an upmarket city-cum-resort right on the beach, with convenient parking and access. Visit Third Street for exclusiv shopping or Tin City for a seaside shanty atmosphere. The **Collier Automo**

Charming Sarasota offers culture and more

Northern Miami Beach has the highrise hotels

tive Museum has an outstanding collection of impeccably displayed automobiles, specializing in sports-racers including the finest Porsche collection outside the factory.

The Everglades

Separating the Gulf Coast from the Atlantic beaches is Pa-Hay-Okee, the Indian name for the 50 mile (80 kilometre) wide 'grassy waters' of the **Everglades**. Inland from Naples on SR846 is **Corkscrew Swamp Sanctuary**, the largest extant stand of virgin bald cypress. Trained Audubon Society volunteers frequent the boardwalk, pointing out the diverse wildlife.

US41 is the Tamiami Trail, which passes through the northern Everglades. Those eastbound first see **Everglades City**, located outside protected areas, where airboats, swamp buggies, and tour boats proliferate. **Shark Valley** is heart of the 'River of Grass', where park rangers narrate a tram tour past water holes teaming with fish, birds and alligators, especially during the drier winter months. Miccosukee Indians made the Everglades their home, many working at **Miccosukee Indian Village**. Located near Shark Valley, the village demonstrates crafts and alligator wrestling while their airboats 'fly' the Everglades.

Everglades Main Park Entrance is near Homestead, south on SR997 from the Tamiami Trail then SR9336. From Miama follow US1 south then SR9336. The park road runs for 38 miles (61km) to Flamingo, with an introductory movie and interpretive exhibits at the visitor centre to help park guests appreciate the Everglade's subtle beauty. Check for special activities, such as guided walks or canoe trips. At Royal Palms two nature walks highlight the diverse ecosystems — the Anhinga Trail passes waterfowl and alligators while the Gumbo Limbo wanders through a dry hardwood hammock. The park trail network includes overland hikes and canoeable waterways. For the renowned bird watching try Mrazek and especially Eco Pond in the early morning, or the mud banks off Flamingo at low tide. **Flamingo Lodge** has clean, comfortable rooms and also self-catering cabins, several being handicapped accessible. A year-round snack bar supplements the restaurant, which closes in summer when few brave the mosquitos. Boat and tram tours are popular, while the lodge rents bicycles and the marina hires small boats and canoes.

Miami

Miami Vice has over-dramatized the glamorous and criminal elements, but Miami has long been famous for its beaches, Caribbean atmosphere, and its cruise ship port, the world's busiest.

Start a tour of Miami at **Bayside Marketplace**, a modern shopping and dining complex overlooking Biscayne Bay. Street performers give a carniva' atmosphere, with sightseeing boats offering daytime and sunset cruises around the bay. Metromover, a few blocks in from the Marketplace, connects with the Metrorail and Metrobus Terminus and also the Metro-Dade Cultura

Getting around Miami

Miami International Airport is well served by domestic and international flights, including onward connections to the Caribbean, Central and South America. Larger hotels have free hotlines, the closer ones offering free transport. The Super Shuttle visits the Miami Beach, Fort Lauderdale, and Palm Beach hotels. Regional Metrorail and Metrobus networks are supplemented with Tri-Rail, which links Miami, Fort Lauderdale, and West Palm Beach.

Miami streets are based on a grid pattern split into four (unequal) quadrants by Flagler Street and Miami Avenue. Most Miami streets run east-west and avenues north-south, both are numbered sequentially. The Metromover encircles downtown Miami, while the Old Town Trolley leaves Bayside Marketplace for a fun and informative tour of Miami, Coconut Grove and Coral Gables, with on-off privileges for Miami attractions.

Center. Inside are the excellent **Historical Museum of South Florida** and unpredictable **Museum of Fine Arts**, whose exhibits are constantly changing, with reduced admission for combined tickets. The terracotta facing of the nearby **Gusman Center** hides a performing arts complex resembling an Italian courtyard.

Key Biscayne off Rickenbacker Causeway is home to the performing dolphins and killer whales of **Miami Seaquarium**. Beyond are several popular parks, including **Bill Baggs Cape Florida**, which supplements beaches and picnicking with tours of its historic lighthouse. On the mainland overlooking Biscayne Bay is **Vizcaya**, the Dade County Art Museum. Conceived as a sixteenth-century Italian Renaissance villa, Vizcaya seemed four centuries old when completed in 1916. Visitors see the mansion and grounds as industrialist James Deering left it. The **Miami Museum of Science & Space Transit Planetarium** is across the road.

For a bohemian atmosphere, visit **Coconut Grove**, which offers al fresco dining at Commodore Plaza. Trendy shoppers make for Mayfair in the Grove and CocoWalk. Nightlife is excellent, and for culture try the acclaimed **Coconut Grove Playhouse**. Early Coconut Grove is relived at **The Barnacle**, a tranquil haven in the midst of bustling Miami. Compare eccentric Coconut Grove with **Coral Gables**, a community planned down to its pink-coloured sidewalks. Tree-lined avenues offer some of Miami's safest driving and bicycling. **Venetian Pool** is undoubtedly one of America's most opulent public baths, with waterfalls and even a wheelchair elevator. The excellent **Lowe Art Museum** is at southern Coral Gables in the University of Miami.

Nearby SW 8th Street is locally known as **Calle Ocho**, heart of the Cuban district, virtually a foreign country within Miami. Sample a *medianoche* (Cuban sandwich) at one of many eateries, watch the games of Domino Park, and see El Credito hand-roll their fine cigars. Northeast of downtown Miami is the **Church of St Bernard de Clairvaux**, a magnificent twelfth-century stone chapel and cloisters brought from Segovia, Spain. **Fairchild Tropical Gardens**, the largest tropical botanical garden in America, is in southeast Miami.

Beyond is **Biscayne National Underwater Park**, with interpretive exhibits, and a glassbottom boat tour of the coral reefs and sponge beds narrated by park naturalists. The shallow waters are perfect for afternoon snorkel trips.

Miami Metrozoo in southwest Miami has cageless, near natural habitats and trained volunteers to answer questions. The white tiger enclosure, resembling a Buddhist temple, and the Wings of Asia, a $1^1/_2$-acre free-flight aviary, are firm favourites. Next door is the **Gold Coast Railroad Museum**, sporting an armoured presidential rail car. Nearby **Weeks Air Museum** restores and presents aircraft from early flight to World War II.

Miami Beach is a city and island unto itself — seaside hotels are on or near Bayshore Drive or Collins Avenue. The **Art Deco National Historic District** boasts numerous 1930s era beachfront hotels, rediscovered by young, arty types who are breathing life back into Miami Beach. Antique and art shops line Lincoln Road, which divides Miami Beach in two near the **Bass Museum of Art**. A 100ft-high mural marks the **Fountainebleau Hilton**, a premier Hilton Hotel and the jewel of Miami Beach. Non-residents are welcome, and the choice of dining and entertainment is excellent.

Port of Miami is gateway to the Caribbean, while shorter trips include a day cruise to the Bahamas and half day cruises to 'nowhere'. Foreign visitors must have a multiple-entry visa to participate.

The Florida Keys

Key comes from *cayo*, 'little island', and there are hundreds of them. The forty-two bridges of the Overseas Highway lead from big Key Largo to arty Key West. Boasting some of the best diving and snorkeling in North America, the Keys offer fantastically coloured fish amongst the exotic coral and half-buried wrecks. Glassbottom boats cater for spectators, while confirmed landlubbers can encounter living coral in the safety of the aquarium.

Little green milemarkers line US1, counting down to 0 in Key West, to which many holidaymakers race. Stop occasionally and enjoy each key in turn, starting with **Key Largo**, the largest. **John Pennekamp Coral Reef State Park** runs the gamut of water-based activities, but most guests take either a narrated glassbottom boat tour or snorkeling expedition, both visiting the coral reefs. John Pennekamp also rents sail and power boats from the marina and caters for certified divers.

The *African Queen* of movie fame is berthed outside the Holiday Inn at MM100, where the marina plays host to the *Key Largo Princess*, another glassbottom boat which visits the coral reefs. Other seafood restaurants, marinas, and resorts lay along US1, including a 200-bed Sheraton bayside resort which combines the three. Resorts and tiki bars line the self-styled 'Purple Isles', centred around **Islamorada**, where dolphins star at **Theater of the Sea** at MM84.5

Grassy Key hosts the **Dolphin Research Center**, a serious marine mammal research centre and sanctuary which, in a previous incarnation, was home to the original Flipper. Proceeds from the amusing and educational tours help maintain the sanctuary. Growing **Marathon** has airport connections to Miami and Fort Lauderdale, and yet more resorts, marinas, and tiki bars. A trio of

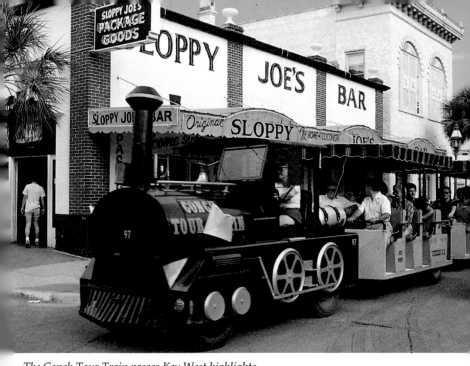

The Conch Tour Train passes Key West highlights

Florida offers some of America's finest diving

fishing tournaments run in November, while the Keys Art League and the Marathon Art Guild exhibit throughout the winter months. **Seven Mile Bridge** is surrounded by a peacock-coloured sea, followed by **Bahia Honda State Recreation Area**, blessed with one of the few natural beaches on the Keys. Water activities include diving and snorkeling; popular pastimes on the boat trip to Looe Key National Marine Sanctuary. Nearby **Looe Key Reef Resort** at MM27.5 is a divers' paradise, with a 5-star PADI training facility.

Cosmopolitan **Key West** is utterly unlike the other keys. It has been a haven for pirates, Bahamians, Cuban refugees, Greek spongers, writers and wreckers — men in the lucrative but dangerous business of salvaging ships. **Mallory Square** is heart of Old Key West, where the Conch Tour Train and Old Town Trolley embark on an excellent orientation tour, the latter providing on-off privileges. Mallory Market has a Shell Warehouse, Sponge Market, and Key West Aquarium. Nearby is **Mel Fisher's Maritime Heritage Museum**, exhibiting the history and treasures of the *Atocha*, a wreck from the Spanish plate fleet. Other attractions include **Audubon House and Gardens**, the **Wrecker's Museum**, and **Ernest Hemingway Home**, the latter a good walk down Whitehead Street or a short hop from the trolley bus stop. The **Key West Lighthouse Museum** offers excellent views atop the 86ft climb.

Fort Zachary Taylor, accessible from Southard Street, preserves the largest extant collection of Civil War cannons, which were incorporated into its walls as the fort was modernized. Providing an excellent overview of the changing arts of fortifications, the fort also exhibits numerous unearthed artifacts. **Key West City Cemetery** has guided tours on weekends at 10am and 4pm. Memorials include the humorous inscription on B. P. Roberts' tombstone — 'I told you I was sick'.

Return to Mallory Pier towards day's end for the Sunset Celebration, where streetwise performers put on a spectacle for the gathering crowd. Another Key West institution, by nightfall everyone has regrouped at their favourite bar or nightspot.

Up the Gold Coast

The scenic coastal route north from Miami Beach is SRA1A. **Fort Lauderdale** is blessed with hundreds of miles of waterways, most navigable, supporting the resort city's claim to be America's largest yacht basin. It also boasts excellent beaches with good parking, especially since the spring break college crowd went elsewhere. The nautical will find the *Jungle Queen*, a For* Lauderdale tradition, at Bahia Mar Marina and Resort. The boat cruises pas: multimillion dollar homes along the canal network; evening cruises com with meal and entertainment.

The **Performing Arts Center** offers productions direct from Broadway, and when at the **Museum of Art** look for the inhumanly realistic 'clones' by loca artist Duane Hanson. The Discovery Center hands-on science exploratoriun expanded as the **Museum of Science and Discovery**, is complete with mult storey IMAX theatre. Central Fort Lauderdale regularly holds culinary gatherings, such as the Seafood Festival and Taste of Fort Lauderdale.

Marathon shopping in Fort Lauderdale includes the upmarket Galleria o

Sunrise Boulevard, with many fine stores. Sawgrass Mills Outlet Mall west of the town offers value shopping, with hundreds of outlet stores along its mile-long corridor. The New River flows south of Las Olas Boulevard, also known for fine shopping. While there visit **Stranahan House**, which spans the transition from frontier trading post to resort city.

The **Fort Lauderdale Historical Museum** offers Saturday morning tours along the New River in conjunction with the water taxis, which also visit fine waterfront restaurants and the Performing Arts Center on their regular beat. Longer cruises leave from Port Everglades; watch the sailings from the beaches and picnic areas of the **John U. Lloyd Beach State Recreation Area**.

Continuing north along SRA1A, the first city within Palm Beach County is **Boca Raton**. Camino Real is a pleasant palm-lined introduction to Addison Mizner's city, famous for its 'wedding cake' Spanish revival architecture. Mizner influence is visible at Boca Raton Resort and Club, originally the Cloister Inn, and Royal Palms Plaza Towers. Inland at Delray Beach is **The Morikami**, which brings ancient and modern Japanese culture and gardens to interested Westerners. Their calendar is crammed with tea ceremony presentations and festivals.

Boca Raton beachside parks include South Beach, Red Reef and Spanish River Parks. Other beach access along A1A between Boca Raton and Palm Beach can be found at Atlantic Dunes Park, Gulf Stream Park, Boynton Public Beach, with parking meters along Delray Beach.

Like Fort Lauderdale, **Palm Beach** is a wealthy residential resort community, but there the resemblance ends — the conservative inhabitants of Palm Beach value tradition over innovation. Synonymous with Palm Beach is **The Breakers**, a resort combining fifteenth-century architecture with the latest spa and business facilities, including access to two world-class golf courses.

Several exclusive Palm Beach golf clubs open to non-members in summer, while the **Henry Morrison Flagler Museum** offers a unique glimpse into Palm Beach society. The lavish home includes $1.5 million worth of furnishings, and a lifestyle few could live up to today. For sheer shopping pleasure, experience **Worth Avenue**. Within walking distance of the Breakers, window shopping is free but prices are rarely displayed.

Shopping can also be exhilarating across the Intracoastal Waterway in **West Palm Beach**, including the **Gardens Mall** on PGA Boulevard and **Palm Beach Mall** on Palm Beach Lakes Boulevard. The quality and variety of restaurants in Palm Beach County is excellent, while art lovers will enjoy the eclectic tastes of the exceptional **Norton Gallery of Art**.

If returning to Orlando after the southern loop, take the Florida Turnpike direct or divert inland on US441 and then US27 north. Attractions en route include **Bok Towers**, with a carillon tower, and fun-packed **Cypress Gardens**, half accredited botanical garden and three-quarters theme park in an antebellum setting. Those taking the northern loop continue up the Florida coast, perhaps visiting Bok Towers and Cypress Gardens after returning to Orlando. Alternatively, follow the scenic SRA1A north along Florida's Atlantic coastline.

Northeast Florida and the Space Coast

No visitors to Florida should miss the immensely interesting and educational
✳ **Kennedy Space Center**. Indisputably number one in value for money (almost
everything is free), its tourist activities are coordinated by **Spaceport USA**.
Exhibits include moon rocks, life-sized rockets, and the Apollo capsule which
docked with the Russian Soyuz. Informative movies and lectures are complemented by paintings from the NASA Art Program.

Options include two bus tours and the **IMAX Film**, which presents dramatic footage shot by the astronauts on space missions. The Red Tour visits
Launch Complex 39, home to Apollo and Space Shuttle Missions — arrive the
week before a scheduled launch to photograph the shuttle on its launch pad.
The Blue Tour encompasses Cape Canaveral's history-making early space
programme, including the Mercury and Gemini series.

Both Kennedy Space Station and Cape Canaveral Air Force Station are
active, so tours may be altered to suit security and launch requirements.
Spaceport USA is closed on launch days until clearance is given by NASA. The
closest launch viewing is along US1 between Titusville and Cocoa, or near
Port Canaveral at Jetty Park. From the USA or Canada call '900-321-LIFT OFF'
for launch schedules.

NASA shares land with the Merritt Island National Wildlife Refuge and
Canaveral National Seashore, accessed via Titusville or New Smyrna Beach.
Port Canaveral is conveniently located for Orlando area and Space Coast
visitors, increasing Florida's cruise options.

Continue up the coast on scenic SRA1A for **Daytona Beach**. Modern day
speedsters watch the fast-paced action at **Daytona International Speedway**,
where Speed Weeks culminate in the fast and furious Daytona 500. Easter is
peak season at Daytona, when spring break brings hordes of college students
in an annual orgasm of fun. To the north is quieter **Ormond Beach**, where John
D. Rockefeller wintered at the **Casements** until his death in 1937. Now a
cultural and civic centre, the drawing room has been restored as Mr
Rockefeller left it.

The coastline from Ormond Beach to St Augustine is less developed, with
✳ plentiful beach access. **Washington Oaks State Gardens** were the plantation
🍀 gardens of George Washington, a relative of the first president. The dolphin
shows at nearby **Marineland** are firm family favourites. **Anastasia State Park**,
popular for beaches and bathing, also hosts the *Cross and Sword*, Florida's
Official State Play. This summer production dramatically re-enacts the 1565
founding of **St Augustine**, the first city in present day United States. Park at
the visitor centre on Castillo Drive, well within walking distance of the **Old
City**. Centuries old buildings in Old St Augustine rub shoulders with handicraft and souvenir shops; where most museums are prefixed with 'oldest'. St
Augustine's Restored Spanish Quarter offers living history displays in a
🏮 collection of historic houses, while the **Lightner Museum**, formerly the
Alcazar Hotel, depicts America's gilded age in a Spanish Revival setting.

The **Oldest House** on St Francis highlights both Spanish and British periods
of occupancy, one of several adjacent museums operated by the St Augustine
Historical Society. The impossible-to-miss **Castillo de San Marcos** is the

oldest masonry fort in continental USA, built after Sir Francis Drake pillaged
St Augustine. The views from its ramparts include Old St Augustine and the
harbour.

Amelia Island, north of Jacksonville along coast-hugging SRA1A, has also
witnessed considerable history. Eight flags have flown over the 11 by 2 mile
island, elucidated by **Amelia Island Museum of History**. **Fernandina Historic District** has late Victorian gingerbread mansions and a colourful shopping district. At **Fort Clinch State Park** rangers in Union army uniforms relive 1864, and the park also offers excellent beaches with modern facilities.

Tallahassee and the Emerald Coast

For a taste of the South, head west on I-10 for **Tallahassee**, the Florida capital.
This charming city is shaded by a canopy of live oaks, and is especially pretty
when dogwood trees bloom in spring. At the **Capitol Complex**, the old
Capitol has been restored to its 1902 grandeur while the new Capitol offers
free tours and views from the 22nd storey observatory. The **Museum of
Florida History** in the R. A. Gray building summarizes Florida's hectic natural
and human history. The interesting **San Luis Archaeological Site** dates to
Florida's Spanish Mission Period, but also has artifacts from the earlier de Soto
encampment.

State parks in and around Tallahassee include the **Alfred Maclay State
Gardens**, with over 160 exotic species of plants and shrubs. **Wakulla Springs
State Park**, just off US61, has glassbottom boats and canoes for exploring the
crystal-clear waterways. During the sixteenth-century the Navarez and de
Soto expeditions reached **San Marcos de Apalache**, now a state historic site.
The remnants of the Spanish fort, modified during the Seminole and Civil
Wars, are interpreted in the museum. Between Tallahassee and Jacksonville
is the Suwannee River, made famous in song by Stephen Foster. The
Suwannee River State Park is a nature lovers' paradise, while the nearby
Stephen Foster Culture Center honours the composer by preserving the
crafts, music, and times of early Florida.

Unless time is short, visit Florida's **Emerald Coast** — a hundred miles of
pure, icing-sugar sand surrounded by a tropi-coloured sea. **Panama City
Beach** immodestly claims the world's best white-sand beach, supplemented
by Miracle Strip Amusement Park. Adjacent St Andrews State Recreation
Area has beach activities in a natural setting. **Fort Walton Beach** is heart of the
Emerald Coast, with more sugar sand all the way to **Gulf Islands National
Seashore** by **Pensacola**. Historic Pensacola Village has a large collection of
museums, homes, and memorabilia around Seville Square, plus its fine
beaches.

Several Gulf Coast treasures are along US19 south of Tallahassee. **Cedar
Key** is a quaint New England style fishing village blessed with the sunshine
and sub-tropical climate of Florida. On winter mornings at nearby **Manatee
Springs State Park**, manatees congregate at the confluence with the
Suwannee River. Visitors can rent a canoe to explore the Suwannee, a lazy
paddle under tree-lined banks festooned with Spanish moss. The manatees at
Homosassa Springs Wildlife Park have been isolated for protection and
studying, and can be seen year-round.

Additional Information

State Tourism Bureaux

Florida Department of
*   Commerce*
Division of Tourism
Collins Building
Tallahassee
FL 32399-2000
☎ 904-488-1810

Florida Division of Tourism
18-24 Westbourne Grove,
First Floor
London W2 5RH
England
☎ 071-727-1661

Regional Information

Florida Keys & Key West CVB
PO Box 1147
Key West FL 33041-1147
☎ 305-296-3811
or 800-FLA-KEYS

Greater Fort Lauderdale CVB
500 East Broward Boul-
evard, Suite 104
Fort Lauderdale FL 33394
☎ 305-765-4466
or 800-356-1662

Greater Miami CVB
701 Brickell Avenue,
Suite 2700
Miami FL 33131
☎ 305-539-3000

Orlando/Orange County CVB
7208 Sand Lake Road
Orlando FL 32819
☎ 407-363-5800

Palm Beach County CVB
1555 Palm Beach Lakes
Blvd, Suite 204
West Palm Beach FL 33401
☎ 407-471-3995

Pinellas County Tourism
4625 East Bay Drive
Suite 109

Clearwater FL 34624
☎ 813-530-6452

Sarasota CVB
655 North Tamiami Trail
Sarasota FL 34236
813-957-1877

Tampa/Hillsborough CVB
111 Madison St, Suite 1010
Tampa FL 33602
☎ 813-223-1111
or 800-826-8358

Local Events

Check locally for exact dates

January
Orange Bowl Football
    Classic
Orange Bowl, Miami

January-February
Gasparilla Festival
Tampa

January-April
Key West's Old Island
    Days
Key West

February
Miami Film Festival
Miami Beach

Florida State Fair
State Fairgrounds
Tampa

Speed Weeks
Daytona Speedway
Daytona

Kissimmee Livestock
Show & Rodeo
Rodeo Grounds
Kissimmee

February-Easter
Black Hills Passion Play
Lake Wales

March
Carnival Miami
Orange Bowl & Calle Ocho
Miami

Medieval Fair
Sarasota

Springtime Tallahassee
Tallahassee

March/April
Easter Festival & Passion
    Play
St Augustine

April
Seafood Festival
Fort Lauderdale

Summer months
Cross and Sword
St Augustine

December
Grand Illumination
St Augustine

Winterfest & Boat Parade
Fort Lauderdale

Places of Interest

Bradenton
De Soto NM
75th St NW
Bradenton FL 34209-0097
☎ 813-792-0458
Open: 8am-5.30pm, Free
Gifts, museum, ♿

Daytona
Daytona International
    Speedway
1801 Volusia Ave,
Drawer S
Daytona Beach FL 32115
☎ 904-253-6711
Open: 9am-5pm Mon-Fri
tours

Delray Beach
*Morikami Museum of
    Japanese Culture*
4000 Morikami Park Rd
Delray Beach FL 33445
☎ 407-495-0233
Open: Tues-Sun 10am-
5pm, except holidays
Donations
Gardens, museum, gifts

Everglades
Everglades NP
PO Box 279
Homestead FL 33030
☎ 305-247-6211
305-221-8455 (Shark Valley)
Main gate open 24hrs
Gifts, walks, tours, ⅋

Flamingo Lodge
Box 428
(SR9336 from Homestead)
Flamingo FL 33030
☎ 305-253-2241 or
813-695-3101
Reduced facilities May-Oct
Cabins, rooms, food, pool,
gifts, boats, tours, ⅋

Fort Lauderdale
*Jungle Queen Sightseeing
    Cruise*
2455 E. Sunrise Blvd
Fort Lauderdale FL 33304
☎ 305-566-5533
Times vary
Cruises, evening meal &
show

Fort Myers
Edison-Ford Winter Homes
2350 McGregor Blvd
Fort Myers FL 33901
☎ 813-334-7419
Open: 9am-4pm Mon-Sat,
12.30-4pm Sun
Homes & gardens,
museum, gifts, ⅋

Kennedy Space Center
*Spaceport USA
(Kennedy Space Center)*
Visitors Center-TWS
Kennedy Space Center
FL 32899

☎ 407-452-2121
Open: 9am-sunset. Free
except IMAX & bus tours
Exhibits, food, gifts, ⅋

Key Largo
*John Pennekamp Coral Reef
    State Park*
Post Office Box 487
(MM102.5)
Key Largo FL 33037
☎ 305-451-1202
Open: 8am-Sunset
Swim, snorkel, scuba,
picnic, camp, parts ⅋

Key West
*Hemingway Home and
    Museum*
907 Whitehead St
Key West FL 33040
☎ 305-294-1575
Open: 9am-5pm
Guided tours, six-toed cats

Old Town Trolley Tours
PO Box 1237
Key West FL 33041
☎ 305-296-6688
Open: 8.55am-4.30pm
On/off privileges

Lake Wales
Bok Tower Gardens
PO Drawer 3810 (off US27)
Lake Wales FL 33853
☎ 813-676-1408
Open: 8am-5pm, selected
evenings
Carillon, gardens, food,
picnic, gifts

Miami
*Biscayne National Under-
    water Park*
North Canal Road
Homestead FL 33030
☎ 305-247-2400
Open: 8am-6pm, call for
tours. Free except boat
tours
Canoe, swim, snorkel, ⅋

Lowe Art Museum
1301 Stanford Dr
Coral Gables

FL 33124-6310
☎ 305-284-3536
Open: 10am-5pm Tue-
Sat, noon-5pm Sun
Kress collection, gifts, ⅋

Miami Seaquarium
4400 Rickenbacker
    Causeway
Miami FL 33149
☎ 305-361-5705
Open: 9.30am-5pm,
grounds 9.30am-6.30pm
Gifts, food, ⅋

Miami Metrozoo
12400 SW 152nd St
Miami FL 33177
305-251-0400
9.30am-5.30pm, last entry
4pm
Gifts, food, tours, ⅋

Old Town Trolley
From Bayside Marketplace
Miami FL 33101
☎ 305-374-8687
Open: 9am-4.30pm
Off-on privileges

SeaEscape
1080 Port Blvd
Miami FL 33132
☎ 305-379-0000
Departures vary
Cruise, meals, shows,
casino, ⅋

*Vizcaya Museum and
    Gardens*
3251 S Miami Ave
Miami FL 33129
☎ 305-579-2813
Open: 9.30-4.30pm,
except Christmas
Tours, gifts, parts ⅋

Orlando
Church Street Station
129 West Church St
Orlando FL 32801
☎ 407-442-2434
Open: 11am-2am daily
Evening cover charge
Entertainment, bars,
food, shopping, ⅋

*Mercado Mediterranean
    Village*
8445 International Drive
Orlando FL 32819
☎ 407-345-9337
Open: 10am-10pm. Free
Shopping, info, food,
entertainment, &

Sea World of Florida
7007 Sea World Drive
Orlando FL 32821
☎ 305-351-3600
Open: 9am daily, closing
varies
Shows & exhibits, food,
gifts, tours, &

Universal Studios Florida
1000 Universal Studios
    Plaza
Orlando FL 32819-7610
☎ 407-363-8000
Open: 9am, closing varies
Studios, rides, food, gifts,
Hard Rock Café, &

Walt Disney World Resort
PO Box 10,040
(off I-4 south of Orlando)
Lake Buena Vista FL
32830-0040
☎ 407-824-4321
Open: 9am, closing varies
Theme parks, resorts,
food, shopping, &

Palm Beach
*Henry M. Flagler Museum
    (Whitehall)*
Cocoanut Row, Box 969
Palm Beach FL 33480
☎ 407-655-2833
Open: 10am-5pm Tue-
Sat, noon-5pm Sun
Home, rail car, tours

Norton Gallery of Art
1451 S Olive Ave
West Palm Beach FL 33401
☎ 407-832-5194
Open: 10am-5pm Tue-
Sat, 1-5pm Sun
Tours, gifts, &

St Augustine
Castillo de San Marcos NM
One Castillo Drive East
St Augustine FL 32084
☎ 904-829-6506
Open: 9am-5.15pm ,9am-
6pm in summer
Exhibits, gifts, part &

Lightner Museum
75 King St
St Augustine FL 32084
☎ 904-824-2874
Open: 9am-5pm daily
except Xmas
Tours, antiques mall in rear

Restored Spanish Quarter
29 St George St
St Augustine FL 32084
☎ 904-825-6830
Open: 9am-5pm except
Christmas
Gifts, tours, living history

St Petersburg
Salvador Dali Museum
1000 Third St South
St Petersburg FL 33701
☎ 813-823-3767
Open: 10am-5pm Tue-
Sat, noon-5pm Sun
Tours, gifts, &

Sarasota
Myakka River State Park
13207 State Rd 72
Sarasota FL 34241-9542

☎ 813-924-1027
Open: 8am-sunset
Airboat, tram, hike,
canoe, snacks, camp, &

Ringling Museum Complex
PO Box 1838
(North on US 41)
Sarasota FL 33578
☎ 813-355-5101
Open: 10am-6pm, 10am-
10pm Thur
Art museum, home, food,
gifts, &

Tallahassee
Capitol Complex
The Capitol
Tallahassee FL 32301
☎ 904-487-1902
Open: 9am-4pm, tours
hourly except 12 noon.
Free
Tours, art, info, &

Tampa
*Busch Gardens The Dark
    Continent*
3000 Busch Blvd
Tampa FL 33674
☎ 813-971-8282
Open: 9.30am-6pm,
extended summer &
holidays
Zoo, rides, food, gifts,
brewery, &

Winter Haven
Cypress Gardens
PO Box 1 (East of US27)
Cypress Gardens FL 33884
☎ 813-324-2111
or 800-237-4826
Open: 9am-6pm with
extensions
Ski show, gardens, food,
boats, &

6
THE GREAT LAKES REGION

Representing the vast heartland of America, the Great Lakes states lead in agriculture and industry. Metropolises include super-slick Chicago, the Michigan motor cities, inland Indianapolis, and the 'Twin Cities' of Minnesota — Minneapolis and St Paul.

Chicago

In summer the 'Windy City' tends more towards balmy. On sunny days the waters of Lake Michigan take on a tropical hue, and Chicago becomes an American metropolis in a Mediterranean setting. Behind beaches and parks tower the skyscrapers, rightly so since Chicago invented them. The city boasts both the oldest and world's tallest.

Chicago rebuilt itself after the Great Fire of 1871, allegedly started by Mrs O'Leary's cow, but a few structures survived. The **Old Water Tower** on North ✳ Michigan and Chicago Avenues is one such landmark, with Here's Chicago Visitor Center in the old pumping station opposite offering information and an introductory film. This section of Michigan Avenue north of Chicago River is the Magnificent Mile, a three-quarter mile stretch of prestigious stores and shopping complexes. Among the latter are 900 North Michigan Avenue, offering six storeys of speciality shops, Water Tower Place and innovative Chicago Place's eight-storey centre.

The **John Hancock Center** has a 94th-floor observatory plus restaurants and lounges on the 95th and 96th, less than 40 seconds from the ground via their express elevators. The Terra Museum of American Art is south on 🏠 Michigan and Erie while the Museum of Contemporary Art is east on Ontario. West of Michigan Avenue, the Near North, Gold Coast, and Old Town areas boast chic boutiques, ethnic dining, and some hot nightspots.

> ### The Great Lakes Region in Brief
> Chicago kicks off this 'tale of twenty cities', the capitals and cornerstones of the Great Lakes region. For extra spice, add gambling cities Fargo and Grand Forks, North Dakota. Excellent air connections make time and distance irrelevant: select desirable destinations then acquire a discount book of air tickets. The Great Lakes states and cities offer four full seasons, winter being least desirable for travelling.

Into and around Chicago

Bustling O'Hare International Airport is gateway to Chicago and the Great Lakes states. Continental Airport Express operates frequent buses to downtown hotels and train stations, while CTA (Chicago Transit Authority) rapid transit goes downtown from beneath O'Hare Terminal 4. The 'El', CTA's elevated light rail, encircles central Chicago, affectionately dubbed the Loop. Evanston line goes clockwise, Ravenswood anticlockwise, the comprehensive CTA system map is helpful if venturing further on the bus, subway, and rail network. When locating a specific address, street numbers begin at State and Madison, divided into north and south by Madison, east and west at State Street.

Chicago is best seen on foot, with public transportation or taxi between areas of interest. Parking is problematic even on weekends, Chicago being a lived-in city, so a car is an encumbrance. Downtown garages are supplemented with parking lots at Navy Pier and Grant Park. Lake Shore Drive, US41, follows Lake Michigan through Chicago, offering a quick route to Lincoln Park north of the city and Jackson Park south, with Grant Park between. I-94 is the main north-south route, with I-290 east leading to the Loop.

✳ South of Chicago River is downtown, its loop being a major city landmark. Another is the **Sears Tower**, with a visitor centre offering the multi-media 'Chicago Experience' and shops and restaurants supplementing the observatory in the world's tallest building. The Chicago Architecture Foundation brings the city's wealth of styles and influences alive through its ArchiTours, highlighting places of note on bus and boat excursions. Their ArchiCenter on South Dearborn and Glessner House on South Prairie Avenue stock books, gifts, and educational toys on Chicago structures, Prairie Avenue Historical District and Victorian Chicago. Downtown museums include the Museum of Broadcast Communications on South Wells and the Museum of Contemporary Photography on South Michigan.

Orchestra Hall, Civic Opera House, Auditorium Theater, and several university venues present performing arts, including the Chicago Symphony, Ballet Chicago, Lyric and Chamber Opera Chicago, and Lake Forest Symphony. Arié Crown Theater stages ballet, concerts and theatre productions, while Mayfair Theatre presents the long running *Shear Madness*, a comedy where the detective audience chooses the murderer. The *Quick City Guide* lists major productions and events. For an open-air cultural experience, Lincoln Park Pavilion holds 'Theatre on the Lake', while Grant Park presents free summer concerts in the Band Shell.

Chicago abuts Lake Michigan: the skyscrapers are a backdrop to the city's fine parks and soft sandy beaches. **Navy Pier** juts into the lake, offering parking, food, a US Navy ship tour and excursion boats along south dock, plus various festivals and events. **Grant Park** is across Michigan Avenue from downtown, home to the respected **Art Institute of Chicago**. South within the park are the Buckingham Memorial Fountain then the notable **Field Museum of Natural History**, **Adler Planetarium**, and **John G. Shedd Aquarium**

Burnham Park's **Soldier Field** hosts the Chicago Bears football, while Cubs and White Sox baseball are respectively played in Wrigley Field and Comiskey Park.

Other lake-hugging parks include Jackson to the south and Lincoln north. Jackson Park offers an 18-hole golf course and other sports facilities, plus the world-class **Museum of Science and Industry**. Boasting some of Chicago's finest beaches, **Lincoln Park** also contains the Conservatory complex and Lincoln Park Zoo. The Chicago Historical Society sits within the park on Clark and North, while the Chicago Academy of Sciences is north. Abraham Lincoln practised law in Illinois before becoming president, and Saint-Gaudens' statues include the standing Lincoln in the park named after him and a sitting version in Grant Park.

Cosmopolitan Chicago is a melee of ethnic cultures, which includes the largest Polish population outside Warsaw concentrated along Milwaukee Avenue northwest of the Loop. Their heritage and contributions are recalled at the Polish Museum of America. Greek Town surrounds Halsted Street while Lincoln and Lawrence Avenues house the German enclave. Another cultural influence is represented at Balzekas Museum of Lithuanian Culture on South Pulaski, while the Morton Weiss Museum of Judaica and the Spertus Museum of Judaica respectively exhibit Iranian Jewish artifacts and Jewish life.

To the west, former **Oak Park** residents include Frank Lloyd Wright and Ernest Hemingway, with tours of the former's home and the surrounding Prairie School of Architecture National Historic District, encompassing 120 buildings in that style. Oak Park Visitor Center on Forest Avenue offers maps and information.

Southwest of Oak Park, Brookfield is home to the renowned **Chicago Zoological Park** (Brookfield Zoo). Further west, Wheaton has several places of interest. The Billy Graham Center displays and underlines the growth of evangelism in America, while others include Cosley Animal Farm, Du Page County Museum, and Cantigny Estate.

South is the University of Chicago, with free tours on weekdays at 10am. Their **Oriental Institute** focuses on the Near East, while the David and Alfred Smart Museum of Art presents an eclectic collection. Robie House is quintessential Frank Lloyd Wright, while the Gothic Rockefeller Memorial Chapel houses a carillon in its tower.

Alternative Great Lakes Region Tour

The main tour highlights the Great Lakes cities, but outdoor enthusiasts may prefer to encircle the lakes, visiting remote picturesque areas in the northern United States and southern Canada. Lakes Huron, Michigan, and Superior offer the best touring, whether taken singly or combined into a 'Great Lakes Grand Pilgrimage'. If enjoying the great outdoors, consider hiring a small motorhome. The cities need not be neglected — select from Chicago, Milwaukee, Duluth, Thunder Bay, Toronto and Detroit. Foreign travellers will require a multiple-entry US visa if visiting Canada.

Wisconsin

Milwaukee comes from the Indian *Millecki*, 'gathering place by waters'. Their Lake Michigan trading site at Milwaukee River's mouth later became home to Italians, Polish, Irish, Scandinavians and German immigrants, especially the latter, whose taste for beer made Milwaukee a brewing stronghold. **Pabst Brewery** and the **Miller Brewing Company** give tours, while the traditional *biergarten* is experiencing a revival.

A powerful group of refugees from Germany in 1848 brought a thirst for culture, today a hallmark of Milwaukee society. The **Performing Arts Center** on Water Street stages the Milwaukee Symphony Orchestra and Milwaukee Ballet, while Florentine Opera are among performers at the Victorian Pabst Theater. Skylight Opera Theatre's repertoire varies from American musical theatre to fine opera. The acclaimed Milwaukee Repertory Theater on East

Chicago sky-scrapers overlook the beach

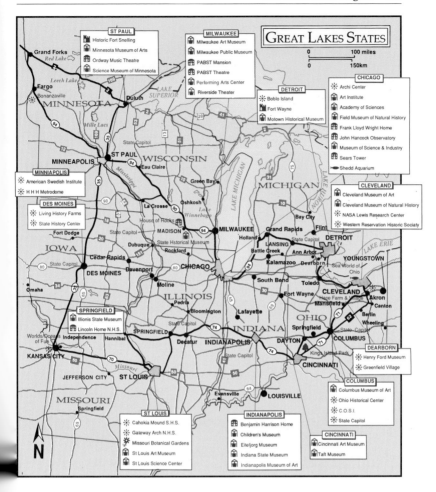

GREAT LAKES STATES

Wells offers parking, dining, and varied productions under one roof. Next Act Theatre and Theatre Tesseract offer entertaining, thought provoking off-Broadway works, while the **Riverside Theater** presents touring shows including Broadway.

Milwaukee boasts numerous fine parks, including several alongside Lake Michigan. The excellent **Milwaukee Art Museum** is housed in the War Memorial Building on Veterans Park, while harbour cruises depart from nearby Municipal Pier. Lakeside beaches are just north in McKinley and Lake Parks, and below at South Shore and Bay View Parks. Inland parks include Charles Whitnall Park southwest of downtown, encompassing the **Boerner Botanical Gardens and Arboretum**, and the **Todd Wehr Nature Center**. Green strips of park also follow the major rivers which meet at Milwaukee, making pleasant drives. Near the junction of US45 and I-94, **Milwaukee County Zoo** provides a near natural environment for their comprehensive assemblage of wildlife. Bird watchers and nature lovers are especially de-

Into and Around Milwaukee

General Mitchell International Airport is some 6 miles south of Milwaukee, with taxi and limousine services supplemented by free shuttles to major hotels. Milwaukee County Transit produces a brochure highlighting places of interest and relevant bus routes. Their Route 80 service links Mitchell Airport to central Milwaukee, an inexpensive option for those not encumbered with heavy luggage.

I-94 runs south to Chicago and west to Madison, the state capitol, while I-43 continues north to Green Bay, running parallel to Lake Michigan's western shore. Milwaukee River divides the city into east and west sections, with north-south running streets west of the river being numbered, the remainder being named. Greyhound operates from 606 North 7th Street, Amtrak from 433 West St Paul Avenue.

lighted at **Schlitz Audubon Center**, with an interpretive centre, observatory tower, and over 5 miles of walks.

A rich collection of structures includes the Flemish Renaissance Milwaukee City Hall, open weekdays, and the Tudor **Charles Allis Art Museum**, exhibiting Oriental, Greek, Roman, European and American works. Italian Renaissance Villa Terrace houses eighteenth-century Americana, while the ornate 37-room **Pabst Mansion** was built for brewing baron Captain Frederick Pabst in Flemish Renaissance style. **St Joan of Arc Chapel** on Marquette University campus, itself over 500 years old, contains the alleged stone which Joan of Arc prayed before. The University of Wisconsin has its own Museum of Art and American Geographical Society Collection. For natural history, visit western downtown's excellent **Milwaukee Public Museum**.

Greater Milwaukee Visitors Bureau on Kilbourn provides maps of the city and its interesting 'Skywalk' system, which even arches across Milwaukee River. Affording a 'traffic-less' shopping environment, Skywalk links **The Grand Avenue** shopping and dining complex west to the Auditorium Arena and MECCA (Milwaukee Exposition and Convention Center and Arena) and east to Riverside Theatre. **Old World Third Street** offers shopping, dining and entertainment in an 'olde worlde' atmosphere, along with the Milwaukee County Historical Center, which traces the city's past.

Madison is the state capital of Wisconsin, situated on a narrow strip of land amid Lakes Mendota, Monona, Waubesa and Wingra. Found due west of Milwaukee on I-94, the city boasts an impressive golden-domed **State Capitol** and informative Wisconsin Historical Museum. The University of Wisconsin hosts the **Elvehjem Museum of Art**, Geology Museum, and the University Arboretum. The university and US Department of Agriculture operate the **US Forest Products Laboratory**, which searches for increasingly efficient uses of renewable forest products. West on US14 at Spring Green is Taliesin, the former home of Frank Lloyd Wright, and **The House on the Rock**. Centerpiece of the latter's monument to tourism is Alex Jordan's eccentric home atop a chimney rock, surrounded by amusements and collections of memorabilia.

Drivers may follow I-94 west, perhaps visiting **Wisconsin Dells**, where the

Wisconsin River has carved a snake-like channel through the picturesque countryside. I-94 continues to Minneapolis, alternatively take I-90 west to St Cross, then follow the scenic Mississippi River north.

Minnesota

Dubbed the 'Land of 10,000 Lakes', Minnesota embraces over 4,000 square miles of water-borne recreation. Visitors to the 'Twin Cities' of Minneapolis and St Paul have ample opportunity to explore scenic waterways, including the mighty Mississippi River and petite Minnehaha, immortalized by Longfellow.

The impressive Minnesota **State Capitol** affords excellent views of the **St Paul** skyline. Also visible southwest is the domed **Cathedral of St Paul**, modelled after St Peter's in Rome. Downtown is a pleasant blend of modern and Victorian architecture, with decorative splashes of art deco, such as **Minnesota Museum of Arts**. The Romanesque Rival Landmark Center houses the art museum's travelling exhibits and Schubert Club's Musical Instrument Museum. Historic buildings include the Governor's Residence and James Hill House, both on Summit Avenue, and Ramsey House on Exchange.

The centerpiece for culture is the **Ordway Music Theater** on Washington Street, offering a variety of productions, while Film in the Cities is amongst the country's top media arts centres. The Museum of Art hosts performances in its Park Square Theater. The informative and educational **Science Museum of Minnesota**, one of the Great Lakes area's finest, combines natural history and science technology, plus an Omnidome Theater. The little ones also love the Children's Museum, which recreates a doctor's office, grocery store and other favourites.

Skywalks make St Paul a four-seasons city, connecting the St Paul Center to Galtier and Carriage Hill Shopping Plazas. **St Paul Center**, largest of downtown shopping complexes, provides a visitor information kiosk. Bandana Square on East Bandana Boulevard incorporates speciality shops and dining in a former railroad building.

Downtown's Town Square Park offers rides on an antique carousel (except Mondays), while Como Park northwest of the Capitol houses a golf course,

Into and Around Minneapolis-St Paul

The Twin Cities share Minneapolis-St Paul International Airport, 10 miles south of Minneapolis and 8 miles southwest of St Paul, with Holden Field (St Paul Downtown Airport) an alternative. Airport Express supplements taxis and limousines to Twin City hotels. Metropolitan Transit Commission services provide bus links between and around the cities. Situated on a main east-west line between Chicago and Portland-Seattle, Amtrak runs from St Paul while both cities have Greyhound terminals. I-94 links the two downtown areas and provides the main east-west route, while north-south I-35 splits into east and west sections, respectively passing through St Paul and Minneapolis before rejoining.

*Make time for
Milwaukee culture*

*The sculpture gard[e]
is a Minnesota
landmark*

lake, a domed conservatory, and free Como Zoo. The burial and ceremonial heaps of Indian Mounds Park are east of downtown. River excursions launch from Padelford Landing, found across the Mississippi from St Paul.

SR5 (7th Street) west leads to **Historic Fort Snelling**, a limestone fortification built to defend America's interests in the northwest. Many restored buildings are open, some providing living history demonstrations. The 1835 **Sibley House** at nearby Mendota (south on SR55 then east on SR13) was built by fur trader and territorial governor Henry Sibley. SR55 leads north to Minneapolis past **Minnehaha Park**, containing the falls named in Longfellow's *Hiawatha*.

Minneapolis is St Paul's thriving sister city, with buildings that bit taller and a slightly quicker pace. Those following SR55 north from the airport or Fort Snelling pass a few blocks west of **Hubert H. Humphrey Metrodome**, where Minnesota Twins baseball and Vikings football games are held. Timberwolves basketball now have their own complex, while the North Stars play hockey in Bloomington.

The Skywalk has been a Minneapolis landmark for 30 years, with shopping concentrated along **Nicollet Mall**. Across the Mississippi are the St Anthony Main and Riverplace shopping and dining complexes and Padelford Packet's river excursions. The University of Minnesota also lies east of the river, with tours available weekdays. The university encompasses the Goldstein Gallery, Bell Museum of Natural History, and an art museum. Other places of interest within Minneapolis include the **American Swedish Institute** on Park Avenue and the Hennepin County Historical Society Museum on South 3rd Avenue. The Minneapolis Library incorporates a planetarium.

Performing arts offerings are commendable, with **Orchestra Hall** hosting Minnesota Orchestra. The respected **Guthrie Theater**, Hennepin Center and Historic State Theatre are supplemented by a collection of innovative theatrical groups. The **Minnesota Society of Fine Arts Park** south on 3rd Avenue accommodates the Children's Theater Company and the excellent Minneapolis Institute of Arts, representing the visual arts in a variety of mediums. Southwest of downtown is the fine **Walker Art Center**, focusing on contemporary art, and the adjacent Minneapolis Sculpture Garden, whose fascinating landmark is a gigantic cherry on a spoon.

Just north of the Walker Art Center, Kenwood Parkway leads to the idyllic Lake of the Isles, especially popular with joggers, cyclists and Sunday drivers. South are Lakes Calhoun and Harriet, beyond which Minnehaha Parkway returns east past Hiawatha Golf Course and Lake Nokomis, which is encircled by another pleasant drive. Of the others, Lake Minnetonka is the largest nearby body of water, found west between US12 and SR7, while Mille Lacs Lake affords an enjoyable day-trip north.

North Dakota

For an interesting diversion, visit the gambling cities of Fargo and Grand Forks. By road, Fargo is under 5 hours away from Minneapolis via I-94, with Amtrak, Greyhound and several air carriers offering alternatives. Drivers could visit Fargo and Grand Forks, seeing Duluth on Lake Superior's westernmost shores before returning south to the Twin Cities.

Places of interest en route include the Kensington-Runestone Museum in Alexandria, Minnesota, with Viking implements and a stone they possibly left. Fargo in North Dakota offers **Bonanzaville**, a reconstructed pioneer village, and the Roger Maris Baseball Museum. Grand Forks riverboat cruises supplement gambling options, while the Myra Museum at Campbell House recalls the pioneering woman's life. Returning through Minnesota, visit the Forest History Center in Grand Rapids. Duluth boasts **The Depot**, an early railway depot and history centre, and picturesque drives along Lake Superior. I-35 south returns to Minneapolis and beyond to Des Moines.

Iowa

Its eastern border delineated by the Mississippi River and western by the Missouri, Iowa is in the heart of America's Midwestern farm belt. With over 90 percent of land given over to agriculture, Iowa comes second only to California for producing farm equipment and processing foodstuffs.

Situated at the confluence of Des Moines and Raccoon Rivers, centrally located **Des Moines** celebrates its farming heritage each August at the Iowa State Fair. The original formula of prize-winning livestock, traditional crafts and thrill rides remains, much expanded with entertainment by show business celebrities, famous bands, car racing, tractor pulling, and various cultural events.

Downtown Des Moines holds the Farmers Market on summer Saturday mornings, but this 'new style American city' is also a major insurance centre. The Civic Center presents symphony music and ballet, supplemented by performances in adjacent Nollen Plaza, the convention centre and Veterans Memorial Auditorium. Des Moines' Skywalk system offers more than three miles of interconnected shopping, dining and business centres — in mid-July the glass spans make viewing platforms for the Des Moines Grand Prix and associated races.

West of Des Moines River is the main downtown area, the Polk County Heritage Gallery and Victorian Hoyt Sherman Place, a Victorian mansion and art gallery. West on Grand Avenue leads to Greenwood Park, encompassing **Des Moines Art Center** and **Des Moines Center of Science and Industry**. Outlying attractions include the **Living History Farms**, portraying past, present and future agriculture off I-35 exit 125.

East of the river is the gold-domed **State Capitol** and nearby **State Historical Museum**. East River Drive leads north to the **Des Moines Botanical Center**, distinguished by its geodesic-domed greenhouse. The SS *Epicure* embarks nearby on lunch, dinner and cocktail cruises along the Des Moines River. South on I-35 leads to Kansas City.

Missouri

Pioneers were lured across the plains by silver tongued orators and over optimistic newspapers. When the grand promises proved to be tall tale many refused to go on, settling in Missouri, the 'Show Me State'.

Despite its name, **Kansas City** is actually two political entities spread over two states and seven counties — the largest portion being in Missouri. Amtrak travellers may reach Kansas City via Chicago or Los Angeles on a route passing through New Mexico and near the Grand Canyon. Numerous carriers operate from Kansas City International Airport, where taxi and limousine services are supplemented by KCI Express shuttle buses, while Downtown Airport offers an alternative to domestic travellers. Greyhound-Trailways' terminal is between 11th and 12th street a few blocks east of City Hall.

Downtown Kansas City, Missouri, offers the **Town Pavilion Shopping Center** on 11th and Main, plus classic opera and symphony at the Lyric on 10th and Central. The *Missouri River Queen* provides excursions along the river to the north. South on Main Street leads to Penn Valley Park, with monuments and memorials to Boy Scouts, Pioneer Mothers and World War I casualties. Liberty Memorial houses a museum of the war and affords views from its 217ft pillar. Across Main Street is **Crown Center**, a shopping and dining complex combined with the **Hallmark Visitors Center**.

Noted Missouri artist Thomas Hart Benton's home and studios are southwest of Penn Valley Park on Belleview Avenue, while the Kansas City's Conservatory of Music, Art Institute, and **Nelson-Atkins Museum of Art** are found east of Main Street, between 44th and 47th Streets. The museum comprises numerous galleries and period rooms, exhibiting an outstanding collection which includes a sculpture garden of Henry Moore bronzes. The museum hosts concerts, films and special events, with a dining room for those spending the day.

The University of Missouri at Kansas City houses the Linda Hall Library, a repository of scientific knowledge, and the Toy and Miniature Museum's collection of antique toys and handcrafted scale models. West of Main on 47th Street is **Country Club Plaza**, with upmarket shops and department stores in a delightful 1920s Moorish-styled complex. State Line Antique and Art Center is just west on 45th. East on 47th leads to Swope Parkway, a tree-lined avenue which turns south to **Swope Park**, Kansas City's finest. Its Starlight Theater and music pavilion stage various performances, including evening concerts in summer. The park contains a nature centre, various walks, a boating lagoon, and Kansas City Zoo. An information centre provides maps and details current events.

Northeast of downtown amid Kessler Park is the **Kansas City Museum**, recalling the city's role in westward expansion. The complex includes natural history and a planetarium, with a separate facility in the Town Pavilion Center. North of the Missouri River off I-435 is **Worlds of Fun** and **Oceans of Fun**, the former a themed amusement park and entertainment centre, the latter a large water park. Northeast is Liberty, with the **Jesse James Bank Museum** and Historic Liberty Jail, where Mormon prophet Joseph Smith spent four months.

Independence, east of Kansas City on Truman Road, was a staging point for Santa Fe and Oregon Trails, plus gold-seeking '49ers. Places of historic interest include the 1859 Marshal's Home and Jail Museum on North Main Street and **Fort Osage** near Sibley, which recalls the first US fort and trading post in the newly acquired 'Louisiana Territory'. Stately homes include Bingham-Waggoner and Vaile Mansions. The Auditorium on River and Walnut is headquarters of the Reorganized Church of Jesus Christ of Latter Day Saints, an offshoot of John Smith's movement, which maintains a visitor centre on Walnut Street. Modern Independence remembers America's favourite son and former President Harry S. Truman with a library and museum on Delaware Street, a multimedia show in the County Courthouse, and the Harry S. Truman National Historic Site, which preserves his home and possessions.

Drivers should head east on I-70 from Kansas City, perhaps detouring south for state capital Jefferson City before pressing on to **St Louis**, at the confluence of mighty Missouri and Mississippi Rivers. **Gateway Arch**, the city's 630ft tall stainless steel landmark, overlooks the Mississippi waterfront from its perch within the **Jefferson National Expansion Memorial**. The memorial and arch honour Thomas Jefferson's trend-setting Louisiana Purchase, the effects of which are recalled in the Museum of Westward Expansion. Those wishing to visit the arch's observation deck should obtain tickets early. Minesweeper USS *Inaugural* is moored near the arch, while Mississippi River excursions depart from the memorial area and north at **Laclede's Landing**, a historic area converted to shopping and dining district. St Louis maintains a visitor centre nearby on Washington Avenue and Memorial Drive.

West from Gateway Arch leads to Market Street and the **Old Courthouse**, where Dred Scott's case was heard before reaching the US Supreme Court. Major sporting events take place at Busch Stadium, which houses the Sporting Hall of Fame. South is the National Bowling Hall of Fame and also the Eugene Field House and Toy Museum, former home of the children's poet who wrote 'Little Boy Blue'. Further west on Market is Memorial Plaza and its Soldiers' Memorial Military Museum followed by Aloe Plaza, where Carl Milles' fountain 'Meeting of the Waters' symbolizes the joining of Missouri and Mississippi Rivers. Across from the plaza is the Amtrak station. North on 15th Street leads to **Campbell House**, recalling the fur trade era.

Olive Street just south of Campbell House leads west to Lindell Boulevard The **Powell Symphony Hall** and **Fox Theatre** are then north on Grand, with the ornate Cupples House, a 42-room Romanesque mansion, south on S Louis University campus. **St Louis Cathedral** is further west on the Lindell which later passes delightful **Forest Park**. Recreational opportunities includ a brace of municipal golf courses and the Steinburg Memorial Skating Rink while a carillon provides background music for the Jewel Box's floral dis plays.

Among Forest Park's excellent cultural centres are **St Louis Art Museun** with its statue of St Louis the Crusader, and the **St Louis Science Cente** which offers a planetarium and outdoor exhibits in addition to state-of-the-a science exhibits. The **History Museum** and **St Louis Zoological Park** wi round off an interesting day at Forest Park, where most museums are free a nominal admission. Muny, the park's outdoor municipal theatre, stages variety of productions with seats upstairs available free, on a first-come basi The **Missouri Botanical Gardens** are southeast of Forest Park.

South of downtown via Broadway is the **Anheuser-Busch Brewery**, whi provides tours and a hospitality suite, except Sunday. Beyond is Chatillo DeMenil House, found just north after Broadway passes beneath I-55. Eve tually Broadway reaches Kingston Drive, where Grant Street leads to Jefferson Barracks Historical Park, originally established to supply western forts. Several buildings have been restored, and picnic facilities are available. The park affords a view of the Mississippi River.

Other places of interest include **Grant's Farm**, found southwest of St Louis on SR30. The farm contains a cabin built by the Civil War general and former president, plus a Clydesdale stable and petting zoo maintained by Anheuser-Busch. Further west of I-44 is **Lone Elk Park**, with drives through a nature area roamed by deer, elk, and bison. Florissant and St Charles, both north of St Louis, give historic peeps into the French fur trapping era and the Louis and Clark expedition. East St Louis, across the river in Illinois, interprets one of the finest examples of Mississippi Indian culture at **Cahokia Mounds State Historic Site**.

I-55 is the quick route to Springfield, Illinois. If time allows take scenic SR79 north along the Mississippi River to **Hannibal**, birthplace of Samuel Clemens, better known to the world as Mark Twain. His birthplace is preserved as a museum, while riverboats still ply 'his' river. Other offerings include a drama about his life, and the cave where Tom Sawyer and Becky Thatcher became lost (now providing guides). Craft and folk festivals pepper the Hannibal calendar, including the National Tom Sawyer Festival, when look-alikes practice their fence painting. US36 leads east across the Mississippi.

Illinois Interior

The Prairie State has much of interest beyond Chicago, as a visit to its capital, **Springfield**, will show. The city is justly proud of its 'son' Abraham Lincoln, whose body was brought from Washington DC to be interred in his adopted city. Gas lighting and wooden sidewalks herald the **Lincoln Home National Historic Site**, which gives free tours on a first-come basis. Related places of interest include the Lincoln Depot Museum, the railway station where former President bid adieu to Springfield, and the Lincoln-Herndon Law Offices, where he worked. Reserve time to see his tomb north at Oak Ridge Cemetery and visit **Petersburg**, where the New Salem Historic Site is a reconstruction of the town where Lincoln lived during the mid-1830s.

Springfield's current **State Capitol** and **Old State Capitol** are both open, the latter providing a living history program in conjunction with the Illinois State Historical Library in its basement. The **Illinois State Museum** has sections on Native Americans plus Illinois art and early life. Dana-Thomas House is an early example of Frank Lloyd Wright's prairie style of architecture. The Governor's Mansion gives tours on Tuesdays and Thursdays, while the Edwards Place Historic Home north on 4th Street is also an art gallery. Historic Clayville, found west on SR125 before Pleasant Plains, offers living history programs in a town restored to its 1850s appearance.

Indiana

As a fledgling United States fresh from the War of Independence, Indiana was Northwest Territory. Awarded statehood in 1816, the site of **Indianapolis** was later chosen for state capital and designed by Alexander Ralston, who assisted Pierre L'Enfant with Washington DC. Although lacking suitable water-borne transportation, railroads brought industry and prosperity, and Indianapolis became (for a time) capital of automobile production. Each Memorial Day recalls that era with America's racing event of the year, the Indianapolis 500.

✳   The **Soldiers and Sailors Monument** in the heart of downtown has an elevator to an observation deck — the views across Indianapolis provide a useful orientation. West down Market Street is the **Indiana State Capitol,**
🏛   while the excellent **Eiteljorg Museum of American Indian and Western Art** is beyond on Washington Street. North from the monument is World War Memorial Plaza and its shrine, with the **Benjamin Harrison Home**, built for the 23rd president, on Delaware just south of 13th Street. Beyond is the noted
🏛   **Children's Museum**, America's largest and perhaps finest, with a wealth of interest for youngsters of any age. From Meridian Street in northern Indianapolis, 38th Street leads east to the State Fair Grounds, which house the delightful **Hooks Historical Drug Store,** while west on 38th is the **Indi-**
🏛   **anapolis Museum of Art**. Set in landscaped grounds, the museum is a complex of pavilions embracing an eclectic selection of the world's art treasures.
     Northeast of the Soldiers and Sailors Monument is the **Indiana State Museum** on Alabama and Ohio, combining natural and Indiana history, plus the
🏛   **James Whitcomb Riley Home** on Lockerbie Street, exhibiting the poets' possessions. South of the monument is **Union Station**, today a bustling shopping, dining and entertainment centre *and* train station. Indiana is the Hoosier State, explaining the name of nearby Hoosier Dome, which hosts major events under its inflated canopy. **Indianapolis City Center** on Capitol
🦌   Avenue provides information and an introductory presentation. Indianapolis Zoo is west of the White River on Washington Street (US40).
     Further from the city centre is **Garfield Park** to the south, with an excellent conservatory boasting a waterfall and exotic plants. Southwest off the I-465 ring road is Indianapolis International Airport, with the **Indianapolis Motor Speedway** west of downtown containing the Indy Hall of Fame Museum Eagle Creek Park and Preserve northwest of US52 has a nature centre and is teaming with wildlife. Outside the city, **Conner Prairie** at Noblesville recreates early Indiana life on the estate of pioneer William Conner. Indianapolis noted for its culture, 'loans' its symphony to Conner Prairie for a summe concert series.

Ohio

As a territory, Ohio land was claimed by many states, its Ohio River providin a vital link west to the Mississippi. Cosmopolitan **Cincinnati**, the 'Quee City', was the largest municipality west of the Alleghenies, comprising mixture of cultures and influences including a certain amount of Germa *schadenfreude*. Cincinnati also has a touch of Southern charm, and those arri ing by air find Greater Cincinnati International Airport is 14 miles southwe in Kentucky, with downtown hotels serviced by Jetport Express. Lunke Airport is an another option for domestic travellers.
     Downtown's Fountain Square on 5th Street between Walnut and Vi

heralds the revitalized Cincinnati. For an scenic overview, ride the elevator to **Carew Tower Observatory** atop Cincinnati's tallest building on 5th and Vine. Also Downtown are the Contemporary Arts Center on 5th and the Cincinnati Fire Museum on Court Street near City Hall. Cincinnati Symphony and Pop Orchestras perform at Music Hall on Elm Street, which also produces opera and ballet. The city's Mississippi River waterfront accommodates the Riverfront Stadium and Coliseum, presenting numerous events, while nearby Showboat Majestic is a floating theatre.

Cincinnati has numerous fine parks and museums, with **Eden Park** split between the waterfront and the larger section northeast of downtown, found by taking 5th Street east to Columbia Parkway, exiting onto Martin Drive. Eden Park houses the noted **Cincinnati Art Museum**, exhibiting an excellent and eclectic collection of great works, with the Cincinnati Historical Society Museum adjoining. Cincinnati Museum of Natural History displays Ohio flora and fauna, with regular planetarium shows. **Playhouse in the Park** offers two theatres, one specializing in European and the other American productions. Behind Krohn Conservatory's floral displays are picnic facilities overlooking the Mississippi River.

Between Eden Park and downtown is the **Taft Museum**, displaying the arts in an 1820 Federal-style home. North on Auburn leads to the William Howard Taft National Historic Site, birthplace of the former president and Supreme Court Chief Justice. Other parks within Cincinnati include the wooded California Nature Preserve east of the city and south of Lunken Airport. Lone Island Water Park and River Downs Race Track are just beyond, while Little Miami Scenic River Park is behind the airport, spread over several sites. **Mount Airy Forest** in the northwest offers pleasant walks and picnicking, while the Mount Airy Arboretum is especially colourful in spring.

Across the Mississippi River is Covington, Kentucky, which recalls its German heritage in **Mainstrasse Village**, an area of restored nineteenth-century homes, some now providing speciality shops or German cuisine. Also within the village are the Gothic German Carillon Tower, with clockwork figures re-enacting the *Pied Piper of Hamlin*, and the Goose Girl Fountain, which portrays a German maiden bringing her geese to market. BB Riverboats offer Mississippi excursions, including lunch and dinner cruises, while Oldenberg Brewery gives tours, except Monday.

Between Cincinnati and Columbus, **Dayton** has the famed **US Air Force Museum** and **Wright Brothers Memorial**, recalling that the flying brothers perfected their techniques here before rewriting world history at Kitty Hawk, North Carolina. **Kings Island** amusement park is a popular day trip from Cincinnati and Dayton, providing a fun-filled day amid some of the world's best thrill rides. I-70 east continues to the next major stop.

Columbus is Ohio's progressive capital, yet the city loves to recall its heritage. **German Village**, found south of downtown off 3rd Street, has been lovingly restored, with Germanic-styled restaurants and *biergartens*. North of the city on I-71 is the **Ohio Historical Center**, offering a reconstructed nineteenth-century rural community with villagers in period costume. A far earlier period is examined north off US23 at **Olentangy Indian Caverns**, a natural shelter utilized by Wyandot Indians, where a museum interprets local finds.

Ohio State Capitol is a downtown landmark, with tours of legislative chambers on weekdays. East on Broad Street leads to **COSI**, the excellent Center of Ohio Science and Industry. After experimenting with their entertaining hands-on exhibits, experience a different view of reality at the **Columbus Museum of Art**, further east on Broad. European and American pieces are supplemented with pre-Columbian and Native American works and a sculpture park. Culture buffs will find that the **Ohio Theater** presents numerous performances, including those by the Columbus Symphony Orchestra. Ohio State University and Vern Riffe Center also stage varied productions. **Franklin Park** offers its famed Conservatory, modelled after the Crystal Palace in London.

Drivers heading for Cleveland will find US62 affords a scenic route through Millersburg. Just beyond is Berlin, heart of Amish Ohio, where 'Plain People' live without modern appliances yet recall a community spirit forgotten elsewhere. Canton was home to William McKinley, with a memorial to the assassinated president and the McKinley Museum next to Monument Park. From Canton, also home to Pro Football Hall of Fame, follow I-77 north to **Akron**. Places of interest include Quaker Square, a shopping and dining

Columbus boasts a modern skyline

precinct amid the refurbished Quaker Oats production facility, and several fine homes including Stan Hywet Hall and Perkins Mansion. Between Akron and Cleveland is **Sea World of Ohio**, found north of Aurora on SR43, and the **Cuyahoga Valley National Recreation Area** between SR8 and I-77. The latter is a parkland reminiscent of rural eighteenth- and nineteenth-century Ohio, where the **Hale Farm and Village** complex demonstrates traditional crafts.

The advent of the Ohio and Erie Canal, followed by John Rockefeller's Standard Oil Company, catapulted **Cleveland** into the Industrial Age. Side

Dearborn's Ford Museum examines the automobile in American culture

effects included generous patronage of the city's fine cultural institutions and a pollution problem culminating in its river catching fire. Modern Cleveland has cleaned up, launching a massive regeneration campaign and converting riverfront properties into entertainment and shopping centres.

University Circle is cultural heart of the city — from downtown skirt Lake Erie east on Cleveland Memorial Shoreway then south on Martin Luther King Jr Drive, passing Rockefeller Park Greenhouse. The exceptional **Cleveland Museum of Art** presents concerts in its auditorium, while the **Cleveland Museum of Natural History** includes an observatory and planetarium. The **Western Reserve Historical Society** maintains an automotive-aviation museum, historical museum and a library. The Garden Center is also at University Circle, as is Severance Hall, home to the Cleveland Orchestra except in summer, when they perform at the open-air Blossom Music Center.

Returning west to central Cleveland on Euclid, **Cleveland Children's Museum** is near the junction with Martin Luther King Jr Drive, with the fascinating **Cleveland Health Education Museum** beyond. Downtown's Tower City Center provides a visitor centre plus the Avenue shopping and dining complex. Armed with a map and directions, visitors can find their way down to **The Flats** for fine nightlife or daytime shopping and cruises on Cuyahoga River.

Drivers returning west may follow US6 along Lake Erie's shoreline, with perhaps a quick detour south for NASA's **Lewis Research Center** outside Cleveland Hopkins International Airport. Continuing west on US6 leads to Sandusky, home of **Cedar Point Amusement Park**. SR2 west passes Crane Creek State Park, with its nature centre and excellent bird watching. Industrial **Toledo** supplements a fine museum of arts, zoological park and historic homes with the *Willis B. Boyer*, one of the largest Great Lakes Freighters and now a museum. North on I-75 leads to the last new state in this tour.

Michigan

Michi Gama, 'Great Lake', is an appropriate name for a state bordering Lakes Erie, Huron, Superior, and Michigan. Boasting more miles of shoreline than many countries, Michigan also contains the mighty motor cities, promising a kaleidoscope of contrasts to its guests.

Detroit comes from French *d'etroit*, a reference to the strait joining Lakes Erie and Huron. From Detroit the Canadian city of Windsor is due south, best viewed from Westin Hotel's observation deck above Renaissance Center. The gleaming black towers of the centre also contain the World of Ford, a showcase of present and future automotive technology, plus a variety of speciality shops and restaurants. The waterfront Civic Center complex encompasses Cobo Hall and the Joe Louis and Cobo Arenas, which together stage sporting events, auto shows, conventions, hockey and ice shows. The visitor information centre in Hart Plaza, between Renaissance Center and Cobo Hall provides maps and information on personal security, which should be heeded. The Detroit People Mover circles downtown, visiting the above and Trapper Alley, a renovated shopping district in 'Greektown'.

Belle Island Park, east on Jefferson then south over MacArthur Bridge, ha a beach, aquarium, nature centre, conservatory and the Great Lakes Museum. **Boblo Island**, across the border in Canada, is a large amusement park reached by ferry from its dock just west of Ambassador Bridge or several points within Canada. Nearby **Fort Wayne** has been restored to the Spanish-American War period, and also contains the Great Lakes Indian Museum. Other places of interest include that famed Detroit trio, the Institute of Arts, Science Center, and History Museum, all located on or near Woodward and Kirby Avenues. **Motown Historical Museum** on Grand Boulevard recalls the Motown sound. **Detroit Zoological Park** is north in suburb Royal Oak.

Nearby **Dearborn**, west of Detroit on US12, was home to Henry Ford, whose estate at the University of Michigan-Dearborn provides tours. Undoubtedly one of the greatest legacies ever bestowed upon the American public is the **Henry Ford Museum and Greenfield Village**. The Ford Museum offers a fascinating glimpse of how technology and especially transportation has affected modern civilization. The outstanding selection of cars traces the automobile's history, pulling no punches in its representation of this now global industry. The museum also exhibits collections of glassware, clocks, ceramics, silver, and pewter.

Greenfield Village embraces perhaps the richest collection of American heritage gathered on one site, including Thomas Edison's Menlo Park laboratory, the Wright Brothers' cycle shop and home, Harvey Firestone's farm, and numerous other accredited national treasures. Henry undoubtedly saved many historic buildings, while his plans to move Philadelphia's Independence Hall galvanized the city into preserving that monument — prompting Henry to build a full-scale replica. Craft demonstrations, shops, train rides and dining at Eagle Tavern add to the enjoyment. If time permits, allow two days.

Those returning to Chicago will find I-94 westbound quickest, about 6 hours nonstop driving. Alternatively, I-96 passes **Lansing**, Michigan state capital, and **Grand Rapids**, with the Gerald Ford Museum. Southwest on I-196 is **Holland**, which retains a hint of its Dutch heritage. After picking up I-94 west allow time to visit the **Indiana Dunes National Lakeshore**, where tall dunes offer a backdrop to Lake Michigan beaches.

Additional Information

State Tourism Bureaux

Illinois Tourist Info Center
310 South Michigan
Suite 108
Chicago, IL 60604
☎ 800-223-0121
or 312-793-2094

Indiana Tourism Development Div
One North Capitol
Suite 700
Indianapolis, IN 46204
☎ 800-289-6646
or 317-232-8860

Iowa Division of Tourism
200 East Grand Ave
Des Moines, IA 50309
☎ 800-345-4692
or 515-281-3100

Michigan Travel Bureau
Dept TPM, PO Box 30226
Lansing, MI 48909
☎ 800-543-2937

Minnesota Travel Info Center
375 Jackson St, 250
Skyway Level
St Paul, MN 55101
☎ 800-657-3700
or 612-296-5029

Missouri Division of Tourism
PO Box 1055
Jefferson City, MO 65102
☎ 314-751-4133

North Dakota Tourism
Liberty Memorial Building
Bismarck, ND 58505
☎ 800-437-2077
or 701-224-2525

Ohio Travel & Tourism
PO Box 1001
Columbus, OH 43266
☎ 800-282-5393
or 616-466-8844

Wisconsin Tourism Dev
123 W Washington Ave
Madison, WI 53707
☎ 800-432-8747
or 608-266-2161

Regional Information

Chicago Office of Tourism
Historic Water Tower
806 North Michigan Ave
Chicago, IL 60611
☎ 800-487-2446
or 312-280-5740

Cincinnati CVB
300 W 6th St
Cincinnati, OH 45202
☎ 800-344-3445
or 513-621-2124

Cleveland CVB
3100 Terminal Tower
Tower City Center
Cleveland, OH 44113
☎ 216-621-4110

Columbus CVB
10 W Broad St, Suite 1300
Columbus, OH 43215
☎ 614-221-6623

Des Moines CVB
309 Court Ave
Des Moines, IA 50309
☎ 800-451-2625
or 515-286-4960

Detroit CVB
100 Renaissance Center,
Suite 1950
Detroit, MI 48243
☎ 313-259-4333

Fargo-Moorhead CVB
PO Box 2164
Fargo, ND 58107
☎ 800-235-7654

Hannibal CVB
PO Box 624
Hannibal, MO 63401
☎ 314-221-2477

Indianapolis CVB
One Hoosier Dome
Suite 100
Indianapolis, IN 46255
☎ 800-323-4639
or 317-639-4282

Kansas City CVB
City Center Square
1100 Main St
Kansas City, MO 64105
☎ 800-767-7700
or 816-221-5242

Madison CVB
615 E Washington
Madison, WI 53703
☎ 800-373-6376
or 608-255-2537

Milwaukee CVB
510 W Kilbourne Ave
Milwaukee, WI 53203
☎ 800-231-0903
or 414-273-3950;
414-799-1177 (recorded events)

Minneapolis CVB
1219 Marquette Ave
Minneapolis, MN 55403
☎ 800-445-7412
or 612-348-7000

Springfield CVB
109 N 7th
Springfield, IL 62701
☎ 800-545-7300
or 217-789-2360

St Louis CVB
10 S Broadway
St Louis, MO 63102
☎314-421-1023 (-2100 events)

St Paul CVB
55 E 5th St
St Paul, MN 55101
☎ 612-297-6985

Local Events

Check locally for exact dates
January
Winterfest
Milwaukee, WI

January/February
Winter Carnival
St Paul, MN

May
May Music Festival
Cincinnati, OH

Indianapolis 500
Indianapolis, IN

Tom Sawyer Riverboat Race
St Louis, MO

June
Chicago Gospel Festival
Chicago, IL

Chicago Blues Festival
Chicago, IL

Celebrate on State Street
Chicago, IL

Lakefront Festival of Arts
Milwaukee, WI

Midsummer Festival
Indianapolis, IN

June-July
Taste of Chicago
Chicago, IL

International Freedom
Festival
Detroit, MI

Veiled Prophet Fair
Louis, MO

Summerfest
Milwaukee, WI

June-August
Grant Park Concerts
Chicago, IL

July
Taste of Minnesota
St Paul, MN

Fargo Street Fair
Fargo, ND

Black Expo
Indianapolis, IN

Taste of Lincoln Ave
Chicago, IL

July-August
Minneapolis Aquatennial
Minneapolis, MN

August
Ohio State Fair
Columbus, OH

Chicago Ethnic Fair
Chicago, IL

Wisconsin State Fair
Milwaukee, WI

Illinois State Fair
Springfield, IL

Iowa State Fair
Des Moines, IA

Indiana State Fair
Indianapolis, IN

Michigan State Fair
Detroit, MI

August-September
Chicago Jazz Festival
Chicago, IL

Minnesota State Fair
St Paul, MN

September
Riverfest
Cincinnati, OH

Cleveland National Air
Show
Cleveland, OH

Montreaux Detroit Jazz
Festival
Detroit, MI

Places of Interest

Chicago, IL
ArchiCenter
330 S Dearborn Ave
Chicago, IL 60611
☎ 312-922-3431
312-782-1776 (recorded)
Open: 9.30am-5.30pm
Mon-Fri, 9am-5pm Sat
ArchiTours, gifts

Art Institute of Chicago
Michigan Ave & Adams St
Chicago, IL 60603
☎ 312-443-3600
(-3500 recorded)
Open: 10.30am-4.30pm
Mon-Fri, 10am-8pm Thu,
10am-5pm Sat, noon-5pm
Sun. Free Tue
Tours, gifts, food, ♿

*Chicago Academy of
Sciences*
2001 North Clark St
Chicago, IL 60614
☎ 312-871-2668
Open: 10am-6pm, 10am-
8pm Fri & Sat. Free Mon
Tours, gifts, food, ♿

Chicago Zoological Park
3300 South Golf Road
Brookfield, IL 60513
☎ 708-485-0263
Open: 10am-5pm,
9.30am-6pm summer.
Free Tue
Zoo, children's zoo, food,
gifts, ♿

*Field Museum of Natural
History*
Roosevelt Rd & Lake
Shore Dr
Chicago, IL 60605
☎ 312-922-9410
Open: 9am-5pm. Free Thu
Tours, gifts, food, ♿

Frank Lloyd Wright Home
951 Chicago Avenue
Oak Park, IL 60302
☎ 708-848-1500
Call for tour times
Tour home & studio,
gifts, food, parts ♿

John Hancock Observatory
875 North Michigan Ave
Chicago, IL 60611
☎ 312-751-3680/1
Open: 9am-midnight
Observatory, shops, gifts,
food, &

*Museum of Science and
Industry*
57th St & Lakeshore Dr
Chicago, IL 60637
☎ 312-684-1414
Open: 9.30am-4pm,
9.30am-5.30 pm summer
& weekends
Omnimax theatre, gifts,
food, &

Sears Tower
233 S Wacker Dr
Chicago, IL 60610
☎ 312-875-9696
Open: 9am-midnight
Observatory, shops, gifts,
food, &

Shedd Aquarium
1200 South Lake Shore Dr
Chicago, IL 60605
☎ 312-939-2438
Open: 10am-5pm, 9am-
5pm summer. Free Thur
Oceanarium, divers, gifts,
&

Cincinnati, OH
Cincinnati Art Museum
Gilbert Ave, Eden Park
Cincinnati, OH 45202
☎ 513-721-5204
Open: 10am-5pm Tue-Sat
Tours, gifts, &

Taft Museum
316 Pike St
Cincinnati, OH 45215
☎ 513-241-0343
Open: 10am-5pm Mon-Sat,
2-5pm Sun & holidays
Tours, garden, picnic

Kings Island Park
Kings Island Dr
I-71 exit 25A
Kings Island, OH 45034
☎ 800-433-1072
or 513-933-1138

Open: 10am-10pm (10am-
11pm Sat) Memorial-
Labor Day
Rides, amusements, food,
gifts, &

Cleveland, OH
Cleveland Museum of Art
11150 E Blvd
University Circle
Cleveland, OH 44106
☎ 216-421-7340
Open: 10am-5.45pm Tue-
Sat, 1-5.45pm Sun
Tours, gifts, auditorium,
&

*Cleveland Museum of
Natural History*
1 Wade Oval Dr
University Circle
Cleveland, OH 44106
☎ 216-231-4600
Open: call for times
Tours, planetarium, gifts,
&

Hale Farm and Village
2686 Oakhill Road
Bath, OH 44210
☎ 216-575-9137
Open: 10am-5pm Tue-
Sat, noon-5pm Sun, mid-
May to Oct
Living history, farm,
gifts, food

*NASA Lewis Research
Center*
21000 Brookpark Rd
Cleveland, OH 44135
☎ 216-433-2001
Open: 9am-4pm Mon-Fri,
10am-3pm Sat, 1-5pm Sun
Tours, gifts, &

Sea World of Ohio
1100 Sea World Drive
(SR43)
Aurora, OH 44202
☎ 800-637-4286
or 216-562-8101
Open: Memorial-Labor
Day, call for times
Shows, exhibits, food,
gifts, &

*Western Reserve Historical
Society*
10825 E Blvd
Cleveland, OH 44106
☎ 216-721-5722
Open: 10am-5pm Tue-
Sat, noon-5pm Sun
Auto, aviation & history
museum, gifts

Columbus, OH
Columbus Museum of Art
480 E Broad St
Columbus, OH 43215
☎ 614-221-6801
Open: call for times,
closed Mon
Tours, gifts, &

*COSI (Science-Industry
Center)*
280 E Broad St
Columbus, OH 43215
☎ 614-228-2674
call for times10am-5pm
Mon-Sat, 1-5.30pm Sun
Tours, gifts, &

Ohio Historical Center
1982 Velma Ave
Columbus, OH 43211
☎ 614-297-2300
Open: call for times
Museum, Ohio Village,
gifts

State Capitol
Broad St & High St
Columbus, OH 43215
☎ 614-466-2125
Open: 7am-9pm Mon-Fri,
9am-5pm Sat-Sun
Free, Tours, &

Des Moines, IA
Living History Farms
2600 NW 111th St
Des Moines, IA 50322
☎ 515-278-5286
Open: 9am-5pm Mon-Sa
11am-6pm Sun, May-Oc
Museum, village, gifts,
food

State Capitol
E 9th St & Grand Ave
Des Moines, IA
☎ 515-281-5591
Open: 8am-4.30pm Mon-Fri, 8am-4pm Sat-Sun
Free, Tours, &

State History Center
E 6th St & Locust St
Des Moines, IA 50319
☎ 515-281-5111
Open: 9am-4.30pm Tue-Sat, noon-4.30pm Sun. Free
Museum, library, gifts, &

Detroit, MI
Boblo Island
C/O 4401 W Jefferson Ave
Detroit, MI 48209
☎ 313-843-8800 (US)
519-252-4444 (Canada)
Open: call for times
Island is in Canada
Amusement park, gifts, food, boat cruise

Fort Wayne
6325 W Jefferson Ave
Detroit, MI 48209
☎ 313-297-9360
Open: 9.30am-5pm Wed-Sun summer
Indian museum, food, gifts

Henry Ford Museum & Greenfield Village
20900 Oakwood Blvd
PO Box 1970
Dearborn, MI 48121
☎ 313-271-1620
Open: 9am-5pm
Museum, village, gifts, food, &

Motown Historical Museum
2648 W Grand Blvd
Detroit, MI 48208
☎ 313-875-2264
Open: 10am-5pm Mon-Sat, 2-5pm Sun
Tour, video, gifts

Fargo, ND
Bonanzaville
I-94 Exit 343 (PO Box 719)
West Fargo, ND 58078

☎ 701-282-2822
Open: 9am-8pm Mon-Fri, 9am-5pm Sat-Sun, Memorial Day-late Oct
Museum, period town, food, gifts

Indianapolis, IN
Benjamin Harrison Home
1230 N. Delaware St
Indianapolis, IN 46202
☎ 317-631-1898
Open: 10am-4pm Mon-Sat, 12.30pm-4pm Sun.
Tours

Children's Museum
PO Box 3000
Indianapolis, IN 46206
☎ 317-924-5431
Open: 10am-5pm Mon-Sat, noon-5pm Sun, closed Mon in winter
Planetarium, exploratorium, gifts, &

Eiteljorg Museum
500 W Washington St
Indianapolis, IN 46204
☎ 317-636-9378
Open: 10am-5pm Tue-Sat, noon-5pm Sun
Tours, gifts, &

Indiana State Museum
202 N Alabama St
Indianapolis, IN 46204
☎ 317-232-1637
Open: 9am-4.45pm Mon-Sat, noon-4.45pm Sun
Free, tours, gifts, &

Indianapolis Museum of Art
1200 W 38th St
Indianapolis, IN 46208
☎ 317-923-1331
Open: 10am-5.30pm Tue-Sat, noon-5pm Sun. Free
Food, gifts, botanic gardens, &

Kansas City, MO
Worlds/Oceans of Fun
I-435 exit 54
Kansas City, MO
☎ 816-454-4444 (Worlds)
816-459-9283 (Oceans)

Open: 10am-6pm Memorial-Labor Day, 10am-late selected nights
Rides, amusements, gifts, food

Madison, WI
House on the Rock
SR23, PO Box 555
Spring Green, WI 53588
☎ 608-935-3639
Open: 8am-dusk Apr-Oct
Home, food, gifts, crafts

State Historical Museum
30 N Carroll
Madison, WI 53707
☎ 608-266-2161
Open: 0am-5pm Tue-Sat, noon-5pm Sun
Tours, gifts, &

Milwaukee, WI
Milwaukee Art Museum
750 N Lincoln Memorial Dr
Milwaukee, WI 53202
☎ 414-271-9508
Open: 10am-5pm Tue, Wed, Fri, Sat; noon-9pm Thur; noon-5pm Sun
Tours, food, gifts, &

Milwaukee Public Museum
800 W Wells St
Milwaukee, WI 53233
☎ 414-278-2702
Open: noon-8pm Mon, 9am-5pm Tue-Sun
Tours, food, gifts, &

Pabst Mansion
2000 W Wisconsin Ave
Milwaukee, WI 53233
☎ 414-931-0808
Open: 10am-3.30pm Mon-Sat, noon-3.30pm Sun; closed Jan to mid-Mar
Tours

Pabst Theater
144 E Wells St
Milwaukee, WI 53202
☎ 414-278-3663
Open: call for times &

Performing Arts Center
929 N Water St
Milwaukee, WI 53202
☎ 414-273-7206
Open: call for times
&

Riverside Theater
116 W Wisconsin Ave
Milwaukee, WI 53203
☎ 414-271-7206
Call for times
&

Minneapolis, MN
American Swedish Institute
2600 Park Ave
Minneapolis, MN 55407
☎ 612-871-4907
Open: noon-4pm Tue-Sat,
noon-8 Wed, 1-5pm Sun
Tours, films, gifts

HHH Metrodome
900 S 5th St
Minneapolis, MN 55403
☎ 612-332-0386
Open: call for events
Tours, sporting events,
food, &

Indiana Dunes, IN
Indiana Dunes National
Lakeshore
C/O 1100 North Mineral
Springs Road
Porter, IN 46304
☎ 216-926-7561
Open: 8am-5pm, 8am-
6pm summer
Walk, picnic, beach,
nature centre

St Louis, MO
Cahokia Mounds SHS
7850 Collinsville Rd
East St Louis, IL 62234
☎ 618-346-5160
Open: 9am-5pm. Free
Tours, food, picnic, &

Gateway Arch NHS
11 N 4th St (offices)
St Louis, MO 63102
☎ 314-425-4465
Open: 9.30am-5.30pm,
8.30am-9.30pm summer
Arch observatory,
museum below, gifts

Missouri Botanical Gardens
4344 Shaw Blvd
St Louis, MO 63110
☎ 314-577-5100
Open: 9am-5pm, 9am-
8pm summer
Food, gifts, plant shop,
tram

St Louis Art Museum
Forest Park
St Louis, MO 63110
☎ 314-721-0067
Open: 1.30-8.30pm Tue,
10am-5pm Wed-Sun
Tours, gifts, food, &

St Louis Science Center
5100 Clayton Ave
(Forest Park)
St Louis, MO 63110
☎ 314-289-4400
Open: 9.30am-5pm Mon-
Thu, 9.30am-9pm Fri-Sat,
11am-5pm Sun
Planetarium, science lab,
gifts, &

St Paul, MN
Historic Fort Snelling
SR5 & SR55
St Paul, MN
☎ 612-726-9430
Open: 9.30am-5pm
summer, reduced winter
Living history, gifts, film

Minnesota Museum of Arts
Kellogg & St Peter
St Paul, MN 55101
☎ 612-292-4355
Open: 10.30-4.30pm Tue-
Fri, 1-4.30pm Sat-Sun
Tours, gifts

Ordway Music Theatre
234 Washington St
St Paul, MN 55102
☎ 612-224-4222
Open: call for times
Opera, concert, theatre

Science Museum of
Minnesota
30 E 10th St
St Paul, MN 55101
☎ 612-221-9400
Open: 9.30am-9pm Mon-
Sat, 11am-9pm Sun,
closed Monday in winter
Tours, Omnitheater, gifts,
&

State Capitol
Cedar & Aurora
St Paul, MN 55101
☎ 612-296-2881
Open: 9am-5pm Mon-Fri,
10am-4pm Sat, 1-4pm Sun
Free, tours, &

Springfield, IL
Illinois State Museum
Spring St & Edwards St
Springfield, IL
☎ 217-782-7386
Open: 8.30am-5pm Mon-
Sat, noon-5pm Sun
Free, Tours, gifts, &

Lincoln Home NHS
426 South 7th St
Springfield, IL
☎ 217-492-4150
Open: 8.30am-5pm. Free
tickets at visitor centre
Ranger tours, gifts

State Capitol
2nd & Capitol Ave
Springfield, IL
☎ 217-782-2099
Open: 8am-5pm Mon-Fri
9am-3.30pm Sat-Sun
Free, Tours, &

7

TEXAS BORDERS

Second only to Alaska in size, during the early 1990s the rapidly growing population of Texas will exceed that of New York State, boosting itself into yet another second place. Of course, Texans prefer to dwell on what they come *first* in, like cattle, crude oil, cotton and cowboy boots. But if Texas produces cowboys then neighbour Oklahoma has the Indians, with some thrilling rodeos, too. Arkansas is famous for the Ozarks, where mountain folk live in a timeless world most of us can only wish for.

Dallas/Fort Worth

Dallas was overshadowed by Fort Worth until it became the temporary terminus for the Texas Pacific Railroad in 1873, although today the growth of either city boosts the other. Europeans attracted by the financial possibilities of a frontier rail-head made Dallas the most cosmopolitan Texan city, firmly establishing it as leader in southwestern banking, insurance and wholesale goods. Against slick Dallas is balanced Fort Worth, self-styled 'cowtown with class'.

Texas Borders in Brief

This tour commences with the Dallas/Fort Worth Metroplex, then visits Houston, Austin, and San Antonio — a contrasting collection of cities. From Corpus Christi and the Gulf of Mexico coast follow the Rio Grande through Laredo and Big Bend National Park to El Paso and its Spanish missions. Those believing Texas is flat learn otherwise at the Guadeloupe Mountains National Park. After New Mexico's Carlsbad Caverns see the Texas panhandle, the most southerly portion of the Great Plains. Visit Indian Territory — Oklahoma — and the Ozark Mountains of Arkansas before returning to Texas.

For this tour, see everything time permits, returning via the nearest interstate to Dallas — never more than a day's drive away. Visitors from abroad must have a multiple-entry US visa to cross into Mexico at Laredo or El Paso. Spring and autumn are the best travelling seasons, while January and February experience the occasional cold spell. Summer day-time highs average low-mid 90s, with humidity varying from a subtropical high in Houston and Corpus Christi to arid in the west.

Into and Around Dallas/Fort Worth

The Dallas/Fort Worth Metroplex incorporates the 'Mid-Cities' of Irving, Grand Prairie and Arlington. The conurbation is some 50 miles across, sharing Dallas-Fort Worth International Airport, 18 miles northwest of downtown Dallas. Bus and taxi services are supplemented by SuperShuttle for airport to hotel connections. Regional airports include Love Field and Red Bird in Dallas, Meacham Field in Fort Worth, and Arlington Municipal.

Both Dallas and Fort Worth are serviced by Amtrak and Greyhound. DART, Dallas Area Rapid Transit, offers an excellent bus network augmented by the McKinney Avenue Trolley. I-30 runs through the heart of the conurbation, with I-20, I-820, I-635 and the Airport Freeway combining to encircle the Metroplex. A good map is essential off the interstates, especially since the cities' grid patterns are non-aligned. Grey Line and Longhorn Tours offer an easy alternative to driving around spread-out attractions.

Reunion Tower is a major **Dallas** landmark, with a revolving restaurant, lounge, and observation deck in its geodesic dome. Nearby Union Station hosts Amtrak and a Dallas visitor centre, while north on Houston Street near Elm is the marker where President John F. Kennedy was assassinated. Neither Dallas nor visitors can forget *that* moment, so the former Texas School Book Depository where the fatal shot was allegedly fired is now the **Sixth Floor Museum**, offering an informative series of films and exhibits.

A log cabin looks incongruous in downtown Dallas, but the reconstruction recalls that built by founder John Neely Bryan. North on Record or Market leads to the Historic West End District and its Marketplace, now a collection of shops, nightclubs and eateries. The McKinney Avenue Trolley runs here from downtown and on to the **Dallas Museum of Art**. In addition to the Reves Collection of impressionist and post-impressionist works, the museum is strong on pre-Columbian artifacts.

Downtown's Neiman-Marcus is more than a Dallas shopping landmark. A purveyor of goods both outrageous and ostentatious, legend surrounds more extravagant sales, such as his and hers camels, while their Christmas catalogue is a collectors item. With over 600 shopping malls and centres to choose from, Dallas boasts the most retail space per capita in America, including **Valley View Center** and the nearby **Galleria**. Having found suitable finery experience Dallas culture at the Meyerson Symphony Center, a summer evening musical at State Fair Park, or a performance at Dallas Theater Center designed by Frank Lloyd Wright.

Dallas boasts some fine squares and parks. Downtown's **Thanks-Giving Square** between Pacific and Bryan has a chapel, carillon, and waterfalls, while a collection of historic buildings form **Old City Park** southeast of downtown. In the northeast, **White Lake Park** offers the Dallas Botanical Garden and pleasant lakeside walks. Marsalis Park, south of Dallas off I-35E, hosts the acclaimed **Dallas Zoo**. A large section recreates the Wilds of Africa, with a major habitats of the African Continent — the monorail offers the best view.

State Fair Park, a legacy of the 1936 Texas Centennial, is one of the world largest art deco districts, with many structures put to interesting uses. Within the park are the Museum of Natural History, Science Place I and II, the Age of Steam Railroad Museum, and informative **Texas Hall of State**. Regular performances take place in the Music Hall, while the Esplanade of State has motifs and statuary symbolizing Texas. The October State Fair is one of America's largest and finest.

Cotton Bowl in Fair Park stages numerous sporting events, including the New Year's Day football classic. Dallas Cowboys take football to new heights at **Texas Stadium** in Irving, while Texas Rangers play baseball in Arlington Stadium. **Arlington** is also home to **Six Flags Over Texas**, a monster amusement park with themed areas representing each flag. If Texas heat gets too much, cool off at nearby Wet 'N Wild. Apart from Cowboys Football, **Irving** has the National Museum of Communications and the **Los Colinas Complex**, with speciality restaurants and shops, plus an equestrian centre and movie studio. Water taxis ply the European-styled canal front, while Williams Square displays the Mustangs of Las Colinas sculpture, nine larger-than-life horses splashing across a raging stream.

At **Grand Prairie**, another 'Mid-City', visitors may drive through the 360-acre International Wildlife Park. Traders Village, a huge flea market, also hosts Metroplex events, such as the April Prairie Dog Chilli Cookoff and National Championship Indian Powwow. A combination ticket is available for the Palace of Wax and Ripley's Believe it or Not! on Belt Line Road. Fans of the television show *Dallas*, will find **Southfork Ranch** north of the city in Plano. East on I-30 from downtown and south on I-635 leads to Mesquite, which holds its famous **Mesquite Rodeo** on Friday and Saturday from April through September.

Fort Worth is mighty civilized for a former cowtown, but pick no fights at **Billy Bob's Texas**, the world's largest honky-tonk. Boasting 600 feet of bar rail to cling onto, Billy Bob's is also an entertainment and dining centre, offering headlining country music stars and big steaks for those with appetites to match. Historic **Fort Worth Stockyards** have been renovated, although stores and eateries retain a Western style and the local museum tells it like it was.

Downtown Fort Worth shows a good collection of C. M. Russells and Remingtons at the **Sid Richardson Collection of Western Art**, as does **Amon Carter Museum of Western Art** out on Camp Bowie Boulevard. Some fine Texas museums are west on Lancaster, including **Kimbell Art Museum**, which concentrates on eighteenth-century portraits and old masters. The Modern Art Museum offers contemporary works, while Fort Worth Museum of Science and History blasts guests into space at the Omnimax Theater. While in the area check events at Will Rogers Auditorium and Coliseum — a statue of Rogers on horseback stands in front of the complex. Amid Trinity and Forest Parks south are the 115 acre **Botanic Garden** and enchanting **Japanese Garden**. A collection of pioneer homes await visitors to the Log Cabin Village, and nearby is Forest Park Zoo.

Follow I-45 to Houston, perhaps pausing en route at Huntsville's **Sam Houston Memorial Museum Complex**. General Sam Houston commanded the Texas Army and became President of the Lone Star Republic, later serving as US Senator and Governor of the state of Texas.

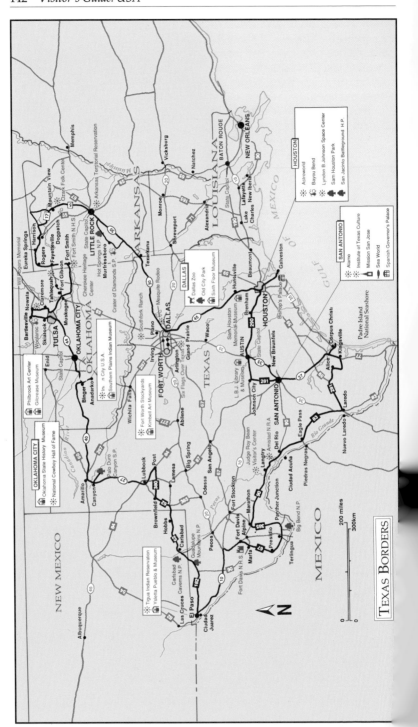

TEXAS BORDERS

Dallas is noted for its modern architecture

Fort Worth is a cowtown with class

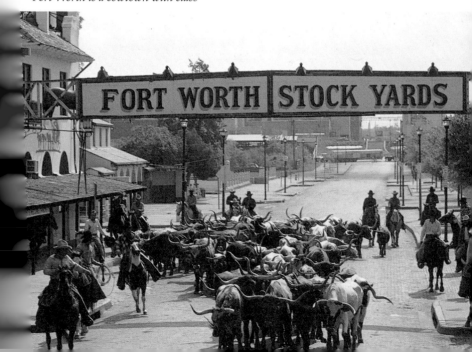

Greater Houston

Houston is mission control to America's space program, but phenomenal growth seemingly launched more skyscrapers than NASA has rockets. Central Houston, Texas Medical Center and several hotel and shopping complexes in west Houston have individual skylines. The medical facilities are world-renowned, while downtown Houston was America's first air conditioned city, where underground concourses link towering monuments to finance.

Houston's theatre district is squeezed between skyscrapers and the freeway system. Surrounding the fountains and towers of Tranquility Park in the **Civic Center** are the Jesse Jones Hall for Performing Arts, housing the Houston Symphonic, Wortham Center, with its grand opera and Houston Ballet, and modern Nina Vance Alley Theater. Also there are the convention centre, and the Sam Houston Coliseum and Music Hall, sporting the larger performances and events. Historic Houston is found at Sam Houston Park west of Civic Center, including several homes and the fascinating **Museum of Texas History**. To the east is Allen's Landing, the original city centre with nineteenth-century buildings renovated as shops and restaurants.

The **Museum District** in and around Hermann Park is southwest of Central Houston. The **Museum of Natural Science** offers exhibits from dinosaurs to offshore oil wells, boasting an IMAX Theatre and Baker Planetarium. The Houston Zoological Gardens and Miller Theatre are also in Hermann Park. Along Main Street are the **Museum of Fine Arts**, which was awarded part of the fabulous Kress Collection, and the Contemporary Arts Museum. The sixteenth- to nineteenth-century works of the **Menil Collection** and abstract expressionist works in Rothko Chapel are north across I-59.

If more action is desired, try **Astroworld**, a 75-acre themed amusement park, or splash-filled Water World, both south of the **Astrodome**. Houston Astros and Oilers play at the world's first indoor stadium, which also hosts the Houston International Livestock Show and Rodeo. Guided tours of Astro-

Into and Around Houston

Houston Intercontinental Airport is 16 miles north of city centre, with Airport Express providing the main bus connections. William P. Hobby Airport is southeast of Houston, both airports maintaining staffed visitor centres. Amtrak services the Washington Avenue station, which also operates the Texas Limited service to Galveston Island. I-10 is the main east-west route, while both airports are off the north-south I-45. Stick to route numbers when navigating around Houston, as freeway names change frequently. For example, the I-610 loop's names reflect compass points.

Central Houston is southeast of I-45 and I-10 crossovers, bounded in the east by US-59. Galveston is south on I-45, while Astrodome and Astroworld are on the southern section of circular I-610, with the famed Texas Medical Center and Herman Park just north. Eastern Houston has a mixture of bayous and oil storage complexes, while the main shopping and hotel complexes are off I-610 west.

dome are available except during afternoon events.

In western Houston, both sides of Westheimer Road off I-610 westbound are lined with shopping centres, restaurants and hotels. Buffalo Bayou lays to the north, and places of interest off Memorial Drive include **Bayou Bend** with its extensive gardens. Also within the grounds, the former home of Miss Ima Hogg, daughter of Governor James Stephen Hogg, reopens in 1993 under the auspices of the Museum of Fine Arts. Memorial Park has a fine municipal golf course, Houston Arboretum, and the Nature Center.

From Houston, I-45 leads southeast to **Lyndon B. Johnson Space Center**. For a guided tour of Mission Control arrive early. Self-guided tours take in a film, moon rocks, the roving lunar 'golf cart' and other interesting exhibits. **Armand Bayou Park and Preserve** is nearby, with a nature centre and walks through various habitats. **San Jacinto Battleground Historical Park** north along the Houston Ship Canal commemorates Sam Houston's defeat of the Mexican Army, with a towering monument and museum beneath. The battleship *Texas* is also there.

I-45 ends at **Galveston**. Home to pirate Jean Laffite then the Texas elite, Galveston was 'Wall Street of the Southwest' until the storm of 1900. A seawall protects the barrier island today, and residential resort Galveston offers a beach, excellent fishing, and numerous historic buildings, the latter saved when Houston became financial capital. Excursion boats include the *Colonel*, a triple-deck paddle wheeler, while *Elissa*, a 400 ton three-masted barque, is a sailing museum when not abroad. Historic places of interest include the elegant and ornate **Bishop's Palace**, listed among America's 100 outstanding buildings by the Institute of Architects. After a major face-lift, performances at the 1894 **Grand Opera House** again benefit from its atmosphere and acoustics. **The Strand** is a colourful collection of 19th century iron-fronted buildings renovated as an art, shopping and dining district. The Galveston Flyer leaves from the Strand Visitor Center.

Take the scenic route from Galveston to Corpus Christi, via inland Austin and San Antonio. From Houston's I-610 freeway loop, take US 290 west, perhaps pausing at **Brenham** for the Blue Bell Creamery's extra-fine ice cream and to visit the St Clare Monastery Miniature Horse Farm.

Capital Austin

Sam Houston was not enamoured with Austin — its central location positioned it in the midst of nowhere. But the city has blossomed into one of the Lone Star State's finest, big enough to offer all cultural amenities, yet with room for trees and greenery. Most international connections are via Dallas or Houston, but nearby Robert Mueller Airport is well served by domestic carriers. Pleasantly situated near the foothills of the Edwards Plateau, the Colorado River—but not that of Grand Canyon fame—passes through Austin.

Start with Austin's **State Capitol Complex**, the dome modelled on the capitol in Washington. Portraits include past governors and five former presidents of the Republic of Texas. Surrounding grounds are full of statuary, memorials, and of greenery. The antebellum **Governor's Mansion** has tours on weekday mornings, missing only the governor's upper floor apartment.

Saturn V at Johnson Space Center

The State Capitol interrupts Congress Avenue, which leads south to **Discovery Hall**, offering hands-on science in a former bus station. Between the Capitol and Discovery Hall, **Sixth Street** was formerly Old Pecan Street, the commercial heart of Austin until the current Capitol was built. The section from Congress Avenue to I-35 really comes alive on weekends, when its shops, galleries, restaurants and night clubs take on a carnival atmosphere. Further south on Congress is the Colorado River, with Lamar Park along its waterfront. Across the river and west is Zilker Park, offering nature and garden centres, a spring-fed swimming pool, and hiking, biking and canoeing trails.

Red River Street runs a few blocks east of I-35, leading north to the **Lyndon B. Johnson Library and Museum**. Films, exhibits, and memorabilia, including his Lincoln limousine, recall the man who became president when John F. Kennedy was assassinated. Johnson's wife, Lady Bird, donated land for the **National Wildflower Research Center**, helping to preserve and propagate special plants. Although most visitors know *The Yellow Rose of Texas*, the bluebonnet is the state flower.

Drivers may follow I-35 south to San Antonio, perhaps visiting New Braunfels for its German heritage, Texas style. Alternatively, take scenic US290 west to Johnson City for the **LBJ Ranch** and **LBJ National Historic Park** before following US281 south.

San Antonio

Settled over a century before its Texan counterparts, San Antonio de Valero began in 1718 as a Franciscan mission and *presidio* (fort), named after the Viceroy of Mexico. The Spanish Government forbade commerce with British colonies, maintaining the ban with the fledgling United States of America. The 1821 Mexican Revolution reversed the embargo, promoting trade and enticing Americans to the scarcely settled land. By then the abandoned mission's name was *Alamo*, Spanish for cottonwood tree. The rest, as they say, is history.

Today the **Alamo** remembers the 187 men who held this fortified mission against 5,000, knowing no quarter would be offered. Each defender took nine attackers, the remainder being mopped up by Sam Houston at San Jacinto. Displays in the museum/memorial trace events leading up to the battle. Embellished versions are available at the nearby Plaza Theater of Wax, while the IMAX Theater presents 'The Price of Freedom'.

San Antonio blends American and Hispanic cultures, **River Walk** being commonly known as Paseo del Río. The redeveloped San Antonio riverfront bustles with shoppers by day and revelers at night. The Hertzburg Circus Museum and Arneson Theatre are along the southern section, the latter seating the audience across the river from the stage. Downtown Hispanic heritage is evident at the **Spanish Governor's Palace** and San Fernando Cathedral.

Maps available from the Alamo Plaza visitor centre include the **Missions of**

South Padre Island off the Gulf Coast of Texas

San Antonio historical trail. First comes Mission Nuestra Señora la Purisima Concepcion, with original wall paintings from the Spanish colonial era. Next is Mission San Jose y San Miguel de Aguayo, 'Queen of the Missions', with restored chapel and outbuildings recreating the mission period. Mission San Juan Capistrano includes the original chapel and the remnants of a larger church which was never completed. Remains of the 1740 irrigation aqueduct are seen at Mission San Francisco de la Espada.

Returning to San Antonio, the **Hemisfair Plaza** was site of the city's 250th anniversary celebrations, holding the 1968 World's Fair. The **Institute of Texan Cultures** highlights the Lone Star State's diverse ethnic input, while the **Mexican Cultural Institute** is dedicated to Central and South American heritage and contemporary art. To find the plaza, head for the 750ft **Tower of the Americas**, with two revolving restaurants and an observation deck.

Brackenridge Park is north of city centre on Broadway. San Antonio River winds through the park, which offers fish-filled pools, a Japanese Tea Garden, entertainment at the Gardens Theater, a golf course, and for youngsters, a skyride, scale model train, and zoological gardens with aquarium. Texas flora and fauna are among natural history exhibits at the Witte Memorial Museum. The **Botanic Gardens** are east from the park on Funston, just before Fort Houston, which has a medical and military museum. The **San Antonio Museum of Art** is just west of Broadway on Jones. Residing in the old Lone Star Brewery overlooking the San Antonio River, there is plenty of space to exhibit its eclectic collection of American, European, Asian and pre-Columbian works.

Sea World of Texas is home to Shamu and friends. Found west on US90 then north on SR151, the theme park combines the best of Sea World San Diego and Cypress Gardens Florida, with a homespun Texan touch. Visitors will find that shows and attractions are constantly updated — Sea World's philosophy involves keeping two steps ahead of the competition.

Corpus Christi

Corpus Christi is an important deep-water port and one of Texas' most popular coastal resort cities. Those who want culture with their sun and sand will find plenty at **Bayfront Arts and Science Park**. Beachcombers should visit Corpus Christi Museum, as among natural history exhibits are examples of local shells. Musicals and Corpus Christi symphony are presented at the Bayfront Plaza Auditorium, while theatrical productions take place at Harbor Playhouse. Add an art museum, eight historic houses, the interesting **International Kite Museum** and excellent **Museum of Oriental Cultures** — then hit the beach.

Padre Island National Seashore preserves 80 miles of pristine barrier island beach, while either end offers typical seaside diversions. Collecting shells and driftwood within the national seashore is allowed (but not historic artifacts). There are primitive campsites along the island, so guests may play being Robinson Crusoe. North on SR35 leads to **Aransas National Wildlife Refuge**, which in winter boasts the world's largest population of whooping cranes. Return to Corpus Christi, perhaps enjoying an excursion cruise or another taste of the seafood before heading inland.

Up the Rio Grande

When travelling from Corpus Christi to Laredo consider a short detour south to **Kingsville**. Kings Ranch is the largest in Texas, occupying some 1,300 square miles and four counties. The ranch produced the Santa Gertrudis, the first strain of cattle developed in the western hemisphere. Guided tours include the ranch house and an old cowcamp. The King Ranch Museum and King Ranch Saddle Shop are downtown. SR141 west to US281 north returns to the main Laredo road at Alice, named after a King Ranch owner's daughter.

Laredo evokes a south-of-the-border image, and if not for the Rio Grande one might wonder where this city stopped and Mexican Nuevo Laredo began. The American side offers the **Nuevo Santander Museum** on Laredo Junior College campus, formerly Fort McIntosh. The museum's four buildings look at regional life of times past and regional military history. The **Museum of the Republic of the Rio Grande** recalls border disputes and revolutionaries who added local spice during the 1840s.

Drivers should leave their cars behind when crossing to **Nuevo Laredo**. Foreign visitors must have a multiple entry US visa, but Mexico rarely requires a visa or special paperwork when visiting a border town. Nuevo Laredo offers bargain basement shopping, and eat where the locals dine for real Mexican cuisine.

By rail to Mexico City

In Laredo, the adventurous can arrange an overnight train ride to **Mexico City**, leaving from either Nuevo Laredo or Ciudad Juarez, near El Paso. Pullman sleeper reservations should be made two weeks in advance (see Additional Information for address). For security, travel in groups and avoid public transport in Mexico City. The Zócalo (Plaza), National Palace, and Alameda area will fully occupy a day or two, Chapultapec Park and Paseo de la Reforma another. Excursions can include the Teotihuacán Pyramids, the mountainside silver city of Taxco, and seaside resort of Acapulco, where imperial Spanish treasure ships unloaded their Pacific plunder.

From Laredo follow US83 northwest, picking up US227 for Eagle Pass and **Del Rio**. Val Verde Winery is the oldest in Texas, producing a selection of table wines and a well received tawny port. Border crossings to Ciudad Acuña are easy, with Avenida Hidalgo, the main shopping street, straight across the bridge. Having returned to the US, boat rentals and other facilities are available at the nearby Amistad International Reservoir, where the Rio Grande is joined by the Devils and Pecos River.

Continue west on US90 to **Langtry** for the **Judge Roy Bean Visitor Center**, where the larger than life judge was 'Law West of the Pecos'. This free and ✳ fascinating centre includes his perfectly preserved courthouse, which doubled as a bar and billiard hall. Dioramas depict how justice was administered and law kept in a highly personalized fashion, where the unruly found their

court fine included, 'a round of drinks for the jury!' Adjacent grounds offer an introduction to cacti and other desert-dwelling plants of western Texas.

Big Bend National Park is south of US90 at Marathon along US385, passing the park visitor centre at Panther Junction. Accommodation at Chisos Mountain Lodge within the park must be booked well in advance, with back-up lodging at Marathon, Study Butte, Terlingua and Lajitas. Hundreds of miles of trails traverse the rugged wilderness, plus several old tracks for four-wheel drive enthusiasts to explore. Scenic paved roads lead to Rio Grande Village for Boquillas Canyon and to Cottonwood/Santa Elena Canyon. Between are the Chisos Mountains, with scenic turnouts named after local features, such as Burro Mesa or Mule Ears. Watch for mule deer, pronghorn antelope and the elusive *javelina*, the local wild boar.

For an in-depth look at the Rio Grande gorge, take El Camino del Rio, the river road, SR170 west from Study Butte. Normally quiet Terlingua gets crowded the first Saturday in November during the International Championship Chili Cookoffs, when most 'spirits' in this mining ghost town are rye whiskey or tequila. From Presidio US67 returns north to Marfa and civilization. The scenic route to El Paso involves driving up SR17 to **Fort Davis**, where the original frontier fort is now a national historic site, complete with costumed volunteers. SR118 leads over the Davis Mountains, passing McDonald Observatory atop Mount Locke en route to westbound I-10.

Watches go back an hour at **El Paso**, the oldest settlement in Texas. Nestled beneath the Franklin Mountains, **Scenic Drive** off Mesa street northwest of

Mexican embroiderer 'South of the Border'

(opposite) The Guadalupe Mountains

downtown offers excellent views across the Rio Grande Valley to Ciudad Juarez, Mexico's fourth largest city. Also behind the city, Fort Bliss Museum is a replica of the original adobe fortification within Fort Bliss.

Whenever a documentary films Mexicans illegally crossing into America, the footage is invariably shot along the El Paso border. The **Border Patrol Museum** examines this phenomenon, a fact of life in El Paso. **Chamizal National Monument** commemorates the friendly Mexican-American border, despite the time when the Rio Grande altered course, 'moving' Mission Nuestra Señora de la Concepcion into Texas.

El Paso has a strong Hispanic and Native American heritage, especially evident in **Ysletta** to the southeast. The Tigua welcome visitors to their adobe pueblo, and guests will find native arts and crafts, plus a restaurant serving Tigua specialities. The reconstructed Ysletta Mission was founded in 1681.

Mexican Ciudad Juarez boasts some fine missions and museums in addition to the shopping and Mexican cuisine. A tour from El Paso simplifies border crossings and access to widespread places of interest.

Northern Texas and Southern New Mexico

From El Paso, US62 returns eastward past **Guadalupe Mountains National Park**. Once Apache hunting grounds, the wildlife is still there, awaiting hardy hikers who penetrate this remote wilderness. Several roads lead into the foothills, providing trailheads for hikers and access to historic ranches and scenic canyons. Visitor centres at Frijole and McKittrick Canyon offer maps and information, and may remind guests to put their watch ahead an hour for Central Time.

The Guadalupe Mountains are remnants of 250 million-year-old Capital Reef, created when this area was sea floor, explaining another 'local' phenomenon. The **Carlsbad Caverns National Park**, located in New Mexico between El Paso and the Texas Panhandle, is one of the world's foremost cave networks. The caverns were born when water percolated through limestone, creating vast underground rooms filled with fantastic shapes coloured by metallic oxides. The Blue Tour descends from the natural entrance on a three-mile meander, while the Red Tour takes the elevator to portions accessible by wheelchair, including the 'basement cafeteria'. Both tours cost the same, and include egress via the elevator, although nothing prevents visitors walking out. At dusk, apart from cold wintry evenings, the famed bats emerge as a gyrating cloud of darkness. By day bats hide in caves off-limits to visitors, with little chance of accidentally meeting one. The town of Carlsbad provides accommodation, dining, tourist amusements, and a prairie dog town in nearby Living Desert State Park.

Continue on US62 into the **Texas Panhandle** to Brownfield, then US380 east to Post, founded by cereal king C. W. Post. Take US84 north, pausing to enjoy scenic views back over the local bluffs. The massive pancake of land disappearing northwards is the Great Plains, ending in Canada. Closer to hand Lubbock is geared more for oil and agriculture than tourists, but burrowing owls and ground squirrels can be found sharing the underground tenements of Prairie Dog Town in MacKenzie State Park. The **Ranching Heritage Cente** at Texas Tech is a collection of thirty historic buildings depicting life in Panhandle Texas.

I-27 makes a fast route north, but do not bypass Canyon. The **Panhandle-Plains Historical Museum** traces the local area from earliest times, including a reconstructed pioneer town. Follow signs for **Palo Duro Canyon State Park** east on SR217, where its vast crevice suddenly appears, swallowing visitors into a grand land of colourfully eroded sandstone shapes. Scenic drives and walks are supplemented on summer evenings by Paul Green's musical *Texas* in the Pioneer Amphitheatre.

Although oil and helium are important in **Amarillo**'s economy, some 600,000 head of cattle still pass through their livestock auction each year. Auctions are usually active early in the week, with Tuesdays the busiest. The chamber of commerce is helpful in obtaining tickets for *Texas* or arranging Western-style horseback trips to the Palo Dura rim, some including meals from a chuckwagon. Amarillo is the world's largest supplier of helium, cashing in on its discovery in 1968, hence the International Helium Timecapsule buried outside the Discovery Center.

Oklahoma

Formerly Indian Territory, one bright spring day in 1889 the plains became suddenly alive with settlers scrambling for parcels of land. The reason — members of the Five Civilized Tribes had lost their land by fighting for the Confederacy. The outcome was that Oklahoma City became a tent town of 10,000 by sundown. Not everyone waited for the official start, and Oklahoma's nickname is the Sooner State, after those arriving 'sooner' than they should have.

Take I-40 east towards Oklahoma City, detouring south on US281 for **Anadarko**. Home of the Apache, Kiowa and Comanche, the Indian Arts and Crafts Board maintain the free and informative **Southern Plains Indian Museum and Crafts Center**. Also of interest is the National Indian Hall of Fame and **Indian City USA**, which recreates several Plains Indian villages. While in Anadarko check events, as several powwows are held annually and Indian City USA often holds celebrations for guests. Those enjoying scenic US281 can return north to Binger, picking up SR37 east and then US81 north across the Canadian River.

Much **Oklahoma City** wealth stems from oil, and even the **State Capitol** has a well. Just south the Oklahoma Historical Society's **State History Museum** shows which tribes were where and when. The nearby Harn Homestead and 1889er Museum, situated on the former estate of a land agent who investigated claim disputes, recall the great land run. Yet further south are **Myriad Gardens**, set amid the business district. Pride of the gardens is Crystal Bridge, a seven-storey conservatory recreating a tropical rainforest.

Oklahoma City is justly proud of its **National Cowboy Hall of Fame and Western Heritage Center**. The museum complex remembers both real cowboys and big screen heroes, like Gene Autry, Roy Rogers and John Wayne. Native Americans are well represented, as is that famous Oklahoma son Will Rogers. The museum displays art works by his hero and friend, C.M. Russell,

Into and Around Oklahoma City

Will Rogers World Airport offers good domestic and growing international connections. Free hotel shuttles often supplement airport transportation services, with major car rentals at both airport and city. The grid pattern extends beyond downtown, interrupted by the State Capitol and occasionally by the excellent freeway network. Numbered streets run east-west, named roads and avenues north-south.

among others. The complex has a western streetfront and buildings, including that plains peculiarity, the sod house.

Other places of interest within Oklahoma City include the **Kirkpatrick Center**, combining education with recreation. The Softball Hall of Fame is northeast near Lincoln Park, the Kirkpatrick Center, and **Oklahoma City Zoo**. Oklahoma Heritage Center is the restored home of Judge R.A. Hefner, and its top floor hosts the Oklahoma Hall of Fame. West of the town is **Enterprise Square USA**, a high-tech hands-on centre teaching the American free-enter-

prise system.

Like Amarillo, auctions are busiest on early weekdays at the Oklahoma National Stockyards. Visitors dressing up for the rodeo will find Western clothing and boots available from several establishments, including Langson's on West Commerce or Cattleman's on Agnew Ave, while Indian art and jewelry are also popular. The State Fairgrounds hold a bevy of events including world-class horse shows. The cowboy's favourite will always be November's **World Championship Quarter Horse Show**, with other dates for Appaloosa and Morgans. The State Fair is an other major event, while Native Americans regularly hold 'powwows', such as June's Red Earth Native American Cultural Festival. *Key Magazine* and *Downtowner* list restaurants and nightspots, with the Civic Center presenting a mixture of classic, pop, and ballet.

Tulsa is also strong culturally, but they had to do *something* with all that oil money. Boasting headquarters or branch offices of most oil conglomerates, the Tulsa skyline is neatly encircled by I-244 and I-444. The Performing Arts Center is heart of downtown, with other events held in the Tulsa State Fairgrounds at Expo Square. Catch a performance of the Rogers and Hammerstein musical *Oklahoma* west at nearby Prattville.

Gilcrease Museum alone would justify Tulsa's fame for fine museums. Brimming with Western Americana from pre-Columbian times until the late nineteenth century, they have an especially fine collection of Remington bronzes and also house the Tulsa County Historical Society Museum. See Italian Renaissance paintings and sculpture from the Kress Collection and other masterpieces at the **Philbrook Art Center**, a Renaissance Villa surrounded by formal gardens. Others include Fenster Museum of Jewish Art, and LaFortune North American Living Museum in Tulsa Zoological Park.

Woolaroc Museum is an interesting and educational oddity left by Frank Phillips, of Phillips Petroleum fame. For a popular day trip from Tulsa, take US75 north, exiting west along SR20 to Skiatook, then north again on SR11 and SR123 towards Bartlesville and the estate. Herds of Bison, elk and deer graze

Red Earth Indian Festival at Oklahoma

Will Rogers Memorial at Claremont

along the drive into the ranch, where carefully sequenced exhibits put south-western history in perspective. Part living history museum, partly a collection of curiosities, Woolaroc contrasts sharply with Phillips' real home on Cherokee Avenue in Bartlesville.

Return to Tulsa on US60 east to Nowata, picking up US169 south for Will Rogers Birthplace. Continue south to Claremore on SR88, where **Will Rogers Memorial** shows films and exhibits on one of America's most beloved men. Rogers State College Library houses the Lynn Riggs Memorial, whose *Green Grow the Lilacs* inspired the musical *Oklahoma*. Also in Claremore is the free Davis Gun Museum.

From Tulsa, head east on Muskogee Turnpike (toll) for Sallisaw. Diversions en route include **Muskogee**'s Five Civilized Tribes Museum and Fort Gibson. Nearby **Tahlequah** is especially rich in Native American Heritage, with **Tsa-La-Gi Indian Village** at Cherokee Heritage Center. From Tahlequah, SR82 makes a scenic route south past Eastern Oklahoma's fine lakes, a fishing and recreational paradise. **Sallisaw** has Sequoyah's Home, inventor of the Cherokee alphabet. Nearby is Robert S. Kerr Lake, with Sequoyah Wildlife Refuge on its western shore. Follow I-40 east for a new state.

Arkansas

The title 'Land of Opportunity' is no misnomer — where else can visitors search for diamonds in a state park and keep their finds? Start with the frontier and **Fort Smith National Historic Site**, a garrison built in case of Indian

uprising but used during the Civil War. Here is the courthouse of 'hanging' Judge Parker, who despite his name only strung up four miscreants a year. The Old Fort Museum on Rogers Avenue traces the town's growth. Follow US71 north to Fayetteville and Rogers, where scenic US62 leads into the **Ozark Mountains**. At Pea Ridge National Military Park, Union soldiers halted a

Confederate march on St Louis, retaining the strategic Missouri River.

Eureka Springs has a continuous holiday atmosphere, augmented by quaint Victorian homes around this health spa and resort. Springs are no longer medically fashionable, but the fresh mountain air soothes and relaxes like no tablets can. Blue Springs is still open to the public, while the Victorian Sampler Tour Home is an excellent example of the old resort's architecture. Always a deeply religious area, temperance campaigner Carrie Nation last spoke here, while the **Great Passion Play**, Bible Museum and several inspira-

tional craft centres are on Statue Road, east of Eureka Springs. Caverns in the region include Onyx Cave Park and Cosmic Cavern, the latter boasting a large underground lake.

Harrison is more rustic than Eureka Springs, where cartoon characters from *Lil' Abner* spring to life at **Dogpatch USA** just south. Local tour operators offer rafting and camping trips along scenic **Buffalo National River**. Follow US6 east as it threads through the Ozark Mountains, taking either SR14 or SR south to Mountain View. **Blanchards Springs Caverns** on SR14 are perhaps the Ozark's finest, with several tours graded according to visitors' abilities.

Shining star of Mountain View is the **Ozark Folk Center**, a living cultural complex preserving local arts, crafts, music and oral history. Artisans utili

ditional methods, and their handicrafts are available in the well-stocked
t shop. May to October is full of activity, with winter quieter apart from
ristmas and special events.

SR5 south meanders past Herber Springs, a lakeside spa resort, on its way
Little Rock. Start a tour with the **State Capitol**, laid out like the Nation's
pitol but hewn from Arkansas marble and granite. City Hall, the Conven-
n Center and **Old State House** are nearer the Arkansas River. The former
pitol is furnished in period style, and evidences the southern heritage of
kansas. Main Street is four blocks east of Broadway, with Metro Center Mall
her side of East Capitol Avenue. **Arkansas Territorial Restoration** is one of
e renovated historical areas comprising the Quapaw Quarter. Of the thir-
n structures, the Woodruff Home Complex is particularly interesting. It
ntains the print shop and residence of William E. Woodruff, whose *Arkansas
zette* is the oldest paper west of the Mississippi River. Other activities
clude cruising along the Arkansas River, touring Victorian Villa Marre, and
joying MacArthur Park with its Science and Arts Centers.

From Little Rock I-30 west returns directly to Dallas, but allow time to
wind at **Hot Springs National Park**. Foreseeing a need to preserve against
croaching tourism, the federal government made the area a preserve in
32, long before the park service was born. The small city of Hot Springs
ers golf courses, waxwork museums and alligator farms, while the park
asts scenic walks, bubbling bathhouses and an observation tower. Hot
rings is a perfect place to unwind after travelling — enjoy a walk then relax
a spa. Masseurs will remove any remaining kinks.

When returning to Dallas, remember to visit **Crater of Diamonds State
rk** near Murfreesboro. Although many scoff, in 1975 one visitor walked
ay with the 16.37 carat Amarillo Starlight. Anything is possible in 'The
nd of Opportunity'.

Additional Information

State Tourism Bureaux

Arkansas Parks & Tourism
1 Capitol Mall
Little Rock, AR 72201
☎ 800-643-8383
or 501-371-1511/7777

*Oklahoma Tourism &
Recreation*
500 Will Rogers Bldg
Oklahoma City, OK
73105-4492
☎ 800-652-6552
or 405-521-2409

Texas Tourism Division
PO Box 12728
Austin, TX 78711
☎ 800-888-8839
or 512-462-9191

Regional Information

Austin CVB
PO Box 2990
Austin, TX 78769
☎ 800-888-8287
or 512-474-5171

Corpus Christi CVB
1201 N Shoreline
PO Box 2664
Corpus Christi, TX 78403
☎ 800-678-6232
or 512-882-5603

Dallas CVB
1201 Elm St, Suite 2000
Dallas, TX 75270
☎ 800-752-9222
or 214-746-6677

El Paso CVB
1 Civic Center Plaza
El Paso, TX 79999
☎ 800-351-6024
or 915-534-0600

Eureka Springs COC
Auditorium Bldg, Box 551
Eureka Springs, AR 72632
☎ 501-253-8737

Fort Worth CVB
Water Gardens Place
100 E 15th St, Suite 400
Fort Worth, TX 76102
☎ 800-433-5757
or 817-336-8791

Hot Springs COC
Box 1500
Hot Springs, AR 71902
☎ 800-643-1570
or 501-321-1700

Houston CVB
3300 Main St
Houston, TX 77002
☎ 800-231-7799
or 713-523-5050

Little Rock CVB
Box 3222 Statehouse Plaza
Little Rock, AR 72203
☎ 501-376-4781

Oklahoma City CVB
One Sante Fe Plaza
Oklahoma City, OK 73102
☎ 800-225-5652
or 405-278-8900

San Antonio CVB
210 S Alamo, PO Box 2277
San Antonio, TX 78298
☎ 800-447-3372
or 512-270-8700

Tulsa CVB
616 S. Boston
Tulsa, OK 74119
☎ 918-585-1201

Local Events

Check locally for exact dates

January
Cotton Bowl Football &
    Parade
Dallas, TX

February-March
Houston Livestock Show
    & Rodeo
Astrodome
Houston, TX

April
Arkansas Folk Festival
Mountain View, AR

Fiesta San Antonio
San Antonio, TX

April-May
Houston International
    Festival
Houston, TX

May
Cinco de Mayo
San Antonio, TX

June
Chisholm Trail Roundup
Fort Worth, TX

Red Earth Native Ameri-
    can Cultural Festival
Oklahoma City, OK

June-August
Oklahoma (musical)
41st St, Prattville
Nr Tulsa, OK

July
Texas Jazz Festival
Corpus Christi, TX

August
American Indian Expositic
Anadarko, OK

Tulsa Pow Wow
Tulsa, OK

Texas Folklife
San Antonio, TX

September
Oklahoma State Fair
Oklahoma City, OK

Cherokee National Holiday
Tahlequah, OK

Old-time Fiddlers Championship
Mountain View, AR

September-October
Texas State Fair
Dallas, TX

October
Bayfest
Corpus Christi, TX

Grand National Morgan Horse Show
Oklahoma City, OK

Tulsa State Fair
Tulsa, OK

Championship Appaloosa Horse Show
Oklahoma City, OK

October-November
Texas Renaissance
Plantersville
Houston, TX

November
Championship Quarter Horse Show
Oklahoma City, OK

Original Ozark Folk Festival
Eureka Springs, AR

Will Rogers Days
Claremore, OK

Places of Interest

Anadarko, OK
Indian City USA
Box 695, SR8
Anadarko, OK 73005
☎ 405-247-5661
Open: 9am-5pm, 9am-pm summer
Indian village, museum, events, gifts

Southern Plains Indian Museum
Box 749, US 62
Anadarko, OK 73005
☎ 405-247-6221
Open: 9am-5pm Tue-Sat, 1-5pm Sun, open Monday in summer
Free, gifts, museum, crafts

Austin, TX
LBJ Library & Museum
2313 Red River
Austin, TX 78705
☎ 512-482-5279
Open: 9am-5pm
Free, exhibits, &

Texas State Capitol
11th St & Congress Ave
Austin, TX 78711
☎ 512-463-0063
Open: 7am-11pm, chambers 7am-5pm
Free, tours, &

Bartlesville, OK
Woolaroc
SR123
Bartlesville, OK 74005
☎ 918-336-0307
Open: 10am-5pm Tue-Sun
Home, museum, gifts, &

Big Bend, TX
Big Bend NP
C/O Supervisor (HQ)
National Park Concessions (lodging)
Big Bend National Park
TX 79834
☎ 915-477-2251 (HQ)
915-477-2291 (lodging)
Open: 8am-5pm, 8am-7pm summers
Lodge, camp, picnic, hike, &

Canyon, TX
Palo Duro Canyon SP
Rt 2, Box 285
Canyon, TX 79015
☎ 806-488-2227 (park)
806-655-2181 (Texas drama)
Open: 8am-10pm, 'Texas'

nightly mid-Jun to late Aug except Sun
Camp, picnic, mini-railroad, amphitheatre

Carlsbad, NM
Carlsbad Caverns NP
3225 National Parks Hwy
Carlsbad, NM 88220
☎ 505-785-2232
Open: 8am-5.30pm, 8am-7pm Memorial-Labor Day
Cave tours, 'bat evenings', food, gifts, &

Claremore, OK
Will Rogers Memorial
W Will Rogers Blvd & SR88
Claremore, OK 74017
☎ 948-341-0719
Open: 8am-5pm. Free
Rogers' memorabilia, gifts, &

Dallas/Ft Worth Metroplex, TX
Dallas Zoo
621 E Clarendon Dr.
Dallas, TX 75203
☎ 214-946-5154
Open: 9am-5pm, 9am-6pm Memorial-Labor Day
Zoo, food, gifts, &

Kimbell Art Museum
3333 Camp Bowie Blvd.
Fort Worth, TX 76107-2744
☎ 817-332-8451
Open: 10am-5pm Tue-Sat, 11am-5pm Sun
Food, gifts, tours, &

Mesquite Championship Rodeo
1818 Rodeo St
Mesquite, TX 75150
☎ 214-285-8777
Open: 8am-10pm Fri & Sat Apr-Sep
Rodeo, petting zoo, food, drink

Old City Park
1717 Gano
Dallas, TX 75215
☎ 214-421-5141

Open: 10am-4pm Tue-
Sat, 1.30-4.30pm Sun
Food, gifts, tours

Six Flags over Texas
PO Box 191, I-30 and SR360
Arlington, TX 76010
☎ 817-840-8900
Open: daily summer,
weekends spring & fall
Rides, gifts, food, ᜓ

The Sixth Floor Museum
411 Elm St
Dallas, TX 75202
☎ 214-653-6666
Open: 10am-5pm, 10am-
6pm Sat
Video & JFK memora-
bilia, ᜓ

Southfork Ranch
PO Box 863773, FM 2551
Plano, TX 75086
☎ 214-442-6536
Open: 9am-6pm Mon-
Thu, 9am-7pm Fri-Sun
Tours, food, gifts

El Paso, TX
*Tigua Indian Reservation/
Ysletta Pueblo & Mission*
119 Old Pueblo Rd
El Paso, TX 79902
☎ 915-859-7913
Open: 9am-5pm Mon-Sat,
9am-3.30pm Sun
Gifts, food, tours, parts ᜓ

Fort Davis, TX
Fort Davis NHS
SR17
Fort Davis, TX 79734
☎ 915-426-3225
Open: 8am-5pm
Fort, museum

Galveston, TX
Bishop's Palace
1402 Broadway
Galveston, TX 77550
☎ 409-762-2475
Open: 10am-5pm Memo-
rial-Labor Day
Tours

Hot Springs, AR
Hot Springs NP
PO Box 1860
Hot Springs, AR 71902
☎ 501-624-3383
Open: centre 9am-5pm
Tower, bathhouse, boat,
gifts, food, ᜓ

Houston, TX
Astroworld
9001 Kirby Dr
Houston, TX 77054
☎ 713-799-1234/3291
Open: 11am-late summer,
10am-late weekends
Sept-May
Rides, food, gifts, ᜓ

Bayou Bend
PO Box 130157
1 Westcott St
Houston, TX 77007
☎ 713-529-8773
Open: 10am-2.45pm Tue-
Fri, 10am-1.15pm Sat,
closed August
Mansion, gardens, fine arts

*Lyndon B. Johnson Space
Center*
Public Service, Code Ap4
Houston, TX 77058
☎ 713-483-4321
Open: 9am-4pm
Free, food, gifts, ᜓ

Sam Houston Park
1100 Bagby
Houston, TX 77002
☎ 713-655-1912
Open: 10am-4pm Mon-
Sat, 1-5pm Sun
Park, Texas History
Museum, food, gifts

*Sam Houston Memorial
Museum*
1836 Sam Houston Ave
Huntsville, TX 77340
☎ 800-289-0389
or 409-294-1832
Open: 9am-5pm Tue-Sun.
Free
Museum, homestead,
outbuildings, parts ᜓ

San Jacinto Battlefield SHS
3800 Park Rd
Baytown, TX 77571
☎ 713-479-2421
Open: 10am-6pm
Memorial, museum

Langtry, TX
*Judge Roy Bean Visitor
Center*
PO Box 160
Langtry, TX 78871
☎ 915-291-3340
Open: 8am-5pm. Free
Saloon, dioramas, cactus
garden, parts ᜓ

Laredo, TX
*Mexican National Railways
Express to Mexico City*
PO Box 3508
Laredo, TX 78004
☎ 512-722-9895
or 800-228-3225
Sleeper & first class tickets

Little Rock, AR
Arkansas State Capitol
W Capitol Ave
Little Rock, AR 72201
☎ 501-682-5080
Open: 7am-4.30pm Mon-
Fri, 10am-4pm weekends
Free, tours, ᜓ

*Arkansas Territorial
Restoration*
214 E. Third St
Little Rock, AR 72203
☎ 501-371-2348
Open: 9am-5pm Mon-Sat,
1-5pm Sun
Tour homes

Mountain View, AR
Ozark Folk Center
PO Box 500
Mountain View, AR 7256●
☎ 501-269-3851
Open: 10am-5pm daily
Apr-Oct & special events
Crafts, gifts, auditorium, ᜓ

Oklahoma City, OK
*National Cowboy Hall of
  Fame*
1700 NE 63rd
Oklahoma City, OK 73111
☎ 405-478-2250
Open: 9am-5pm, ex-
tended summers
Tours, gifts, ♿

*Oklahoma State History
  Museum*
2100 N Lincoln
Oklahoma City, OK 73105
☎ 405-521-2491
Open: 8am-5pm Mon-Sat
except holidays
Free, tours, gifts, ♿

San Antonio, TX
Alamo
PO Box 5299
300 Alamo Plaza
San Antonio, TX 78205
☎ 512-225-1391
Open: 9am-5.30pm Mon-
Sat, 10am-5.30pm Sun. Free
Mission-fort, tours,
books, ♿

Institute of Texas Cultures
PO Box 1226
Hemisfair Plaza
San Antonio, TX 78294
☎ 512-226-7651
Open: 9am-5pm Tue-Sun
Free, Texas gifts, ♿

Mission San Jose
6539 San Jose Drive &
  Mission Rd
San Antonio, TX 78214
☎ 512-229-4770
Open: 9am-5pm, 9am-
6pm summer

Sea World of Texas
10500 Sea World Dr
San Antonio, TX 78251
☎ 800-422-7989
or 512-523-3611
Open: 10am-10pm
Memorial-Labor Day,
weekends Mar-May &
Sep-Nov
Shows, exhibits, food,
gifts, ♿

Spanish Governor's Palace
105 Plaza de Armes
San Antonio, TX 78205
☎ 512-224-0601
Open: 9am-5pm Mon-Sat,
10am-5pm Sun Tours

Tahlequah, OK
Cherokee Heritage Center
Box 515
Tahlequah, OK 74465
☎ 918-456-6195
Open: 10am-5pm Mon-
Sat, 1-5pm Sun, extended
summers
Indian village, homes,
outdoor drama, gifts

Tulsa, OK
Gilcrease Museum
1400 Gilcrease Museum Rd
Tulsa, OK 74127
☎ 918-582-3122
Open: 9am-5pm Mon-Sat,
1-5pm Sun
Indian & Western art,
gifts, ♿

Philbrook Art Center
2727 S. Rockford Rd
Tulsa, OK 74152
☎ 918-749-7941
Open: 10am-5pm Tue-
Sat, 1-5pm Sun
European & Indian art,
gifts, ♿

8
THE GREAT PLAINS

The gently rolling Great Plains sweep down from the Rocky Mountains to the mighty Mississippi, ranging from central Canada to the Texas panhandle. Once filled with thundering herds of buffalo and the proud Plains Indians, the coming of the railroad foretold their doom. Shanty towns sprang up around gold mines and railheads, and after a brief but bawdy period of lawlessness the settlers came, replacing the brand with barbed wire.

Yet the Great Plains are not entirely tamed, and modern cities remember their colourful past. Cowboys still attend the world's largest outdoor rodeo at Cheyenne, while gambling at Deadwood still tests skill and luck, a hundred years after Wild Bill Hickok was gunned down playing poker.

Denver, Colorado

Denver rests squarely on the Great Plains, yet within easy reach of the Rocky Mountains. Denver's ideal situation has made it *the* city between Chicago and the Pacific Coast, and its circumstances have occasioned its outlook. From the late 1850s, 49ers were returning east from California while many easterners were heading west. Denver is a unique blend of Yankee ingenuity and Californian lifestyle.

❋   Commence sightseeing at the massive, golden domed **State Capitol**. The altitude engraved on the western entrance's thirteenth step supports Denver' title of 'mile high city'. Tours are informative, afterwards climb the ninety

---

The Great Plains in Brief

From 'mile high' Denver, Colorado, visit fabled Cheyenne and old Fort Laramie en route to the fabulous Black Hills of South Dakota. Follow the Mormon and Oregon Trails through Nebraska to notorious Dodge City, where Wyatt Earp kept the law, western style. Return to Denver via Colorado Springs. Options include the super scenic Rocky Mountain Loop (Chapter 9).

Two weeks should be sufficient; if time is less stick to Colorado and Cheyenne. The Great Plains can be combined with the southwest tour i desired. The best travelling time is June to September, with rodeos, count fairs, and other activities peaking around 4 July. Summer days are gener ally hot and sunny, evenings cool.

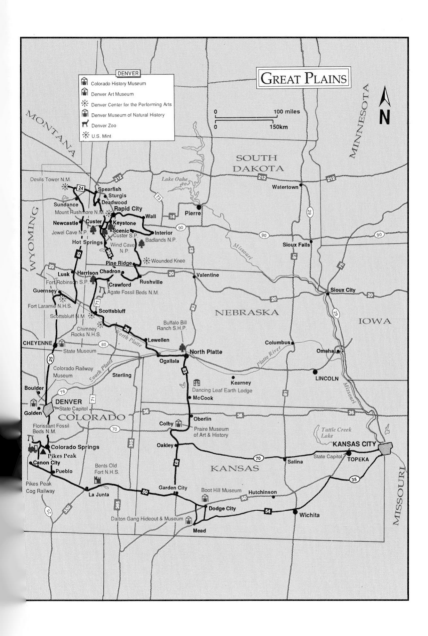

DENVER
- 🏛 Colorado History Museum
- 🏛 Denver Art Museum
- ☀ Denver Center for the Performing Arts
- 🏛 Denver Museum of Natural History
- 🐕 Denver Zoo
- ☀ U.S. Mint

GREAT PLAINS

0   100 miles
0   150km

N

MONTANA

SOUTH DAKOTA

MINNESOTA

Lake Oahe

Watertown

Devils Tower N.M.

Spearfish
Sturgis
Deadwood
Sundance
Mount Rushmore N.M.   Rapid City
Wall   Pierre

WYOMING

Newcastle   Custer   Keystone
Jewel Cave N.P.   Scenic   Interior
Hot Springs   Custer S.P.
Wind Cave   Badlands N.P.
N.P.

Sioux Falls

Pine Ridge   Wounded Knee

Lusk Harrison Chadron
Fort Robinson S.P.   Valentine
Guernsey   Crawford   Rushville
Agate Fossil Beds N.M.

Sioux City

Fort Laramie N.H.S.
Scottsbluff

Scottsbluff N.M.   NEBRASKA   IOWA

Chimney   Buffalo Bill
Rocks N.H.S.   Ranch S.H.P.
CHEYENNE   Lewellen   Columbus
State Museum   Omaha

North Platte
Colorado Railway   Ogallala
Museum   Sterling   LINCOLN
Boulder   Kearney
Dancing Leaf Earth Lodge
DENVER   McCook
Golden   State Capitol
COLORADO
Florissant Fossil   Colby   Oberlin
Beds N.M.   Prairie Museum   Tuttle Creek
of Art & History   Lake   KANSAS CITY
Colorado Springs   Oakley
Pikes Peak   State Capitol TOPEKA
Canon City   Bents Old   Salina
Pueblo   Fort N.H.S.   KANSAS
Pikes Peak
Cog Railway   La Junta   Garden City Boot Hill Museum Hutchinson
Dalton Gang Hideout & Museum   Wichita
Dodge City
Mead

MISSOURI

Into and Around Denver

Denver International Airport, 18 miles east of the city, is scheduled to open during 1993. Meanwhile, Stapelton International Airport, 8 miles northeast of Denver, continues to greet air arrivals. Amtrak east-west rail connections are excellent from Denver, the westerly route being particularly scenic. In winter the Rio Grande Ski Train provides weekend passenger service to Winter Park. Union Train Station is on 17th Street and Denver Bus Terminal on 19th and Arapaho; local buses leave from the 16th Street Mall. Car parks are relatively inexpensive, while parking meters are scarce and offending vehicles clamped with the 'Denver Boot'.

Streets run north-south and avenues east-west except downtown, where numbered streets go northwest-southeast and named streets northeast-southwest. Colfax Avenue passes through the government complex and alongside the visitor centre, marking the transition from diagonal streets to east-west. Speer Boulevard diagonally bisects Colfax — heading westerly on either connects with I-25, the primary route north or south from Denver. I-70, the major east-west route, runs to the north of Denver, and is reached quickly via I-25.

three steps to the dome for, weather permitting, an excellent view over Denver to the Rocky Mountains. Maps and tourist information is provided at a kiosk outside the Capitol and west on Colfax Avenue at the Denver Metro Convention and Visitor Bureau.

 Places of interest around the Capitol area include the restored Victorian **Molly Brown House**, home of the 'Unsinkable Molly Brown', survivor of the Titanic disaster. **Colorado History Museum** offers an excellent overview of Colorado past, while the **Denver Art Museum** building itself is considered a masterpiece. Inside is an eclectic collection of the world's art, including local flavour with the Native American works and western art. The adjacent **Byers-** **Evans House** is operated by the Colorado Historical Society, and tours link Denver's growth with several generations of the Evans family. A tour of the **US Mint** shows billions of cents being made, but forget free samples. Bars of Denver gold are on display, and the gift shop sells medals and special proof sets of coins. The Denver Firefighters Museum is across Colfax Avenue from the Mint, just west of the visitor centre.

The **Museum of Western Art** includes a collection of Remingtons and Russells, and for a fresh approach to visual and performing arts, experience the **Museum of Outdoor Arts**. The **Black American West Museum and Heritage Center** remembers a west forgotten by the movies and school books. The **Children's Museum of Denver** is both entertaining and educational while Elitch Gardens Amusement Park offers a floral-themed fun park, refreshing Water World, and child's sized Tiny Town. Everyone will enjoy the Denver Museum of Miniatures, Dolls and Toys on Gaylord and **Fourne Transportation Museum**, located in and around the former Denver Tramway Powerhouse building.

Culture has a front row seat at the **Denver Center for the Performing Art** Theatre, dance, symphony and opera punctuate the Denver social calenda

housed in a modern complex near the Convention Center. Numerous Denver clubs offer disco or live music — for a taste of the west try the country offerings of Grizzly Rose or Country Dinner Playhouse, with a musical revue before each performance. Culture within reach of Denver includes excellent theatre at Central City Opera House and the midsummer Colorado Shakespeare Theater in Boulder. Golden has family entertainment at Heritage Square Music Hall, while **Park of the Red Rocks**, west of Denver near Morrison, offers a summer concert series in a red sandstone setting. *The Dining Directory* and *What's Going On in Denver Tonight?* list special events and entertainment at Denver nightspots.

City Park, established in 1881, is home to **Denver Zoo**, near natural home to some 400 exotic species. At nearby **Denver Natural History Museum**, an IMAX Theatre and planetarium supplement the dioramas of Native Americans, natural history, Egyptian artifacts, and mineral displays. Also within City Park are a public golf course and bandstand for summer concerts. Budding botanists should visit the **Denver Botanic Gardens**.

Denver is justly proud of its parks and tree-lined streets. For a driving tour of upmarket Denver, go east on 17th Avenue Parkway from City Park. Turn right onto Monaco Street Parkway and right again onto 6th Avenue Parkway. The expanse of green north (right) on Williams Street is Cheesman Park, while the private Denver Country Club is due south. **Cherry Creek** and **Cherry Creek North** shopping malls are found where Speer Boulevard becomes 1st Avenue, east of the Denver Country Club. Both offer an 'upscale shopping and dining experience', with numerous specialty shops and boutiques to supplement the quality department stores.

Downtown Denver shopping includes **16th Street Mall** (watch for buses). **Tabor Center** on Lawrence has the unusual Bridge Market, while **Larimer Square** is the revitalized heart of old Denver's retail district. The gaily decorated structure on Auraria Parkway and 9th Street is **Tivoli**, which combines dining and shopping with themed exhibits in a former nineteenth-century brewery. Bargain hunters will find trivia and treasure at the Mile High and Dog Track Flea Markets.

Presents with a local flavour include Native American jewelry and art, western wear, and various items labelled 'Made in Colorado'. The Native American Trading Company is a leading source for Indian artifacts, a curio shop with museum quality gifts. Check out the *Denver Official Visitors Guide* or the galleries promoting local artists.

Outdoor enthusiasts enjoy the largest per capita collection of sporting goods outlets, and plenty of action, too. **Mile High Stadium** presents Denver Broncos football and Zephyrs baseball in their respective seasons, and the stadium is also open for tours. Bandimere Speedway has motor sports in summer, while downtown hosts the Texaco/Havoline Grand Prix of Denver in late August. Golfers can contact the Colorado Golf Resort Association for information on semi-private clubs, while the city operates six public courses. Denver presents the National Western Stock Show and Rodeo in mid-January. Colorado's downhill and cross-country skiing is legendary, many resorts being detailed in the next chapter.

A number of tour operators provide effortless sightseeing in the Denver environs. Gray Line Tours are extensive and well subscribed, while smaller

Denver skyline, with the Rockies in the background

The State Capitol, Denver

companies provide specialized trips, such as cycling down Mount Evans or a private horse-drawn carriage tour of Denver. Those without transportation will find several operators provide excursions within the Denver environs and to the Rocky Mountains.

Denver Environs

Connoisseurs of decades past drove to **Golden,** Colorado, even from Boston or San Diego, returning with a cache of Coors beer. Nowadays Coors is available everywhere — no excuse for not visiting **Coors Brewery**, one of the world's largest. Take Colfax Avenue west from Denver, following signs for Golden. The city grew up from placer mines along Clear Creek, a 'golden' era recalled at DAR Pioneer Museum, the **Colorado Railroad Museum**, and **Heritage Square**, an 1880s flavoured entertainment and shopping centre. Also in Golden are the interesting exhibits at the School of Mines Geology Museum. Western fun peaks during Buffalo Bill Days in mid-July. The great scout and showman is interred nearby on Lookout Mountain, with excellent views to complement **Buffalo Bill Memorial Museum and Grave**.

Boulder is a fun loving college town surrounded by serious research centres attracted by nearby University of Colorado. **Pearl Street Mall**, heart of Boulder, offers unparalleled people watching, riotous street performers, and pleasant shopping and dining. For formal entertainment, sample productions at the **Colorado Dance Festival**, **Colorado Music Festival**, and **Colorado Shakespeare Festival**. Each calendar varies, overlapping the last three weeks of July when the **Gilbert and Sullivan Festival** takes place.

Golden and Boulder may be visited separately, using Denver as a base, incorporated with the Rocky Mountain Scenic Loop (Chapter 9) or visited while heading north on the Great Plains tour. From Colorado, follow I-25 north for Cheyenne.

Wyoming

America's nineth largest state has the lowest population of any, hovering around the half million mark. Known as the 'Cowboy State', working and dude ranches are plentiful, but Wyoming is also the 'Equality State', where women could vote even during its territorial days. This tour encompasses the eastern plains, commencing with the capital.

Cheyenne sprang into being during 1867, when the Union Pacific Railroad came. The lawless period packed considerable excitement into a few short years, but by 1869 Cheyenne had become capital of Wyoming territory and eventually of the state. Gold from the Black Hills of Dakota came to Cheyenne on the Deadwood Stage, providing gold leaf for the State Capitol dome.

The state visitor centre off I-25 offers maps of state and town, plus information on current events. Largest of these is Cheyenne Frontier Days, held the last full week of July. Accommodation should be pre-booked, as some 300,000 visitors are attracted to Cheyenne. Frontier Days parades and rough and tumble 'Daddy of 'em All Rodeo' are complemented by downtown shootouts,

Indian dances, and plenty of entertainment, including an air show at nearby Warren Air Force Base.

The **Wyoming Capitol** tour offers a concise history of the state and Cheyenne. Look for hidden pictures in Mike Kopriva's mural, *Wyoming, the Land, the People*, and for fossils in the Italian marble flooring. Next visit the free **State Museum and Art Gallery** at the Barrett Building, which supplements well displayed memorabilia with western and local art. Now open to the public, former residents of **Historic Governor's Mansion** on East 21st Street include Nelly Tayloe Ross, first woman state governor in America.

Cheyenne's three main parks offer recreation with a slightly different focus. Holiday Park has Union Pacific engine No 4004 *Big Boy*, the largest steam locomotive in the world. Lions Park offers a golf course and other athletic facilities. Frontier Park hosts the Frontier Days' Daddy of 'em All Rodeo, and County Fair. The **Frontier Days Old West Museum** has a renowned collection of carriages and rodeo memorabilia dating back to 1897. Also within Cheyenne are the National First Day Cover Museum, which specializes in rare first edition stamps and original artwork, and the Wyoming animals of Wildlife Visitor Center.

Laramie is a popular day trip from Cheyenne. The University of Wyoming sports free geological, art, and anthropology museums. The **Wyoming Territorial Park** living history program recreates 1872 Laramie, including the much needed territorial prison. As the railroad terminus, Laramie was commonly referred to as 'Hell-on-Wheels'. Laramie Plains Museum is located in Edward Ivinson Mansion.

I-25 north from Cheyenne roughly parallels the first section of the old Deadwood Stage route. Turn east on US26 for Guernsey, where **Oregon Trail** wagons ruts may still be seen. Nearby Register Cliff has markings made by early passers-by, some from the 1840s. An uneasy truce existed between Indians and wagoners during that period, at first forestalled by US government annuities to the Sioux. **Fort Laramie National Historical Site** recalls how misunderstandings in 1854 occasioned the Grattan massacre, where thirty soldiers died in hostilities which did not end until decades later at Wounded Knee. Fort Laramie interpretive centre gift shop is well stocked with books on the Plains Indians.

From Fort Laramie follow US85 north for 154 miles (248 km), perhaps relaxing at Lusk or Newcastle before following SR585 to **Sundance. Crook County Museum** historical exhibits include the trial of Harry Longabaugh, the Sundance Kid. The name comes from Sundance Mountain, a Sioux ceremonial site. The museum gallery exhibits local artists' works. An 85-mile loop drive from Sundance encircles **Devils Tower National Monument** which featured prominently in the movie, *Close Encounters of the Third Kind*. Erosion has revealed this 867ft (264m) high volcanic plug. Visitors may walk around the base, but technical skills and equipment are required to ascend the tower.

South Dakota

The **Black Hills of South Dakota** are a mixture of wild mining towns, un bashed tourism, and superb recreation in a national forest environment. Follow I-90 east to the state welcome centre, and on to Spearfish, summer home to the **Black Hills Passion Play**, portraying Christ's final days.

Scenic Alternate US14 winds up **Spearfish Canyon** before dropping down into Lead. Pronounced 'leed' and derived from lode, as in vein of gold, Lead is a modern mining town straddling the Black Hills. A nearby chairlift raises visitors to Terry Peak, while the Black Hills Mining Museum takes them down into a simulated mine. The mother lead (lode) was in Homestake Gold Mine, one of the western hemisphere's largest mines and open for surface tours.

If Lead is too peaceful, try **Deadwood**. Wild Bill Hickok and Calamity Jane rest at Mount Moriah Cemetery alongside lesser known but equally colourful characters. Gambling is once again legal in Deadwood, with increasingly sophisticated casinos and innumerable nickel and quarter slot machines. Saloons are lively and local entertainment includes 'The Trial of Jack McCall', reenacting the final days of Wild Bill Hickok's murderer. **Adams Memorial Museum** portrays the area's fascinating history through a trove of memorabilia spread over three floors. Their informative and amusing video highlights local characters, including Potato Jonny, a diminutive Welsh miner with the golden touch, and cigar smoking Poker Alice. A horse and buggy ride, trip on the steam powered Deadwood Central Railroad, or tour of Broken Boot Gold Mine rounds off a busy day or two at Deadwood.

Poker Alice came from Sturgis, which in early August holds the **Black Hills Motorcycle Classic**. The hillside reverberates as innumerable motorcyclists, all on their very best behaviour, overflow from Sturgis into the surrounding countryside. Trouble is rare, the main difficulty being a shortage of campsites and accommodation in the northern Black Hills. Sturgis also holds a steam rally in mid August and Jeep Jamboree in late September. History buffs will enjoy Old Fort Meade Museum, situated in the early army post.

From Deadwood take US385 south through less developed sections of the Black Hills National Forest. Hill City has the Call of the Wild Museum and the popular **1880 Train**, with steam locomotives pushing century-old passenger cars through Pleasant Valley to Keystone.

Although the Crazy Horse Monument is unfinished, the informative museum complex is open daily. Beyond is **Custer**, central gateway to numerous local attractions. To the south is **Wind Cave National Park**, offering regular cave tours below ground plus bison and other wildlife above. Wind Cave and nearby **Jewel Cave National Monument** are supplemented by numerous privately operated caverns. Custer's 1881 courthouse is now a historical museum, while the National Museum of Woodcarving houses the amusing and often animated creations of Dr Niblack. Cartoon characters come to life at Flintstone's Bedrock City.

South of Custer is Hot Springs, celebrating a hundred plus years of bathing at **Evans Plunge**. Older still is **Mammoth Site**, although the archaeological digs are more recent. Visitors can view their comprehensive collection of mammoth and other Ice Age remains *in situ*, as the beasts dropped. The scenic route to Mount Rushmore is via Alternate US16 east from Custer through **Custer State Park**. America's second largest state park offers accommodation, wildlife, and various activities, including the Black Hills Playhouse. Bison roam the southern sections while the scenic Needles Highway is north.

Alternate US16 pierces the Black Hills, perfectly framing the **Mount Rushmore National Memorial** through its tunnels. The four presidents carved in living rock, Washington, Jefferson, Lincoln and Roosevelt, symbolize America, and her respective phases of independence, growth, unity, and conservation. The complex boasts a supermarket-sized gift shop, restaurant with a view, and the artist's studio museum, which exhibits techniques used in 'carving' the monument. The memorial is illuminated at night, and in summer park rangers conduct campfire talks at the amphitheatre.

Keystone's pride is the **Rushmore-Borglum Story**, which looks behind the scenes at Mount Rushmore and its creator. Also here is the Parade of Presidents Wax Museum and Big Thunder Gold Mine, plus Keystone is terminus for the 1880 steam train from Hill City. The narrow but lively town of Keystone is full of motels, restaurants and bars.

Nearby US16 is lined with tourist attractions en route to **Rapid City** — Bear Country, Black Hills Gold, Reptile Gardens, and Marine Life Aquarium are among the roadside wonders. The Rapid City Convention and Civic Center houses the visitor bureau. The **Museum of Geology** at the School of Mines has an excellent collection of minerals from the Black Hills and fossils from the nearby Badlands, with changing exhibits at the New Gallery. The comprehensive **Sioux Indian and Minnilusa Pioneer Museum Complex** is across town, with quality Native American gifts at the Tipi Shop. Dhal Fine Arts Center has a special viewing room for Bernard Thomas's 200ft mural, depicting the past 200 years of American History. Rapid City Parks are diverse, including one populated with storybook characters and another with dinosaurs. **Ellsworth Air Force Base Air and Space Museum** is found east of Rapid City.

Cheyenne Rodeo brings the crowds to Wyoming

Mount Rushmore is an American landmark

Follow I-90 east to Wall, home of the world famous, city block-sized store called **Wall Drug**. The restaurant's dining rooms seat hundreds while stocks of gifts and novelties run to millions. Their western outfitter supplies jeans, cowboy hats, and saddles — they even have a pharmacy. Wall Drug has a fascinating collection of post war amusements and oddities, which like its ice cold water are free to the public.

SR240 south from Wall visits the heart of **Badlands National Park**, where accommodation and fuel is limited. Start early with a *full* tank to enjoy the sculptured beauty of the badlands. Farmers ignored the vast tracts of eroded shale and clay, but Native Americans survived in the tortured terrain, as do a surprising variety of animals. Watch for prairie dogs and pronghorns (American antelope), bison and birds of prey.

Park officials prefer guests to keep to paths, such as the informative Fossil Trail (wheelchair accessible). Several longer walks start near the **Ben Reifel Visitor Center**, while Sage Creek Rim Road offers a mini-adventure on a well-maintained dirt track. South at Sage Creek wilderness, bison live off the native grasses which once blanketed the Great Plains.

From Ben Reifel Visitor Center head south to Interior, following signs for Scenic, where a left turn continues south. The White River Visitor Center is across the silt-laden creek it was named after. The displays and informative video on the Sioux Indians is in keeping with the location — heart of the Pine Ridge Indian Reservation. Both SR33 and SR27 south from White River pass through **Wounded Knee**. A large historical marker outlines the history of the massacre, while Sioux Chief Big Foot and his tribe are interred in a mass grave at the nearby cemetery.

Continue south from Wounded Knee, then turn right for Pine Ridge, where a short detour north leads to Holy Rosary Mission and Red Cloud School Displays of contemporary Native American art are boosted in July and August by the Red Cloud Indian Art Show; many interesting works are for sale Return south through Pine Ridge for Whiteclay, Rushville, and a new state

Nebraska

The lucrative trade in furs, sometimes called 'soft gold', brought the first white men into what is now Nebraska. For an understanding of that era, follow US20 west from Rushville to Chadron, visiting the **Museum of the Fur Trade**. A reconstructed sod house stands on the foundations of the original Bordeaux Trading Post. The museum boasts an outstanding collection of flintlocks and portrays the complete history of the fur trade, including oft neglected Russian and Spanish efforts. Nearby Chadron relives its frontier days in mid-July with a Fur Traders Rendezvous. Both Chadron and Crawford provide circular tour maps of local sites.

West of Crawford is **Fort Robinson**, Nebraska's largest and most popular state park. Among its museums and refurbished buildings is where Crazy Horse was mortally wounded. Fort Robinson Museum is concerned with fort life, documenting clashes between settlers, soldiers, and Indians. The nearby Trailside Museum specializes in geology and natural history. Scenic drives pass elk, bighorn sheep, and bison, while activities include horseback riding bicycling (rentals available), jeep rides, a tour train, chuckwagon cookouts and, on selected days, free rodeo events. Lodging and camping is available with dining facilities augmented by fun breakfast activities. Reservations are recommended in summer.

Pioneers soon followed fur traders once the Rockies had been crossed by wagon. Both Oregon and Mormon Trails followed the Platte River, as did the celebrated but short lived Pony Express. While heading south from Harrison on SR29, contemplate crossing the vast Great Plains on foot. Have a rest at **Agate Fossil Beds National Monument**, where prehistoric beavers created the 'Devil's Corkscrews', then continue south. Cross the Platte River on SR29 and turn east (left) onto SR92 for **Scotts Bluff National Monument**. Early pioneers struggled to achieve 65 miles per week, so the tall landmark remained on their horizon for days. The visitor centre has various exhibits including the fuel of the prairies — buffalo chips — and interesting extracts from pioneer diaries and letters. Both the road and path up Scotts Bluff are 1.6 miles (2.6 km) long, with excellent views over the Platte River Valley.

SR92 east joins US26, which parallels the Oregon Trail to Bridgeport before crossing the North Platte River to the Mormon Trail side. Just beyond Lewellen on US26 is Ash Hollow Cemetery, with a small stone marking the grave of pioneer Rachael Pattison. Next comes **Ash Hollow State Historical Park**, offering a cave with early Indian drawings and an excellent historical overview of the pioneer era settlers, soldiers, and Indians in the visitor centre. Full brakes and chained wagon wheels were required for steep **Windlass Hill**, where deep ruts are still evident.

North Platte is east from Ogallala. Take either US30 or I-80, putting watches forward an hour for Central Time. In June the city celebrates NEBRASKAland Days, with parades, craft fairs, and good old fashioned country fun culminating in the PRCA Buffalo Bill Rodeo at the Wild West Arena. North Platte is also home to the **Buffalo Bill State Historic Park**, called 'Scouts Rest' by William Π Cody. The famous scout, hunter, and entertainer recuperated there between hectic Wild West Shows, entertaining American celebrities and European royalty in his heyday. Buffalo Bill's former house is open for tours, the barn is a museum, and visitors can opt for buggy rides and a buffalo stew cookout.

Lincoln County Historical Museum Complex near Scouts Rest displays Indian artifacts to World War II memorabilia, preserving several historic 🏠 buildings. Hidden within Cody Park across town is the Railroad Museum, home to *Challenger* No 3977. This massive Union Pacific steam engine performed the work of two until retired. North Platte's Union Pacific Bailey Yard has an observation deck overlooking one of the world's largest rail classification complexes — a rail enthusiast's dream.

Between North Platte and McCook is Dancing Leaf Earth Lodge. Primitive Native American life is the focus, where visitors experience first hand the food, tools, customs, herbal remedies, and spirituality of pre-contact natives. Tours take two or more hours, and the adventurous may sleep in the authentically reconstructed lodge. Call ahead for reservations and directions.

Friendly **McCook** provides services to farmers and ranchers as far as Kansas. Their Red Willow County Fair includes a country music jamboree in late July. McCook has preserved the former home of celebrated Nebraska senator George Norris, while the Museum of the High Plains on Norris Street portrays early prairie life. Heritage Hills Golf Course has a reputation as one of America's best, boasting an imaginative layout over difficult terrain. South on US83 the rolling countryside flattens at the Kansas border.

Kansas

Welcome to the 'Land of Ahhhs', as Kansas calls itself. Stop at Oberlin for travel information, a Kansas map, and the Last Indian Raid exhibit at the Decatur County Museum. Unfortunate settlers in Oberlin were caught out in 1878 by Cheyenne escaping from Indian Territory, now Oklahoma, en route to traditional hunting grounds north.

Detour west (right) onto US24 for Colby and their excellent **Prairie Mu-** 🏠 **seum of Art and History**. The specially designed museum houses the extensive Kuska Collection of dolls and china, while various buildings illustrate prairie life, including the surprisingly comfortable sod house, a single room school house, and the recently acquired Cooper Barn, Kansas' largest. Return to southbound US83 via I-70 east, following signs for Oakley. At the free and fun **Fick Fossil and History Museum** even the unusual 'paintings' are made 🏠 from fossils.

The endless plains tire even the locals, who will drive hundreds of miles for the sight of the Chalk Castles. For a glimpse, drive 4 miles east (left) at the sign and 2 miles south (right) along a dirt road. Incidentally, the eroded ramparts have provided numerous fossils for Fick and other museums. Return by taking the first right beyond the 'Castles' and left (south) onto US83.

From Garden City, follow the **Santa Fe Trail** east on US50, which has visible ruts signposted by Kansas Historical Markers. Follow this once important trade route to infamous **Dodge City**. Wyatt Earp, Doc Holiday, and Bat Masterson were just a few living legends who brought their own brand of justice to Dodge City, haven of buffalo hunters, gamblers, and prostitutes. Boot Hill was born in 1872 when two cowboys fought at their campsite above the town, the penniless loser being buried on the spot, boots and all.

Time has changed Dodge City. Fire demolished the wooden Front Street and the bodies at Boot Hill were removed to the public cemetery. Movie westerns, followed by *Gunsmoke,* brought a renewed interest in the town's bad old days. Today the **Boot Hill Museum** complex offers a reconstructed Front Street, plus selected historic buildings and a restored portion of old Boot Hill. Entertainment and activities include an introductory movie, medicine show, and the obligatory gun fight. Optional extras include a stage coach ride, evening variety show at Long Branch Saloon, and a chuckwagon dinner. The complex is also a living museum, where displays help separate fact from legend.

Consider one last diversion before returning to Colorado. South from Dodge City on US283 and west on 54 leads to Mead for the **Dalton Gang Hideout and Museum**. After the Dalton Gang became too ambitious, several dying while simultaneously robbing two Coffeyville banks, the house was abandoned. New owners found strangers suddenly appearing from nowhere, and like them visitors may follow the secret tunnel from house to barn, part of the museum. Take SR23 north, then US50 west (left) along the Arkansas River to Colorado.

Southeastern Colorado

Follow signs onto SR194 west for **Bent's Old Fort National Historic Site**. Built in 1833 and destroyed in 1849, a reconstructed adobe fort recreates the early fur trading post and Santa Fe Trail waystation, where Kit Carson worked as hunter and scout. During summers the park service operates a living history program. Nearby **La Junta**, Spanish for junction, was named after the cross-roads of the Santa Fe and Navajo trails. La Junta is a major cattle and produce shipping centre, where Koshare Indian Kiva offers an excellent introduction to southwestern Indian culture, including Native American crafts and Koshare Indian dances on summer Saturday nights.

The next major stop is **Colorado Springs**, centre of an activity packed area which includes Manitou Springs and the celebrated Pikes Peak. Downtown Colorado Springs has the Pioneer and Numismatic Museums, plus the McAllister House. Theatrical performances and concerts take place at the Pikes Peak Center and Colorado Springs Fine Arts Center. At the **US Olympic Complex** on Boulder Street, young athletes compete for a place on the American team. An informative video outlines the purpose of the complex, proceeds from the gift shop help the athletes, and trials are often public.

Nearby **Manitou Springs** is mecca to tourists visiting the Pikes Peak area

The Manitou Springs and Old Colorado City end of Colorado Avenue is studded with motels of all shapes and sizes, many offering very reasonable rates, with numerous attractions lining the road or nearby on 21st Street. The **Manitou Cliff Dwellings Museum** protects the remnants of an Anasazi Indian town. These early cliff dwellers are believed to be the ancestors of southwestern Pueblo Indians. Other attractions include the Buffalo Bill Wax Museum, Miramont Castle, Cave of the Winds, Hall of Presidents Wax Museum, and the Deer Creek Nature Center. Toll roads lead to Cheyenne Mountain, with a zoo and shrine to Will Rogers, and Pikes Peak. The latter climbs the 14,110ft (4,300m) mountain Zebulon Pike claimed could never be scaled. For a relaxed ascent take a tour bus from Colorado Springs or the scenic and spectacular Pikes Peak Cog Railway from Manitou Springs.

The old gold mining village of **Cripple Creek** is accessible via US24 west of Colorado and Manitou Springs. Those with strong nerves and ideally a four-wheel drive vehicle may take the Gold Camp Road over the mountains. Cripple Creek offers mine tours, museums, a rail excursion, and even a Victorian melodrama or two. Not all mines are abandoned, many operate whenever gold prices are favourable.

Depending upon one's interests, before returning to Denver visit the **Pro Rodeo Hall of Fame**, **Garden of the Gods**, or the **US Air Force Academy**, all ✳ outside Colorado Springs. They respectively offer a peep into the wild world of the rodeo, stunning formations of eroded red sandstone, and a chance to see Air Force Cadets on parade.

Additional Information

State Tourism Bureaux

Colorado Tourism Board
1625 Broadway, Suite 1700
Denver, CO 80202
☎ 800-433-2656
or 303-592-5510

Kansas Travel & Tourism Division
Dept of Commerce
400 S W 8th St, 5th Floor
Topeka, KS 66603-3957
☎ 913-296-7091

Nebraska Travel & Tourism Office
PO Box 94666
Lincoln, NE 68509
☎ 800-228-4307
or 402-471-3796

South Dakota Tourism
711 Wills Avenue
Pierre, SD 57501-3335
☎ 800-843-1930
or 605-773-3301

Wyoming Division of Tourism
I-25 at College Dr
Cheyenne, WY 82002
☎ 307-777-7777

Regional Information

Cheyenne COC
Box 1147, 301 W 16th St
Cheyenne, WY 82001
☎ 307-638-3388

Colorado Springs CVB
104 S. Cascade, Suite 104
Colorado Springs, CO 80903
☎ 800-888-4748
or 719-635-7506

Deadwood-Lead COC
735 Main St
Deadwood, SD 57732
☎ 605-578-1876

Denver Metro CVB
225 W Colfax
Denver, CO 80202
☎ 303-892-1112

Dodge City CVB
PO Box 1474
Dodge City, KS 67801
☎ 316-227-2176

North Platte CVB
PO Box 968
North Platte, NE 69103
☎ 308-532-4966

Rapid City CVB
PO Box 747,
444 Mt Rushmore Rd
Rapid City, SD 57709
☎ 605-343-1744

Local Events

Check locally for exact dates

January
National Western Stock
Show & Rodeo
Denver, CO

June
Donkey Derby Days
Cripple Creek, CO

NEBRASKAland Days
Buffalo Bill Rodeo
North Platte, NE

June-August
Black Hills Passion Play
Spearfish, SD

Colorado Shakespeare
Festival
Boulder, CO

July
Black Hills & Plains
Indians Pow Wow
Rapid City, SD

Pikes Peak or Bust Rodeo
Colorado Springs, CO

July-August
Frontier Days' Daddy of
'em All Rodeo
Cheyenne, WY

Dodge City Days
Dodge City, KS

August
Black Hills Motorcycle
Classic
Sturgis, SD

Denver Grand Prix
Denver, CO

Colorado State Fair
Pueblo, CO

Places of Interest

Cheyenne, WY
Wyoming State Museum
24th & Central
Cheyenne, WY 82002
☎ 307-777-7014
Open: 8.30am-5pm Mon-
Fri, weekends in summer
Gifts, art gallery, ♿

Colby, KS
*Prairie Museum of Art &
History*
1905 S Franklin
(Frontage Rd)
Colby, KS 67701
☎ 913-462-6294
Open: 9am-5pm Tue-Fri,
noon-5pm weekends
Museum, outbuildings,
gift shop, ♿

Colorado Springs, CO
Pikes Peak Cog Railway
PO Box 1329 (US24)
Colorado Springs
CO 80901
☎ 719-685-5401
Open: May-Oct
Gift shop & food at summit

Crawford, NE
Fort Robinson State Park
US20
Crawford, NE 69339
☎ 308-665-2660
Lodging, food, trails,
horse & wagon rides,
gifts, ♿

Custer, SD
Custer State Park
HC 83 Box 70
Custer, SD 57730
☎ 605-255-4515
Open: hours vary
Lodging, camp, hike,
wildlife, ♿

Denver, CO
Colorado History Museum
1300 Broadway
Denver, CO 81416
☎ 303-874-5787

Open: 10am-4.30pm Mon-
Sat, noon-4.30pm Sun
Gift shop, ♿

Colorado State Capitol
200 E Colfax
Denver, CO 80203
☎ 303-866-2604
Open: 9am-3.30pm Mon-
Fri
Views, ♿

Denver Art Museum
100 West 14th Avenue Pkwy
Denver, CO 80204
☎ 303-640-2793
Open: 10am-5pm Tue-
Sat, noon-5pm Sun
Gift shop, ♿

*Denver Center for the
Performing Arts*
1425 Champa St
Denver, CO 80204
☎ 303-893-4000
Call for times
Theatre complex, food, ♿

*Denver Museum of Natural
History*
2001 Colorado Boulevard,
City Park
Denver, CO 80205
☎ 303-322-7009
Open: 9am-5pm
Gift shop, ♿

Denver Zoo
East 23rd & Steele St
City Park
Denver, CO 80205
☎ 303-331-4110
Open: 10am daily
Gift shop, restaurant, ♿

United States Mint
320 W Colfax
Denver, CO 80204
☎ 303-844-3582
Open: 8.30am-3pm
Free, gifts, ♿

Dodge City, KS
Boot Hill Museum
Front St
Dodge City, KS 67801
☎ 316-227-8188
Open: 8am-8pm summer,

reduced winter
Museum, gifts, food,
shows, &

Fort Laramie, WY
Fort Laramie NHS
Fort Laramie, WY 82212
☎ 307-837-2221
Open: 8am-4.30pm, 8am-
7pm summer
Visitor centre, gifts, part
&

Golden, CO
Colorado Railroad Museum
17155 W 44th Ave
Golden, CO 80402
☎ 303-279-4591
Open: 9am-5pm, 9am-
6pm summer
Gifts, occasional rides

Hot Springs, SD
Wind Cave NP
RR1, Box 190-WCNP
Hot Springs, SD 57747-9430
☎ 605-745-4600
Open: call for times
Gifts, cave tours, &

Interior, SD
Badlands NP
PO Box 6
Interior, SD 57750
☎ 605-433-5361
Open: 8am-5pm
Gifts, camp, trails,
wildlife, &

Keystone, SD
Mount Rushmore NM
PO Box 268
Keystone, SD 57751
☎ 605-574-2523
Open: 8am-5pm, 8am-
10pm summer
Free, gifts, restaurant, &

North Platte, NE
*Buffalo Bill State Historic
Park*
Buffalo Bill Ave
North Platte, NE 69101
☎ 308-535-8035
Open: 9am-5pm Mon-Fri,
1-5pm weekends in
summer
Museum, home, gifts

Scottsbluff, NE
Scotts Bluff NM
PO Box 427 (SR 92)
Gering, NE 69341
☎ 308-436-4340
Open: 8am-5pm
Visitor centre, gifts, &

Stockville, NE
Dancing Leaf Earth Lodge
Box 121
Stockville, NE 69042
☎ 308-367-4233
Call for reservation
Pre-contact Indian lodge,
gifts

9
AMERICAN SOUTHWEST

Welcome to the romantic Southwest, the fabled 'Four Corners' — where Colorado, Arizona, Utah, and New Mexico meet. Here is the promised land of Brigham Young and the Rocky Mountains, backbone of America. Cowboy landscapes stretch to the horizon, dotted with Indian pueblos and divided by the Grandest Canyon of all.

Colorado — The Rocky Mountain Scenic Loop

'Mile high' Denver should not be missed — its places of interest are detailed in Chapter 8. The main southwest tour commences with Rocky Mountain High — this scenic loop can be experienced immediately or savoured on return.

US36 north from Denver quickly reaches Rocky Mountain National Park, missing almost everything between. Instead, follow US6 to Golden, described in Chapter 8, then continue on US6 through the scenic gorge carved by Clear

American Southwest in Brief

After landing in Denver, experience a real 'Rocky Mountain High', from the great National Park to the ski and summer resorts of Vail and Aspen. Relive the old West at Durango and charming Santa Fe, Spanish capital of New Mexico. Beyond the indescribable Grand Canyon and super-spectacular Bryce Canyon and Zion National Park is the Mormon Temple Square of Salt Lake City.

Allow three weeks for the 3,000 mile tour, two weeks for just Colorado, New Mexico and the Grand Canyon. Those with more time may add the Great Plains route for a grand tour of the American West. If time is short, chose the area of greatest appeal and nearest gateway: Denver, Phoenix, Albuquerque or Salt Lake City.

Spring and autumn offer comfortable touring weather, while summers are hot but generally dry. The Grand Canyon is busiest from mid-June to mid-September — reserve accommodation well ahead. Winter skiing in Colorado is legendary, with slopes and conditions to suit *everyone*. Adventurous and warmly dressed travellers who follow the route (with alterations for road closures) in winter will find Santa Fe, Taos, and Albuquerque particularly enchanting at Christmas.

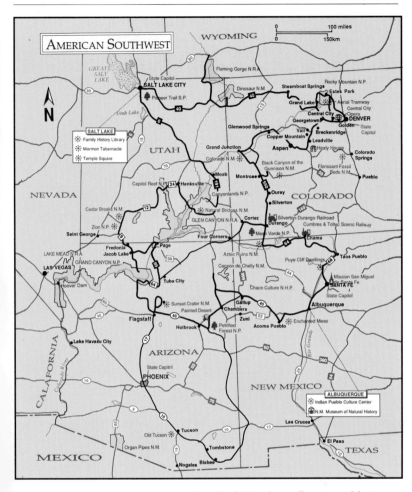

Creek. Turn north (right) onto SR119 for Black Hawk, a still active gold mining community, then west (left) for **Central City**. The grand old buildings of Central City proclaim its heyday as the 'Richest Square Mile on Earth', when its raucous population outnumbered Denver's. The city's fortunes ran out with the gold, but tourism has revived the town, sparked by the **Central City Opera**. Classic operas by some of America's finest voices fill the house, as they did over a century ago, with tours except during performances. Several Victorian homes are open to the public, a steam engine ventures through canyons lined with abandoned mines, and the Historical Society Museum recalls those earlier days.

Continue north on the **Peak-to-Peak Highway**, initially SR119, which winds through the scenic Roosevelt National Forest. At Netherlands turn north on SR72 and at Raymond north again on SR7, still following the Peak-to-Peak Highway. Frequent changes of perspective, unusual rock formations and glimpses of higher mountains make this the most visually rewarding route to the Rockies. Longs Peak, the highest point in Rocky Mountain National Park at 14,255ft (4,345m), is left after Olive Ridge.

Estes Park, eastern gateway to the Rockies, offers resort accommodation, dining, golf, boating, tours of the park, an aerial tramway, riding stables, skiing in winter, and a brace of trout farms — no fishing license required. Estes Park makes a good base for exploring the Rocky Mountain National Park, which has campgrounds but no lodgings.

Begin the **Rocky Mountain National Park** experience at the US36 visitor centre west of Estes Park. Park maps highlight roads, peaks and trails, while park newspapers list ranger-led activities and seasonal events. **Moraine Park** and **Bear Lake** areas offer a pleasant introduction to the Rockies, with gentle to moderate walks aiding acclimatization to ever increasing altitudes. Trailheads en route to Bear Lake are popular, sometimes overcrowded in summer, so park at Moraine Park Museum and take the free shuttle. Trails around the lower lakes are gentle, while Emerald Lake trail from Bear Lake will stretch walkers legs in preparation for more strenuous walks. Hikers intending to take the more adventurous walks up to the glaciers or across the Rocky Mountains should be experienced, fit, acclimatized to the altitudes, and must obtain a wilderness camping permit.

Trail Ridge Road, closed from late fall to mid-spring, crosses the Rocky Mountains, opening up what would otherwise be wilderness to the day visitor. Traversing a series of ridges overlooking the canyons below, scenic stops are many but trails few off higher sections of road, which reaches 12,183ft (3,713m). The Tundra Trail passes through alpine meadows full of blossoming plants in mid-summer, a gentle stroll along the ridge. The Alpine Visitor Center offers warming cups of coffee and snacks, then the road gradually drops to under 8,500ft at the Kawuneeche Visitor Center near Grand Lake. Moderate trails along the Cache la Poudre and Colorado Rivers are perfect for unhurried forays into the Rockies.

Grand Lake refers both to the water and the resort town surrounding it, a base for exploring the western Rockies. Altitude at lakeside is still 8,367ft (2,550m), but if walking proves tiring, travel on horseback. Facilities are similar to Estes Park, but offering a more rustic, relaxed atmosphere. Recreation is not confined to the Rocky Mountain National Park. The lakes, trails and timberlands of the **Arapahoe National Forest** are next door, as are popular ski resorts **Winter Park** and **Breckenridge**. Take US40 southeast over Berthoud Pass to I-70. Denver is east, while this tour goes west.

Rocky Mountain High

I-70 is Colorado's scenic corridor west through the Rockies, with interesting diversions along the way. **Georgetown** is one of Colorado's best preserved mining towns, with Victorian Hamil House, mine tours, and the Hotel de Paris, now a museum. Steam engines on the Georgetown Loop tie themselves in knots en route to Silver Plume. I-70 exits for **Breckenridge** and **Copper Mountain** are followed by **Vail**, its distinctive clock tower recognizable from the Interstate. Breckenridge is a former gold town turned resort, while Alpine styled Vail is as famous for shopping as skiing. All three resorts run chair lift or gondolas in summer, offering spectacular views and opportunities to hik without the long climb.

To explore the Rockies further, take US24 south to **Leadville**, at 10,188ft (3,105m), America's highest incorporated city. Lacking the 'cuteness' of the mountain resorts, Leadville recalls both raucous and respectable aspects of nineteenth-century mining. Tour Victorian **Healy House**, National Mining Hall of Fame, Tabor Opera House and Matchless Mine Cabin, or take the Leadville, Colorado & Southern Railroad, a scenic ride to the Colorado River headwaters. West on SR82, Independence Pass (closed in winter) enjoys magnificent views across to 14,433 foot (4,399 metre) Mount Elbert, Colorado's highest peak.

From Denver, getting to **Aspen** by road is half the fun; although non-drivers will find year-round flights from Denver and beyond supplemented during winter ski season. Boasting fine shopping, dining and active nightlife, Aspen is *the* place to buy the latest resort or ski wear. Culturally, their calendar is always full, culminating in the summer-long **Aspen Music Festival**. Outdoor activities include horseback riding and hiking, with opportunity for the latter by taking **Maroon Bells Bus Tour** to a particularly scenic portion of White River National Forest.

Of Aspen area ski resorts, **Buttermilk** offers the most scope for beginners without neglecting others. **Aspen Highlands** has a good mix centred around competent skiers, while nearby **Snowmass** caters for all. **Aspen Mountain** challenges the best intermediates and experts alike, but no experience is required to enjoy the **Silver Queen Gondola** in summer.

The massive Hot Pool at Glenwood Springs is a bather's delight. From there, take westbound I-70 along the Colorado River to **Grand Junction**. **Colorado National Monument**'s eroded terrain is a prelude to the Grand Canyon, while the town itself boasts the informative Museum of Western Colorado and Dinosaur Valley. US50 is the main route south, with a slight backtrack for SR65 offering a scenic alternative through Grand Mesa National Forest.

Montrose is main gateway to **Black Canyon of the Gunnison**, a dark, brooding defile whose sheer granite walls plummet 2,700ft (823m) to the Gunnison River. A permit is required for hiking down, but most are satisfied with views from roadside overlooks. Take US550 south through the rugged countryside, which boasts several 14,000ft peaks. The Ouray to Silverton section is the 'Million Dollar Highway', referring either to extracted mineral wealth or perhaps former high tolls. Forays into surrounding countryside, including remote ghost towns, are provided by Colorado West and San Juan Jeep Tours of Ouray, with 4WD rentals for the adventurous.

San Juan County Museum at Silverton remembers when Bat Masterson was imported to curb unruly elements. Today the town is terminus of **The Silverton**, the famous narrow gauge train which steams up from **Durango**. Advance bookings are essential between mid-June and Labor Day. Diamond Circle Theater and other structures give downtown Durango a Victorian holiday atmosphere. Durango is also prime gateway to the **Four Corners** — the only point where four states meet. Visitors can explore the region independently, while several operators offer tours.

Four Corners boasts scenery straight from a movie western, and is incredibly rich in Native American heritage. Take a short detour west on US160 to explore the **Mesa Verde National Park**, where Anasazi culture reached its

Rocky Mountain National Park

The Southwest is a firm favourite with rafters

zenith during the twelfth and thirteenth centuries. Dwelling literally on cliff faces, their story is told at Far View Lodge. Cliff Palace is the largest and best ת known site, while ruins road and petroglyph trail provide additional help in understanding this lost culture. The University of Colorado Center at nearby Cortez has information on other sites, and the town holds regular Indian dances in summer. Optionally, visit Anasazi Heritage Center in Dolores and ת while there, ask directions to Lowry Ruins.

If time is short, US160 west is shortest route to the Grand Canyon. Otherwise, continue south on US550 from Durango.

New Mexico

The 'Land of Enchantment' is also rich in Anasazi and Chaco sites, including the **Aztec Ruins National Monument** and **Chaco Culture National Histori-** ת **cal Park**, a short detour south. From Bloomfield take US64 west to Chama, which offers the **Cumbres & Toltec Scenic Railroad**.

The unique factors which created New Mexico are most evident across the Rio Grande gorge in **Taos**. The rich melange of Spanish and Native American influences are everywhere, especially the plaza area. Buildings are of hybrid Pueblo/Spanish Colonial architecture, with muted colors and gentle curves. Strings of red-hot chilies add colour and spice, while scores of galleries explode with ceramic story tellers, silver jewelry and brightly decorated kachina dolls. When dining, sample local blends of Mexican and Native American cuisines — such as the blue corn *tostada*. If that is too adventurous, Taos has several tour operators offering river rafting and other excursions.

Structures of interest include the Kit Carson Home, Martinez Hacienda, and Mission St Francis de Assisi. **Taos Pueblo** is true living history, where Pueblo ✳ Indians have retained their lifestyle and tradition. Outsiders may visit their village and even view selected ceremonies, but permits are required for photography. The Ernest Blumenschein Home recalls a founder of Taos Society of Artists, now exhibiting works he influenced.

Chillies spice up
New Mexico
decorations

SR68 follows the Rio Grande south to enchanting **Santa Fe**, capital (
'American' New Mexico, as it was under Spanish and Mexican rule. Th
Capitol Building is unusually round, reminiscent of the state flag's Zia su
design. The Museum of New Mexico covers four areas: fine arts, internation
folk art, Indian arts and culture, and Palace of the Governors. The Center fc
Contemporary Arts, Institute of American Indian Arts, and Weelwrigl
Museum of the American Indian also exhibit local and native art. Like Tao
Santa Fe is home to many artists.

The beauty and interest of Santa Fe owes much to its Spanish heritage, i
name coming from **Mission San Miguel de Santa Fe**, founded in 1610. Le:
remains of the Tesuque Pueblo Mission to the north, but Indians still use th
sacristy. Other sites include Santuario de Guadalupe, Cathedral of St Franc
de Assisi, and Santa Fe cemetery. *Luminarias*, paper bags aglow with cand
light, are a quaint custom, making Christmas a charming event in Santa Fe

Albuquerque is New Mexico's largest city, yet retains its historic charact€
in **Old Town**, west of the new city centre. Horse drawn carriages, gas lamp·
and adobe architecture offer respite from the bustle of a modern cit·
Albuquerque Trolley runs tours through the historic section. Several winerie
offer tastings in the surrounding area, while the climate is near perfect fc
ballooning, the International Balloon Fiesta being the largest meet.

One of Albuquerques's finest museums is the **New Mexico Museum** (
Natural History, with local art, native and Hispanic history, and the usu.
dinosaur bones. Others include the **Albuquerque Museum** and several at th
University of New Mexico. The excellent **Indian Pueblo Cultural Center**
owned and operated by the Pueblo tribes. The centre helps visitors unde
stand differences between seemingly similar groups of Pueblo Indians, higl
lights traditional crafts, and stages Native American events.

To see Pueblo culture in an usual setting, follow I-40 west, taking exit 1C
to **Acoma**. Called 'Sky City', their high mesa offered protection, only recentl
becoming accessible by road. Visitors take their bus and walking tour, whic
includes Acoma village and Mission San Esteban Del Ray (small addition₃
charge for cameras). Return to I-40 west, following the Atchison, Topeka, an
Santa Fe railway.

Coronado came to **Zuni Pueblo** in search of the legendary seven cities (
Cibola, but discovered that their golden walls were adobe. Today the Zuni a⋅
masters of silver and turquoise, but check at Gallup that the pueblo remair
open to guests before diverting south. Then continue west on I-40.

Arizona

Several places of interest are reached before the Grand Canyon. At Gallup (
Chambers travellers may opt to visit the **Canyon de Chelly National Monu**
ment. Situated in the Navajo Indian Reservation, the red sandstone walls (
Canyon de Chelly and adjoining Canyon del Muerto have evidence of India
occupation going back to fourth-century Basket Weaver Culture. Nava;
guides and/or park rangers must accompany visitors except at the whit
house ruins, while organized tours leave from Thunderbird Lodge. Note th₃
daylight savings time applies on reservations, but not to the rest of Arizon.

The Petrified Forest National Park straddles I-40. The northern section offers the colourful Painted Desert, while the badlands and fossilized trees are south. Collecting within the park brings stiff fines, but local shops sell colourful varieties of polished petrified wood from outside the park's boundaries. From the southern park exit take US180 to Holbrook, continuing west on I-40.

Flagstaff is the largest city in the Grand Canyon area, and also the gateway to other outdoor adventures. SR179 leads to Alternate US89, a spectacular drive through Oak Creek Canyon, while other offerings include winter skiing in the Arizona Snow Bowl and exploring an old volcano at Sunset Crater National Monument. Nearby sites include Lowell Observatory, which in 1930 discovered the planet Pluto, and Riordan Mansion, now a state historic park.

The mile-deep defile of the **Grand Canyon** strips away 2 billion years of history, unearthing past epoches for the delight of geologists and spectators alike. The canyon separates the national park into two distinct entities — North and South Rims. Most tour operators and first time visitors opt for South Rim, which therefore offers the most facilities but suffers crowding. Some 10 percent reach North Rim, which being higher offers a different but no less spectacular perspective. Traveller may see both, if desired, except in winter when the North Rim is closed.

SR180 leads from Flagstaff through Coconino National Forest to **South Rim**. Just before the park entrance is 'Grand Canyon — the Hidden Secrets', on a seven-storey IMAX screen. Some prefer the real thing first, but the film does simulate a raft trip down the Colorado — available in real life through several tour operators. Most visitors first view majestic Grand Canyon from **Mather Point**, an overwhelming experience. Colours and textures alter with view point and time of day, as well as weather and season. Most rangers have favourite spots for sunrise and sunset, ask at Grand Canyon Village Visitor Center. The centre also has maps, schedules of ranger-led activities, and informative exhibits on canyon formation.

From the village, South Rim Drive goes both east and west. In summer west drive is closed to private vehicles, but a free shuttle bus is available, as is the **Rim Trail**, a level walk along the canyon's edge. Another walk, **Bright Angel Trail**, plummets 4,460ft (1,360m) down to the Colorado River. Advance reservations are necessary both for food and lodging at **Phantom Ranch** below, and also for the mule trip, which in winter does not reach the bottom.

Grand Canyon Tips

Accommodation within the park should be booked well in advance, ideally the January before travelling. Grand Canyon National Park Lodging operates South Rim, while TW Recreational Services provide lodging at North Rim (see Additional Information). Accommodation is available outside the park in Tusayan, and further away in Flagstaff (170 miles round-trip) and Williams (120 miles). The latter offers the **Grand Canyon Railroad**, an exhilarating trip leaving some three hours at the canyon. Camping reservations are made through Ticketron; permits are required for backcountry camping. Only attempt Bright Angel and other strenuous trails if fit and carrying sufficient water.

With a full fuel tank, follow South Rim Drive eastbound (SR64), pausing for scenic overlooks, Tusayan Indian Ruins and Museum, and the Watchtower, highest point on South Rim. US89 travels north through Navajo country, a region of colourful sandstone cliffs. For Navajo handicrafts, take the 10 mile detour east on US160 to Tuba City.

Those visiting the **North Rim** of the Grand Canyon follow Alternate US89 west, taking Navajo Bridge across Marble Canyon and past abandoned stone houses before turning south at Jacob Lake. Lodging, trails, and overlooks at North Rim look down upon the South Rim. Return north to Fredonia, taking US89 into Utah. Those *not* visiting North Rim may follow US89 to Page, gateway to **Glen Canyon National Recreation Area**. Glen Canyon Dam has impounded the 180 mile (290km) Lake Powell, which can be cruised by boat but is best comprehended by air. Continue north and west on US89.

Utah

When Brigham Young and his Mormon followers reached Utah, they declared, 'This is the place!' Utah scenery is straight from a Zane Grey Western — he based many novels here — and the 'Beehive State' is understandably proud of its five gems: Zion, Bryce, Capitol Reef, Canyonlands, and Arches National Parks. Visitors fresh from the Grand Canyon may wonder whether Utah can do better, and the answer for many is yes. Each Utah park offers a

(opposite) Mule trekking at Supai Indian Village, Grand Canyon

The Grand Canyon reveals two billion years of history

Tips for Utah's National Parks

Zion and Bryce Canyon have lodging within the park operated by TW Recreational Services, while Moab offers accommodation near Arches and Canyonlands, with lodging at Torrey near Capitol Reef. All parks have campgrounds, but most have limited facilities and fill by mid-day in peak season. Hikers should carry water, taking early morning or late evening walks in summer, when midday temperatures often exceed 100°F (38°C).

different, more personal experience than the often overwhelming Grand Canyon; each is on a grand yet somehow more human scale.

The scenic beauty of Utah is not restricted to its national parks, and the area surrounding Kanab, including Coral Pink Sand Dunes, was popular with Hollywood filmmakers for Westerns. Travel further west on SR9 through Zion tunnel (motorhomes and buses must be escorted) to **Zion National Park**. The Virgin River has carved a defile through Navajo sandstone, narrowing to 300ft at Temple of Sinawava. Hikers following the 'Gateway to the Narrows' (first check for possible flooding) will find the gap reduces to 20ft. The entire 16 mile (26km) trail takes days, but the first mile is an easy, paved path. The climb to Angels Landing is rewarded by incredible views of Zion Canyon, not a trail for the giddy. If pressed for time, I-15 offers a rapid route north, either to Salt Lake City or east on I-70 back to Denver. Otherwise return east, following US89 north to SR12.

At **Bryce Canyon National Park**, the scenic drive to Rainbow and Yovimpa Points overlooks a variety of fantastically eroded shapes. Nearer the entrance is an interconnecting network of trails, where visitors walk among the incredible figures. Evening activities include a walk during full moon and stargazing at new moon. From Bryce, continue east on SR12 through Dixie National Forest, turning east again onto SR24 for **Capitol Reef National Park**. The massive sandstone abutments were likened to a sleeping rainbow by the Navajo. The name comes from an unusual white sandstone formation said to resemble the American Capitol. Despite the seeming inhospitable location, early Mormon pioneers settled here, and their trees in the park still bear fruit.

At Hanksville, Bicentennial Highway offers a scenic route over the Colorado River past Natural Bridges National Monument before connecting to US191, where Moab is north. **Canyonlands National Park** has a paved road to Grand View Point, overlooking the serpentine erosions surrounding the confluence of the Colorado and Green Rivers. Numerous dirt roads lead into the park and surrounding countryside, and four-wheel drive vehicles may be rented from Moab. Most sandstone formations in **Arches National Park** are visible from scenic drives, although some, such as Delicate Arch, are best approached by the excellent trail network. If time is pressed, return east to Denver via I-70. Otherwise, US6 offers a quick route north.

Salt Lake City

Founded by Brigham Young's followers in 1847, **Salt Lake City** and its outposts played an important role in settling the vast American west. Chiefly remembered for once practicing polygamy, 'Mormons' are members of Church of Jesus Christ of Latter Day Saints, LDS for short. Those wishing to learn more should visit **Temple Square**. Inside is the Mormon Temple, open only to the LDS, and the great Mormon Tabernacle (see information section for recital times). Fresh faced LDS volunteers take visitor groups on tours through the complex, which has two visitor centres, the Tabernacle, an assembly hall-cum-temple open to the public, and monuments to pioneers and their benefactors, the seagulls. Parking is provided on North Temple between West Temple and Main Streets.

Across from Temple Square on West Temple Street is the Museum of Church History and Art. The **Family History Library** is highly regarded by genealogists. On the opposite side along South Temple Street is Brigham Young Monument and one block east, Eagle Gate. Between them is Beehive House, original residence of Brigham Young. The towering building on North Temple is the LDS Church headquarters, with a 26th-floor observatory deck.

The **State Capitol** is perched on a hill overlooking the downtown area. Just west is Pioneer Memorial Museum, while other places of interest include Utah Historical Society and Pioneer Craft House. Cottage industries were important to the 'Beehive State', and the craft house focuses on that heritage. The University of Utah east of Salt Lake City was founded by Brigham Young. Here shade-giving trees are part of the State Arboretum of Utah, while museums include the Utah Museum of Fine Arts and the flora, fauna, and fossils of the Natural History Museum. In the vicinity is **Pioneer Trail State Park**, which has collected and restored the homes and households of Old Deseret. The 'This is the Place' Monument has a highly informative audio presentation tracing the Mormon exodus to Utah.

Return east on US40. After Vernal, gateway to Uintas Mountains and Flaming Gorge National Recreation Area, comes Dinosaur National Monument in Colorado. Further east is ski and summer resort **Steamboat Springs**. The healthy atmosphere and thermal waters bubbling up from over 150 springs enticed visitors from around the world, including European guests who introduced skiing and ski jumping. To experience Rocky Mountain National Park again, take US34 east then return to Denver on US36.

Additional Information

State Tourism Bureaux

Colorado Tourism Board
625 Broadway, Suite 700
Denver, CO 80202
☏ 800-433-2656
☏ 303-592-5510

Arizona Office of Tourism
100 W Washington St
Phoenix, AZ 85007
602-542-TOUR

Utah Travel Council
Council Hall, Capitol Hill
Salt Lake City, UT 84114
☏ 801-538-1030

New Mexico Tourism & Travel
Joseph Montoya Building
1100 St Francis Dr
Santa Fe, NM 87503
☏ 800-545-2040
or 505-827-0291

Regional Information

Albuquerque CVB
PO Box 26866
Albuquerque, NM 87125
☏ 800-284-2282
or 505-243-3696

Aspen Resort Assn
303 E Main St
Aspen, CO 81611
☏ 303-925-1940

Denver Metro CVB
225 W Colfax
Denver, CO 80202
☎ 303-892-1112

Durango Area Resort Assn
PO Box 2587
Durango, CO 81302
☎ 303-247-0312

Estes Park Area Chamber
PO Box 3050
Estes Park, CO 80517
☎ 800-443-7837
or 303-586-4431

Flagstaff COC
101 West Santa Fe
Flagstaff, AZ 86001
☎ 800-842-7293
or 602-774-4505

Grand Junction CVB
360 Grand Ave.
Grand Junction, CO
81502
☎ 303-242-3214

Grand County Travel
   Council
805 N Main St
Moab, UT 84532
☎ 801-259-8825

Salt Lake City CVB
180 S West Temple
Salt Lake City, UT 84101
☎ 801-521-2822

Santa Fe CVB
PO Box 909
Santa Fe, NM 87504-0909
☎ 800-777-CITY
or 505-984-6760

Local Events

Check locally for exact date

January
Ullrfest & World Cup
Freestyle
Breckenridge, CO

Winterskol
Aspen, CO

February
Winter Carnival
Steamboat Springs, CO

June
New Mexico Arts &
   Crafts Festival
Albuquerque, NM

Stampede and Air Show
Steamboat Springs, CO

Strawberry Days
Glenwood Springs, CO

Utah Arts Festival
Salt Lake City, UT

June-August
Aspen Music Festival
Aspen, CO

Festival of the Arts
Flagstaff, AZ

June-September
Festival of Native Arts
Flagstaff, AZ

July
Pioneer Day
Salt Lake City, UT

July-August
Central City Opera Festival
Central City, CO

August
Purgatory Music Festival
Durango, CO

September
Colorfest
Southwest Colorado

Fiesta de Santa Fe
Santa Fe, NM

New Mexico State Fair
Albuquerque, NM

Southern Utah Folklife
   Festival
Zion NP, UT

Utah State Fair
Salt Lake City, UT

September-October
Taos Fall Art Festival
Taos, NM

October
Albuquerque Balloon
   Festival
Albuquerque, NM

November
Lighting of Temple
   Square
Salt Lake City, UT

December
Luminaria Tours
Taos, Santa Fe &
Albuquerque, NM

Places of Interest

Acoma, NM
Pueblo of Acoma (Sky City)
PO Box 309 (SR 23)
Acoma, NM 87034
☎ 505-252-1139
Open: 8am-4pm, 8am-
7pm summer
Tour pueblo, mission

Albuquerque, NM
*Indian Pueblo Culture
   Center*
2401 12th Street, NW
Albuquerque, NM 87102
☎ 505-843-7270
Open: 9am-5.30pm except
major holidays
Museum, Native crafts &
gifts, food, &

*New Mexico Museum of
   Natural History*
1801 Mountain Road NW
Albuquerque, NM
☎ 505-841-8837

Arches, UT - see Moab

Bryce Canyon, UT
Bryce Canyon NP
Superintendent's Office
Bryce Canyon, UT 84717
☎ 801-834-5322
or 801-586-7686 (lodging

Open: 8am-4.30pm, 8am-6pm summer
Lodging, food, camp, hike, ♿

Canyon de Chelly, AZ
Canyon de Chelly NM
PO Box 588
Chinle, AZ 86503
☎ 602-674-5213
Open: 8am-5pm, 8am-6pm summer
Camp, picnic, Indian petroglyphs & ruins

Canyonlands, UT - see Moab

Capitol Reef, UT
Capitol Reef NP
Superintendent's Office
Torrey, UT 84775
☎ 801-425-3791
Open: 8am-4.30pm, 8am-6pm summer
Visitor centre, camp, hike, ♿

Central City, CO
Central City Opera
200 Eureka St
Central City, CO 80427
☎ 303-292-6700
Call for times Tours

Chama, NM
Cumbres & Toltec Scenic Railroad
PO Box 789
Chama, NM 87520
☎ 505-756-2151
Call for times & reservation
Food, gifts

Durango, CO
Silverton-Durango Railroad
479 Main
Durango, CO 81301
☎ 303-247-2733
Call for times & reservation
Food, gifts, ♿

Grand Canyon, AZ
Grand Canyon NP
Superintendent's Office

Grand Canyon, AZ 86023
☎ 602-638-7888
Open: visitor centre 8am-5pm, 8am-8.30pm summer
Picnic, camp, summer shuttle, hike, ♿

Estes Park, CO
Aerial Tramway
420 E Riverside Drive
Estes Park, CO 80517
☎ 800-443-7837
or 303-586-3675
Open: 9am-6.30pm
Memorial-Labor Day
Gifts, views, ♿

Grand Canyon NP Lodging
Box 699
Grand Canyon, AZ 86023
☎ 602-638-2401
South Rim services,
Phantom Ranch bookings
Lodging, food, mule trips, tours, ♿

TW Recreational Services
PO Box 400
Cedar City, UT 84721
☎ 801-586-7686
or 602-638-2611
Grand Canyon North
Rim, Bryce, Zion services
Lodging, food, mule trips, tours, ♿

Mesa Verde, CO
Mesa Verde NP
Supervisor
Mesa Verde, CO 81330
☎ 303-529-4461
Open: 8am-5pm, 8am-6.30pm summer
Museum, hike, camp, summer lodging, ♿

Moab, UT
Arches NP
Box 907
Moab, UT 84532
☎ 801-259-8161
Open: 8am-4.30pm, 8am-6pm summer
Visitor centre, camp, hike, ♿

Canyonlands NP
Superintendent's Office
Moab, UT 84532
☎ 801-259-7164
Visitor centre hours vary
Visitor centres, hike, ♿

Montrose, CO
Black Canyon of the Gunnison
2233 East Main (HQ)
Montrose, CO 81401
☎ 303-249-7036
Open: 8am-5pm
Visitor centre, hike, camp, picnic

Petrified Forest, AZ
Petrified Forest NP
Superintendent's Office
Petrified Forest NP
AZ 86028
☎ 602-524-6228
Open: 8am-5pm, 8am-8pm summer
Visitor centre, gifts, ♿

Rocky Mountain NP, CO
Rocky Mountain NP
US 34 & 36
Estes Park, CO 80517-8397
☎ 303-586-2371
Open: 8am-5pm, 8am-9pm summer
Gifts, snacks, trails, camping, ♿

Salt Lake City, UT
Family History Library
35 North West Temple St
Salt Lake City, UT
☎ 801-240-2331
Open: 7.30am Mon-Sat
Free genealogical research, ♿

Mormon Tabernacle
50 West North Temple
Salt Lake City, UT
☎ 801-240-2534
Recitals noon & 4pm
weekdays. Choir rehearsals 8pm Thu. Broadcast 9.15am Sun. Concerts 7.30pm Fri & Sat

Pioneer Trail State Park
2601 East Sunnyside Ave
Salt Lake City, UT
☎ 801-584-8391
Open: Old Deseret noon-
5pm summer; centre
10am-4.30pm
Tours, living history, gifts

Temple Square
50 West North Temple
Salt Lake City, UT
☎ 801-240-2534
Open: 9am-9pm. Free
Visitor centres, tours, &

Santa Fe, NM
*Mission San Miguel de
    Santa Fe*
401 Old Santa Fe Trail
Santa Fe, NM 87504
☎ 505-983-3974
Open: 9am-4.30pm Mon-
Sat, 1-4.30pm Sun
Tours, gifts

Zion, UT
Zion NP
Superintendent's Office
Springdale, UT 84767
☎ 801-772-3256
or 801-586-7686 (lodging)
Open: visitor centre 8am-
4.30pm
Lodging, food, camp,
hike, &

Ski Resorts

Aspen/Snowmass, CO
Aspen Highlands Ski Area
PO Box T, 1600 Maroon
Creek Road
Aspen, CO 81612
☎ 800-525-8955
or 303-925-5300
Open: late Nov-early Apr
3,800ft drop; 23% begin-
ners, 48% intermediate,
29% advanced
9 double chairs

Aspen Mountain Ski Area
PO Box 1248
Aspen, CO 81612
☎ 800-525-6200 (reserva-
tions), 303-925-1220 (info)
Open: late Nov to mid-Apr
3,267ft drop; 0% begin-
ners, 35% intermediate,
65% advanced
Gondola, 3 quad, 4
double

Buttermilk Ski Area
PO Box 1248
Aspen, CO 81612
☎ 800-525-6200 (reserva-
tions), 303-925-1220 (info)
Open: late Nov-late Mar
2,030ft drop; 35% begin-
ners, 39% intermediate,
26% advanced
6 double chairs

Snowmass Ski Area
PO Box 1248
Aspen, CO 81612
☎ 800-525-6200 (reserva-
tions), 303-925-1220 (info)
Open: late Nov to mid-Apr
3,615ft drop; 9% begin-
ners, 51% intermediate,
40% advanced
3 quad, 2 triple, 9 double
chairs

Breckenridge, CO
Breckenridge Ski Area
PO Box 1058
Breckenridge, CO 80424
☎ 800-US-SKIER (reserva-
tions), 303-453-2368 (info)
Open: mid-Nov to mid-Apr
3,398ft drop; 20% begin-
ners, 31% intermediate,
49% advanced
4 quad, 1 triple, 8 double
chairs

Copper Mountain, CO
*Copper Mountain Ski
    Resort*
PO Box 3001
Copper Mountain, CO
80443
☎ 800-458-8386 (reserva-
tions), 303-968-2882
(info)
Open: mid Nov-late Apr
2,760ft drop; 25%
beginners, 40% interme-
diate, 35% advanced
2 quad, 6 triple, 8 double
chairs

Steamboat Springs, CO
Steamboat Ski Area
2305 Mt Werner Circle
Steamboat Springs
CO 80487
☎ 800-922-2722 (reserva-
tions), 303-879-6111
(info)
Open: late Nov-early
Apr
3,600ft drop; 15%
beginners, 54% interme-
diate, 31% advanced
Gondola, 1 quad, 7
triple, 9 double chairs

Vail, CO
Vail Ski Area
PO Box 7
Vail, CO 81658
☎ 800-237-0643 (reserva-
tions), 303-476-5601
(info)
Open: late Nov to mid-
Apr
3,250ft drop; 32%
beginners, 36% interme-
diate, 32% advanced
Gondola, 9 quad, 2 triple
& 6 double chairs

10

CALIFORNIA AND NEVADA

Named after a legendary island inhabited by blonde Amazons, the reality of California transcends the myth. Spanish Missions and Silicon Valley, gold rushes and the glamour of Hollywood — all are part of the California experience. In Nevada, Las Vegas and Reno are a glittering beacon to showgoers and high rollers.

Greater Los Angeles

Called a collection of suburbs in search of a city, Los Angeles is a diverse collection of neighbourhoods, but with a heart. Start at **El Pueblo de Los Angeles Historic Park**, the city's birthplace. Also known as Olvera Street, the park is a riotous, colourful introduction to Los Angeles and its Hispanic heritage. Street vendors sell Mexican snacks and delicacies while al fresco dining may include an impromptu mariachi band. Certain historic buildings house shops while others, like Olveras Adobe, recreate Spanish Alta (Upper) California. The Visitor Information Center in Sepulveda House shows an orientation film.

The Hispanic heritage of Los Angeles is indisputable, but other cultures have also contributed. For authentic oriental cuisine, **Chinatown** is north of El Pueblo Historic Park along North Broadway, while **Little Tokyo** surrounds San Pedro and 2nd Streets. Little Tokyo boasts fine shopping, a Japanese Garden, and the Japanese American Cultural and Community Center. West

California and Nevada in Brief

Choose between two routes, each two/three weeks long. The Southern California tour includes Los Angeles, San Diego, Las Vegas, the oasis of Palm Springs and Death Valley. The Northern California tour incorporates San Francisco, Big Sur Coastline, Gold Rush Country, Yosemite, Reno, Lake Tahoe, and the wine valleys of Napa and Sonoma. Combine routes for a grand tour of California.

Los Angeles is the gateway for the southern tour. The desert blooms during late winter and early spring, while beaches (and desert) sizzle in summer. Northern gateway San Francisco is always refreshing — bring a warm layer even in summer. Except for skiing trips, tour May to October, remembering that July and August are peak season at Yosemite.

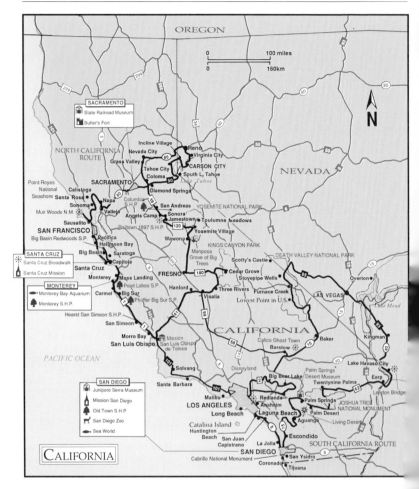

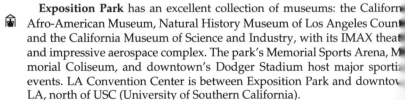

and North of Little Tokyo are respectively the major centres for finance and government.

Music Center and associated theatres bring numerous productions into downtown LA. The Sunday *Los Angeles Times* calendar supplement detail events there, at LA Theatre Centre near Little Tokyo, and 'abroad' at Universa and Century City. Los Angeles Times offers tours on weekdays, while **Wel Fargo History Center** off Grand Avenue has a stagecoach and gold rus exhibits. Also downtown are the Museum of Contemporary Art and Chi dren's Museum.

Exposition Park has an excellent collection of museums: the Californ Afro-American Museum, Natural History Museum of Los Angeles Count and the California Museum of Science and Industry, with its IMAX theat and impressive aerospace complex. The park's Memorial Sports Arena, M morial Coliseum, and downtown's Dodger Stadium host major sporti events. LA Convention Center is between Exposition Park and downtov LA, north of USC (University of Southern California).

Into and Around Los Angeles

LAX, Los Angeles International Airport, is in southwestern LA. Super Shuttle and Prime Time provide door-to-door transportation over Los Angeles and Orange Counties, while the Airport Coach has connections to local and Anaheim (Disneyland) hotels. Amtrak operates from Union Passenger Terminal, across Alameda Street from El Pueblo Historic Park, while Greyhound's transportation centre is southwest on 6th and Los Angeles Streets.

Interstates form a major part of the sometimes frantic freeway system, linking outlying areas and acting as traffic arteries within greater Los Angeles. A map is essential, and drivers should orientate themselves before setting off, following freeway numbers en route, not their names.

The famous sign on Santa Monica hills proclaims **Hollywood**. The main drag, Hollywood Boulevard, is paved with names of stars while their hand and footprints are outside **Mann's Chinese Theatre**. Hollywood offers T-shirt and memorabilia vendors, wax museums, and tours of homes once owned by movie stars. North of Hollywood on Highland Avenue or US 101 leads to **Mulholland Drive**, take it west. Waysides along this scenic route over the Santa Monica hills overlook the natural amphitheatre of **Hollywood Bowl**, south across Los Angeles and north to San Fernando Valley. Take Coldwater Canyon Drive south (left) down to **Beverly Hills**. The ultimate shopping experience, **Rodeo Drive**, is a few blocks southwest off Sunset Boulevard. Further west on Sunset is Bel Air and UCLA, University of California Los Angeles.

The Queen Mary,
*now a tourist
attraction and hotel
at Long Beach*

Seaside **Santa Monica** is southwest of Beverly Hills, with sandy beach, shops, restaurants, and the amusements of Municipal Pier. The Museum of Flying is by the local airport while the Heritage Museum is on Main Street near Ocean Park. South is Venice Beach, especially popular with the younger set. At Marina del Rey beyond the wealthy overlook their yachts from towering condominiums. Nearby Fisherman's Village is a shopping and dining complex off Lincoln Boulevard and Fiji Way.

The oceanside resort communities of **Malibu** and **Pacific Palisades** are west from Santa Monica. LA County Parks and California Department of Natural Resources administer public coastline, saving them from the hyper-development of privately owned sections. Behind is the **Santa Monica Mountains National Recreation Area**, a collection of county, state, and federally owned land. Topanga and Malibu Creek State Parks offer good hiking and cycling in cooler seasons. **Will Rogers State Historic Park**, the late star's former home, includes a collection of C. M. Russell's paintings. The **J. Paul Getty Museum** houses an incredible collection of Greek and Roman antiquities in a replica Roman villa. Advance parking reservations (1-2 weeks ahead) are required for this free museum. Pedestrians are allowed if they show their bus transfer ticket — do *not* park outside and walk in.

Wilshire Boulevard returns east from Santa Monica to downtown LA. Eclectic art collections along Wilshire include the **Armand Hammer Museum** and **County Museum of Art** — both excellent. The **George C. Page Museum of La Brea Discoveries** displays a wealth of fossilized remains from La Brea tar pits. Visitors also view the paleontology lab, where new discoveries are cleaned and catalogued. East of downtown is the flashy **Museum of Neon Art**.

Griffith Park off I-5 in northern LA boasts plenty to do. The 'Gene Autry Western Heritage Museum** compares the 'real' Wild West with Hollywood's version, including memorabilia from many Westerns. Films new and old are shown in the museum theatre. Also within Griffith Park, summer concerts by famous singers regularly take place at the Greek Theatre, while the star-struck should visit Griffith Observatory and Planetarium. Travel Town is a transportation museum with rail connections to **Los Angeles Zoo**, one of California's largest. Activities within Griffith Park include picnicking, hiking, and horse riding, the latter rented at the Equestrian Center across Ventura Freeway.

LA County is peppered with movie sets and television studios, especially around Burbank and Universal City. Set aside a full day for **Universal Studios**, where the world's largest studio complex combines instantly recognizable movie and television sets with high-tech hi-jinks launching guests into movieland's special effects. For a sneak preview of forthcoming scenes without distractions, take **Warner Studios VIP Tour**. Tranquility is ensured at picturesque **Mission San Fernando Rey de Espana**, located in Mission Hills north of Burbank. The restored chapel and museum recall the Spanish Missionary era of Alta California.

Pasadena is home to the **Rose Bowl**, which holds huge flea markets between football matches. Tournament House, home of chewing gum magnate William Wrigley Jr, has Rose Bowl game and parade memorabilia. Also in Pasadena are Norton Simon Museum's art exhibits and Oriental cultural displays in the Pacific Asia Museum. Between Los Angeles and Pasadena on Freeway 110 are the excellent **Southwest Museum**'s Native American art and artifacts, representing Californian, Northwestern, Plains, and Pueblo Indian cultures. Charles Lummis, founder of Southwest Museum and co-founder of Sierra Club, hand-built **Lummis Home**, now operated by Historical Society of Southern California. Nearby is Heritage Square, a collection of preserved Victorian buildings.

Undisputed monarch of urban resort **Long Beach** is the *Queen Mary* — ✳ floating hotel, restaurant, and tourist attraction in one. Most visitors tour the liner and Howard Hughes' flying boat, the *Spruce Goose*, while upper sections of the Queen Mary are open for dining in evenings, with views across San Pedro Bay to Long Beach. Long Beach Harbor offers regular boat trips to **Santa Catalina Island**, more reminiscent of a Greek island village than an American resort. Boats to sunny Santa Catalina also leave from **San Pedro**, the Los Angeles Harbor.

Disneyland is just outside LA in **Anaheim**, heart of Orange County. Dis- ✳ neyland offers a very full day of enjoyment; arrive early as ticket sales commence *before* posted opening hours. Continuously refurbishing and improving, Disneyland remains as fresh and more entertaining than when opened in 1955. Themed areas are packed with pop-up Disney characters, Audio-animatronics adventures, fun-packed rides and truckloads of Disney memorabilia.

Knott's Berry Farm in Buena Park is the 'other' theme park, combining an ✳ old western ghost town, the latest thrill rides and, for the younger set, Camp Snoopy. Knott's is also famous for 'home-made' jams, preserves, and chicken dinners 'like mom used to make'. Nearby attractions include the Mediaeval ⊓ Times dinner extravaganza, Movieland Wax Museum, and Hobby City Doll and Toy Museum.

South to San Diego

Huntington Beach is the first Orange County beachside resort along coast-hugging SR1 south towards San Diego. Huntington and Bolsa Chica State Beaches have massive car parks to cope with summer crowds. Seaside **Newport Beach** hosts the nautical set, perfect for yacht spotting or shopping at Fashion Island. Beachside Balboa offers amusements and entertainment, plus harbor cruises and excursions to Santa Catalina; they lack only parking space. Artist colony Laguna Beach holds its Festival of Arts and Pageant of the Masters, a mid-summer celebration by local artists. Dana Point was named after the celebrated author of *Two Years Before the Mast*, describing life along Alta California. Orange County Marine Institute has a replica of his ship, the ⬗ *Pilgrim*.

Mission San Juan Capistrano is most famous for the swallows which arrive on 19 March, St Joseph's Day. Founded by Father Serra in 1776, visitors find delightful combination of restored chapels, historic exhibits and peaceful gardens. San Juan Capistrano town sports quaint shops and Mexican restaurants, a quick hop from Los Angeles via Amtrak.

Take I-5 south to easy, outgoing **San Diego**. The city began at **Old Town San Diego State Historic Park**. Part living history museum and part carnival, tours of Old Town start from Robinson-Rose House, the park visitor centre.

The majority of adobe homes and historic structures in the park and surrounding area are free, as are the 2pm guided tours. **Bazaar del Mundo** is a colourful collection of Mexican-style shops and restaurants surrounding an open-air courtyard. Behind the Old Town is Presidio Hill, site of the first mission and fort. **Junipero Serra Museum** commands an excellent view from its tower gallery, which has photographs of old San Diego for reference. Sometimes mistakenly identified as **Mission San Diego**, which is further inland where Father Serra moved it, Serra Museum traces the development of early San Diego in exhibits and art.

Balboa Park, site of several international expositions, is the gem of San Diego Parks. Balboa is best explored on foot, with plentiful parking in the northeast corner, near **San Diego Zoo**. Famed for hundreds of exotic species in natural settings, an optional guided bus tour introduces visitors to the 100-acre zoo, with the deluxe ticket also including the educational Children's Zoo and aerial rides on the Skyfari. Adjacent to the formal gardens south of the zoo is Spanish Village, where Hispanic and other artisans exhibit and sell their crafts.

An exceptional assemblage of museums await visitors to Balboa Park. The **Natural History Museum** and **Ruben H. Fleet Space Theater and Science Center** are world class, as is the **San Diego Museum of Art**. For classic works of art visit the Timken Gallery and for local artists, try San Diego Art Institute. Both are free, as is the tropical Botanical Building. **Museum of Man** traces human evolution, while the **Aerospace Historical Center** exhibits early flying machines, including a replica of Charles Lindberg's *Spirit of St Louis* made by the original San Diego company. Car buffs head to the Automotive Museum, while Casa de Balboa houses the San Diego History Museum among others. If visiting multiple museums, purchase a reduced price passport. Most museums have one free Tuesday per month, on a staggered basis.

Balboa Park also houses the **San Diego Visitor Center** and **Simon Edison Centre for the Performing Arts**, whose three theatres celebrate the Old Globe Theatre Festival each summer. The Houses of Pacific Relations are a cluster of cottages representing some thirty nations, with ethnic music and dance on Sundays. Spreckels Organ Pavilion gives free concerts on Sundays at 2pm.

Mission Bay Park is more activity oriented, with boats and bike rentals in several locations. A visitor centre on East Mission Bay Drive lists park activities and places of interest. Several resort hotels and Campland on the Bay campground resort are adjacent to the park, as is **Sea World**. Killer whales Shamu and family welcome guests to this first Sea World, packed with educational exhibits and a variety of entertaining shows.

Downtown's Convention and Performing Arts Center is on C Street, with Symphony Hall on B. **Horton Plaza Center** offers some of San Diego's finest shopping in modern surrounds. The nearby Gaslamp Quarter was heart of downtown at the turn of the century and is bouncing back as a shopping and dining district with an 1890s touch. **Villa Montezuma** was built for musician and spiritualist Jesse Sheppard. Today this elaborate Victorian mansion found east of I-5 on K Street, is worth a visit for its fabulous furnishings and stained windows alone.

Seaport Village along the **Embarcadero**, or waterfront, offers another fine shopping experience. North along Harbor Drive are commercial fishing ve sels, naval ships, and **Broadway Pier** followed by the **Cruise Ship Terminal**. Boat tours of San Diego Bay leave from Broadway, while cruise ships leave the terminal for the other California — Baja, Mexico. **Maritime Museum** has three fine ships: square-rigged *Star of India*, reputedly the oldest merchant ship afloat; the *Medea*, a steam powered yacht; and ferryboat *Berkeley*. The museum's exhibits and replica ships are displayed on the *Berkeley*, where volunteers are often constructing additional models.

The **Cabrillo National Monument** is within San Diego County, found south of Mission Bay on Point Loma. This monument to California's discoverer has interesting walks, tide pools to explore (carefully), and views across to San Diego. Other points within the county include the Old Ferry Terminal shopping and dining complex in Coronado, reached by car on SR75 or by ferry boat from Broadway Pier. Nearby are Coronado and Silver Strand State Beaches, followed by Border Field State Park.

The well-to-do resort community of **La Jolla** (pronounced La Hoy-ah) is north of Mission Bay. Again shopping is heavily featured, with the added opportunity of exploring sea-eroded caves. La Jolla has the respected Museum of Contemporary Art, while up the coast off La Jolla Shores Drive is the educational Scripps Aquarium-Museum. The aquarium is administered by the Scripps Institute of Oceanography, part of nearby UCSD (University of California San Diego).

If travelling 'South of the Border' to **Tijuana**, park in San Ysidro, the US border city, or take the LRT (Light Rail Transit) south line from downtown San Diego. Converting currency is optional as dollars are universally accepted, but check the exchange rate. Picture identification is required when returning, and visitors from abroad must ensure their visa allows multiple entries to the US. A Mexican permit is only required if venturing beyond Tijuana. Main

The Joshua Tree grows well in the damp Mojave Desert

activities in Tijuana include people watching, bargain shopping, and sampling Mexican cuisine and cocktails. Pari-mutuel betting is practised on dogs, horses, and people (*jai alai*) — check at the border information booths.

Across the Desert to Las Vegas and Back

The hot desert air draws life-giving moisture, so carry and drink plenty of non-alcoholic fluids, especially in summer. Desert tours are best between late fall to early spring. If touring southern California in mid-summer, I-15 north to Las Vegas should pass sufficient desert, otherwise consider the following scenic route.

From San Diego follow I-15 north to **Escondido**, where the **San Diego Wild Animal Park** is located east off Rancho Parkway. African and Asian animals roam 1,800 acres, recreating a natural environment viewed from a monorail or at lookouts along a walking trail. The **Lawrence Welk Resort Theater** offers a 330-seat dinner theatre and museum with exhibits on the inventor of 'Champagne Music'. Several California wineries can also be found around Escondido.

Follow I-15 north then SR76 east towards the mountains. Mission San Antonio de Pala has been restored, and is used by Pala Reservation Indians. SR6 climbs **Mount Palomar** to the famed observatory, where images from the 200in Hale telescope are exhibited in the free Greenway Museum. Continue east on SR76 through Cleveland National Forest past Lake Henshaw, then northwest on 79. At tiny Aguanga turn right (northeast) onto SR371 then 74, winding through the San Jacinto Mountain section of San Bernardino National Forest. Winter snow is not unknown along the heights, which in summer offer respite from desiccating desert heat. From quaint resort Mountain Center follow SR243 through Idyllwild.

Gradually, then dramatically the road winds down to Banning, where I-10 east passes thousands of giant wind-driven turbines, which produce electricity for **Palm Springs** and the desert resort communities. Intensely green lawns and golf courses are watered from natural underground reservoirs. Apart from golf and tennis, recreation includes the **Palm Springs Aerial Tramway** which lifts visitors up the San Jacinto Mountains for some 50 miles of trails and another network of walks through scenic canyons, courtesy of the Agua Caliente Indian Reservation. To learn more about desert animals and ecology visit **Palm Springs Desert Museum** and **Living Desert** in Palm Desert. Check current productions at **Bob Hope Cultural Center**, which incorporate McCullum Theatre for the Performing Arts.

The Cottonwood Springs entrance to **Joshua Tree National Monument** east on I-10, with a visitor centre offering maps a few miles north. There is no accommodation within the monument, just (waterless) primitive campgrounds, so an early start from Palm Springs with a full fuel tank advisable. The monument protects an important buffer zone between the dryer Chihuahuan Desert and higher and thus marginally more humid Mojave, where Joshua Trees grow — likened by Mormon pioneers to Joshua in supplication. Other activities within the 870 square mile monument include exploring a former horse thieves' hideout, scenic overlooks, rock climbing and numerous hiking trails (carry water). Accommodation is available in Twentynine Palms or 150 miles (240km) further east.

From Twentynine Palms follow SR62 east across the Mojave Desert, where the lifeblood of Southern California, the Colorado River Aqueduct, can be seen. In Earp take Parker Dam road north and cross the dam into Arizona, where watches should be advanced one hour. SR95 north leads to desert resort **Lake Havasu** and **London Bridge**, brought stone by stone from England. The   ✳ planned resort has a 'Tudor English Village' next to the bridge, and golf courses and hotels on either side. Continue North on SR95, taking I-40 east to Kingman, then US93 for the massive **Hoover Dam**. Wind watches back that hour and after sampling **Lake Mead Recreation Area**, continue north.

For a dramatic entrance, reach **Las Vegas** under cloak of night, when the glittering **Strip** sets the desert sky on fire; colourful cascades of light and water, with' starbursts of neon as each casino tries to out-dazzle the competition. Inside, a good casino is determined by other factors, thus glamorous cocktail waitresses and big name entertainment are sometimes secondary to a phenomenon known as 'Super-Loose Slots'. Casinos have them, laundramats have them-even instant wedding chapels have them. Slot professionals wear gloves and hold *big* buckets. Casinos also have crap tables and roulette wheels, keno games and poker hands, with free sets of rules for the asking. Casino guests learning a new game occasionally receive 'practise chips'.

Las Vegas is famous for big name entertainment, and for the biggest shows it sometimes pays to stay at that particular resort. Big casinos have free entertainment in their lounges, while people-watching or promenading along the Strip at night is excitement enough for many. Fine dining is available in large hotels, but firm favourites are the massive buffets offering hundreds of items for bargain-basement prices. The bright desert sun drowns the Strip's neon by day, but a wealth of recreation lurks around its borders.

Interesting rock formations and high desert animals are found along the   🐎 drive and trails of **Red Rock Canyon**. Hire horses at **Bonnie Springs Ranch** in the canyon, which re-lives Nevada past with an Old West town and staged   ♣ gunfights. **Overton**, founded by Mormon pioneers, is gateway to **Valley of Fire State Park**. Shifting rays of sunlight set rugged canyon walls alight, especially towards sunrise and sunset. Various groups of Indians inhabited the area, and the **Lost City Museum of Archeology** has restored sections of   🏛 Pueblo Grande, remnants of an early civilization that vanished, possibly re-emerging as the Chaco Canyon and Mesa Verde cliff dwellers of the Four Corners area.

Returning to Las Vegas, the **Old Mormon Fort** has seen the transition from frontier outpost to railway town to gambling mecca. In sharp contrast are the **Imperial Palace Auto Collection** and **Liberace Museum**. Sightseeing flights   🏛 from nearby McCarran International Airport offer a bird's-eye view of the **Grand Canyon**. Add 800 miles (1,285 km) round-trip if driving to the Grand Canyon from Las Vegas, albeit on fast western roads. If taking the super-scenic Grand Canyon diversion, follow US93 southeast to Kingman, where I-40 leads east to Flagstaff. Follow Chapter 9's Grand Canyon tour, returning to Las Vegas on I-15 southbound from Utah, having visited Zion National Park.

Death Valley National Monument is easiest reached by following US95   ♣ north, then SR374 west through Hells Gate. Furnace Creek has the visitor

Death Valley

Catch a San Fransisco cable car up Hyde Street

centre, accommodation, camping, and food. Interpretive museums examine plants and animals which survive in the harsh desert environment, and also interpret the twenty mule team borax operations. Historic Stovepipe Wells and Scottys Castle are north, then leave south via SR178, passing through the Badlands, lowest elevation in the United States at 282ft (86m) below sea level. Outside Death Valley, follow SR127 south to Baker.

There are several points of interest along I-15 en route to Los Angeles. **Calico Ghost Town** in Barstow boomed when silver was discovered and died when prices plummeted, having been resurrected since by tourism. The Bureau of Land Management operates an interesting California Desert Information Center, while artifacts uncovered at Calico Early Man Archaeological Site may be from North America's earliest inhabitants.

If touring the whole of California, take SR58 west to Bakersfield then Freeway 99 north, joining SR198 towards Sequoia National Park. Follow the narrative from the High Sierras. Otherwise continue west on I-15.

The San Bernardino and San Gabriel Mountain Ranges tower above the communities of Greater Los Angeles and San Bernardino, offering boundless recreation and respite from the heat. From I-15, SR138 offers two slightly different excursions. East leads to **San Bernardino National Forest**, boasting several resort towns along SR138 west, which also passes Silverwood, Gregory, Arrowhead, and popular Big Bear Lakes. Complete the scenic loop by following SR38 south to Redlands, where I-10 returns to LA. West on SR138 through **Los Angeles National Forest** in the San Gabriel Mountains. Lacking the lakes and larger resort communities, LA Forest is better for quieter activities, especially long or short walks and picnics. SR2 threads its way west over ridges and around peaks, with a short detour to **Mount Wilson Observatory** ✳ before dropping down to La Canada Flintridge, near Pasadena, where Los Angeles is south on I-210 then I-110.

San Francisco & the Bay Area

The northern California tour starts at San Francisco. Rome was founded on seven hills, but San Francisco has forty. Developers ignored the topography during the gold rush boom, laying San Francisco in straight grids over irregular terrain. When horse and cart balked at the resulting gradients, the cable car was born. Today, San Francisco is renowned for its ethnic experiences, delicious dining, and sensational sightseeing.

The San Francisco experience begins at the hotel doorstep, especially in Fisherman's Wharf and Union Square areas. **Union Square** is heart of the downtown shopping district, surrounded by scores of specialty shops and upmarket department stores on or near the confluence of Post, Geary, Powell, and Stockton Streets. Other shops and fast food emporiums line bustling Market Street, south of the square. Hallidie Plaza on Market and Powell has the **San Francisco Visitor Information Center**. The **Old Mint** is across Market and a few blocks south on 5th Street, now a free gold rush museum. Two cable car lines run from Hallidie Plaza and Union Square: Powell-Mason to Fisherman's Wharf, and Powell-Hyde past the crookedest street to Hyde Pier and its ✳ National Maritime Historic Site.

Into and around San Francisco

San Francisco International Airport is in San Mateo County, south of the city. Hotel connections are provided by Airporter Coaches, plus Good Neighbors and Super Shuttle mini-bus services. Cable cars and buses are supplemented by BART, Bay Area Rapid Transit, with links around San Francisco Bay. MUNI sells a good transit map, which includes handicapped access information, and special passes at book-stores, supermarkets, and department stores. Trans-Bay Terminal at Market Street and First has Greyhound buses and connections to Amtrak rail links in Oakland, while CalTrain runs from Townsend and Fourth, south of the Moscone Convention Center.

US101 is the main north-south route, while I-80 leads east over Oakland Bay Bridge. For the tourist, San Francisco starts just south of busy Market Street and continues north to Fisherman's Wharf. Sightseeing tours provide useful orientation, but San Francisco's vibrant atmosphere is better sampled on foot. Allow several days and wear comfortable shoes, utilizing the excellent public transport to jump between areas. Visit outlaying points later along the acclaimed 49-mile drive. Smart visitors to blustery San Francisco bring several warm and/or windproof layers, even in summer.

A block east of Union Square and north on Grant Street leads to the impressive archway to **Chinatown**, boasting the western hemisphere's largest Chinese community. Some visitors never get beyond the restaurants and novelty shops lining Grant Street. East on Clay and Kearny, Chinese Culture Center offers culinary and cultural tours. Center handouts list excellent restaurants, some specializing in delectable Dim-Sum. Locals shop one block west of Grant on Stockton Street, more reminiscent of Canton or Hong Kong than America. A few blocks further east on Washington is the free **Cable Car** **Museum**, where massive motors pull cables through underground San Francisco. Returning east, Columbus Avenue cuts a diagonal swath through Grant Street, the beginning of Italian North Beach district. Despite pressure from a growing Chinese population, the area around Washington Square on Columbus still offers a great Cappuccino coffee. Those in cars or with strong legs can detour east on Lombard and up **Telegraph Hill**, whose Coit Tower represents a fire hose nozzle. The hill has limited parking, but excellent views across the bay to Alcatraz.

Continue north on Stockton to **Fisherman's Wharf**, where shopping and sea food are only part of the excitement. **Pier 39** adds a colony of sealions and the multi-media **San Francisco Experience**, a colourful romp through the city's past. The **Blue & Gold** fleet cruises the bay from Pier 39, while the **Red & White** line departs between Piers 43 and 44. **Alcatraz Island**, former prison home of 'Bird Man' Robert Stroud, is now a national park; purchase tickets at Pier 41. Ferry boats to Sausalito leave behind the World Trade Center, near Market Street.

Inland from Fisherman's Wharf are the Cannery and Ghirardelli Square shopping complexes in a former Dole cannery and a one-time chocolat factory, respectively. Also in the Fisherman's Wharf area are Ripley's Believ

It or Not! Museum, and the Wax Museum.

The three-masted *Balclutha* and other ships moored at Hyde Street Pier are part of **San Francisco Maritime National Historical Park,** their free maritime 🏛 museum being east on Beach Street. The Powell-Hyde cable car amasses long afternoon queues at the Hyde Street turnabout; those returning to Union Square may prefer a number 30 bus from nearby Ghirardelli Square. If fit, consider walking up Hyde to **Lombard Street,** 'crookedest street in the world.' Views of the bay are excellent, and a cable car climbing the hill offers an excellent photo-opportunity, plus a ride back to Union Square.

Follow the **49 Mile Scenic Drive** for remaining points of interest. Just west of Fisherman's Wharf from the drive is **Fort Mason.** Buildings in this former military complex house numerous ethnic and artistic cultural centres — Fort 🏰 Mason Center details current activities. The Palace of Fine Arts, built for the 1915 Panama-Pacific exhibition, houses the innovative **Exploratorium,** a hands-on science centre for the whole family. Beyond the Presidio comes **Golden Gate Bridge,** where metered parking allows visitors to walk across or ✳ examine the famous landmark close up. Baker Beach and Point Lobos are part of **Golden Gate National Recreation Area,** the world's largest urban park — stop at the Cliff House to see seals and sea lions.

Golden Gate Park is indisputably one of America's finest. Sporting pur- ♣ suits include golf, tennis, and baseball, with model yachting in Sprechels Lake and boating on Stow. On Sundays many roads are closed, dedicating the park to strollers, skaters, cyclists, and joggers. The cerebral and contemplative should allow days for the museums and gardens. **California Academy of** 🏛 **Science** has a world-class natural history museum, aquarium, and plan- etarium. **De Young Museum** concentrates on American art while its sister museum, **Palace of the Legion of Honor** in Lincoln Park, leans toward European works, including a collection of Rodin sculptures. One admission includes both museums if visited on the same day, plus the excellent **Asian Art** 🏛 **Museum** adjacent to De Young. Learn the tea ceremony at the Japanese Tea Garden, or stroll in the Strybing Arboretum, found across Martin Luther King Drive. The Conservatory of Flowers on Kennedy is based on a Kew Gardens design, while nearby McLaren Lodge is park headquarters.

The windy coastline south of the park is perfect for kites and hang gliders, while nearby San Francisco Zoo has a children's section. After **Twin Peaks** the 🦌 scenic drive passes **Japantown,** found between Post and Geary. Best explored on foot, this thriving community offers several shopping areas and plenty of restaurants.

Several bay area magazines list cultural events, with the **Civic Center** offering performances at the Opera House and Symphony Hall. The Museum of Modern Art is next door in the Veterans War Memorial building until 1995, when it moves to Third Street near Moscone Center. The scenic drive misses the old Spanish **Mission Dolores** on Dolores and 16th Streets, and **Candle- stick Park** south off US101, where 49ers football and Giants baseball events take place.

Coasting down California

The Santa Cruz Mountains form the backbone of the San Francisco Peninsula, with several scenic options for the southbound — start early as both offer plenty to see. SR1 follows the coastline, passing Pacifica, Half Moon Bay and other seaside communities en route to Santa Cruz, with an optional hike or nature walk at **Point Ano Nuevo State Reserve**. Alternatively, I-280 south leads to SR35, aptly named Skyline Boulevard. At Saratoga Gap, the adventurous head west on SR9 and then 236 along a winding mountain road amongst the tall trees of **Big Basin Redwoods State Park**. SR236 returns to SR9, which passes south through mountain resorts Boulder Creek and Felton. The latter is home of **Roaring Camp & Big Trees Narrow-Gauge Railroad**, with scenic rides into the mountains or down to Santa Cruz.

Santa Cruz sightseers make for the **Boardwalk**, a collection of beachfront rides and amusements. Beyond municipal pier is **Steamer Lane**, where surfing was introduced from Hawaii. UCSC (University California Santa Cruz) is up in the hills, with interesting productions at the Barn Theatre and Performing Arts Center, where their summer Shakespeare festival is held. **Mission Santa Cruz** is off SR1 on Mission Street east. Shoppers love the boutiques and oddity shops of nearby **Capitola**, while beach goers find Santa Cruz Beach supplemented with Natural Bridges to the west and Capitola, New Brighton, and Seacliff to the east. SR1 passes the fishing village of Moss Landing en route south.

Historic **Monterey** was capital of Spanish and Mexican California. Amid the downtown one way-system is **Monterey State Historical Park**, a fascinating if widespread collection of adobe buildings. A new maritime museum and state park visitor centre is scheduled for 1993, until then Pacific house doubles as a visitor centre. Exhibits at Customs House recall early maritime trade, while restaurants at nearby **Fisherman's Wharf** serve up other treasures from the sea. The acclaimed **Monterey Bay Aquarium** brings the region's diverse marine life to visitors, centred around a three-storey kelp habitat. Learn to recognize the lovable Sea Otter before proceeding down the coast. The aquarium is on **Cannery Row**, whose raucous fish-packing heyday is graphically described by John Steinbeck, although modern visitors dine and shop in comfort. Ocean Boulevard is a free and picturesque drive along Monterey Peninsula, or opt for famed 17 Mile Drive past the golf courses and exclusive homes of Pebble Beach.

Clint Eastwood was mayor of nearby **Carmel**, a seaside resort with a quaint village atmosphere and excellent shopping. Father Serra, founder of California's mission system, is interred at **Carmel Mission**. Depending upon season wildlife off Point Lobos State Reserve to the south includes whales, sea-otters sealions and pupping seals. Year-round activities offer exploring tide pools and some excellent hikes. In winter, hoards of monarch butterflies congregate along the Californian coast, especially on the 'butterfly trees' of Pismo Beach

After Carmel, SR1 winds south along the rugged **Big Sur** coastline — bring plenty of film and gas, a picnic lunch, and do not rush. Apart from scenery highlights include walks at Pfeiffer Big Sur State Park and a visit to **Hearst Sa Simeon State Historic Monument**. Tours of William Randolph Hearst unfinished castle fill early, so forward bookings through MISTIX are advise

Cathedral Rocks, Yosemite National Park

Tenaya Lake in the Yosemite National Valley

(see Additional Information). If time is short, the free visitor centre museum has exhibits on the Hearst family and construction of the castle, but if possible visit La Cuesta Encantada (the enchanted hill). Tour 1 is a general introduction, best for first time visitors.

Morro Bay, named after the nearby rock, is a seaside resort and fishing village. Inland is **San Luis Obispo**, the county's primary retail centre and home to **Mission San Luis Obispo de Tolosa**. Called 'Prince of the Missions', admission includes the chapel, flower gardens, and a museum of the Chumash Indians and mission era. Continue inland to the High Sierra unless touring the whole of California, when US101 south passes Dutch Solvang and red-roofed Santa Barbara before continuing at Malibu and Los Angeles.

High Sierra

The northern loop leaves the California coast. Follow US101 north then SR41 east across the San Joaquin (pronounced San Hwah-keen) Valley, agricultural heartland of California. Follow SR198 east through Hanford and Visalia for **Sequoia/Kings Canyon National Parks**. Accommodation is available at the aforementioned towns, Three Rivers, and within the parks at Giant Forest, Grant Grove, and Cedar Grove Villages.

Sequoia's pride are its massive trees, including General Sherman, the largest living thing on earth. General Grant in Kings Canyon is America's official Christmas tree, with other magnificent specimens along walks threading through the groves. Ash Mountain, Lodgepole and Grant Grove visitor centres have information on longer hikes. A 35 mile (56km) road from Grant Grove Village leads deep into the Sierra Nevada along Kings Canyon (closed in winter). Trails along the canyon and into the Sierra are less crowded here, as fewer visitors take this detour.

Leave Kings Canyon on SR180 west and from Fresno, raisin capital of America, take SR41 north to **Yosemite National Park**. First within the park is the Mariposa Grove, a collection of Sequoia, followed by Wawona and its Pioneer History Center. Glacier Point Road (closed in winter) climbs to an excellent view of Yosemite Valley. First timers might prefer to enjoy the valley from below first, and then see it from above.

The sheer granite cliffs of **Yosemite Valley** have been carved by glaciers,

---

Yosemite Tips

The park service must balance conservation efforts with rocketing attendance figures. The crush is worst on holiday weekends from Memorial to Labor Day, when incomparable Yosemite Valley becomes hopelessly overcrowded. Visitors without accommodation have been turned away, prompting some to bypass Yosemite altogether. Avoid weekends and American holidays, especially if combined, and ideally arrive before mid-June (except around Memorial Day) or after mid-September. For accommodation, book in January, while campers should make reservations through Ticketron 8 weeks in advance.

leaving much photographed features like Half Moon Dome and El Capitan. Of all the dramatic waterfalls, Yosemite is perhaps finest. Spring flows are strongest, when a full moon creates a rainbow at Yosemite Fall's base on clear nights. By day, the free shuttle bus circles main points of interest, such as Ansel Adams Gallery and Yosemite Museum near the visitor centre, or the food and outdoor clothing shops of Curry Village. Mirror Lake is a pleasant stroll up Tenaya Creek, while the John Muir and Mist Trails up to Vernal and Nevada Falls offer more challenge. The very fit can reach Half Dome, Upper Yosemite Falls, or Glacier Point, although the latter is attainable by car, saving some 3,250ft (991m) of climbing.

Tioga Road (SR120) crosses east over the High Sierra to **Tuolumne Meadows**, a delight of alpine flowers in July and early August. Tioga Pass is typically closed between October and June, but the tour follows SR120 west then 49 north for a new experience.

Gold Country begins near Yosemite and ends the other side of Sacramento, one long vein which promised instant riches to hopeful '49ers. Former boom towns like **Sonora** and **Jamestown** recall the gold rush era, and the coming of the iron horse in **Railtown 1897 State Historic Park**. **Columbia State Historic Park** engulfs most of Columbia, with panning for gold and old mine tours complimented by authentic period hotels and family 'saloons'. Mark Twain's 'Celebrated Jumping Frog of Calveras County' came from Angels Camp, an event still celebrated at the County Fair. Travellers rest easier after the town of San Andreas proclaims, 'It's not our fault!' Continue through Gold Country on SR49 to Diamond Springs, then take US50 over the Sierra Nevada to South Lake Tahoe.

Lake Tahoe, America's largest alpine lake, sprawls across the California-Nevada border, with cruises available from Tahoe City and South Tahoe. From South Lake Tahoe, SR89 follows the timbered western shoreline past aptly named Emerald Bay and Bliss State Parks en route to **Tahoe City**, one of the northern resorts. Continuing clockwise around the lake, Incline Village across the Nevada state line is home of Ponderosa Ranch, of *Bonanza* fame. SR431 is shortest route to Reno, but if time permits continue around the lake, taking US50 east for **Carson City**, capital of Nevada. Remain on US50 east then take SR341 north to **Virginia City**, home of the Comstock Lode. Bluish clay slowed gold mining at the Comstock — until wiser prospectors bought out the claim to cash on an inestimable fortune of high-grade silver ore. Later facing decline, Virginia City was saved by tourism, a sort of 'resort ghost town'.

Reno calls itself America's 'Biggest Little City'. Much of the action is south of I-80 on or near Virginia Street, with Bally's Reno out on Glendale the main exception. Bally's, Harrah's, the Flamingo Hilton and the Nugget produce big time shows, while virtually all casinos have cabaret lounges. Many US airlines operate from Reno Cannon International Airport, as Reno is a year-round resort. Lake Tahoe ski areas include Squaw Valley USA, Tahoe Donner, Sugar Bowl, Northstar-at-Tahoe, and Mount Rose — rent skis and equipment at the resort or in Reno. Many big ski centres offer cross-country as well as downhill runs, and California and Nevada State Park summer trails are often groomed for skiing in winter.

Sacramento and the Napa Valley

♣ Return to California via I-80, taking SR20 to Nevada City then Grass Valley, visiting the excellent **Empire Mine State Historic Park**. Complete the loop by following SR49 south through Gold Country to Coloma, where **Marshall Gold Discovery Site** commemorates the find with a full-size replica of Sutter's Mill and other exhibits.

Sacramento, California's capital, is east on US50. Numbered streets run roughly north-south, alphabetic streets east-west, with the **State Capitol** and surrounding park at 11th and Capitol Avenue, found between L and N streets. The Sacramento River is west, where **Old Sacramento State Historic Park** is located. Many historic buildings house shops, while the new **California State Railway Museum** includes the old Central Pacific Passenger Station and a world-class museum complex where railway engines, cars, and memorabilia are exhibited. Hastings Museum is in the former Wells Fargo Pony Express office, while the History Center examines the city's past.

Other Sacramento gems include **Crocker Art Museum** in the Crocker family's former mansion, **Towe Ford Museum**, and **Sutter's Fort**. Marshall, who discovered the gold, and Sutter, who owned the fort and mill where gold was found, both became casualties of the gold rush, which actually started in 1848. The restored fort recalls that era, with the informative and interesting **State Indian Museum** next door.

Continue West on I-80, then SR12 and 29 north for Napa. Famous for wines, **Napa Valley** Chamber of Commerce details tours through the wine country. Hot air balloon rides and the **Napa Valley Wine Train** are other options. SR29 continues north through the valley, as does the less busy Silverado Trail. Large wineries cater to tour buses and have wider selections; smaller operations offer more personalized service but may require an appointment. After pausing for heath-resort Calistoga, turn left from SR29 onto Calistoga Road towards Santa Rosa and the delightful **Sonoma Valley**. After visiting local attractions, such as Luther Burbank Gardens and Sonoma County Museum

♣ follow SR121 south to , visiting **Jack London State Historic Park** en route. Jack made the 'Valley of the Moon' his home, and the site exhibits his belongings and travel mementos. Sonoma Valley wines are gaining the reputation they deserve — Californian viticulture began there. Sonoma itself was founded by General Vallejo, and has the only mission established under Mexican rule **Sonoma State Historic Park** includes the general's home, Sonoma Mission and the garrison's barracks. General Vallejo surrendered on 14 June 1846 to American sympathizers in the bloodless Bear Flag Revolt, which gave California its flag.

Return towards San Francisco, spending a few days exploring Marin Peninsula before crossing Golden Gate Bridge, if time permits. **Muir Woods National Monument** preserves an easily accessed grove of *Sequoia Sempervirens*

♣ — the gigantic coastal redwoods. **Point Reyes National Seashore**, found north on SR1, has an extensive network of trails, an elk herd, and a lighthouse plus a replica Miwok Indian village next to the Bear Valley Visitor Center Olema. Sausalito, a bayside artist's colony, and Vallejo, named after the general, have ferry links to San Francisco. Vallejo hosts **Marine World Africa USA**, a family-oriented zoological park with marine mammal shows.

Additional Information

State Tourism Bureaux

Nevada Tourism
Capitol Complex
Carson City, NV 89710
☎ 702-885-4384
or 800-237-0774

California Office of Tourism
PO Box 9278, Dept A1003
Van Nuys, CA 91409
☎ 916-322-2881
or 800-862-2543

Regional Information

Anaheim Area CVB
800 W Katella Avenue
Anaheim, CA 92802
☎ 714-999-8999

*California Deserts Tourism
Association*
37-115 Palm View RD,
PO Box 364
Rancho Mirage, CA 92270
☎ 619-328-9256

Las Vegas CVB
310 S. Parade RD
Las Vegas, NV 89109
☎ 702-733-2323

Los Angeles CVB
515 S Figueroa St, 11th Floor
Los Angeles, CA 90071
☎ 213-624-7300

Los Angeles Visitor Center
695 S Figueroa St
Los Angeles, CA 90071
☎ 213-689-8822

Monterey Peninsula CVB
380 Alverado St
PO Box 1770
Monterey, CA 93942
☎ 408-649-1770

Napa Valley COC
1556 First St, PO Box 636
Napa, CA 94559
☎ 707-226-7455

Reno/Sparks CVB
PO Box 837
Reno, NV 89504
☎ 702-827-7366
or 800-367-7366

Sacramento CVB
1420 K Street
Sacramento, CA 95814
☎ 916-449-6711

San Diego Visitor Center
11 Horton Plaza
San Diego, CA 92101
☎ 619-232-1212

San Francisco Visitor Center
Hallidie Plaza
Powell St & Market St
San Francisco
CA 94101-6977
☎ 415-291-2000

Local Events

Check locally for exact dates

January
Tournament of Roses
Pasadena, CA

February
Chinese New Year
San Francisco, CA

April
Cherry Blossom Festival
San Francisco, CA

Renaissance Pleasure Faire
San Bernardino, CA

May
Cinco de Mayo
Statewide CA

Calveras County Frog
Jumping
Angels Camp, CA

June
Monterey Bay Blues Festival
Monterey, CA

July
Summer Rose Bowl
Spectacular
Pasadena, CA

Central Coast Renaissance
Faire
San Luis Obispo, CA

August
Napa Town & Country Fair
Napa, CA

California State Fair
Sacramento, CA

September
Napa Wine Festival &
Crafts Fair
Napa, CA

Monterey Jazz Festival
Monterey, CA

Valley of Moon Vintage
Festival
Sonoma, CA

November
Grand Prix of Southern CA
Del Mar, CA
Tickets ☎ 619-259-5119

Places of Interest

Anaheim, CA
Disneyland
1313 Harbor Blvd
Anaheim, CA 92803
☎ 714-999-4565
Open: 10am-6pm Mon-
Fri, 9am-midnight
weekends & holidays
Theme park, food, gifts, ♿

Barstow, CA
Calico Ghost Town
PO Box 638
Yermo, Barstow
CA 92398
☎ 619-254-2122
Open: 9am-5pm except
major holidays
Shops, restaurant, train

Big Sur, CA
Pfeiffer Big Sur SP
Hwy 1
Big Sur, CA 93920
☎ 408-667-2315
Open: 8am-10pm
Lodge, food, picnic, trails, ♿

Boulder Creek, CA
Big Basin Redwoods SP
Hwy 9
Boulder Creek, CA
☎ 408-338-6132
Open: 8am-sunset
Museum, picnic, hike,
camp, gifts, ♿

Buena Park, CA
Knott's Berry Farm
8039 Beach Blvd
Buena Park, CA 90620
☎ 714-220-5200
Open: 10am-6pm, extended
weekends & summer
Ghost town, rides, food,
gifts, ♿

Coloma, CA
Marshall Gold Discovery Site
SR49
Coloma, CA 95613
☎ 916-0622-3470
Open: 10am-5pm
Visitor centre, museum,
gifts, ♿

Columbia, CA
Columbia SHP
PO Box 151
Columbia, CA 95310
☎ 209-532-4301
Open: 8am-5pm, 8am-
6pm summer. Free
Museum, gifts, food,
lodging, ♿

Death Valley, CA
Death Valley NM
National Park Service
Death Valley, CA 92328
☎ 619-786-2331
Open: 8am-5pm, 8am-
8pm winter
Gifts, museums, food,
lodging, ♿

Felton, CA
*Roaring Camp & Big Trees
  Railroad*
Graham Hill RD
PO Box G-1
Felton, CA 95108
☎ 408-335-4400 or 4484
Train times vary
Store, BBQ, picnic

Huntington Beach, CA
Huntington SB
Pacific Coast Hwy
Huntington Beach, CA
☎ 714-536-1454
Open: 9am-10pm
Beach, surf, picnic, cycle,
♿

Jamestown, CA
Railtown 1897 SHP
PO Box 1250
Jamestown, CA 95327
☎ 209-984-3953
Open: 10.30am-4.30pm
mid-May to Labor Day
Rides on weekends,
museum, gifts, ♿

Joshua Tree NM
Joshua Tree NM
74485 National Monu-
  ment Dr
Twenty-nine Palms
CA 92277
☎ 619-367-7511
Open: visitor centres
8am-5pm
Climb, hike, camp, ♿

Greater Los Angeles, CA
El Pueblo de Los Angeles
Olvera St
Los Angeles, CA 90012
☎ 213-628-1274
Open: 10am-8pm, muse-
ums close early. Free
Visitor centre, shops,
food

*Gene Autry Western
  Heritage Museum*
Griffith Park, 4700 Zoo Dr
Los Angeles, CA 90027
☎ 213-667-2000

Open: 10am-5pm Tue-Sun,
except major holidays
Gifts, restaurant, cinema,
♿

Hollywood Bowl
2301 N Highland Ave
Hollywood, CA 90078
☎ 213-850-2000 (info)
213-480-3232 (tickets)
Philharmonic July-Sept.
Amphitheatre, picnic,
museum

*Los Angeles County
  Museum of Art*
5905 Wilshire Blvd
Los Angeles, CA 90036
☎ 213-857-6111
Open: 10am-5pm Tues-
Fri, 10am-6pm weekends.
Free 2nd Tues. of month
Gifts, food, tours, ♿

Mann's Chinese Theater
6925 Hollywood Blvd
Hollywood, CA 90028
☎ 213-461-3331
Cinema show times vary

*Page Museum of La Brea
  Discoveries*
5801 Wilshire Blvd
Los Angeles, CA 90036
☎ 213-936-2230
Open: 10am-5pm Tues-
Sun except major holidays
Tar pits, Gifts, ♿

J. Paul Getty Museum
17985 Pacific Coast Hwy
Malibu, CA 90265
☎ 213-458-2003
Open: 10am-5pm Tues-
Sun except major holi-
days. Free, book ahead
'Roman villa', gifts, food,
♿

Queen Mary/Spruce Goose
PO Box 8/Pier J
Long Beach, CA 90801
☎ 213-435-3511
Open: 10am-6pm, hotel
24hrs
Hotel, food, gifts, tours,
part ♿

Southwest Museum
234 Museum Dr
Los Angeles, CA 90065
☎ 213-221-2163
Open: 11am-5pm Tues-Sun
Gifts, library, part ♿

Universal Studios Hollywood
3900 Lankershim Blvd.
Universal City, CA 91608
☎ 818-508-9600
Open: 8am summer, 9am
rest of year
Tours, stunts, gifts, food, ♿

Will Rogers SHP
14253 Sunset Blvd
Pacific Palisades, CA 90272
☎ 213-454-8212
Open: 8am-6pm, 8am-
7pm summer except
major holidays
Home, trails, picnic, part ♿

Monterey, CA
Monterey Bay Aquarium
886 Cannery Row
Monterey, CA 93940
☎ 408-648-4888
Open: 10am-6pm except
Xmas
Aquarium, gifts, food, ♿

Monterey SHP
20 Custom House Plaza
Monterey, CA
☎ 408-649-7118
Open: times vary
Gifts, tours, part ♿

Palm Springs, CA
Living Desert
47-900 Portola Ave
Palm Desert, CA 92260
☎ 619-346-5694
Open: 9am-5pm, closed
summer
Gifts, picnic, wildlife park

Palm Springs Desert Museum
101 Museum Dr
Palm Springs, CA 92262
☎ 619-325-7186
Open: 10am-4pm Tues-
Fri, 10am-5pm weekends.
Free 1st Tues of month
Gifts, art, ♿

Sacramento, CA
State Railroad Museum
111 I St
Sacramento, CA 95814
☎ 916-448-4466
Open: 10am-5pm
Railway station, gifts, ♿

State Capitol
10th St & Capitol Mall
Sacramento, CA 95814
☎ 916-324-0333
Open: 10am-4pm
Free, tours, ♿

San Diego, CA
Junipero Serra Museum
2727 Presidio Dr
Presidio Park
San Diego, CA 92138
☎ 619-297-3258
Open: 10am-4.30pm Tue-
Sat, noon-4.30pm Sun,
except major holidays
Museum in replica
mission, gifts, views

Mission San Diego
10818 San Diego Mission RD
San Diego, CA 92108
☎ 619-281-8449
Open: 9am-5pm except
major holidays
Mission, museum, gifts

Old Town SHP
4002 Wallace St
San Diego, CA 92110
☎ 619-237-6770
Open: visitor centre
10am-5pm
Gifts, food, part ♿

San Diego Zoo
Balboa Park
San Diego, CA 92112
☎ 619-234-3153
Open: 9am-4pm, 9am-
5pm summer
Tours, food, gifts, part ♿

Sea World
1720 S Shores Rd
San Diego, CA 92109
☎ 619-226-3901
Open: 9am-dusk, 9am-
11pm summer
Exhibits, shows, food, ♿

San Francisco, CA
Alcatraz Island
Pier 41, Fisherman's Wharf
San Francisco, CA
☎ 415-546-2896 (info)
415-392-7469 (res)
Times vary, book ahead
Cassette tour extra, gifts

Asian Art Museum
Golden Gate Park
San Francisco, CA 94118
☎ 415-668-8921
Open: 10am-5pm Wed-
Sun
Gifts, ♿

Blue & Gold Fleet
Pier 39, Fisherman's Wharf
San Francisco, CA 94133
☎ 415-781-7877
Sailings vary

Cable Car Museum
Washington St & Mason St
San Francisco, CA
☎ 415-474-1887
Open: 10am-5pm, 10am-
6pm Apr-Oct. Free
Visitor centre, gifts, ♿

*California Academy of
   Sciences*
Golden Gate Park
San Francisco, CA 94118
☎ 415-750-7145
Open: 10am-5pm, ex-
tended in summer
Museum complex, gifts,
food, ♿

Golden Gate NRA
Park HQ, Building 201
Fort Mason
San Francisco, CA 94123
☎ 415-556-0560
Open: visitor center
9.30am-4.30pm. Free
Beaches, hike, seals, ♿

Mission Dolores
3321 16th St
San Francisco, CA 94114
☎ 415-621-8203
Open: 9am-4pm
except major holidays
Basilica, museum,
cemetery, gifts

Red & White Fleet
Pier 41, Fisherman's Wharf
San Francisco, CA 94133
☎ 415-546-2655
Sailings vary
Ferry service, Bay tours

San Francisco Maritime Park
Hyde Street Pier
San Francisco, CA 94123
☎ 415-556-3002
Open: 10am-5pm, 10am-6pm summer. Museum free
Ships, gifts, part ♿

San Juan Capistrano, CA
Mission San Juan Capistrano
Ortega Hwy & Camino
Capistrano
San Juan Capistrano
CA 92675
☎ 714-493-1424
Open: 8.30am-7pm summer; else 7.30am-5pm
Chapels, museum, garden, gifts

San Luis Obispo, CA
Mission San Luis Obispo
782 Monterey St
San Luis Obispo, CA 93401

☎ 805-543-6850
Open: 9am-5pm except major holidays
Museum, garden, gifts

San Simeon, CA
Hearst Castle
PO Box 8
San Simeon, CA 93452
☎ 800-444-7275 (reservations)
Open: hours vary, book ahead
Tours, gifts, food, museum
♿ — make reservations

Santa Cruz, CA
Santa Cruz Boardwalk
400 Beach St
Santa Cruz, CA 95060
☎ 408-423-5590
Open: from 11am daily in summer
Amusements, rides, food, shops

Santa Cruz Mission
126 High St
Santa Cruz, CA 95060
☎ 408-426-5686
Open: chapel 9am-5pm
Donations

Sequoia/Kings Canyon, CA
Sequoia/Kings Canyon NP
PO Box 789
Three Rivers, CA 93271
☎ 209-561-3314
Open: visitor centres
8am-5pm
Food, lodging, shops, hike, camp, ♿

Sonoma, CA
Sonoma SHP
Spain St & 3rd
Sonoma, CA 95467
☎ 707-938-1578
Open: 10am-5pm except major holidays
Mission, home, gardens, gifts

Yosemite, CA
Yosemite NP
PO Box 577
Yosemite NP, CA 95389
☎ 209-372-0264 (info), 209-252-4848 (lodging)
Shuttle bus 9am-10pm summer, 10am-9pm rest of year
Lodge, camp, hike, picnic, food, gifts, ♿

11

THE NORTHWEST PASSAGE

European powers sent their finest ships and captains in search of the legendary Northwest Passage, to no avail. Furs, gold, and fertile valleys lured pioneers to Oregon Territory, as it was then known. Civilization is a recent development, and many unspoilt wilderness areas have been set aside. To tour the Northwest is to experience the cutting edge of the new America — where cities co-exist harmoniously with their surrounding magnificence.

Seattle and Washington State

The skyline of rapidly growing Seattle has altered considerably since the Space Needle was erected for the 1962 World's Fair. Consistently rated among America's most livable cities, cosmopolitan Seattle blends metropolitan culture with rugged outdoor adventure.

Get a feel for Seattle at **Pike Place Market**. Selling everything from fresh produce to designer T-shirts, the sea food section offers an excellent introduction to local specialities, worth following up later in the restaurants. The

The Pacific Northwest in Brief

The Northwest Passage combines the scenery and cities of Washington State, Idaho, Montana and Oregon with the grandeur of northwest Wyoming's Yellowstone and Grand Teton National Parks. A minimum of three weeks, ideally four, is required for the entire 4,400 miles. Alternatively, subdivide this monster of a trip into a two-week tour of Washington and Oregon, and another of Idaho, Montana and the Wyoming parks. Options include a visit to British Columbia or a cruise to Alaska.

The principal gateway city is Seattle in Washington state, although Portland in Oregon, or Vancouver in British Columbia may be substituted. Visits to Yellowstone and Grand Teton National Parks are best in May, June, September, and early October. Accommodation in Yellowstone must be booked well advance, especially during July and August.

The acclaimed Going-to-the-Sun Road in Glacier National Park opens mid to late June and closes in October, with alternative routes available. Snow is rare along the Oregon and Washington coasts, but inland even interstates may be temporarily closed. Book a complete winter sports package, including transportation.

Getting to and around Seattle

Sea-Tac (Seattle-Tacoma International Airport) connects to downtown hotels via Gray Line Airport Express or Shuttle Express, plus the usual rental companies and taxi/limo services. I-5 is the major north-south route, while I-90 heads east over the Cascade Mountains. Seattle's east-west streets possess names while north-south avenues generally have numbers. US99, Alaskan Way Viaduct, separates downtown from waterfront piers and park. Meter parking is available in the downtown area, but restrictions apply during morning and afternoon rush hours. Metro buses are free in the downtown area, or explore the self-styled Emerald City on foot or tour bus. Washington State Ferries extend the highway system across the colourful waters of Puget Sound.

✳ waterfront is down from the market via the Hillclimb, or park under Alaskan Way Viaduct. **Seattle Aquarium**, the **Omnidome**, and **Waterfront Park** are popular with visitors, as are the seafood restaurants and specialty shops of Piers 59 and 70. Ferry excursions include Victoria BC departures from Piers 48 and 69, and Washington State Ferries to Bremerton and Bainbridge Island from Pier 52. Harbour tours leave from Piers 54-57, including one to Blake Island's **Tillicum Indian Village**. The latter combines the rich culture of Northwestern Native Americans with a tasty salmon bake. Melbourne trolleys along the waterfront offer feet relief.

Central Seattle is awash with construction sites and office buildings, but the city has not forgotten its heritage. **Pioneer Square Historic District** south of downtown dates back to 1889, when a great fire swept through Seattle. Today the restored buildings house antique shops, art galleries, specialty shops and restaurants, while the statue of Chief Seathl (Seattle) looks on. View older Seattle with a different perspective — from below — on the **Underground**
Π **Tour. Klondike Gold Rush National Historical Park** commemorates the arrival of the gold laden *Portland*, which sparked Seattle's early growth. East and south is the **International District**, where Chinese cuisine and other eastern fare may be sampled. The Wing Luke Asian Museum represents the different Oriental cultures.

Seattle Center is heart of the city, albeit displaced northwest. From downtown, take the monorail from Westlake Center shopping and dining complex
✳ or head for the **Space Needle**. The observation deck and circling restaurants look across the Puget Sound to the Olympic Mountains and south to Mount Rainier (weather permitting). Youngsters love the amusement park, Chil-
✳ dren's Museum, and the educational **Pacific Science Center**. The latter combines hands-on science exhibits with a laser light show and planetarium, plus a multi-storey IMAX Theater. Culture is ranked high in Seattle, and the Opera House, Bagley Wright Theater, the Playhouse, Coliseum, and Arena are all in Seattle Center complex. The Seattle Arts Festival, known affectionately as **Bumbershoot**, erupts into hundreds of events and performances.

🏛 Visual arts are better represented outside Seattle Center. **Seattle Art Museum** trebled its capacity to display a growing permanent collection on relocation to the Venturi-designed museum on University Street. The respected Frye Museum in Seattle and Bellevue Art Museum, east across Lake Washington, supplement Seattle's artistic offerings, as do hundreds of galleries.

Northwestern Seattle is divided by the **Lake Washington Ship Canal**, which links inland Lakes Union and Washington to Puget Sound. Discovery Park offers nature trails, a beach, and the West Point Lighthouse, the latter open weekend afternoons. Inland bound ships negotiate the **Hiram M. Chittenden Locks**, as do trout and salmon. The visitor centre and botanical garden are on the northern bank, fish viewing windows on the south.

The Fishing Terminal on the canal's south side is home to Seattle's commercial fleet, while the nearby waters of Lake Union fill with the flash of sails on sunny weekends. The Seattle side of Lake Washington is lined with parks, from popular Seward Park which juts into the lake, to the long, narrow strip of Washington Park. The University of Washington Arboretum in the northeast is pleasant for picnicking and strolling, with a Japanese Garden in its southern section. Tree-lined Interlaken and Washington Boulevards are nearby, popular with cyclists and drivers.

Excursions from Seattle

The excellent **Museum of Flight** is south of Seattle at Boeing Field, also called King County International Airport. Exhibits include early thoughts on flight, historic aircraft, and a hands-on design centre for budding engineers. Boeing is the largest employer in the Seattle area.

North in **Everett**, Boeing 747-767 Division gives a 90-minute tour of the world's largest production facility and aircraft they construct. Video cameras and children under 10 are excluded, and tours fill quickly, so arrive early or book ahead through a tour operator. Everett is a base for exploring scenic **Whidbey Island**, a short ferry hop away. Whidbey is Puget Sound's largest island, lined with charming coves and communities. At Deception Pass State Park, Captain Vancouver's sailing master, Joseph Whidbey, proved that it was an island. Fort Casey, once part of the Puget Sound Defense System, is now a state park.

Washington State Ferries sail from Anacortes to **San Juan Islands**, with flights from Sea-Tac and Bellingham Airports also available. Friday Harbor on San Juan Island is a good introduction for first-time visitors, with a whaling museum and daily whale-spotting boat excursions. In summer look for whales from Lime Kiln State Park. Orcas, Shaw, and Lopez are other populated islands serviced by ferry, while some fifty smaller isles comprise the San Juan Islands National Wildlife Refuge. Most cyclists prefer gently rolling Lopez Island, while others attack the strenuous climb up Mount Constitution in Moran State Park, Orcas Island.

Bellingham is a harbour city overlooking Bellingham Bay to San Juan Islands. The Whatcom Museum of History and Art on Prospect offers exhibits of Eskimo and Northeast Indian artifacts plus logging and regional history. Revitalized Fairhaven district shops on 11th Street sell crafts, books, and cards. Chuckanut Drive (SR11) hugs the Samish Bay coastline, with excellent views of Puget Sound and the islands. Harris Avenue in Bellingham is southern terminus for **Alaska Marine Highway**, offering connections to Juneau

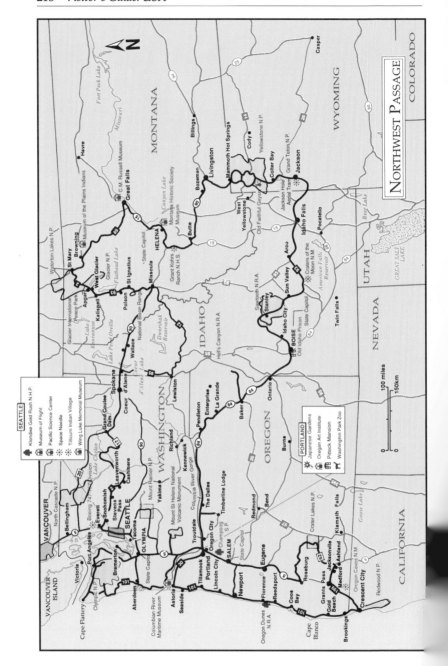

and other places of interest via the famed 'Inside Passage'.

Picturesque **Olympic Peninsula** will fill several days of enjoyable exploration — start from Seattle taking I-5 south. **Tacoma** is en route, boasting Point Defiance Park's Fort Nisqually, a replica Hudson Bay Company outpost, and the Washington State Historical Society Museum on Stadium Way. **Olympia**, capital of Washington state, is smaller than Seattle — beer, oysters and government are among its diverse industries. Tours of the **State Legislative Building** are conducted daily, and the domed structure is taller than the Capitol in Washington DC. The **State Capitol Museum** on 21st Avenue is the former mansion of Clarence Lord, one time mayor and president of Capitol National Bank. Other activities include tours of Olympia Brewing Company, hikes through Nisqually National Wildlife Refuge, and sampling tasty Olympic oysters.

Follow US101, the Olympic Highway, north around the peninsula. After Shelton US101 hugs the shoreline of the Hood Canal. If time permits, visit Port Townsend, with its Victorian architecture and fort.

Port Angeles is the nearest port to Victoria BC, and gateway to northern **Olympic National Park**. Only trails penetrate the heart of this glaciated park, but for a spectacular peep, visit **Hurricane Ridge** after collecting information from the Pioneer Memorial Museum and Visitor Center. Mount Olympus is visible from the ridge. While technical skills and equipment are required to climb that mountain, most visitors enjoy the walks along the ridge. In summer the fields are covered in sub-alpine flora, with plenty of marmot and deer at dusk. Please do not feed them.

US101 is especially scenic along Lake Crescent, where a $^3/_4$ mile trail to

Seattle skyline

Marymere Falls leaves from Storm King Information Station. The turnoff for Sol Duc Hot Springs is beyond Lake Crescent. Most northwesterly point within the contiguous United States is a half hour walk from SR112 at Neah Bay, itself a 74 mile (119km) detour off US101. Those making the effort will find the Makah Indian Reservation, and should visit their local Culture and Research Center.

Hoh and Quinalt valleys along the western Olympic Mountains sport one of the world's few temperate rain forests. Trails at the **Hoh Rain Forest Visitor Center** lead visitors through different sections of the forest, while the adventurous may walk all or part of the 16.9 miles (27km) to the base of Mount Olympus. Permits are required for wilderness camping, but the path along Hoh River makes a pleasant day hike. US101 continues south to twin cities of Hoquiam and Aberdeen, where the driver should take US12 east to SR8. Either continue east to Olympia, returning to Seattle on I-5, or return to Shelton on SR108 and follow SR3 for Bremerton, home of the northern Pacific Naval Fleet, then catch the ferry back to Seattle.

Over the Cascades to Spokane

Three scenic east-west routes pass through the Cascade Range, a jagged, mostly volcanic chain of mountains. I-90 leaves Seattle and crosses the Cascades at **Snoqualmie Pass**, Washington's busiest ski area. Drivers on the interstate will miss Grand Coulee Dam.

Alternative US2 heads east from Everett, passing near Snohomish, noted for its Victorian-era homes, and Skykomish, a historic railway town. **Stevens Pass** is this route's most popular ski area. Proceeding downhill on US2, watch the Wenatchee River spill through Tumwater Canyon in a spectacular series of cascades. Rafting and tubing are popular sports, but start below the dam and dangerous sections if rafting independently.

Leavenworth faced demise before adopting a Bavarian village façade. Now formerly deserted streets are packed with *bierkellers*, chalet hotels, specialty shops, and restaurants. Beyond is quaint **Cashmere**, where the Aplet and Cotlet Candy Factory provides tours and samples of their Turkish Delight derivatives. The well presented **Liberty County Historical Museum** offers two storeys of Natural History and Native American artifacts, plus pioneer-era buildings.

US2 follows the eastern bank of the mighty Columbia River north o. Wenatchee, heart of Washington apple country. Sightseers may prefer Alternate US97, which runs parallel to the western bank, providing views of 55 mile long **Lake Chelan**. *Lady of the Lake* and *Lady Express* boat tours leave Chelan early mornings for Stehekin in Lake Chelan National Recreation Area. Continuing on US97, Fort Okanagon State Park offers Indian trading relics, plu excellent views over the Columbia river valley.

Return to US2 via SR17 south, taking SR156 north for the massive canyo of Grand Coulee. Banks Lake irrigates the lava rich, semi-arid soil of th Columbia Basin with water from the **Grand Coulee Dam**. Tours start at th visitor centre and water is spilled 'over the top' just after lunchtime fo tourists. A free laser light spectacular illuminates the dam on summer ev nings. Return to US2 via SR174, following the grass-covered plains to Spokane.

The third and most scenic route over the Cascade Mountains is via Northern Cascades National Park and the **Ross Lake National Recreation Area** on SR20 (closed in winter). If taking SR20 east, follow SR17 south to US2 at Coulee City and visit Grand Coulee Dam. Fewer cities and services line SR20, making it a scenic and remote drive.

Spelt **Spokane** but pronounced 'spo-can', the city provides goods and services over several states and into Canada. The visitor centre on Sprague Avenue provides maps and information. Downtown department stores are connected by enclosed skywalks, providing year-round comfort to shoppers. Museums include **Chenny Cowles** and the **Museum of Native American Cultures**. The 'new' city is some 10 miles southeast of the original trading post, site of **Spokane House Interpretive Center**. Expo '74 was hosted at Riverfront Park, which now boasts a science centre with an IMAX Theater, children's rides, a gondola, and a friendly marmot colony. Cliff Park in southern Spokane provides views of the city, while Manito Park has several pleasant gardens, including one Japanese.

Idaho Panhandle

The semi-arid countryside of eastern Washington is magically transformed into rolling forested hills at the Idaho border. Some of America's finest natural lakes are within striking distance of I-90. The most famous is **Coeur d'Alene Lake**, literally 'Heart of the Awl' referring to the sharp bargaining natives, although the lakeside city is now a major tourist destination. Accommodation and campsites are available to suit most budgets, with world-class **Coeur d'Alene Resort** offering a welcome respite from the road. Tour and rental boats ply the cobalt waters, alternatively follow scenic SR97 along eastern Coeur d'Alene Lake to Harrison. Extracurricular activities include fishing in or parasailing over the lake, a floating boardwalk and unique floating green at the resort golf course, **Museum of North Idaho** within the city, plus reliving the good old days at Silverwood Theme Park.

If time permits, detour south along US95 to Lewiston for a jet boat trip into the spectacular **Hell's Canyon**. Nearby is the Nez Pierce National Historic Park, which contains a campsite used by Lewis and Clark. Get information at the park visitor centre in Spaulding, as the park occupies several sites. From Lewiston to Missoula in Montana take the scenic Lewis and Clark Highway (2) east through Clearwater National Forest.

If travelling to Missoula from Coeur d'Alene, take I-90 east to **Old Mission** **State Park** for the Sacred Heart Jesuit Mission, Idaho's oldest standing structure. Further east are the mining communities of Kellogg, now a winter ski resort with summer rides on Silver Mountain gondola, and Wallace. The latter displays its heritage at the Sierra Silver Mine Tour and Coeur d'Alene District Mining Museum.

Montana

Welcome to 'Big Sky' country, where the Rocky Mountains divide the land, separating western lakes and forests from the Great Plains, which sweep down to the east. I-90 follows St Regis River through the Lolo National Forest to **Missoula**, with an information centre signposted from the Van Buren exit. The University of Montana campus makes Missoula the educational and cultural centre of western Montana, while the importance of forestry is emphasized by parachute-trained fire fighters of the Aerial Fire Depot. Missoula also has a historical museum, an art museum, and a county courthouse with paintings of the old west. St Francis Xavier Church was built in 1889, the year Montana attained statehood.

Return west on I-90 then head north on US93. The Flathead Indian Reservation boasts more white settlers than Native Americans, but their land also supports about 400 buffalo at the **National Bison Range**. Turn left onto SR200 and right onto 212 for the preserve's entrance and visitor interpretive centre. The two hour scenic loop drive over hilly grazing land includes a festival of wildflowers well into July, with numerous large game animals and bison (buffalo). Retrace the route back to US93 then continue northbound, pausing at St Ignatius for the Mission Museum and Flathead Indian Trading Post.

Polson is gateway to southern **Flathead Lake**, the largest natural freshwater lake in western America. Excursions include *Polson Princess* jaunts across the lake and the Glacier Raft Company's half-day trips down Flathead River. Accommodation is available in Polson and **Kalispell**, 10 miles north of Flathead Lake. The 23-room Victorian Conrad Mansion is open for tours on Woodland Avenue in Kalispell.

Glacier National Park is east on SR2 then a left turn at West Glacier. Apgar the park's western support centre, offers lodging, camping, shops, boa rentals, and an information centre. Apgar rests beside icy blue Lak McDonald, which may be further enjoyed along Going-to-the-Sun Road. Thi serpentine scenic drive through the Rocky Mountains is best started morn ings; if lodgings in Apgar are full, try West Glacier. The road is closed fror October to mid-June, but US2 is an alternative route.

The incomparable **Going-to-the-Sun Road** offers numerous diversior along its winding 50 miles (80km). Lake McDonald Lodge, a Swiss-sty chalet, offers full facilities, including fuel and wrangler conducted horsebac

---

Glacier National Park Tips

Hiking is extremely popular, with over 700 miles of trails, long and short Strenuous hiking is required to experience glaciers first hand, but excellen examples are visible from the road and marks of ancient glaciers are everywhere. Park lodging must be booked early in the year. Campsites are first-come first-served, and fill by mid-morning during July and Augus Usual national park restrictions about backcountry camping and agains feeding wildlife apply — Glacier is definitely 'bear country'. Bicycles ar prohibited on sections of Going-to-the-Sun Road between 11am and 4pm Vehicle combinations may not exceed 30ft in July and August, 35ft otherwise.

The Montana Frontier as portrayed by C. M. Russell in the museum at Great Falls

The fantastic formations of Mammoth Hot Springs in the Yellowstone National Park

rides. Sacred Dancing Cascade and Trail of the Cedars are both short nature walks, with ample opportunity for spotting wildlife. The road doubles back at The Loop, offering fantastic views, followed by the visitor centre at Logan Pass, high point at 6,680ft (2,036m). At Sunrift Gorge look for the American dipper (water ouzle), a cheerful grey bird splashing through the icy mountain stream. Sun Point promises a sweeping panorama of St Mary Lake and the eastern Rockies, including Going-to-the-Sun Mountain, the road's namesake. Rising Sun, another full service lodging and camping area, offers boat tours on St Mary Lake, weather permitting.

If time is available, consider the US89 north diversion to Many Glacier, on Lake Sherburne. Activity levels vary from horse riding and hiking to watching glacier reflections in the lake. Chief Mountain International Highway on 89 leads to Waterton Lakes in Canada (foreigners must have multiple-entry visas). Return to St Mary to continue the tour.

Following US89 south, note the slow transition from Rocky Mountains to foothills and the sudden emergence of the **Great Plains**. Pause at Browning for the free **Museum of the Plains Indians**, with excellent displays of Indian clothing and handicrafts.

The city of **Great Falls** sits astride the mighty Missouri River, the highway used by Lewis and Clark. Although Great Falls cherishes those famous explorers, Charles M. Russell is the most celebrated 'local'. An artist capable of working in any medium, Russell captured the Cowboy and Indian era of the West, and was treated as brother by both. The **C. M. Russell Museum** complex includes the artist's home, his log cabin studio, and a museum to house his works. Russell's letters help outsiders understand his humour and charisma.

Helena, state capital of Montana, is a scenic drive south on I-15 alongside the Missouri River. The city was founded after disheartened miners hit paydirt in 'Last Chance Gulch'. Tours of the **State Capitol** start on the hour, and the domed edifice has paintings from Montana history and legend. The latter includes a large mural by C. M. Russell, with more of his art displayed at the nearby **Montana Historic Society Museum**, which also offers an excellent walk through the Big Sky State's past. Last Chance Gulch historic tours depart from the museum front. Other interesting sights include the Original Governor's Mansion and Cathedral of St Helena. Frontier Town is a replica western pioneer village about 15 miles from Helena on US12. Beyond there pick up I-90 south.

Visit **Deer Lodge** for **Grant-Kohrs Ranch National Historic Site**, and after learning about one of the area's first major ranching operations, spend time in Old Montana Prison. Towe Ford Museum has an excellent collection, including Henry Ford's own Lincoln camper. Nearby Anaconda was a strong contender for state capital during a financial tug-of-war match between Copper Kings Marcus Daly and William Clark.

Although gold and silver drew miners to **Butte**, 20 billion pounds of copper minted the city's fortunes. Enough shafts and tunnels were dug to link New York City to Los Angeles, with connections to Boston and Chicago. The chamber of commerce on the Harrison Street exit of Interstate 15 provides tour map of historic Butte. The 32-room Victorian home of William A. Clark is open for tours as **Copper King Mansion**, also offering lodgings and restaurant. William Clark constructed a scaled down French chateau for h son, Charles. Now the **Arts Chateau**, admission includes a tour of the chateau and changing art exhibits.

Butte's free Mineral Museum is on Montana Tech campus, with the World Museum of Mining and Hell Roarin' Gulch complex nearby. Check with the chamber of commerce for mine tour information, or view the mile-wide Berkeley Pit. The 90ft **Our Lady of the Rockies** glows from a nearby peak by night, watching the city's transition from mining town to transportation and service centre.

Stop at **Bozeman** on I-90 eastbound before rushing to Yellowstone. Their **Museum of the Rockies** includes a planetarium, western art exhibits, and an excellent collection of natural, Native American, and pioneer history. Gallatin County Pioneer Museum houses memorabilia in the old county jail. The town of Livingstone in Paradise Valley is the northern gateway to Yellowstone National Park, situated 56 miles (90km) south via US89. Alternatively visit Billings, Montana's largest city, stopping to see the Western Heritage Center and Yellowstone County Historical Museums. Then take US212 over the super-scenic Bear Tooth Highway (closed in winter) to Yellowstone.

Yellowstone and the Grand Tetons

The world's first national park spills over the Wyoming border into Montana and Idaho. Best known for Old Faithful Geyser, certainly the colourful, some-times awesome, displays of thermal energy draw the crowds. Yet Yellowstone preserves 3,742 square miles (9,690 square km) of wild country and wildlife. Deer, elk, and bison keep video cameras rolling — but do keep back.

Yellowstone and Grand Teton Tips

John D. Rockefeller Jr Memorial Parkway links Grand Teton National Park to Yellowstone, with admission valid in both parks for seven days. During busy July and August, many visitors spend evenings in search of accom-modation. Lodging facilities within the parks should be booked the pre-ceding January, with alternative accommodation available at West Yellowstone, Gardiner, and Livingstone (all Montana), or Cody and Jackson (Wyoming). Except for Bridge Bay all campgrounds are on a first-come basis, most being full by early morning. Yellowstone has greatly reduced its infamous 'bear problem' at the expense of bears' lives. Feeding wildlife is strictly prohibited, as is approaching large mammals — bring a 200mm or longer camera lens.

Altitude precautions apply in both parks: avoid strenuous activities, drink non-alcoholic beverages, smokers and those with breathing difficul-ties take extra care. Keep to boardwalks and pathways — thin crusts prevail in areas of thermal activity, with steam and boiling water beneath. Check at ranger stations for times of geyser eruptions and schedule activi-ties accordingly. Over 1,000 miles of trails are available in Yellowstone alone, but obtain free permits for backcountry camping and follow precau-tions for protecting food.

Start the Yellowstone experience at **Mammoth Hot Springs**, where a series of boardwalks overlook chromatic terraces of travertine, deposited by piping hot, mineral-rich water spilling down them. The Park Service offers ranger conducted activities and a good selection of illustrated books. The resort was once Fort Yellowstone, which explains various military looking buildings, but the lodgings, shopping and dining facilities are excellent. Horse rentals are nearby, complete with a guide, while bus tours offer sightseeing options.

Beyond Mammoth is **Grand Loop Road**, a 142 mile (228km) figure of eight encompassing the majority of Yellowstone's attractions. If time is very short an inverted 'S' will suffice. From Mammoth follow signs for Tower-Roosevelt, which has comparable facilities. Pause at the petrified tree or walk to Tower Falls before continuing south to Canyon Village, another support centre. Scenic drives visit both rims of the awesome **Grand Canyon of the Yellowstone**. Walks line sections of the canyon rims, where paths lead down to overlooks of Yellowstone River's Upper and Lower Falls. Camping at Canyon Village fills before Mammoth, and reservations are almost always required for accommodation at this central spot.

For the most spectacular areas of thermal activity, head west towards **Norris Geyser Basin**, where the museum explains how geysers work. Steamboat, the world's largest geyser, may take years to erupt while Echinus Geyser is active approximately hourly (check times then see other thermal features while waiting). Fountain Paint Pot and Firehole Lake Drive are south on Grand Loop Road, as is the polychromatic Grand Prismatic Spring at Midway Geyser Basin. The ever popular **Old Faithful** complex is beyond less frequented areas of thermal activity. Old Faithful is a misnomer, the geyser being neither ancient nor a good timekeeper — eruptions take place every 30 to 95 minutes. If Old Faithful puts on a poor show, try again later, perhaps after visiting the museum and gift shops, enjoying a meal, and visiting other local thermal features. About one eruption in eight is exceptional, but the occasional misfire occurs. Early morning cyclists may accompany a ranger, who combines the latest technology and considerable experience to estimate geyser eruption times.

West Thumb and Grant Village, at the southern end of Grand Loop Road, offer activities at massive Yellowstone Lake, as does Lake Village to the north. Additional food, lodging and a taste of the old west is available 80 miles (129km) away at Cody Wyoming, founded by Buffalo Bill. Grand Loop Road returns to Canyon Village and Norris Geyser Basin, then completes the loop back to Mammoth Hot Springs via Obsidian Creek. The fire of 1988 burned a considerable area of forest along the Great Loop Road; now boasting grass and wildflowers between the remaining trees. This change to Yellowstone scenery, occasionally over-emphasized by the press, makes wildlife easier to spot.

Grand Teton National Park offers an equally compelling yet different spectacle. The jagged peaks of the Tetons rise abruptly above Jackson Hole, a 50-mile long, 4/5-mile wide depression, with no foothills to dilute the views. The Tetons provide a spectacular backdrop for hiking, horseback riding, or lazy motoring along Jackson Hole. While the Tetons require technical climbing skills and equipment, available trails range from gentle to challenging. **Colter Bay** rests on the shores of Lake Jackson. Facilities including gi

Old Faithful in the Yellowstone National Park, can put on a spectacular display

The glorious Grand Tetons make a dramatic backdrop

shops, accommodation, dining, a marina with boat and canoe rentals, and a visitor centre, offering information on current activities. Horseback riding is popular, whether for short rentals or multi-day expeditions. A pleasant two mile (3.2km) nature walk circumnavigates a local island, and other level walks abound. South of Colter Bay is Jackson Lake Lodge, also lakeside, offering numerous amenities.

Choose either combined Highways 26, 89, and 191 or, better still, opt for the **Teton Park Road**. The latter passes Signal Mountain Lodge and Chapel of the Sacred Heart before the one-way scenic drive to **Lake Jenny**, which abuts the Tetons. Again hourly or multi-day horse rides are available, while a boat ferries visitors across Lake Jenny, offering hikers a 2-mile shortcut on popular Cascade Canyon Trail. Excellent for a day hike or longer, the trail penetrates into the Tetons, leading hikers to meadows of alpine flowers.

Beyond Moose Visitor Center near Grand Teton National Park's southern border is **Jackson**. This western-style resort town is ideally situated for recreation in the Grand Tetons and nearby Bridger-Teton National Forest. Downhill and cross country skiing are available in winter, while innumerable outfitters offer Snake River rafting, with gentle trips within the park and white water further down the Snake River. **Jackson Hole Aerial Tram** reaches the 10,450ft top of Rendezvous Mountain, affording excellent views of the Tetons and Jackson Hole. Wagons West and Teton County Prairie Schooner give passengers a feel of the old West, travelling by wagon and camping under stars. Accommodation and excursions fill rapidly; pre-book through Jackson Convention and Visitors Bureau.

Jackson has art and wildlife museums, while local events include Old West Days in spring, Jackson Hole Shootout throughout summer, and the respected **Grand Teton Music Festival** next door at Teton Village in July and August. Professional skiers compete at several major events in winter, when the nearby National Elk Refuge is home to thousands of wapiti. Although elks leave before summer, other wildlife may be spotted. From Jackson, Follow US26 southwest along Snake River, returning to Idaho.

Southern Idaho

The fertile southern Idaho soil is of volcanic origin, irrigated by the Snake River. Interstates 15, 86 and then 84 west trace the river's route past farmland interspersed with outcroppings of crumbling lava. Idaho Falls, Pocatello, and Twin Falls punctuate the small communities which 'follow the Snake'. The scenic route to Boise follows US20 west from Idaho Falls, passing the aptly named **Craters of the Moon National Monument**. Virtually every type of volcanic activity is explained at the visitor centre and seen along its 7 mile (11km) drive. Take SR75 north for **Sun Valley**, one of the west's foremost ski and summer resorts. Innumerable recreational activities, including excellent skiing, draw visitors from around the world to this Swiss-styled Shangri-la. Together with nearby Ketchum and Stanley in the north, they make a good base for exploring **Sawtooth National Recreation Area**. From Stanley take SR21 west to gold rush town **Idaho City**, which in 1862 vied for being the most populated town north of the California gold fields.

Boise is the governmental and commercial capital of Idaho, and also growing as a university town. Start with the **State Capitol**, offering guided tours, except Sunday. The 'City of Trees' has many parks and gardens. Within or around popular Julia Davis Park are the Boise Art Museum, City Zoo, Historical Museum, and Discovery Center of Idaho. Doing time in Old Idaho Prison includes admission to the History of Electricity in Idaho and Idaho Transportation Exhibits, while the Botanic Gardens are nearby. Boise may be explored on the tour train or floating down the Boise River. Float trips may be arranged, or rent an inner tube at Barber Park and jump in. The summer-long Idaho Shakespeare Festival is a riverside event, as is the Boise River Festival in late July. Before leaving, check current performances at Morrison Center for the Performing Arts or reserve a tour of Peregrine Fund World Center for Birds of Prey. One of the largest concentrations of raptors in the wild is at Snake River Birds of Prey Natural Area, to which there are several guided trips from Boise. Then continue west on I-84 for a drive along the Columbia river gorge.

Oregon

Travellers should not expect gigantic spruce and douglas fir at the Oregon border, they are a coastal phenomenon. The visitor centre in Ontario provides maps and information on Oregon. Agriculture along the Snake River is the region's economic mainstay, while popular pastimes include fishing, hunting, and rock-hounding.

Paint Your Wagon was filmed at **Baker**, Oregon gateway to Hell's Canyon. Other diversions include the Blue Mountains, Sumpter Valley Railroad excursions during summer weekends, and visits to gold mining ghost towns. The US National Bank has a free gold exhibit, while the Oregon Trail Regional Museum displays local rocks and minerals. **La Grande** is a staging point for forays into Enterprise, Joseph, and the Wallowa Lake Area. Ranger stations give information on scenic drives through Wallowa-Whitman National Forest, while Wallowa Lake Tramway lifts visitors to the top of Mount Howard. Professional packers provide trips into Eagle Cap Wilderness.

Pendleton is in Oregon wheat country, but the name conjures up images of quality woollens, with tours round the Pendleton Woollen Mills. The area has an authentic western feel, with September's Pendleton Round-Up crowning the year's events in a week-long celebration of rodeo, Happy Canyon Indian Pageant, and parades, plus bronco and stagecoach races — book accommodation ahead.

Early travellers on the Oregon Trail were forced to abandon the relative safety of land, taking their belongings by raft down the **Columbia River**. The Dalles remembers that past at Fort Dalles Museum, last remnant of the 1850 fort, and at old Wasco County Courthouse. The Dalles Dam is open for tours. Port Marina Park at the **Hood River** exit of I-84 has a county historical museum with interesting exhibits. In the background windsurfers crisscross the Columbia River. The local visitor centre gives information on the town of Hood River, gateway to the scenic Mount Hood Loop Highway. A complete circle is not necessary to appreciate that **Mount Hood** (11,235ft, 3,425m) dominates northern Oregon. The Hood River County Scenic Route leads to

A dramatic sunset at Crown Point in the Columbia River Gorge

Jackson Hole, Wyoming, offers winter recreation

Panorama Point Park, overlooking the orchards and gardens of the Hood River Valley, an incredible contrast to semi-arid eastern Oregon. Mount Hood Railroad offers alternate transport up the Hood River Valley.

Those wishing to drive the Mount Hood Loop Road should take SR35 south, then SR26 west, following the Oregon Trail through the dense Mount Hood National Forest. Timberline Lodge on the side of Mount Hood offers year-round skiing, rentals, and a tow to 7,000ft. Timberline is a popular trailhead for Mount Hood; check conditions before climbing. Rather than miss the best Columbia River Gorge scenery, retrace the route to Hood River or, if armed with a good map, from Zig Zag drive north over Lolo Pass (check road conditions first).

Cascade Locks are west of Hood River, and although dams have submerged the cascades, the locks are in a park-like setting. The local history museum exhibit includes the *Pony*, first steam locomotive in the west. The **Historic Columbia River Highway** was an engineering marvel in its day, with sections still open to traffic. Numerous waterfalls line the most popular section, found at the Ainsworth State Park exit off I-84. Multnomah Falls are best appreciated from the top, Bridal Veil from the base, the latter the easier walk. Most pictures illustrating **Columbia River Gorge** are taken from Crown Point. The Historic Columbia River Highway returns to I-84 at Troutdale, a short hop from Portland.

Greater Portland

The greenery which surrounds **Portland** continues into the tree lined streets, offering pleasant strolls to visitors and locals alike. The self-styled 'City of Roses' has parks ranging from tiny Mill Ends Park, a mere 24in across, to the aptly named Forest Park, some 5,000 acres of trees. Central Portland straddles the Willamette River, encircled by I-5 (east) and I-405 (west). Downtown is south of Burnside Street and west of the Willamette, with Old Town just north and Skidmore Historic District in the waterfront area between.

Walking is enjoyable within Portland, but the city also has an award-winning transportation network. TRI-MET offers connections across three counties, with free transport in downtown Portland in the 'Fareless Square'. Most TRI-MET buses pass through the downtown transit mall on Southwest 5th & 6th Streets, and kiosks help sightseers plan travels. MAX links downtown to the Lloyd district across the Willamette, where the convention centre and 'America's first' shopping mall are found. TRI-MET operates vintage electric trolleys on selected routes, while several tour boats cruise the Willamette River. Portland International Airport is expanding to meet increases in visitor levels. Taxis, limousines and major rental cars are supplemented by free shuttles to many hotels and regular bus links to downtown.

The visitor information centre is on Salmon and Front Streets. Across Front Street is Tom McCall Waterfront Park by the Willamette River. The **Oregon Art Institute** and **Oregon Historical Museum** are on Jefferson, which runs inland from Front Street south of the visitor centre. Tree lined Park Avenue and Broadway are perpendicular to Jefferson, and the Portland Center for the performing Arts sprawls across Broadway. Arlene Schnitzer Concert Hall houses Oregon Symphony Orchestra and hosts travelling concerts and dance troups. The two stages of New Theatre Building offer varied productions, while Portland Opera and Oregon Ballet perform in the Civic Auditorium.

Check out the lighthearted weather station at **Pioneer Courthouse Square**. Helia shines on clear days, a dragon follows stormy weather, and the blue heron heralds Portland's more changeable days. Surrounding the square is some of Portland's finest shopping. Pioneer Pavilion has fine stores, with Galleria a few blocks away. Portland has a lively city centre, perfect for people-watching or leisurely shopping. Even tall office buildings house ground level specialty stores or al fresco cafés, and Portland boasts a wealth of public art.

Places of interest around West Burnside include the **Portland Saturday Market, wh**ich fills the Skidmore Fountain Area on weekends. New Market Village is one of the recycled buildings in Portland's former financial and commercial centre. The gateway to Chinatown is on Burnside and 4th, with the Columbia River Maritime Museum towards the Willamette River.

A TRI-MET bus beats an uphill walk from West Burnside to Portland's pride, **Washington Park**. No 'City of Roses' would be complete without the 400 species at the **International Rose Test Gardens**. An authentic tea house awaits visitors to the **Japanese Gardens**, where snow-capped Mount Hood substitutes for Mount Fuji. Hoyt Arboretum claims the largest collection of conifers within the USA, including long-lived Bristlecone Pine. **Washington Park Zoo** is a walk or drive down from the gardens, or take the park train. The century-old zoo offers diverse modern environments, from tropical rainforest and arctic tundra, with unrivalled success in breeding Asian elephants. Nearby **OMSI**, Oregon's Museum of Science and Industry, and **World Forestry Center** offer hands-on learning. Up from Washington Park on Burnside is the French Renaissance **Pittock Mansion**, with panoramic views and a fascinating floor plan.

The Oregon Coast and Capital Loop

From Portland, US30 follows the Columbia River west towards the Pacific Ocean. Despite centuries of searching for the Northwest Passage, the Columbia remained undiscovered until 1792. American Captain Robert Gray sailed over a sand bar which British Captain Vancouver had ignored just weeks before, and the Lewis and Clark expedition supported the American claim for Oregon Territory. Despite a setback during the War of 1812, when John Jacob Astor sold his fur company holdings to the British for a song, Oregon became part of America. **Astoria** remembers its heritage as that frontier post, with sections of Fort Astoria reconstructed. **Columbia River Maritime Museum** highlights centuries of Northwestern maritime history. Other places of interest include Captain Flavel's restored Victorian mansion and Heritage Center Museum. Coxcomb Hill has excellent views and **Astoria Column**.

Fort Clatsop National Memorial is off US101, Oregon's primary coastal route. The fort and visitor centre commemorate the Lewis and Clark expedition, which wintered here before returning with news of fertile Oregon. For Clatsop rangers and volunteers relive the Lewis and Clark encampment during the warmer months of summer. Follow US101 south, past the popular resort of **Seaside**. Offshore rocks at Tillamook Head in Ecola State Park support sea lion colonies, while wading birds and waterfowl frequent estua ies along the Oregon Coast.

Tillamook is a major dairy centre, with two cheese processing plants and a Pioneer Museum full of fascinating memorabilia. The scenic **Three Capes Road**, found by turning right (west) at 3rd Street, passes the Cape Meares State Park lighthouse, which gives tours. Cape Lookout State Park has a beach and $2^1/_2$ (4km) mile walk to the cape's head. Nestucca River cuts through quaint Pacific City, where local fishermen still launch dories from the beach. Three Capes Road rejoins US101 followed by another turnoff to Three Rocks, where waterfalls plunging from Cascade Head into the Pacific may be reached by trail.

Continuing south, Lincoln City boasts the longest developed section of Oregon beach, while Depoe Bay claims the world's smallest harbor. At Cape Foulweather, named by Captain Cook during a March gale, the resorts of Otter Rock nest near a temperate rain forest.

Newport is a good base for exploring the central coast area. Behind the chamber of commerce is the Lincoln County Historical Museum and adjacent Burrows cottage, with Victorian furnishings and gifts. Beachside Newport offers Yaquina Bay State Park and tours of a haunted lighthouse. Bayside are fish markets, seafood restaurants, tourist attractions, and several charter and tour boats.

Travellers may take US20 inland to shorten the coastal loop, but should first cross the Yaquina River and visit both the **Hatfield Marine Science Center** and **Oregon Coast Aquarium** for an excellent introduction to life beneath the coastal waters. Those continuing south have plenty to see — pinnipeds at seal rock, fishermen leaving harbor at Waldport or Yachats, and the Siuslaw National Forest visitor centre at Cape Perpetua.

Sea lions breed only on islands and at **Sea Lion Caves**, a tourist attraction where neither staff nor visitors may feed or otherwise disturb the resident stellar seals. Admission includes the summertime viewing platform and elevator into their cavernous winter refuge.

Florence is the northern gateway to **Oregon Dunes National Recreation Area**, a 40 mile (64km) stretch of coastline hiding mountains of sand. Off road vehicle rentals line US101, while cars may access the beach via South Jetty Road below Florence and at Horsefall Lake near Glasgow. The headquarters at Reedsport provides picturesque trail guides, with the 2 mile (3.2km) round-trip walk from Oregon dunes overlook an excellent introduction. Umpqua Dunes Trail from North Eel Campground crosses an unmarked 2-mile wide stretch of 400ft-high dunes, literally a shifting sea of sand — exhilarating but carry water and compass.

The quaint fishing village of Charleston is a detour west from busy Coos Bay. The nearby wildlife sanctuary of South Slough, a National Estuarine Preserve, has an active and educational visitor centre. Artists gather at **Bandon**, attracted by the rugged coastline, while beachcombers collect agates and semi-precious stones along its beaches.

Cape Blanco, off US101, is the most westerly point in the contiguous United States. Walk there from the picnic area or drive past the campground to the fully operational (therefore closed to visitors) 1870 lighthouse. The cape offers grey whale and sea lion spotting, the latter having an off-shore colony.

A storm in 1861 washed away placer gold from **Gold Beach**. Today the natural beauty of the Oregon coast is supplemented with jetboat excursions up the **Rogue River**, leaving early mornings and, during July and August, shortly after lunch. The most exhilarating trek is 52 miles up Rogue River to Blossom Bar Rapids, beyond which no power boats go.

Gold Beach to Brookings offers Oregon's most scenic coastline, with vista points perched on cliffs and coastal trails to sheltered coves. The California agriculture quarantine station is south of Brookings, the 'Banana Capital of Oregon', so purchase no roadside or self-pick fruit or vegetables.

The northern **California** coastline resembles southern Oregon's, but adds primeval forests of old growth redwood. The overwhelming majesty of *Sequoia Sempervirens*, the coastal redwood, is best experienced south on US101 in **Del Norte State Park**, where stately redwoods form a roadside honour guard. At **Prairie Creek Redwoods State Park**, Roosevelt Elks feed across from the visitor centre, while an excellent trail network passes beneath virgin stands of redwood. **Redwood National Park** visitor centre offers numerous interpretive activities during summer months. The world's tallest tree is in the remote Tall Trees Grove, but more accessible redwood groves satisfy most visitors.

Travellers should return north on US101 then take US199, the redwood highway. **Jedediah Smith Redwoods State Park**, named after the famous mountain man and trapper, is parted by the wild and scenic **Smith River**. Winding US199 bisects the Six Rivers National Forest before diving through the Collier Tunnel.

Once back in Oregon, consider the 20 miles (32km) detour to **Oregon Caves National Monument**, west of Cave Junction via SR46. The guided, moderately strenuous, walking tour includes all classic cave formations. Meals are available at the chateau dining room, while child care is provided for under sixes. Return via Holland Loop Road to sample several of southern Oregon's Wineries.

Like Gold Beach, **Grants Pass** offers jet boat trips on the Rogue River, some venturing all the way to Hells Gate. Rafting expeditions on the Rogue vary from outings to four day trips. The Grants Pass Visitor and Convention Bureau match traveller's desires and abilities with professional guides. Before returning north to Washington, consider one of the following diversions.

From Grants Pass, I-5 offers a scenic route southeast to Ashland, holders of the acclaimed **Oregon Shakespeare Festival**. Performances (which include modern plays) take place from February to October, ideally booked in advance. Ashland also offers other theatre groups and the Shakespeare Art Museum, where exhibits coincide with the Festival's productions. **Jacksonville**, a gold mining town between Ashland and Grants Pass has retained its historic buildings and character. Visitors to **Jacksonville Museum of Southern Oregon History** on Fifth and D Streets may then follow their self guided tour through the town, including the period Beekman House.

Crater Lake National Monument is 70 miles east of Medford on SR62. Formed 7,000 years ago when Mount Mazama erupted violently, today the crater contains a deep, brilliantly blue lake surrounded by a 26 mile (42km) long cliff of lava. The visually rewarding 31 mile (50km) crater rim drive is always popular (snowbound sections open around mid-July), while the strenuous but rewarding climb up Wizard Island awaits the very fit. Ste

Pioneer Square is a popular Portland rendezvous

Scientists keep a careful watch on the Mount St Helens volcano

Center interpretive facilities are open year-round, but during mid-summer visitors gravitate towards the rim village, starting point for many trails. Seek local advice before venturing into the wilderness surrounding Crater Lake.

Return north on I-5, reached from Crater Lake by scenic SR138. **Wildlife Safari** at Roseburg is a popular stop, with drives through 600 acres of zoological park. Eugene and Springfield form a major cultural centre within southern Oregon, hosting the Oregon Bach Festival during late June and early July. The University of Oregon has a Museum of Art and Museum of Natural History.

Salem, capital of Oregon, makes a good base for exploring scenic Willamette River Valley. **Mission Mill Village** on Mill and 12th Streets offers mill tours, except Monday, and also houses the Salem Visitor Center, a history museum and selected shops. Park at the mill to explore Salem on foot. Start at the park-like Willamette University between 12th and Winter Streets, then meander north towards State Street and the **State Capitol Building**. Tours may be booked or self-guided, and Oregon's history in art is displayed both inside the capitol building and out. Downtown Salem, just blocks from the Willamette River, has an interesting selection of shops. Return to the mill via Mission Street, pausing for the Rose Gardens and Italinate residential Bush House at Bush's Pasture Park.

For a tour of Willamette Valley, follow scenic SR99W north instead of I-5. McMinnville is the self-styled capital of Yamhill Wine Country, heart of Oregon's wine industry. At Newburg turn off 99W for **Champoeg State Park** (pronounced 'shampooee'). Today an archaeological site, Champoeg would have been Oregon State Capital *and* end of the Oregon Trail but for its devastating floods. The park interpretive centre remembers the narrow vote at Champoeg which set Oregon on course to join the United States.

The Oregon Trail officially ends in **Oregon City**, where the excellent Interpretive Centre will be supplemented by a new Oregon Trail Museum, both offering exhibits of pioneer life. Nearby McLoughlin House recalls the man who helped pioneers find land, build a home, and prosper at the end of the Oregon Trail.

Southern Washington

Return north on I-5, perhaps visiting America's newest National Volcanic Monument — **Mount St Helens**. The main visitor centre is 5 miles (8km) east on SR504 (I-5 exit 49), well back from the volcano itself. Exhibits highlight the destructive 1980 eruption and gradual revegetation since. A new centre within the national monument is planned, but volcanic activity has not totally subsided. Check with rangers before hiking into the monument — permits are required to climb Mount St Helens. Drivers will find the best views, at least until SR504 is restored, west on SR25 to Windy Ridge (closed in winter). Activities in the southern section of Mount St Helens Monument include exploring Ape Cave and the surrounding Mount St Helens National Forest.

The glaciated volcano of **Mount Rainier National Park** is Washington's highest mountain, dominating the surrounding countryside for many miles. Nisqually, the main entrance on SR706, leads to the Longmire Museum then Henry Jackson Visitor Center in Paradise, the nearest driveable point to th dormant giant. The 92 mile (148km) Wonderland Trail encircles Mount Rainier, passing exquisite canyons and waterfalls, with optional detours onto glaciers. Day walks are also available while many enjoy exploring roads through the national forests. The winding White River Road leads to Sunrise Visitor Center on the mountain's east side. Many roads and trails are open to cross country skiing in winter, while in summer SR410 leads drivers along the White River from Mount Rainier towards the coast, where I-5 returns to Seattle.

Vancouver Detour

Given the friendly border between the United States and Canada, travellers may sample the pleasures of British Columbia before returning home. Visitors from abroad should possess multiple entry United States visas before crossing into Canada. At the border I-5 becomes Highway 99, leading directly to Vancouver. The border information centre provides maps, accommodation guides and currency exchange facilities. Those arriving by air will find Vancouver International Airport southwest of the city. Airport buses to downtown Vancouver hotels leave from Level 2, hotel shuttle buses from Level 1.

Greater Vancouver has undergone considerable growth, sprawling over the rich Fraser River delta and forested hills overlooking the rugged Pacific coastline. Downtown Vancouver sits on a peninsula jutting into Burrard Inlet, where the classic glass and steel skyline is best appreciated by a harbour boat trip.

The main Vancouver Travel InfoCentre on Dunsmuir Street provides maps and helps visitors choose accommodation and tours. Sightseeing within Vancouver is easily combined with international class shopping and dining. Handcrafted artifacts bring home a flavour of Northwest Canada. **Robson Street** offers fashionable boutiques and continental shops, while **Pacific Centre** between Howe and Granville offers three blocks of specialty shops and eateries.

Harbour Centre Mall on West Hastings has a harbour viewing tower with a restaurant. Fine dining with views of Vancouver are available at the Vancouver Hotel, the Sheraton Landmark, and the Ramada Renaissance. In good weather cross to North Vancouver for Grouse Mountain Chalet, where the dining room offers excellent views.

Vancouver is the major cultural centre of Western Canada, with regular concerts and drama at the **Queen Elizabeth Theatre** and **Vancouver Playhouse**, both within the Civic Theatres Complex, and the **Orpheum Theatre**, a refurbished 1927 opera house which gives tours. **Vancouver Art Gallery** on Hornby Street exhibits classical and contemporary art, including works by the noted Canadian artist Emily Carr.

Summer cruises depart from **Canada Place** to northern British Columbia, Alaska and beyond, while sea planes depart from the nearby British Columbia Floatplane Terminal. Canada Place houses the World Trade Centre, shops, restaurants, a hotel, Vancouver Convention Centre, and an IMAX theatre. The **Science Centre** offers the curved dome of an OMNIMAX theatre, plus hands-on exhibits.   ✳

Gastown, restored heart of Old Vancouver, offers shopping for art and antiques plus dining in cozy restaurants lining the cobblestone streets. Gastown straddles Water Street east of downtown Vancouver. Next door on East Pender Street is North America's second largest **Chinatown**, with opportunities for people watching, sampling the cuisine, and relaxing in the Ming dynasty styled **Dr Sun Yat-Sen Chinese Garden**.

Stanley Park offers Vancouverites a respite from the pressures of modern living. Minutes from downtown, the park encompasses 80 miles of roads and paths plus two large lakes. Park at the Georgia Street entrance for the free zoo, much acclaimed **Vancouver Aquarium**, and **Malkin Bowl**, an open-air theatre with summertime performances. The scenic drive passes a forest of totem poles and 9 o'clock gun, with excellent views of Vancouver across the harbour. Prospect point offers good views of West Vancouver and Lions Gate Bridge, while beaches, lawn bowling and tennis courts are at the southwestern corner of Stanley Park along English Bay.

Vanier Park has the **Maritime Museum** and **H. R. MacMillan Planetarium-Vancouver Museum Complex**. From Stanley Park bear right from Beach Avenue onto Pacific Boulevard, then right again onto Burrard. **St Roch National Historic Site** adjacent to the Maritime Museum offers illuminating tours of the first ship to cross from Atlantic to Pacific via the Arctic. The well preserved vessel is seemingly supplied for another fantastic voyage.

Beaches, parks, and yacht clubs line Point Grey, with the University of British Columbia at its western tip. The Japanese **Nitobe Memorial Garden** is acclaimed for its accuracy, while **Main Garden** offers alpine, native British Columbian, contemporary, food, winter and Asian Gardens, with reduced admission for Nitobe and Main Gardens. The **Museum of Anthropology** exhibits artifacts from northwest coastal Indians as part of its People of the Pacific Collection.

South of downtown Vancouver across Cambie Street Bridge is the much loved **Queen Elizabeth Park**. A former quarry is now an exquisite sunken garden, while the hilltop offers unimpeded views of Vancouver. The educational and enjoyable **Vandusen Botanical Gardens** are several blocks west on Oak Street.

Other parks in the Vancouver environs include the free Lynn Canyon Park and exhilarating Capilano Suspension Bridge and Park. **Grouse Mountain** operate their aerial tramway year-round, with excellent views of Vancouver, weather permitting. All are located in North Vancouver. Art in Deer Lake Park includes the Burnaby Art Gallery and exhibitions along Summer Set Lane during warmer months. A Village Museum with numerous pioneer buildings and exhibits is at Burnaby park.

Before returning to the United States via Highway 99, consider the waters surrounding Vancouver. Cruises should be booked in advance, but other options include the ferries and sightseeing trips from Coal Harbour. **Victoria** provincial capital of British Columbia, may be reached by the Tsawwassen Ferry and a bus ride from Swartz Bay. Victoria was a riotous boomtown during the Canadian Gold Rushes, but the railroad made Vancouver the growth town, and Victoria evolved into a charming city. Retaining its British character, Victoria offers magnificent floral displays at Government House Gardens, Butchart Gardens, Fable Cottage, and Crystal Gardens. Visit stately hotel for 'high tea', and reserve time for the **Royal British Columbia Museum** — one day is rarely enough.

Alaskan Excursion

Whether visited separately or as an extension to the Northwest Passage, Alaska is a trove of breathtaking vistas, boasting a rugged terrain within easy access of civilization. Travel is simple within Alaska — highways begin where cruise ships dock, and where the road ends, Alaskans take to the air. Follow the sun north, where summer days are all but endless.

Cruise liners and ferries ply the famed **Inside Passage**, the island-studded waterways of southeastern Alaska. Most cruise options depart from Vancouver, British Columbia, reaching Glacier Bay National Park before returning. **Alaska Marine Highway** connects Bellingham in Washington (north of Seattle) and Prince Rupert in British Columbia to Alaskan towns, taking passengers and cars through the picturesque passage. Both liners and ferries visit interesting sites en route.

Ketchikan is famous for salmon, high rainfall, and Northwestern Native artifacts, especially totem poles. Totem Bight Historical Site is 10 miles from town, while Totem Heritage Center is on Deermount Street. Saxman Native Village south of the town displays native crafts, including totem carving, plus tribal dances if numbers are sufficient. **Sitka**, once capital of Russian America, recalls its heritage at the **Sitka National Historical Park**, which includes the Russian Bishop's House and Southeast Alaska Indian Culture Center. New Archangel Dancers perform Russian dances in the Centennial Building, while St Michael's Cathedral has a wealth of Russian Orthodox art, icons and antiques. Sitka tours offer local sightseeing and harbour cruises, while the town holds regular events including the All Alaska Logging Championships, Sitka Salmon Derby, and the Sitka Summer Music Festival.

Juneau is Alaskan state capital and first of the gold rush towns. Places of interest include the State Capitol and excellent **Alaska State Museum**, chronicling Eskimo, Indian, American and Russian culture. House of Wickersham is a Juneau landmark, exhibiting early Alaskan memorabilia. Juneau Douglas City Museum revues the city's mining methods and history, while 'Lady Lou Revue' presents a humorous look at the gold rush days. The 1894 St Nicholas Russian Orthodox Church is on Gold Street.

Popular tours from Juneau include nearby **Mendenhall Glacier**, with a visitor centre observatory affording excellent views. Helicopters and airplane-floatplane operators provide excursions to more isolated areas, including **Glacier Bay National Park**, also visited by luxury liners and daylight cruises from Juneau, Haines and Skagway. The **Forest Service Information Center** in Juneau's Convention Center on Egan Drive offers interesting exhibits, current road and trail conditions, plus reservation information on campsites and cabins within southeastern Alaska.

Haines and Skagway provide something other Inland Passage towns lack, a road north, albeit occasionally gravelled until the Alaska Highway is reached. Haines offers Chilkat Bald Eagle Preserve, Sheldon Museum and Cultural Center, and Fort William Seward. This frontier army post now hosts

Chilkat Indian Dances and a tribal craft centre in the old hospital. **White Pass & Yukon Route** connects **Skagway** to Whitehorse, British Columbia, via a super-scenic narrow gauge railway along the Klondike Gold Rush trail. Skagway also offers **Klondike Gold Rush National Historical Park**, the Trail of '98 Museum, and Skagway '98 Days with 'Soapy Smith', recreating gold rush entertainment at Eagle's Hall. Those driving to 'mainland' Alaska from Skagway or Haines may take SR1 to Anchorage, then continue north to Fairbanks on SR3 passing Denali National Park, returning via SR2 to the Alaskan Highway. If the long trek is daunting, consider flying from Juneau.

   Anchorage, cultural and commercial heart of Alaska, is the ideal base for exploring 'The Last Frontier'. The Log Cabin Visitor Center on 4th and F offers maps and tour information, plus places of interest, such as **Anchorage Museum of History and Art**, depicting Alaskan heritage and history through a variety of media. Different pioneers are remembered at the Alaska Aviation Heritage Museum, near Anchorage International Airport. Alaska Experience Theater offers 'Alaska the Greatland', with scenes sure to encourage armchair travellers to get out and experience the wonders. Before departing, visit **Alaska Public Lands Information Center** on 4th Avenue for information and use of their touch-screen trip planners.

   Outside Anchorage, 495,000 acres of **Chugach State Park** surround the city on three sides, with visitor centres north at Eagle River and south at Potter Point. Air and floatplanes visit local landmarks and otherwise unreachable wilderness areas. Cruising options are considerable with even Gray Line, known for coach tours, operating boat excursions. The **Alaska Marine Highway** links Valdez, Cordova, Whittier, Homer and Seward, to **Kodiak Island**, boasting Kodiak National Wildlife Refuge, and the **Aleutian Archipelago**. Boats from the picturesque port of Seward visit Resurrection Bay and the glaciers of **Kenai Fjords National Park**. Valdez is southern terminus to the **Alaskan Pipeline**, with tours provided by Gray Line. The main Valdez access road, Richardson Highway (SR4), passes **Worthington Glacier** with an overlook at milepost 28.7, the most accessible glacier in Alaska.

   Fairbanks can be reached from Anchorage via SR3 or the **Alaskan Railroad**, which several operators package with side trips to the **Denali National Park and Preserve**. Denali is Indian for 'the tall one', referring to 20,320ft-high Mount McKinley, highest peak in North America. No road leads to its summit, and the main park road is closed to private vehicles, but the free shuttlebus connects to places of interest. The visitor centre lists current activities, while Denali Air offers a Mount McKinley fly-by. **Fairbanks** offers more excursions, by air, land and water, the latter including rafting and the sternwheeler Riverboat *Discovery*. Locals sleep little in summertime, and the Goldpanners play their Summer Solstice Baseball Game at midnight without lights. Perhaps the perfect ending for an Alaskan excursion would be a quick trip north into the **Arctic Circle** before returning home.

Additional Information

State Tourism Bureaux

Alaska Division of Tourism
Dept 901, PO Box 110801
Juneau, AK 99811-0801
☎ 907-465-2010

Idaho Travel Council
700 West State St
Boise, ID 83720
☎ 800-635-7820
or 208-334-2470

Oregon State Tourism
775 Summer St, NE
Salem, OR 97310
☎ 800-547-7842
or 503-373-1270

Travel Montana
1424 9th Ave
Helena, MT 59620
☎ 800-541-1447
or 406-444-2654

Washington Tourism Division
101 G.A. Building, AX-13
Olympia, WA 98504-0613
☎ 800-544-1800
or 206-753-5600

Wyoming Division of Tourism
I-25 at College Dr
Cheyenne, WY 82002
☎ 307-777-7777

Regional Information

Anchorage CVB
1600 A St, Suite 200
Anchorage, AK 99501-5162
☎ 907-276-4118

Southwestern Idaho Travel Assn
PO Box 2106
Boise, ID 83701
☎ 800-635-5250

Bozeman COC
Box B
Bozeman, MT 59014
☎ 800-228-4224
or 406-586-5421

Butte CVB
2950 Harrison Ave
Butte, MT 59701
☎ 406-494-5595

Coeur d'Alene COC
PO Box 850
Coeur d'Alene, ID 83814
☎ 800-232-4968

Crescent City CVB
1001 Front St, PO Box 246
Crescent City, CA 95531
☎ 707-464-3174

Fairbanks CVB
550 First Ave
Fairbanks, AK 99701-4790
☎ 907-456-5774

Grants Pass CVB
PO Box 1787, 1501 6th St NE
Grants Pass, OR 97526
☎ 800-547-5927
or 503-476-5510

Helena COC
201 E Lyndale
Helena, MT 59601
☎ 800-543-5362
or 406-442-4120

Jackson CVB
Box E, 532 N Cache
Jackson, WY 83001
307-733-3316

Juneau CVB
369 South Franklin St (office)
134 Third St (visitor centre)
Juneau, AK 99801
☎ 907-586-1737/2201

Kodiak Island CVB
100 Marine Way
Kodiak, AK 99615
☎ 907-486-4782

Missoula CVB
Box 7577
Missoula, MT 59807
☎ 406-543-6623

Olympia CVB
PO Box 7249
Olympia, WA 98507-7249
☎ 206-357-3370

Pendleton CVB
25 SE Dorion
Pendleton, OR 97801
☎ 800-547-8911
or 503-276-7411

Portland CVB
26 SW Salmon
Portland, OR 97204
☎ 800-345-3214
or 503-222-2223

Salem CVB
1313 Mill St SE
Salem, OR 97301
☎ 800-874-7012
or 503-581-4325

Seattle/King County CVB
520 Pike Street, Suite 1300
Seattle, WA 98101
☎ 206-461-5800/5840

Spokane CVB
West 926 Sprague Ave,
Suite 180
Spokane, WA 99204
☎ 509-624-1341

Central Idaho Rockies Assn
PO Box 2420
Sun Valley, ID 83353
☎ 800-634-3347

Vancouver CVB
Suite 665, Two Bentall Centre
555 Burrard St
Vancouver, BC V7X 1M8
☎ 604-682-2222

Local Events

Check locally for exact dates

February-October
Oregon Shakespeare
   Festival
Ashland, OR

February
Anchorage Fur Rendezvous
Anchorage, AK

April
Alaska Folk Festival
Juneau, AK

Dogwood Festival
Lewiston, ID

May
Missoula Heritage Days
Missoula, MT

Washington Apple
Blossom Festival
Wenatchee, WA

Indian Pow-wow
Bozeman, MT

Buffalo Feast & Pow-wow
St Ignatius, MT

Fred Murphy Days
Coeur d'Alene, ID

Old West Days
Jackson Hole, WY

Northwest Folklife Festival
Seattle, WA

Sitka Salmon Derby
Sitka, AK

May-June
ArtFest
Spokane, WA

June
Sitka Summer Music
   Festival
Sitka, AK

Rose Festival
Portland, OR

Alaska Festival of Music
Anchorage, AK

Boise River Festival
Boise, ID

Montana Roundup Days
Great Falls, MT

All Alaska Logging
Sitka, AK

College National Finals
   Rodeo
Bozeman, MT

June-July
Oregon Bach Festival
Eugene, OR

June-August
Idaho Shakespeare Festival
Boise, ID

July
North American Indian
   Days
Browning, MT

King County Fair
Enumclaw, WA

Golden Days
Fairbanks, AK

Great State Art Fair
Salem, OR

Grant-Kohrs Ranch Days
Deer Lodge, MT

Bellevue Jazz Festival
Bellevue, WA

High Country Cowboy
   Festival
Grand Targhee Resort
Jackson Hole, WY

State Fiddlers Contest
Polson, MT

July-August
Sun Valley Music Festival
Sun Valley, ID

Seafair
Seattle, WA

Grand Teton Music Festival
Teton Village
Jackson Hole, WY

August
Montana Fair Billings, MT

Coeur d'Alene Indian
   Pilgrimage
Cataldo Mission SP
Coeur d'Alene (East), ID

A Taste of Portland
Portland, OR

Western Idaho Fair
Boise, ID

Oregon State Fair
Salem, OR

August-September
Seattle Arts Festival
(Bumbershoot)
Seattle, WA

September
Kodiak State Fair & Rodeo
Kodiak, AK

ArtQuake
Portland, OR

Pendleton Round-Up
Pendleton, OR

Chelan County Fair
Chelan, WA

Places of Interest

Anchorage, AK
*Anchorage Museum of
   History and Art*
121 W 7th Ave
Anchorage, AK 99501
☎ 907-343-4326
Open: 10am-6pm Tue-Sat,
1pm-5pm Sun summer
Free, tours, gifts

Arco, ID
Craters of the Moon NM
PO Box 29
Arco, ID 83213
☎ 218-527-3257
Open: 8am-4.30pm,
extended summer
7 mile drive mid Apr-Nov

Astoria, OR
Columbia River Maritime Museum
1792 Marine Drive
Astoria, OR 97103
☎ 503-325-2323
Open: 9.30am-5pm
Museum, ship, gifts, &

Fort Clatsop NM
Route 3, Box 604-FC
Astoria, OR 97103
☎ 503-861-2471
Open: 8am-5pm, 8am-6pm summer
Replica fort, gifts, parts &

Boise, ID
Idaho State Capitol
State St
Boise, ID 83702
☎ 208-334-2411
Open: 8am-5pm Mon-Sat except holidays
Free, tours

Old Idaho Prison
Penitentiary Road
Boise, ID 83705
☎ 208-334-2844
Open: noon-4pm
Prison, various museums, gifts

Browning, MT
Museum of the Plains Indian
PO Box 400
Browning, MT 59417
☎ 406-338-2230
Open: 9am-5pm, reduced winter. Free
Exhibits, Indian Crafts , &

Cave Junction, OR
Oregon Caves NM
SR46
Cave Junction, OR
☎ 503-592-3400
Open: 8am-7pm summer, reduced winter
Cave tours, food, lodge, hike

Crater Lake, OR
Crater Lake NP
Box 7
Crater Lake, OR 97604

☎ 503-594-2211
Open: hours and facilities vary seasonally
Drive, lodging, boat tours, hike, camp, food, &

Crescent City, CA
Redwood National Park HQ
1111 Second St
Crescent City, CA 95531
☎ 707-464-6101
Open: 9am-5pm, extended summer
Tours, gifts, hike, camp, &

Denali Park, AK
Denali NP
Box 9-A
Denali Park, AK 99755
☎ 907-683-2686
Road open June-mid Sep
Store, filling station, shuttle bus

Everett, WA
Boeing 747-767 Division
Everett Plant, SR 526
Everett, WA 98201
☎ 206-342-4801
Call for tour times
Tours, no videos or children under 10

Fairbanks, AK
Riverboat Discovery
PO Box 80610
Fairbanks, AK 99708
☎ 907-479-6673
Open: call for times
River cruise, Indian village, food, &

Glacier, MT
Glacier NP
Attn Supervisor
West Glacier, MT 59936
☎ 406-888-5441
Open: mid-June to mid-Sept main season
Lodging, food, gifts, camp, hike, tours, &

Grand Teton, WY
Grand Teton NP
PO Drawer 170
Moose, WY 83102
☎ 307-733-2880
Open: 8am-4.30pm, 8am-7pm summer
Gifts, hike, camp, swim, &

Grand Teton Lodge Co
Grand Teton NP
PO Box 240
Moran, WY 83013
☎ 800-628-9988
or 307-543-2855
Lodge, food, horse rentals, &

Great Falls, MT
C. M. Russell Museum
400 13th St North
Great Falls, MT 59401
☎ 406-727-8787
Open: 9am-6pm Mon-Sat, 1-5pm Sun, reduced winter
Museum, home, log cabin, gifts, &

Helena, MT
Montana Historic Society Museum
225 N Roberts St
Helena, MT 59601
☎ 406-444-2694
Open: 8am-6pm Mon-Fri, 9am-6pm Sat-Sun, reduced winter
Free, gifts, library, &

Montana State Capitol
6th & Montana
Helena, MT 59601
☎ 406-444-2694
Open: 8am-5pm
Free, tours, food, &

Jackson, WY
Jackson Hole Aerial Tram
SR 390, Teton Village
Jackson, WY 83001
☎ 307-733-2292
Open: 9am-7pm summer
Ride, gifts, food

Juneau, AK
Alaska Marine Highway
Box R
Juneau, AK 99811
☎ 800-642-0066
or 907-465-3941
Call for cruise times
Car & passenger ferry,
staterooms, food, gifts, ♿

Alaska State Museum
395 Whittier St
Juneau, AK 99801-1718
☎ 907-465-2901
Open: 9am-6pm Mon-Fri,
10am-6pm Sat-Sun summer
Tours, gifts, ♿

Mount Rainier, WA
Mount Rainier NP
Star Route, Tahoma Woods
Ashford, WA 98304
☎ 206-569-2211
Open: 9am-6pm
Gifts, hike, drive, camp

Mount St Helens, WA
Mount St Helens Volcanic NM
Route 1, Box 369
Amboy, WA 98601
☎ 206-247-5800/5473
Open: 9am-5pm. Free
Visitor centre, hike

National Bison Range, MT
National Bison Range
Range Manager
Moiese, MT 59824
☎ 406-644-2211
Open: daylight mid-May
to mid-Oct. Free
Scenic drive, wildlife, ♿

Newburg, OR
Champoeg SP
Champoeg Rd
St Paul, near Newburg
OR 97137
☎ 503-678-5537
Open: hours vary
Replica homes, gifts,
pageant

Olympia, WA
State Capitol Museum
211 W 21st St
Olympia, WA 98501
☎ 206-753-2580
Open: 10am-4pm Tue-Fri,
Noon-4pm Sat-Sun
Free, memorabilia, home

Port Angeles, WA
Olympic NP
600 East Park Ave
Port Angeles, WA 98362
☎ 206-452-4501
Open: 6.30am-4pm,
6.30am-6pm summer
Gifts, hike, camp, rainforest, ♿

Portland, OR
Japanese Gardens
611 SW Kingston
Washington Park
Portland, OR 97221
☎ 503-223-1321/9233
Open: 10am-4pm, extended summer
Garden, parts ♿

Oregon Art Institute
1219 SW Park Ave
Portland, OR 97204
☎ 503-226-2811
Open: 11am-5pm Tue-Sat, 1-5pm Sun
Tours, gifts, ♿

Pittock Mansion
3229 NW Pittock Dr
Portland, OR 97210
☎ 503-823-3624
Open: 1-5pm
Tours, views

Washington Park Zoo
4001 SW Canyon Rd
Portland, OR 97221
☎ 503-226-7627
Open: 9.30am, closing varies
Train, food, gifts, ♿

Reedsport, OR
Oregon Dunes NRA
855 Highway Ave
Reedsport, OR 97467
☎ 503-271-3611

Open: 9am-5pm
Free, hike, beach, camp

Salem, OR
Oregon State Capitol
Court St
Salem, OR 97301
☎ 503-378-4423
Open: 8am-5pm Mon-Fri,
9am-4pm Sat, noon-4pm
Sun
Free, tours, ♿

Seattle, WA
Klondike Gold Rush NHP
117 S Main
Seattle, WA 98104
☎ 206-422-7220
Open: 9am-5pm
Free, films, gifts, ♿

Museum of Flight
9404 E. Marginal Way S
Seattle, WA 98108
☎ 206-764-5720
Open: 9am-5pm
Tours, gifts

Pacific Science Center
200 Second Ave N
Seattle, WA 98109
☎ 206-443-2001
Open: 10am-5pm Mon-Fri,
10am-6pm weekends
Planetarium, IMAX, gifts,
♿

Space Needle
5th Ave N & Broad St,
Seattle Center
Seattle, WA 98109
☎ 206-443-2100
Open: 10am-midnight,
extended summer
2 restaurants, gifts, views,
♿

Tillicum Indian Village
Pier 56 (tours)
2200 6th Ave, Suite 804
(offices)
Seattle, WA 98121
☎ 206-443-1244
Open: 11.30am; plus
4.30pm & 6.30pm summer
Indian village, food, gifts

Washington State Ferries
Colman Dock
Seattle, WA 98104
☎ 800-542-0810
or 206-464-6400
Call for schedules
Passenger & car ferries

*Wing Luke Memorial
  Museum*
407 Eighth Ave
Seattle, WA 98104
☎ 206-623-5124
Open: 11am-4.30pm Tue-
Sat, noon-4pm Sun
Asian folk art & culture,
gifts

Skagway, AK
White Pass & Yukon Route
PO Box 435
Skagway, AK 99840
☎ 800-343-7373
or 907-983-2420
Open: May-Sep, 9am &
1.30pm
Skagway to Fraser rail-
road, bus to Whitehorse

Twin Falls, ID
Sawtooth NRA
1520 Addison Ave
Twin Falls, ID 83301
☎ 208-733-3698
Open: 9am-6pm. Free
Hike, ski, wilderness

Yellowstone, WY
Yellowstone NP
PO Box 168
Yellowstone NP, WY 82190
☎ 307-344-7381
Open: hours vary,
sections closed in winter
Hike, camp, gifts, ranger
activities, ♿

TW Recreational Services
(Lodgings)
Yellowstone NP, WY 82190
☎ 307-344-7901
Lodgings, food, shops,
tours, horse rental, ♿

12

HAWAII

The Hawaiian Islands comprise America's most southerly state, sharing the same tropical latitude as Hong Kong, Mexico City, and Calcutta. Boasting a year-round balmy climate, sun-drenched days are mellowed by gentle trade winds.

To perfection, resort cities add hot nightspots, clubs sporting top-name celebrities, and the Luau — an orgy of food, drink and entertainment. All islands have the unique blending of Polynesian, Asian, and Western Culture which is Hawaii, but each offers a different atmosphere worth experiencing. Oahu, Maui, and Big Island (Hawaii) are most popular, while visitors to Kauai, Molokai, and Lanai are growing in number.

Oahu

Oahu *is* 'the gathering place', bringing millions of visitors annually to America's only tropical state. Honolulu is the state capital while adjacent Waikiki is the heart of island tourism. Alaskans, Europeans, Midwest farmers, Japanese, and even Californians come, bejewelling the streets of Waikiki with exotic beachware and tropi-coloured *muu-muus*.

Honolulu is state capital of Hawaii and America's most exotic city. Otherwise lacking an indigenous palace-building royalty, **Iolani Palace** is especially popular with Americans. Iolani ('Royal Hawk') was built by King Kalakaua, boasting an impressive colonnaded architecture amalgamated from the king's visit to Europe. The 1969 **State Capitol** is now the seat of government, while the Iolani Palace is also open for guided-tours (book the day before).

Hawaii in Brief

Hawaii is both a major tourist destination and Mid-Pacific refueling stop, with Honolulu airport offering the majority of connections. Island tour operators will tailor make flight-car-accommodation packages which offer excellent value. Sample the Hawaiian Islands — select a few then book an island-hopping tour on arrival. If starting in Honolulu, allow a few days to relax in Waikiki then, after a week or more of island hopping, explore remaining Oahu. Temperatures drop only imperceptibly in winter, which experiences a few more showers along with bigger surfing waves.

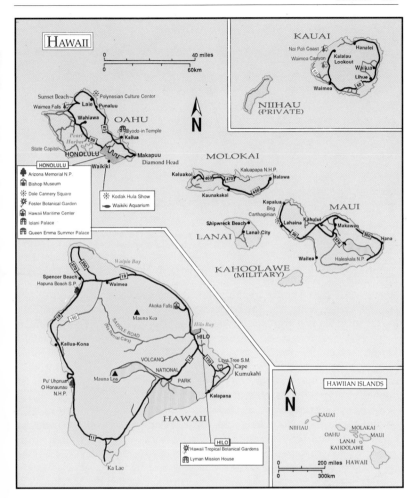

The palace grounds are pleasant, a large portion shaded by the massive banyan tree. West of the palace is the Royal Bandstand, built for the king's coronation, while the Royal Household Guards resided in the barracks behind. Across from the Iolani Palace is the **Statue of King Kamehameha**, first ruler to unite the Hawaiian islands. On 11 June his black and gold statue is festooned with fragrant *leis*, long floral necklaces. Behind is **Aliiolani Hale**, commissioned for King Kamehameha V and now the State Judiciary Building.

East on Merchant Street is the state library, and beyond is **Kawaiahao Church**, where services in Hawaiian are still held. Coral blocks were used after a drunken sailor burned down the grass church during the whaling and missionary period. Kawaiahao Church demonstrates the missionary's efforts, while the **Mission Houses Museum** depicts the lives they led. The Frame House was prefabricated in Boston, shared by up to four families. The Printing House has a replica of Hawaii's first press, where energetic missionaries created a Hawaiian alphabet and taught islanders to read their language. The

Into and around Honolulu-Waikiki

Honolulu International Airport is the prime gateway to Hawaii, sandwiched between Honolulu and Pearl Harbor. Get current information on agriculture quarantine if returning to mainland USA, especially before purchasing tropical plants and pineapples. Taxis offer quick transportation to downtown and Waikiki hotels.

Rental cars are inexpensive, but should be pre-booked and are a luxury in Waikiki and downtown Honolulu, where an excellent bus network operates. Waikiki offers the holiday resort atmosphere, while Honolulu hotels mostly cater for business people. Pre-book accommodation, as local prices have risen since new hotel developments were curtailed. Prices drop noticeably at hotels and condominiums three or more blocks inland.

Binghams, Judds and others came from New England, and many museum members are descendants.

South of downtown Honolulu is the **Hawaii Maritime Center** at Pier 7. Their *Falls of Clyde* may be the only fully-rigged four-masted sailing vessel afloat, while double-hulled sailing canoe, *Hokule'a* ('Star of Gladness'), is exhibited when not at sea. The latter completed a return journey from Tahiti to Hawaii 1976, proving that Hawaii could have been settled by Tahitians. Nearby is Honolulu's equivalent of the Statue of Liberty. The ten-storey Aloha Tower, built in 1926, recalls when incoming steamers were met by the Royal Hawaiian Band, boys diving for coins, and arrivals being *leied* by well-wishers. Today the 9th floor houses the **Maritime Museum**, while the 10th floor affords views of harbour and city.

The nearby Oceania Floating Restaurant, towed from Hong Kong in 1972, heralds **Chinatown**. Bounded by Mauna Kea and Nuuanu Streets (running north-south), and Beretania and Hotel Streets (east-west), by day Chinatown is sleepy. At night topless bars and strip joints open for locals and GIs, but the areas boasts some fine Chinese restaurants (travel by taxi).

Pearl Harbor is several miles west of Honolulu. Together the National Park Service and Navy provide an excellent and free boat service to the USS *Arizona* memorial, plus an informative museum to peruse while awaiting the shuttle. The memorial is a moving experience, with rusting gun turrets jutting from water tinged with an oily rainbow. Public buses from Waikiki and Honolulu stop outside the *Arizona* Memorial Visitor Center, which is near the USS *Bowfin* and Pacific Submarine Museum. Private companies do not dock at the memorial, instead offering extended tours around Pearl Harbor.

The **Bishop Museum**, located on Bernice Street off Likelike Highway, houses the personal effects of Charles Bishop's late wife, Princess Bernice, and her cousin, Queen Emma. Containing the finest collection from Hawaii's royal era, the museum also boasts a hands-on learning centre of the islands and Polynesian culture, plus a heritage theatre and planetarium. Another fine cultural centre is **Honolulu Academy of Arts**, which balances European masterpieces with an excellent collection of oriental works.

Other places of interest around Honolulu include the **Punchbowl**, National Cemetery of the Pacific, with Tantalus Drive behind leading to Tantalus and

Round Top Mounts plus the Puu Ualakaa Wayside. When returning, the Contemporary Museum is nearby, exhibiting modern art works. **Cannery Square** beneath Dole Pineapple Tower offers the Dole Theatre, telling how Jim Dole changed the islands, plus shops and food. **Foster Botanic Garden** on Vineyard was founded by Queen Kalama, while **Queen Emma Summer Palace** and its Shinto Temple is up the Pali Highway.

Waikiki offers $2^1/_2$ miles of beach, backed by an urban resort six to ten blocks deep and full of entertaining diversions. Waikiki is also the ideal base for exploring Oahu, but allow time to acclimatize to Hawaii's slower pace. Of the beaches, Kuhio is most popular for swimming, within an enclosure to keep out surf. Waikiki beach proper, near the Sheraton and DeRussy complexes, offers much needed space for sun worshippers. Waves get higher beyond Diamond Head, frequented by windsurfers and other 'board' enthusiasts.

Below Diamond Head is **Kapiolani Park**, a pine and palm-shaded park within a coconut's throw of Waikiki. The Royal Hawaiian Band performs at the bandstand on Sunday afternoons, while the Waikiki Shell offers various performances, especially during Aloha Week Festivities. Visitors learn Hawaiian music and dance at the free and fun **Kodak Hula Show**. Learn the hula, missionary version, and do take some photographs! **Honolulu Zoo** and Queen Kapiolani Hibiscus Garden are inland, along the park's outskirts. Nearer the beach are **Fort DeRussy Army Museum** and **Waikiki Aquarium**.

Evening entertainment is centred around larger hotels, boasting tropical revues, Hawaiian celebrities or mainland stars. The **Luau** offers an evening of drinking, eating, and entertainment — Hawaiian style. Germaine's and Paradise Cove Luaus combine a fun mixture of Polynesian culture and ceremonies with American audience participation. Both Luaus include all you could wish to drink *and* transportation to their beachside hideaways, while several large Waikiki hotels offer local Luaus.

Waikiki is famous for its tropical shopping, especially its floral shirts and colourful hand-printed *muu-muus*, specialities of **Hilo Hattie**. Boasting numerous speciality shops, the **Royal Hawaiian Shopping Center** is on Kalakaua Avenue, as is trinket-filled International Market and Waikiki Shopping and Business Plazas. Royal Hawaiian often provides free entertainment, as does **Ala Moana Shopping Center** over the Ala Wai Canal towards Honolulu. Smaller shops and street vendors fill in niches inadvertently left by large shopping malls.

Condominiums have kitchens, but most visitors dine out, sampling the great variety offered by this crossroads of the Pacific. Hawaiian sounding dishes are really American-Polynesian, while true Hawaiian food such as *poi* is an acquired taste. Inexpensive restaurants abound, while the best hotels offer fine dining with a choice of cuisines.

Around Oahu

Oahu alters dramatically away from Honolulu and Waikiki, best sampled over a two or three day driving tour. A driving loop around Makapuu Point makes a pleasant day's outing or a start around Oahu, commencing with a visit to **Diamond Head**. From Waikiki travel east along the coast then inland

HAWAII

The Kodak Hula Show is a family favourite

Sunswept Waikiki offers an urban resort atmosphere

following the signs. Calcite crystals were the 'diamonds' this extinct volcano was named after. Trails wind up to the summit, while the crater is a national guard depot. US72 follows the Oahu coast, and beyond Diamond Head the crowds gradually thin.

Swimmers should check that beaches are safe from waves, undertow, rocks, and surfers. **Hanauma Bay State Underwater Park** offers protected swimming and snorkeling, interesting coral, and tame tropical fish. Tour companies visiting Hanauma provide snorkeling gear, independents visitors may rent or purchase equipment in Waikiki. Changing facilities, toilets, picnic tables, a food concession and life guards are provided.

Visitors should leave bodysurfing at nearby Sandy Beach and Makapuu Beaches to the experts — 10ft waves can break necks. Around Makapuu Point is **Sea Life Park**, with displays of marine plants and animals, plus shows by trained marine mammals. The 300,000 gallon Hawaiian Reef Tank hosts innumerable creatures, from lion-fish to moray eels. Their Pacific Whaling Museum has a scrimshaw display.

If just out for the day, return to Waikiki via the **Pali Highway**, pausing at **Nuuanu Pali State Park**, where King Kamehameha drove his enemies over the 1,000ft drop. The views are spectacular, but bring a warm layer as the air is decidedly invigorating. Otherwise continue north toward the windward coast.

Just off SR83 in the Valley of the Temples is **Byodo-In Temple**. Built to mark the centenary of the first Japanese immigrants, the temple is a replica of the far older Byodo-In of Uji, Japan. Sheer *pali* (cliffs) provide a green backdrop for the Buddhist temple and grounds. SR83 becomes the Kamehameha Highway at the coast. This is rural Oahu, a far cry from bustling Waikiki. Dirt roads wind up into hidden valleys, where Hawaiian families keep small-holdings. Developers are kept at bay by the showers which saturate windward hills.

Continuing north along the coast, all travellers instantly recognize the floating mountain called Chinaman's Hat. It can be reached at low tide via **Kualoa County Regional Park**, which also offers safe swimming, good snorkeling and fishing. The buses parked beyond the sugar mill ruins are outside the Crouching Lion. After a few drinks at nearby Crouching Lion Inn the rock appears more feline, but avoid the Inn's lunchtime crush.

Pat's at Punaluu offers accommodation, rare along the windward coast, with condominium-style rooms and a restaurant. Out front are golden sand, safe swimming and nearby coral reef, with special rates for longer stays. **Sacred Falls** are a mile or so beyond Pat's, where a moderately strenuous hike through a narrow valley is rewarded by the 90ft high falls. The sun sets early over western hills, so morning starts are advisable.

The **Polynesian Cultural Center** offers seven model villages, depicting life in Hawaii, Tahiti, Tonga, New Zealand, Samoa, Fiji, and the Marquesas. Festivities here last all day, from the morning's welcoming *lei* to the evening's optional 'This is Polynesia' extravaganza. Attention to detail and demonstrations of traditional skills are the centre's strong point, encouraged by the LDS (Mormon) organizers. Nearby **Laie** hosts **Brigham Young University**, serving students throughout Polynesia, and the most visited **Mormon Temple** complex outside of Salt Lake City, which includes a history of the Laie colony (non-LDS visitors may enter the visitor centre but not the temple).

Laniloa Lodge offers accommodation in Laie, while Kahuku boasts the self-contained Turtle Bay Hilton resort, offering excellence for those who can afford it. Otherwise north shore lodging is generally limited to surfer's shacks. **Sunset Beach** is first of the surf beaches. Next door is Ehukai Beach Park, and between them the famous **Banzai Pipeline**. Winter is best for surfing or to watch — bring a telephoto lens to capture the action.

A scenic road leads inland from Waimea to **Puu O Mahuka Heiau** (temple). Designated a State Historical Site, *Ti* leaf offerings may still be seen at this five acre *heiau*. A separate road inland from SR83 leads to the **Waimea Falls Park**. This lush valley is now a large botanical garden and recreational area, boasting several pleasant walks. Entertainment includes hula lessons and a professional diving 55ft into Waimea Falls pool. Return towards Honolulu/Waikiki south along SR99, the inland Kamehameha Highway. En route are several pineapple centres and **Wahiawa Botanical Gardens**.

Hawaii

Twice the combined size of the other islands, Hawaii is often called **Big Island** to avoid confusion with the state of Hawaii. Although fiery eruptions vary with volcanic goddess Madam Pele's mood, Big Island is still pouring lava into the sea, slowly growing. Hilo, the largest city, is surrounded by lush vegetation and rainbows brought by windward showers. Leeward Kona Coast resorts offer a sunnier if less tropically exuberant climate, while the 'Old West' still lives in the ranches of Waimea.

A circular tour of Big Island may start at Hilo International Airport, with Keahole Airport offering an alternative on the western Kona coast. **Hilo** makes a good base for exploring the area's luxuriant tropical foliage and flowers, but start first with the town. The airport access road leads to Kanoelehua Road, SR11, the main route south to the volcanoes. Turn right (north), crossing Kamehameha Avenue onto one way **Banyan Drive**, which weaves beneath an overgrown hedge of banyans, each tree named after a notable American. The drive follows Waiakea Peninsula, where many of Hilo's best hotels line Banyan Golf Course's perimeter.

Hilo Bay is best appreciated from formal Japanese **Liliuokalani Gardens** and nearby **Coconut Island**, both on Banyan Drive. Lunchtime visitors may bring a picnic or sample the *mahimahi* (meaty fish) at a local restaurant. At 7.30am the **Suisan Fish Market** on Banyan Drive and Lihiwai Street sells the catch of the day to housewives and restauranteurs; the nearby snack shop provides coffee to stimulate early risers.

Lyman Mission House and Museum on Haili Street, built in 1839 and extended in 1856, exhibits missionary life. Personal artifacts include bright autumn leaves for Lyman children, who might never see New England. Next door the museum displays pre- and post-contact island heritage, plus a massive collection of minerals, rocks, and miscellany from Polynesia. Legend claims mighty King Kamehameha once raised the **Naha Stone** at nearby Hawaii Public Library on Waianuenue Avenue. On sunny days **Rainbow Falls** lives up to its name, while the **Boiling Pots** are a series of cascades, both inland from the library.

Most visitors to Big Island hope to experience a live volcano, with helicopter tours offering views of active areas otherwise unreachable (check current activity before booking). SR11 goes south from Hilo into Puna District, where Hawaii's hottest property is found.

If time permits, sample the rural atmosphere of Big Island's **Cape Kumukahi**. Turn left consecutively onto SR130 then 132 for a pleasant mixture of forests and farmland. Two centuries ago a river of lava engulfed a wooded area, creating **Lava Tree State Monument**, where upright lava tubes act as memorials for the trees. Cape Kumukahi Lighthouse nearly succumbed to the 1960 lava flow. Recent legend says Madam Pele, disguised as an old woman, was turned away by a nearby town but treated kindly by the lighthouse keeper — thus Kapoho village was devastated but the lava parted around the lighthouse.

East along coastal SR137 passes Kaimu Beach Park, offering a picturesque, if disconcerting, jet black sand beach lined with palms. Kalapana hosts Star of the Sea Catholic Church, called the **Painted Church**. Father Damien's statue is outside, a saintly man who founded a grass church and local school before giving himself to Molokai's leper colony. Father Everest Gielen, who built the Painted Church, painted biblical scenes within his church to inspire Hawaiians. Beyond Kalapana, the 1987 flow buries the road in crusty *pahoehoe* lava until the highways commission battle with Madam Pele once more (or she moves mankind further from her doorstep). Head inland on SR130 then continue south on SR11.

Volcanoes National Park visitor centre gives the latest information on volcanic activity, also available on (808) 967-7977. Within the park, **Crater Rim Drive** encircles massive Kilauea Caldera, once a mass of molten lava, with its crisscrossing flows labelled by rangers. Those with respiratory difficulties should keep away from the steam and sulphur vents. Trails include a short walk to Thurston Lava Tube and 11 mile (17^1/$_2$km) Crater Rim Trail, which is roughly parallel to the drive. Halemaumau Trail crosses Kilauea Caldera to Halemaumau Crater — a shorter walk from Halemaumau Crater overlook.

Kilauea Iki rained molten lava over *ohi'a* forest, now crossed by Devastation Trail, a half-hour walk highlighting subsequent plant regeneration. South of Kilauea Iki is **Chain of Craters Road**, which once joined SR130. Higher craters may still be visited, but the flows in 1987-9 obliterated lower sections, including Waha'ula Visitor Center.

Beyond the volcanoes, SR11 continues south then turns north towards Big Island's western Kona Coast. **Ka-Lae**, southern most point in the United States, is an 18 mile (29km) round-trip detour from the route. The climate is dryer in leeward (western) Hawaii, sitting in the rain shadow of 13,680ft (4170m) Mauna Loa. Accommodation is limited before the Kona Resort, but if night approaches, do return for **Pu'uhonua O Honaunau**, House of Refuge. Strict *kapu* laws covered every aspect of island life, with severe punishment or death for law breakers lest gods become angry. Early kings including the great-grandfather of King Kamehameha were buried here, their powerful *mana* (spirit) purging 'sin' from refuge seekers. The National Park Service have faithfully restored Pu'uhonua O Honaunau, offering a fascinating glimpse into old Hawaii.

The Captain Cook Memorial rests across Kealakekua Bay, just visible from

Hikiau Heiau, the Hawaiian temple where Cook performed the island's first Christian funeral. Mistaken for the Hawaiian god Lono, unfortunate events culminated in Cook's death, his *mana* digested by natives including King Kamehameha. Local stalls sell coral necklaces and cooling, fragrant *leis*.

Kailua-Kona offers sun-drenched resorts and quality shopping, plus a few hidden treasures. The *ali'i*, elite rulers of Hawaiian society, lived here and worshipped Lono, god of fertility and bane of Captain Cook. King Kamehameha was interred nearby in a secret grave, protecting his *mana*. A 112ft steeple marks **Mokuaikaua Church**, with huge *ohi'a* beams plus pews and pulpit of beautiful *koa* wood. Near Kailua Bay is the Victorian **Hulihee Palace**, with many original furnishings. Kamehameha spent his last years at **Ahuena Heiau** on Kailua Bay, the temple reconstructed through the Bishop Museum. King Kamehameha Hotel, adjacent to the temple, offers tours. Do sample the coast before leaving, **Ali'i Drive** offers a scenic route studded with resorts.

North on SR19 leads past an area devastated by lava flows to **Hapuna Beach State Park**, with an excellent stretch of sand (watch for rip-tides in winter). Before Spencer Beach comes **Pu'ukohala Heiau**, dedicated to blood-drinking war god Kukailimoku. Nearby is John Young's home, whose advice on guns and cannons helped Kamehameha take the other islands. Adopted by Hawaiians, Young's granddaughter became Queen Emma. **Spencer Beach** offers protected swimming, popular with families and snorkelers. A detour up SR270 and back SR250 visits North Kohala, boasting the original King Kamehameha statue intended for Honolulu, now honouring the king's birthplace.

East on SR19 towards Hilo passes Waimea, ranching capital of Big Island.

Hike through a Hawaiian moonscape

ae Hawaiians are a friendly people

The **Kamuela Museum** captures the early pioneering spirit, while **Parker Ranch** runs a visitor and ranch centre, museum, and herds of cattle. Continuing towards Hilo, the brown scrub of cowboy country gradually gives way to lusher vegetation. Another diversion north on SR240 visits Kukuihaele, where a four-wheel drive shuttle offers tours of the picturesque **Waipio Valley**. Legends and myths abound, telling how *mana* from ancient kings protects locals from *Lua o milu*, gateway to the dead.

 Savour the lush Hamakua coastline slowly. After Kolekole Beach Park is the turn for 400ft-high **Akaka Falls**, with a circular walk among the verdant vegetation. Just outside Hilo, Four Mile Drive offers a picturesque route closer to the coast, passing **Hawaii Tropical Botanical Gardens**. The botanical gardens offer an excellent selection of native and introduced species. Hilo is just south on SR19.

The other inter-island route, **Saddle Road**, is prohibited for most rental cars. SR200 crosses the saddle between 13,796ft (4,205m) Mauna Kea and marginally lower Mauna Loa, hence the route's name. Four-wheel drive vehicles may climb Mauna Kea in summer, while trails lead to Mauna Loa's peak, two from Volcanoes National Park and another from saddle road — all climbs being difficult, potentially dangerous.

Maui

In Hawaiian Legend, Maui was a larger-than-life hero who went fishing, pulling up a huge behemoth which became the island of Maui. In reality, Maui is formed by two volcanoes with a valley between. Mile-high Puu Kukui is dwarfed by 10,023ft (3,055m) Haleakala, actually 30,000ft from the sea bed. Kahului in the valley has the main airport, while Kapalua-West Maui Airport serves western resorts.

SR36A east from Kahului Airport passes the Kanaha Bird Sanctuary, where a gentle right onto Haleakala Highway leads to SR36 then 32 through twin cities of Kahului and Wailuku. SR32 becomes 320, passing Maui Historical Museum en route to **Iao Valley State Park**. Walks lead to Iao (supreme light) Needle, which pierces the tropical foliage while valley gardens and swimming holes await below. Return east, taking SR30 south past **Maui Tropical Plantation** with its express tram, marketplace, and nursery.

Western Maui is a coastline hugging the slopes of sleepy volcano Puu Kukui, with the former capital Lahaina and northern resorts Kaanapali and Kapalua nestled between. Lahaina is an old whaling port which tourism has rescued, rather than spoiled. *Carthaginian* along the waterfront is a replica square-rigger and floating museum, with exhibits on the whaling industry. The whale populations have since bounced back, and spotting tours depart from the harbour. The massive Banyan Tree behind provides pleasant shade around mid-day. The nearby courthouse offers an art gallery, and other notable buildings include Pioneer Inn and **Baldwin Home Museum**. Downtown Lahaina, careful to retain its old town atmosphere, has integrated numerous art galleries, restaurants, and shops, perfect for an evening stroll. North of Lahaina are fine beaches and several self-contained retreats, including Kapalua Resort, Hyatt Regency, and Sheraton-Maui.

Haleakala has an affinity with the sun god, best appreciated by arising before dawn and experiencing the sunrise atop it. Nowhere else is there so short a road from the coast to the virtually two-mile high summit. Bring warm clothes, camera, perhaps a few hotel blankets, and arrive *early*, an hour before sunrise for best effect. From Lahaina follow SR30 south to SR380 then 37, 377, and 378. Tours are available for non-drivers, some provide bicycles for a ride down afterwards. The national park's visitor centre has a rare silversword, others may be seen along the trail network. For breakfast, return down 378, taking 377 then 365 to **Makawao**, a town with a western feel in Upcountry, a ranching district.

Continue north on SR365, turning east on SR36, the **Hana Highway**, weaving through an almost magical tapestry of sights and tropical scents. Waysides boast waterfalls and pools, parks, nature walks, tropical fruit stands, caves, and gardens — the secret of enjoying the Hana Road is starting early and stopping often. Many visitors press past **Hana**, although a few visit the old-time Hasegawa General Store and Hana Culture Center, with local history exhibits. Beyond is the scenic O'heo Gorge and the Seven Sacred Pools, which feed into each other and make excellent swimming holes, but check with rangers first. Walks lead into the tropical rainforest, and to Wailua Falls. Return to Kahului via the Hana Road, first putting another film in the camera.

The Other Islands

Three additional islands, Kauai, Molokai, and Lanai, are off-the-beaten tourist path, and offer a slower pace. One or more make for a relaxing grand finale to the island-hopping.

'Garden Island' **Kauai** is roughly circular and boasts many striking natural features, including **Waimea Canyon** (Mark Twain's 'Grand Canyon of the Pacific') and the incomparable Na Pali Coast. Although roads provide access to Waimea Canyon, most of the countryside is rugged and best seen by air, boat and on foot. 'Wilderness Experiences' and helicopters may be arranged in **Lihue**, the county seat. Rangers of Lihue-Koloa Forest Reserve offer advice on the numerous walks, some being potentially dangerous. West on SR50 leads to **Waimea**, site of Cook's first landing. Inland is Waimea Canyon and Kokee Natural History Museum, while further west is leeward Kauai, which would be arid except for the irrigation. North from Lihue is **Wailua**, where Smith's Tropical Paradise offers 30 acres of gardens and boat rides up Wailua River. The area boasts waterfalls, a fern grotto, and a restored Hawaiian temple. Continuing along the coast, check in Hanalei for excursions around the incredibly rugged **Na Pali Coastline**. Beautiful Hanalei Bay has captured many hearts, and movie fans may recognize shots there from *South Pacific*.

Molokai is the closest island to old Hawaii, apart perhaps from off-limit Niihau. At its western edge, Kaluakoi is a growing resort in a ranching area. Kaunakakai, central to the southern coast, is the largest town, with excursions north to **Kalaupapa National Historical Park**, where Father Damien gave a beleaguered leper colony hope and self-respect. A steep $3^1/_4$ mile ($5^1/_4$ km) trail leads down to the site, or opt for the Molokai Mule Ride, which starts early but includes picnic lunch. The eastern side remains refreshingly unchanged, the northeast being accessible only on foot apart from the coastal route to Halawa.

Lanai is the 'Pineapple Island', boasting the world's largest pineapple plantation on one of the smaller islands. Lanai is best explored in a four-wheel drive or on foot, ideally both. Hotel Lanai plus a few newcomers supply accommodation and provide amusements. Lanai City is the commercial and geographical heart of the island, with places of interest around the outskirts, such as Keomuku ghost town near Shipwreck Beach.

Additional information

Visitor Information

Hawaii Visitors Bureau
2270 Kalakaua Ave
Honolulu, HI 96815
☎ 808-923-1811

Local Events

Check locally for exact dates

January
Cherry Blossom Festival
Honolulu

March/April
Merry Monarch Festival
Hilo

May-June
Hawaii State Fair
Honolulu

June
Kamehameha's Birthday
Honolulu

August
Hula Festival
Waikiki

September-October
Aloha Week Festival
Celebrated everywhere

Places of Interest

HAWAII (BIG ISLAND)

Hilo
Hawaii Tropical Botanical Gardens
PO Box 1415 (Onomea Bay)
Hilo, HI 96720
☎ 808-946-5233
Open: hours vary
Garden, tour

Lyman Mission House
276 Haili St
Hilo, HI 96720
☎ 808-935-5021
Open: 9am-5pm Mon-Sat
Museum, gifts

Honaunau
Pu'uhonua O Honaunau
(City of Refuge)
PO Box 129
Honaunau, HI 96726
☎ 808-328-2288
Restored village

Volcano
Volcanoes NP
PO Box 52
Volcanoes NP, HI 96718
☎ 808-967-7311
Open: hours vary
Museum, lodging, food, gifts, &

MAUI

Lahaina
Brig Carthaginian
PO Box 338 (Lahaina Waterfront)
Lahaina, HI 97676
☎ 808-661-3262
Open: 9am-4.30pm daily
Tall ship museum, gifts

Makawao
Haleakala NP
PO Box 369
Makawao, HI 96768
☎ 808-572-9306
Lodgings, gifts, camp

OAHU

Haleiwa
Waimea Falls Park
59-864 Kam Hwy
Haleiwa, HI 96712
☎ 808-638-8511
Open: 10am-5.30pm daily
Gardens, food, walk, tours

Honolulu
Arizona Memorial NP
1 Arizona Memorial Place
Pearl Harbor
Honolulu, HI 96818
☎ 808-422-0561
Open: visitor centre
7.30am-5pm. Free
Museum, boat, gifts,
food, part &

Bishop Museum
1525 Bernice Street
Honolulu, HI 96817
☎ 808-847-3511
Craft demos 9am-3pm
Museum, planetarium,
gifts, food, ♿

Dole Cannery Square
650 Iwilei Rd, PO Box 2780
Honolulu, HI 96817
☎ 808-543-6500
Open: 9am-5pm daily
Shop, food, tour

Foster Botanical Garden
50 N Vineyard Blvd
Honolulu, HI 96817
☎ 808-533-3214
Open: 9am-4pm daily
except major holidays
Garden, tours

Germaine's Luau
1451 S King St, Suite 508
Honolulu, HI 96814
☎ 808-941-3338
Open: evenings
Luau, free transfer

Hawaii Maritime Center
Pier 7, Honolulu Harbor
Honolulu, HI

☎ 808-523-6151 & 536-6373
Open: 9am-5pm daily
Tall ship, gifts

Hilo Hattie
700 Nimitz Hwy
Honolulu, HI 96817
☎ 808-537-2926
Free. Aloha-wear shop,
free transfer

Iolani Palace
364 S King St
Honolulu, HI 96813
☎ 808-522-0832
Open: 9am-2.15pm Wed-Sat
Palace tour

Paradise Cove Luau
1580 Makaloa, Ste 1200
Honolulu, HI 96815
☎ 808-973-3539
Luau, free transfer

*Queen Emma Summer
Palace*
2913 Pali Hwy
Honolulu, HI 96817
☎ 808-595-3167
Open: 9am-4pm daily
Palace tour

Kaneohe, HI
Byodo-In Temple
Valley of the Temples
Memorial Park
Kaneohe, HI 96744
☎ 808-239-8811 & 239-5570
Gardens & temple, gifts

Laie, HI
Polynesian Culture Center
SR83
Laie, HI 96815
☎ 808-923-2911
Open: 12.30am-9pm
Mon-Sat
Show, tram, food, part ♿

Waikiki, HI
Kodak Hula Show
Monsarrat Ave
Waikiki Shell
Waikiki, HI 808-833-1661
Open: 10am Tue-Thu.
Free, arrive early
Show, film sales, ♿

Waikiki Aquarium
2777 Kalakaua Ave
Waikiki, HI 96815
☎ 808-923-9741
Open: 9am-5pm daily
except major holidays

Common Hawaiian Words

Friendly Hawaiians beam when visitors speak the 'old tongue', even if only a few words. Pronounce words like *humuhumunukunukuapua'a* (a tiny fish) by splitting the word into short syllables. With the following words, the *malihini* is half-way to becoming *kama'aina*.

a'a	rough lava	*kokua*	help
aikane	friend	*komo mai*	come in
aloha	welcome, farewell	*lanai*	porch
hale	house	*lei*	floral or shell garland
haole	Caucasian	*luau*	feast
hauoli	happy	*moana*	ocean
heiau	temple	*mahalo*	thank you
honi	kiss	*malihini*	newcomer
hula	Hawaiian dance	*muu-muu*	roomy, colourful dress
huhu	angry	*ono*	delicious
imu	earthen oven	*nui*	big, much
ipo	sweetheart	*pali*	cliff
kapu	taboo, keep out	*pau*	finished
kane	man	*pahoehoe*	smooth, ropy lava
kama'aina	islander, blue-blood Hawaiian	*pu pu*	appetizer
kaukau	food	*wahine*	woman
keiki	child	*wikiwiki*	quickly, hurry

USA FACT FILE

Accommodation

Hotels and Motels

American hotels and motels typically charge by the room, with a small surcharge for additional occupants. Older hotels usually offer only single, twin, or double beds; while more modern hotels and motels typically have rooms with two double beds - great value for families or couples travelling together. The management can often supply an additional single bed or crib, but this should be verified while booking. Most rooms have private bathrooms, telephones, television, and air-conditioning.

Prices and services vary according to hotel/motel chain, location, the season, and whether AAA (American Automobile Association) or senior citizen discounts are available. Visitors from abroad will find that many chains have pre-paid voucher schemes. These offer excellent value, but ensure that the hotel coverage is suitable. Surcharges may apply to guests in up-market hotels or major cities. Most pre-paid schemes must be booked before departure, but fly-drive brochures often list participating chains.

Hotels and motels with a restaurant may offer American Plan (full board) or Modified American Plan (half board). Those without often give the American continental breakfast — donuts and coffee — free in the lobby. Efficiencies are a special type of hotel/motel room where cooking facilities are available, varying from a hot plate and sink to full kitchens complete with garbage disposals and ice makers.

Toll-free telephone numbers for major hotel/motel chains who can supply details of their hotels are listed below, but before booking check available discounts, and also restrictions if travelling with children or pets.

Best Western International	800-528-1234	La Quinta Motor Inns	800-531-5900
Budgetel Inns	800-428-3438	Marriott Hotels & Resorts	800-228-9290
Clarion & Comfort Inns	800-228-5150	Omni Hotels	800-843-6664
Days Inn	800-325-2525	Quality Inns	800-228-5151
Econo Lodges of America	800-446-6900	Ramada Inns	800-228-2828
Embassy Suites	800-362-2779	Scottish Inns	800-251-1962
Hilton Hotels	800-445-8667	Sheraton Hotels & Motor Inns	800-325-3535
Holiday Inns	800-465-4329	Susse Chalet Motor Lodges & Inns	800-258-1980
Howard Johnson's Motor Lodges	800-654-2000	Super 8 Motels	800-843-1991
Hyatt Hotels	800-233-1234	Travelodge Hotels	800-255-3050
		Westin Hotels & Resorts	800-228-3000

Condominiums
These are apartments, often high-rise, with one or more separate bed-rooms, giving greater privacy than one room efficiencies. They typically have one or more bathrooms and a kitchen/lounge/dining room area with a fold-out double bed or two. Agencies in popular resort areas specialize in renting condominiums, usually requiring visitors to stay by the week or month. They can be found via local newspapers or 'Condo for Rent' signs.

Resorts
Top class cuisine, entertainment, and accommodation are offered by most resorts, with enough extracurricular activities to satisfy the most ardent sporting enthusiasts or health fanatics. Some of America's best resorts are exclusive hotels nestled in a pro-designed golf course.

Bed & Breakfast and Guest Houses
Brought back by American visitors to Britain, the B&B has become popular in many areas, although bargain motels often offer the same facilities for less. Bed and breakfast organizations have sprung up to ensure standards are maintained and to promote the concept, and their addresses may be obtained from the nearest USTTA (United States Travel and Tourism) office or the local tourist authorities listed at the end of each chapter.

Guest Houses are sometimes known as boarding houses, and a large network exists throughout the USA. For details contact:
The Director
Tourist House Association of America
PO Box 355-AA
Greentown
Pennsylvania 18426

Youth Hostels and the YMCA
These provide inexpensive accommodation for all ages, although foreign visitors should become members of their own country's Youth Hostel organization before travelling. The YMCA is busy, especially during peak seasons, and should be booked well ahead to avoid disappointment and additional expense. Contact:

American Youth Hostels Inc
1332 Eye Street NW
Washington DC 20013-7613
☎ 202-783-6161

or the YMCA via
The Y's Way
356 West 34th Street
New York, NY 10001
☎ 212-769-5856

Camping
This is another popular way to see America. For those hiring a motorhome, many private campsites have full hookups, which include water, sewage, electricity, and a television cable. National and state parks and forests provide campsites in natural settings, with facilities ranging from full hookups to primitive sites, sometimes free in remote areas. The Woodall's or Rand McNally campsite guides, usually included with the hire, offer comprehensive lists of sites. Camping or tenting alongside the road may require special permission, varying by state, and is potentially dangerous.

Campsites near major national parks and cities may become fully booked in summer, except in the southernmost areas, which fill in winter. Not all sites allow tents, but Woodall's produce a special guide for tenters.

Climate

America has not one, but many climates. The northeastern US has four distinct seasons peppered with variable weather, which has occasioned the adage, 'If you don't like the weather, wait a minute.'

The southeast has hot summer days interspersed with cooling mid-afternoon showers. Autumn, winter and spring are less distinct and gradually blend into each other. Travelling south towards Florida, frosts become rarer and 'snow birds', Northerners escaping the winter, are abundant. Florida summers are hot, humid, and best spent on a beach or near an air-conditioner. Heading west across Texas the air becomes less humid away from the Gulf of Mexico, while the American Southwest varies from dry to desert. Average winter daytime temperatures are pleasantly warm, with occasional cold snaps. Spring and autumn are excellent times to tour the southwest, while summers are hot and dry.

Northern California, Oregon and Washington have sunny summer days interspersed with occasional showers or fog. Snow-free coastlines and short drives to ski resorts make for ideal winter recreation. From late spring to early autumn is best for touring the northwest interior, and also the 'Heartland of America', that massive sweep from the Great Plains to the Great Lakes States. Greater Denver offers excellent outdoor recreation, with the agenda set by the season. Hawaii is another year-round destination, with a balmy climate and trade winds to sway the coconut fronds.

Clothes

Dress is casual; only top restaurants insist upon a jacket and/or tie for men. One or two warm layers are essential, regardless of location or season — the hottest destinations have arctic air-conditioned restaurants, hotels, and shopping centres. Winter visitors in the north should wear overcoats, boots or rubber overshoes with non-skid soles, gloves, and earmuffs or a hat. Winter sports participants *should* be prepared for cold weather, but business travellers and those visiting relatives are sometimes taken unawares.

Driving Styles and Tips

For pre-trip planning, the *Rand McNally Road Atlas (United States, Canada and Mexico)* has state and city maps, distances between major cities, scenic routes and major sites of interest. The AAA (American Automobile Association) provides free maps and accommodation guides to its members and affiliated foreign club members.

Driving is generally relaxed and pleasant over America's excellent road network, and freeways help relieve traffic congestion. Visitors may find distances deceptive: Boston to Miami is further than London to Rome

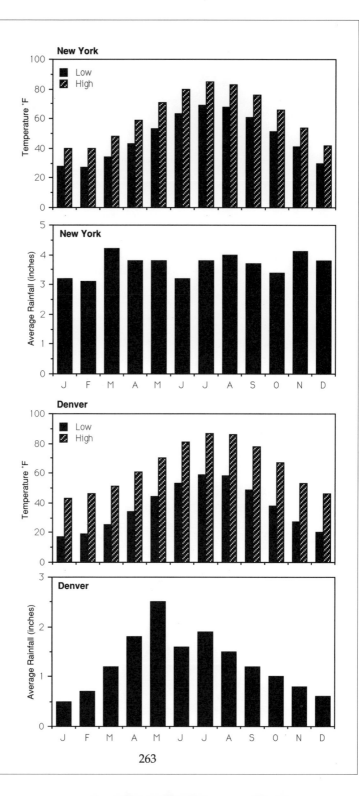

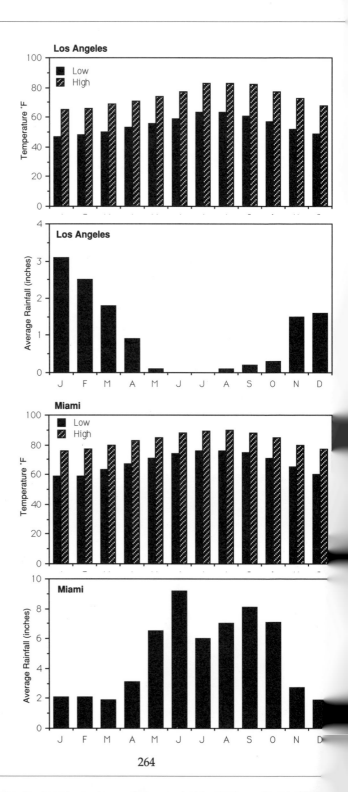

States in the east are smaller, with distances between cities generally less. Apart from major cities, Western roads are uncrowded, allowing drivers to travel further without undue fatigue.

Interstates in America are restricted access, multi-lane arteries between the states; typically coloured blue or red on road maps. Green-coloured lines are turnpikes, which charge a toll but are otherwise similar to interstates. Freeways are restricted access arteries into and through dense urban areas. Speed limits for limited access highways are normally 55mph, rising to 65mph in specified rural areas.

US highways are not necessarily multi-lane, and often cross towns rather than bypassing them. Traffic lights and strip development along urban highways slow traffic considerably, but faster interstates and turnpikes are normally less visually rewarding than rural highways. Speed limits are typically 45-55mph in the countryside, 15-35mph in urban areas.

Road numbering and signs can confuse the unwary. Each state and many counties have their own roads, whose numbers change when crossing a border. Signs for US highways, interstates, and turnpikes have a numbered shield with three points at the top, and are respectively white, blue, and green. Even-numbered highways go east-west, while odd-numbered highways run north-south. The state outline appears on many state highway signs, while county roads have numbers in a box or circle. To reduce confusion, road numbers within this guide are preceded by 'US' to designate a US highway, 'SR' for a state or county road, and 'I-' for interstates.

Emergencies

Breakdowns
In the event of a malfunction, coast onto the hard shoulder (breakdown lane), lift the car's hood (bonnet), at night use emergency flashers, and await assistance in a locked car. As soon as possible, notify the hire company and ask for a replacement. PPI insurance, if taken out, may cover hotel and incidental expenses while waiting. Members of an overseas automobile association can contact the AAA through the yellow pages or, for breakdown assistance, on 1-800-AAA-HELP.

Accidents
If involved in an accident, get the particulars of other drivers and any witnesses. State law requires the police to be notified if damage exceeds a nominal amount or in event of personal injury, and the hire company must always be informed. Some insurance policies become void if the driver admits liability, and saying, 'I'm sorry,' could be considered an admission of guilt. Leave medical help to those who are trained and insured.

Illness and Injury
Medical insurance documents should be kept safe and preferably with the traveller. Call 911 (or 0 for operator) in emergency. Remain calm.

For non-emergencies the operator or medical referral agencies in the

Yellow Pages can help the independent traveller, as can an overseas visitor's consulate. Advance payment may be required for those without medical insurance.

While hiking in remote areas, the group should have a minimum of three people so that one person can remain with the injured while another goes for help. In the highly unlikely event of a bite from a poisonous snake or spider, always: remain calm, treat victim only for shock, and seek immediate medical attention. Permanent injury from a poisonous bite is highly unlikely, especially if proper medical attention has been sought *without* attempting a tourniquet or other treatment without professional advise. A course of rabies injections may be the outcome of feeding, petting, or molesting domesticated or wild fur-bearing animals. If bitten, seek a doctor immediately.

Theft and Lost Property

Common-sense rules on avoiding theft include using the hotel safe for valuables, reserves of cash or traveller's cheques, travel vouchers, and airline tickets. Dress casually, wearing the minimum of jewellery. Keep passports and reclaim forms separate from credit cards and traveller's cheques. Lock car doors and keep windows shut while travelling to prevent car theft and hand bag snatchers. Travel in groups, and check with hotel staff for areas of potential trouble (and local points of interest).

In case of theft, report details to police. Use travel or credit card insurance to replace lost or stolen articles. Contact your embassy immediately if a passport is lost or stolen, and also for financial help in an emergency. Traveller's cheque replacement will be far easier if the company is represented in the United States. When notifying credit card companies of a loss, most companies have toll free numbers, while those abroad will accept a collect call. Several companies offer credit card protection schemes, where one call notifies relevant credit card companies.

American airports, hotels, and restaurants are very good with lost property, but also leave details with the police lost-and-found department.

Handicapped Facilities

Public buildings, national, and state parks must, by law, provide access facilities to the handicapped. In addition the major hotels and many private attractions, such as Walt Disney World, provide facilities and access for the disabled which are unsurpassed. However, planning is poor in many American towns and cities: sidewalks are nonexistent and pedestrians must cross at odds with turning traffic. Vehicular mobility is a must for the independent traveller, whether physically handicapped or not, but there are alternatives: join a tour group, cruise on a ship, or stay in one of the many resorts. If requested, Walt Disney Company provides handbooks identifying special facilities within their theme parks.

Major rental car companies such as Hertz and Avis can provide automobiles with special controls if contacted in advance. An increasing number of states include information regarding handicapped access to points o interest in their vacation planning guides. However, many states charge a fee for handicapped access parking permits — an unfortunate nuisance to those visiting more than one state.

National and State Parks and Forests

America's 'crown jewels' are on permanent public display. Her state and national parks, monuments and historic sites are open to all. Summers are usually the busiest periods, while spring and autumn bring cooler temperatures and fewer people. National forests in mountainous areas boast some of America's finest ski resorts, often open for year-round recreation. Those who *must* visit a popular park in the summer should book accommodation or campsites months ahead. Even the Grand Canyon has niches where quiet contemplation is possible, away from car parks and bus stops.

Admission to most national parks is $5 per carload, valid for seven days. The Golden Age and Golden Access passes are free respectively to those over 62 and handicapped individuals, excluding foreign nationals, with discounts for campsites and certain tours. The $25 Golden Eagle Pass allows unlimited access — including foreign nationals — for one calendar year but gives no camping or tour discounts.

National Park Service information is available from the American tourist offices abroad, or from:
The National Park Service
PO Box 37127
Washington, DC 20013-7127

Renting a Car

Renting a car is easy and, especially in Hawaii and Florida, inexpensive. Pre-booking an automobile via a fly-drive package or through a major rental company is safest, especially during peak season. Rent-a-Wreck style companies offer lower prices, but may sting unwary drivers with high mileage charges and/or inadequate insurance.

Third-party insurance is normally included in the price but CDW (collision damage waver) may not be. CDW pushes rental prices up $9-16 per day, but does insure against damage to the vehicle and loss of use charges. Travellers who utilize their own insurance policies may find themselves paying hire charges for damaged cars being repaired. PPI (Personal Protection Insurance) provides additional liability coverage and may pay accommodation costs in the event of a breakdown or accident.

Cars rented in Florida may not be insured to leave the state — check first. Special insurance arrangements and permission may also be required if crossing into Canada. In general, hire cars are not allowed into Mexico, and private vehicles may go only if covered by Mexican insurance.

Restrictions may apply to drivers under 25 years old, travellers without a major credit card, and anyone whose driving privileges have been revoked — they should inform the rental company or tour operator while booking.

Renting a Motorhome

Seeing the United States by RV (recreational vehicle or motorhome) has become so popular that many Americans live permanently in these mansions on wheels. Hiring an RV is simple, with similar restrictions to car hire. Both Cruise America and Go Vacations offer motorhomes which may be booked directly or through various travel agencies abroad.

The RV is ideal for groups and families who enjoy travelling together, whether or not they enjoy the 'great outdoors'. Far from spartan, these vehicles offer full kitchens, bathrooms, ample cupboard space, comfortable beds, and air-conditioning. Most come with a microwave and television, which can be linked to cable or satellite at many commercial campgrounds.

The temptation to hire the largest vehicle possible should be resisted. Wise 'RVers' chose a vehicle just large enough to meet their needs — a 35ft motorhome is difficult to manoeuvre in tight spaces. Power steering and automatic transmissions help enormously, but drivers should practice in quieter locations before attempting a major city.

For Overseas Visitors

Currency and Credit Cards

The American unit of currency is the dollar, divided into 100 cents (¢), with coins in the value of: 1¢ (penny), 5¢ (nickel), 10¢ (dime), 25¢ (quarter), 50¢ (half dollar) and $1 (dollar). Bank notes are available in denominations of $1, $2 (rare), $5, $10, $20, $50, and $100. Larger notes exist in limited quantities, but many establishments will not accept notes larger than $20. Each bank note is the same size and colour, regardless of value, so take care to give the correct note and always check the change.

Bank hours are 9 am to 3 pm, Monday to Friday, except national holidays. Buy American dollars as cash or traveller's cheques before leaving home. American Express, Thomas Cook, and certain banks provide currency exchange, but in generally only in major cities, and tracking them down can waste valuable holiday time. Dollar traveller's cheques are treated as cash, and offer protection against loss. American Express are popular and widely accepted, while traveller's cheques from 'obscure' foreign banks may be more difficult to cash.

Major credit cards reduce the problems of currency exchange and dangers of carrying large quantities of cash. American Express, Diners Club, Visa, and Mastercard are the most popular, although a few establishments which accept Mastercard have refused to honour foreign Access Cards. Non-resident American Express card holders may cash foreign cheques (amount varies by card and country) once every three weeks. Dollar cash advances on a credit card may be obtained from participating banks and affiliated cash dispenser networks, although interest or transaction charges are levied. Certain ATM networks, such as the PLUS system, withdraw funds directly from home accounts without an interest penalty.

Customs

America is very strict on controlled substances (non-prescription drugs), meat, dairy products, fruit and vegetables. Check with the consulate or embassy before bringing firearms, ammunition or animals. British visitors should note that America does have rabies, and returning pets will be subject to extended quarantine.

There are no restrictions on the amount of currency brought into or taken from the United States, but a declaration form must be filled in when the value exceeds $10,000.

The following goods may be imported duty free into the USA:

Either 200 cigarettes, 50 cigars, 2kg of tobacco, or proportionate amounts of each; 1 litre of alcoholic beverage for those 21 or over; gifts up to a value of $100, which may include 100 cigars in addition to the tobacco allowance. Gifts must be available for inspection, and thus should not be wrapped.

At major international airports, such as Miami, Chicago, and New York's JFK, there are red and green customs channels. American Customs Officers are not chosen for their sense of humour — adopt a business-like attitude and save jokes for an appreciative audience.

Documents

Passports and Visas

All travellers visiting America from abroad, whether on business or holiday, must have a full passport which will remain valid six months beyond the date they are scheduled to return. Canadian citizens and British subjects resident in Canada or Bermuda do not require an American visa if arriving from most Western Hemisphere countries. Mexicans arriving from Canada or Mexico do not require a visa if they are in possession of a form I-136.

A visa may not be necessary for nationals of the United Kingdom, certain EEC countries, and Japan when arriving by air or sea via a carrier participating in the United States Visa Waiver Program. Travellers intending to re-visit America are advised to apply for a visa. Those staying beyond 3 months must have a visa, as must students on exchange programmes and citizens of countries not participating in the Visa Waiver Program.

Postal applications for visas are typically processed within 10 days, but for safety allow 4 weeks. Travel agencies can often obtain American visas within 48 hours, but acquiring an 'instant' visa by personally visiting the United States Consulate General may no longer be possible — check first. The standard multiple-entry visas are valid indefinitely, and will be transferred from an expired passport to a new one so long as both passports are presented when entering the United States. Visas may be obtained by writing to an American Consulate:

United States Consulate General
Visa Branch
5 Upper Grosvenor Street
London W1A 2JB
United Kingdom
☎ 071-499-7010

United States Consulate General
Visa Branch
1155 Saint Alexandra
Montreal, Quebec H22 I22
Canada
☎ 514-398-9695

United States Consulate General
Visa Branch
36th Floor, Electricity House
Park & Elizabeth Streets
Sydney, NSW 2000
Australia
☎ 02-261-9200

United States Consulate General
Visa Branch
4th Floor, Yorkshire General Building
CNR Shortland & O'Connell
Auckland
New Zealand
☎ 09-303-2724

Upon admission to the United States, visitors have a departure form stapled to their passport. When leaving, especially if departing overland into Canada or Mexico, ensure the emigration official retrieves the form. The alternative is to be branded an illegal alien, making re-entry to America most difficult.

Driving Documents

For foreign visitors and Americans alike, the most popular way to see the United States is from behind a steering wheel. A valid driving license should always be carried with the driver. An International Driver's Permit is not necessary for those coming from an English-speaking country, and is invalid unless accompanied by a driving licence.

The AAA (American Automobile Association) has reciprocal arrangements with many non-American automobile associations and clubs. Visitors bringing proof of membership enjoy AAA services, such as free maps, trip-tiks (a series of strip maps following the drivers intended route), area guidebooks, and breakdown help. AAA affiliated members may receive discounts from car hire companies, tourist attractions, and hotels. (Other discounts are often available to senior citizens, students, the military, and members of various travel clubs).

Essentials

Travellers taking medication should bring their prescription, which can be used for an emergency top up and also to prove the medication is prescribed. Replacement glasses or contact lenses and their prescription are also recommended. Electrical appliances must work at 110 volts and fit the US two/three pronged plug. European or British plugs, including 'universal' electric shavers, will require an electrical socket adapter. Drinking the water is not a problem, and water fountains are standard in most shopping centres and parks.

For travel security, one should make a list of phone numbers, issuer's addresses, and identification numbers for passports, airline tickets, insurance policies, credit cards, travellers cheques, AAA or equivalent member ship, and travel vouchers. Keeping the list secure and separate from the above items will greatly simplify replacing lost or stolen items.

Insurance

Good personal health and accident insurance is essential for medical coverage and general peace of mind. American hospital treatment is excellent, but it may be unobtainable unless proof of insurance is demonstrated or costs are pre-paid. Those with existing health problems should consult both their doctor and the travel insurance company to ensure they are adequately protected. Check that personal accident insurance indemnifies travellers against third-party law suits.

Injections are not required to visit America, nor are vaccination certificates except where travellers have recently visited a country where yellow fever or similar is endemic. Bring or buy a small first aid kit, protection from the sun, and mosquito repellant.

For UK citizens a 24-hour *emergency-only* service is available via: British Consul General, Suite 2700, 245 Peachtree Center Ave, Atlanta, GE 30302. ☎ 404-524-5856

Legal Advice

This is very expensive in America, and best avoided where possible. Purchased travel insurance should indemnify against personal law suites. If legal advice is necessary, check the yellow pages for legal referral specialists. Visitors from abroad should consult their embassy or consular offices.

Language

American accents vary, as does word usage compared to 'English'. Here are selected British words and their American equivalents:

British	American	British	American
biscuit	cookie	lift	elevator
car boot	trunk	motorhome	RV
car bonnet	hood	pavement	sidewalk
car wing	fender	post	mail
chips	french fries	petrol	gasoline (or gas)
cot	crib	public school	private school
(see also single bed)		public toilet	rest room,
crisps	(potato) chips		bathroom
egg fried one side	sunny side up	reverse-charge call	collect call
egg fried both		road	pavement
sides, yolk soft	over easy	scone	biscuit
egg fried both		single bed	cot
sides, yolk hard	over hard	sweet	candy
grilled	broiled	tap	faucet
ground floor	first floor	tights	panty hose

Mail

Post Offices will hold mail sent to travellers for 30 days, so long as it is addressed with the recipients name and includes 'c/o General Delivery'. Most large cities have several post offices, with only one handling general delivery mail.

Holders of American Express Cards or Traveller's Cheques may have mail delivered to themselves care of *participating* AMEX offices, again held for 30 days. Mail should be addressed to the recipient and marked 'Client Mail'.

Note that some US addresses now use the new nine-digit zip code, which should not be confused with the telephone number.

Photography

Film is often less expensive in America than abroad, and most types are readily available. In major cities bargain if purchasing large quantities or buy from discount stores. Film prices increase significantly near major tourist attractions. Many theme parks offer free or rental cameras, usually courtesy of Kodak. Foreign visitors should check that process-paid film may be developed at home.

Hot sunny days turn cars into ovens, and can ruin film whether inside the camera or out.

Public Holidays

The following are public holidays:

New Year's Day	1 Jan
Martin Luther King Day	16 Jan
President's Day	Third Monday in February
Memorial Day	Last Monday in May
Independence Day	4 July
Labor Day	First Monday in September
Columbus Day	Second Monday in October
Veteran's Day	11 November
Thanksgiving	Last Thursday in November
Christmas	25 December

Regional holidays and special events are listed at the end of each chapter.

Sales Tax

Foreign visitors are often surprised to find their purchases cost more than the price tag indicated. State Sales Tax is automatically added when paying and, as if to prove each state's constitutional right to be different, the amount varies from 0 to 10 percent.

Telephones

The emergency code is 911, and if that fails, dial 0 for Operator.

All American (and Canadian) telephones have a three-digit area code, and a seven-digit phone number. Area codes are only used when calling between areas. The area code 800 is reserved for toll free calls, usually valid only from America or Canada. Major airlines, hotels and car rental companies have toll free numbers listed in the Yellow Pages. Long distance and toll free calls are normally preceded with 1.

Direct dialing of calls, even international ones, are possible from most hotels and public pay phones. The international code 011 and the country code is followed by the phone number, minus the leading zero. To telephone 071-784-9659, a ficticious London number, dial 011 (International Direct Dialling Access), 44 (the United Kingdom Country Code), 71-784-9659 (the London Number, less the leading zero).

Not all pay-phones are operated by AT&T, and rules for long distance dialing vary, but most phones provide instructions. International direct dialing from a public phone box requires a fistful of quarters, up to $10 worth for a short call. AT&T make calling home easier with their Direct Service. Collect or telephone credit card calls may be made to the United Kingdom by dialing 1-800-445-5667.

For directory enquires, dial 411 for local numbers, or the area code and 555-1212 for long distance numbers. To find the toll free number of an airline, hotel, or car rental firm, dial 1-800-555-1212 and ask for their number.

Time and Dates

Continental USA is divided into four time zones. From east to west they are: Eastern, Central, Mountain, and Pacific — 5 to 8 hours respectively behind (less than) Greenwich Mean Time. Mainland Alaska is 9 hours behind GMT, and Hawaii 10 hours behind.

Daylight Savings Time comes into effect on the first Sunday in April, with the clocks moving ahead one hour, and reverts back to standard time on the last Sunday in October. Arizona, Hawaii, and parts of Indiana do not observe Daylight Savings Time.

Americans write their dates in the format: month, day, year. Thus Christmas Day in 1999 is December 25, 1999, or in shorthand 12/25/99.

Tipping

15 percent is the standard tip for taxis, restaurants, and bar staff, while exceptional service or luxurious surroundings now command 20 percent. Restaurant service charges are not normal except for large groups, which then take the place of tipping. Cover charges are not service charges, and tips are still expected.

Toilets

Usually referred to in a hushed voice as the rest room, bathroom, or often the ladies' and men's room. Public toilets are found in shopping malls, large department stores, recreational parks, and at rest areas on major highways (often indicated on state maps). Fast food emporiums are useful in emergencies, although some now charge non-customers.

Tourist Offices

Main American tourist offices are at the following addresses. For those countries not listed, contact the American Embassy.

United States Travel & Tourism
   Administration
United States Department of Commerce
Washington, DC 20230
USA

United States Travel & Tourism
   Administration
Suite 602, 480 University Avenue
Toronto, Ontario M5G 1V2
Canada
☎ 416-595-5082

United States Travel & Tourism
   Administration
P.O. Box 1EN
London W1A 1EN
United Kingdom
☎ 071 495 4466

United States Travel & Tourism
   Administration
Suite 6106, MLC Centre
King & Castlereagh Streets
Sydney, NSW 2000
Australia
☎ 02-233-4055

Travel — Getting to the United States

Air

Most travellers reach America by air. The diversity of carriers, rates, and routes is bewildering, with new routes and packages added almost daily. A travel agent can help decipher the offerings, but some general guidelines may help. Packaged tours generally offer the best value, without necessarily sacrificing the flexibility the independent traveller demands. A basic fly-drive package will leave the visitor in a rental car, this guide book propped open, with the whole of America ahead. Check before departing for hotel voucher bargains, which usually include a certain number of nights in a particular chain of motels at a special price. Those preferring a more fixed arrangement can still see more of America by opting for a fly-drive or bus tour itinerary with places of interest, hotels, flights and transfers included.

Land

Travellers arriving in America overland via Canada or Mexico must have visas, unless they are Canadian Citizens, British Canadian Residents, Mexicans with form I-136, or naturalized Americans. The Visa Waiver Program does not apply to overland arrivals. Both borders are friendly crossings and visitors occasionally have to prompt officials, especially about collecting the departure forms when leaving America.

Sea

Qunard's *Queen Elizabeth II* still plies the waters between Southampton and New York. A reduced fare option allows cruising one direction and flying the other. It is also possible to join a Mediterranean to Caribbean cruise and fly to America from there, or visit Hawaii on a Pacific cruise.

Travel — Getting around the United States

Long Haul Public Transport
Air

America's air network has innumerable routes and carriers. Deregulation has increased competition between airlines, and the traveller often benefits with reduced rates. Numerous airlines give reductions for senior citizens, to whom they offer blocks of tickets for the cost of a few flights. Rates are significantly reduced when booking a week or more in advance if the return flight involves a weekend stopover — shop around. Non-residents should check for special deals available from local travel agencies, whether a package holiday which visits several American cities or a United States airline which offers reduced price air passes.

Rail (Amtrak)

Travellers booking from abroad may take advantage of Amtrak's USA Rail Pass. Each pass is valid for 45 days, allows unlimited stopovers, and takes in America's largest passenger rail network. A region may be as small as Florida or as large as continental USA, and the price varies accordingly. With the potential for unlimited travel comes restrictions, additional charges apply for luxuries such as sleeping car accommodation, and the large network can be difficult to negotiate.

Amtrak also offer packaged trips which include sightseeing tours of the major cities and national parks. Visitors from Australia and New Zealand should contact Thomas Cook, while Amtrak may be reached in the UK on (071) 978-5222. In America write to:

Amtrak
60 Massachusetts Ave NE
Washington, DC 20002
☎ 202-383-3000 or 1-800-USA-RAIL

Greyhound Buses

Armed with a Greyhound Ameripass (purchased before leaving home) and a sense of determination, much of America can be seen by bus. The Greyhound (and participating carriers) network is extensive, but travellers may face poor public transport at final destinations, as the Greyhound network is city to city, not accommodation to attraction.

Short Haul Public Transport

San Fransisco has the most options regarding public transport, with the world famous cable cars supplemented by the underground BART (Bay

Area Rapid Transit) and an excellent bus system. Chicago has its rapid transit network, Washington the Metro, and Boston the 'T'. Every major city has a bus network, supplemented in many with light rail. Even Los Angeles has a rail link to Long Beach, with plans for extending the network.

While travel can be dangerous during off-peak hours in any city, the New York Subway has a legendary reputation for violence not entirely deserved. In all cities, stick to well travelled routes and at night, use taxis.

Motoring Laws and Tips

The essential law for foreign visitors is to drive on the right-hand side of the road. On multi-lane highways keep right when not overtaking, and when changing lanes watch for cars passing on either side, which is legal in many states. Unless otherwise posted, drivers at a red traffic light may turn right after stopping in the majority of states. But do not turn if interfering with other traffic or pedestrians.

One crucially important law relates to school buses. Whenever a school bus flashes red warning lights drivers going in *either direction* must stop! Children expect all traffic to come to a standstill, and often race across the road without looking.

Radar, airplanes and other methods of speed control are extensively used by the police forces. Intoxicated drivers and lead-footed speedsters will find that on-the-spot fines may be supplemented with prison and/or confiscation of the offending vehicle. Especially avoid speeding on turnpikes as the time-stamped tickets are checked when paying tolls at the other end, and fines are charged if the driver arrives too quickly. Tough policies on drunk driving in many states means that drivers below the legal drinking age (generally 21) will lose their licence if *any* alcohol is detected.

Driving is actually a very pleasant way to see America — the *only* way to see some parts. The most likely problem drivers confront is fatigue, caused by the temptation to go 'just a little further'. Rest stops (with toilet facilities) and pullovers (without) are plentiful along the interstates and scenic highways, and regular stops will refresh tired drivers.

Many gas stations insist upon paying before pumping. Lower priced stations, often combined with convenience stores, only accept cash and travellers cheques. Since the station attendant (and customers) would be at risk during a hold-up, chances are minimized by mechanically whisking paper money into a safe. The attendant thus cannot change large dollar bills or travellers cheques — bring small denominations.

A surcharge may apply for using credit cards, and at 'full service' pumps a per gallon premium is charged in exchange for a windscreen wash, checking engine fluid levels and possibly the tyres, and a smile. Hire cars use readily available unleaded fuel, but older vehicles use leaded fuel which can be difficult to find.

Weights and Measures

The American system of weights and measures was derived from the British Imperial system, thus they are similar if not identical. The metric system is making gradual inroads, but road distances are in miles, not kilometres. Produce, whether dry or liquid, usually has both metric and American weights or volumes indicated.

Liquid measure differs between America and Britain. 1 US Gallon = 0.833 Imperial Gallons = 3.8 litres. Women's clothing sizes vary, with American sizes two less than the British. Thus a size 12 dress in Britain is only 10 in America, and a size 36 sweater is 34. Women's shoes are the opposite, so a dainty British size 4 becomes an American 6. Ounces and pounds are the same in the UK as the United States, but Americans do not use the stone.

A Note to the Reader

Thank you for buying this book; we hope it has helped you to enjoy your visit. We have worked hard to produce a guidebook which is as accurate as possible. With this in mind, any comments, suggestions or useful information you may have would be appreciated.

Please send your letters to:

The Editor
Moorland Publishing Co Ltd
Moor Farm Road West
Ashbourne
Derbyshire
DE6 1HD

MPC The Travel Specialists

INDEX

ACKNOWLEDGEMENTS

The author is deeply indebted to 50 states and some 500 cities for their assistance in compiling this guide. A heartfelt thankyou is also due Virgin Atlantic Airways for coping admirably with our greaty revised travels.

This work is dedicated to Cathy and Kimberley, who are departed but not forgotten and to those family members without whom such endeavers would be meaningless. Travellers following the routes will please think kindly of Jackie, who drove 34,000 miles this trip, and who still wants more.

Illustrations have been supplied by: Biltmore Estate: 82; Dennis Breedon: 99 lower, 199; Fontainbleau Hilton: 103 lower; John Hartman: 11 lower; Jackie Merritt: 14 lower, 15, 19 lower, 47 lower, 78 lower, 83, 86 lower, 151, 166 lower, 183, 202 lower, 223 lower, 250, 254, 255; MPC Picture Collection: 39, 59 lower, 186, 187, 195, 202 top, 207; Newman Associates: 107 top; Opreyland: 86 top; C. M. Russell Museum: 223; Sea World: 99 top; and the visitor bureaux and tourism divisions of Atlanta: 78 top; Boston: 19 top; Chicago: 118; Denver Metro: 166 top, 182 top; Detroit: 131; Durango: 182 lower; Fort Lauderdale: 107 lower; Maryland: 27; Milwaukee: 122; Minnesota: 122 lower; New Hampshire: 26, 30 top; New York State: 47 top; Ohio: 130; Oklahoma: 155; Oregon: 230; Portland (Larry Geddis): 235 top; Portland: 30 lower; Sarasota: 103 top; South Dakota: 171; Tennessee: 11 top; Texas: 14 top, 143, 146, 147, 150; Washington DC: 58 top: Washington State: 219, 235 lower; Wyoming: 170, 227, 230 lower.

Visitor's Guides
Tour & Explore with MPC Visitor's Guides

Austria
Austria: Tyrol & Vorarlberg

Britain:
Cornwall & Isles of Scilly
Cotswolds
Devon
East Anglia
Guernsey, Alderney & Sark
Hampshire & the Isle of Wight
Denmark
Jersey
Kent
Lake District
Scotland: Lowlands
Somerset, Dorset & Wiltshire
North Wales and Snowdonia
North York Moors, York & Coast
Northumbria
Northern Ireland
Peak District
Sussex
Yorkshire Dales & North Pennines

Crete
Egypt
Finland
Florida

France:
Alps & Jura
Corsica
Dordogne
Loire
Massif Central
Normandy Landing Beaches
Provence & Côte d'Azur

Germany:
Bavaria
Black Forest
Rhine & Mosel
Southern Germany
Iceland

Italy:
Florence & Tuscany
Italian Lakes
Northern Italy
Mauritius, Rodrigues & Reunion
Peru

Spain:
Costa Brava to Costa Blanca
Mallorca, Menorca, Ibiza & Formentera
Northern & Central Spain
Southern Spain & Costa del Sol

Sweden
Switzerland
Tenerife
Turkey
Yugoslavia: The Adriatic Coast

World Traveller
The new larger format Visitor's Guides

Belgium & Luxembourg
Czechoslovakia
France
Holland
Norway
Portugal
USA

**A complete catalogue of all our travel guides to over
125 destinations is available on request**